Surfing in the Movies

Surfing in the Movies
A Critical History

JOHN ENGLE

McFarland & Company, Inc., Publishers
Jefferson, North Carolina

LIBRARY OF CONGRESS CATALOGUING-IN-PUBLICATION DATA

Engle, John, 1950–
Surfing in the movies : a critical history / John Engle.
        p.   cm.
Includes bibliographical references and index.

ISBN 978-0-7864-9521-4 (softcover : acid free paper) ∞
ISBN 978-1-4766-2284-2 (ebook)

1. Surfing in motion pictures.   2. Surfing films—History and criticism.   I. Title.
PN1995.9.S83E75 2015   791.43′6579—dc23   2015032792

BRITISH LIBRARY CATALOGUING DATA ARE AVAILABLE

© 2015 John Engle. All rights reserved

*No part of this book may be reproduced or transmitted in any form
or by any means, electronic or mechanical, including photocopying
or recording, or by any information storage and retrieval system,
without permission in writing from the publisher.*

Cover image © iStock/Thinkstock

Printed in the United States of America

*McFarland & Company, Inc., Publishers
Box 611, Jefferson, North Carolina 28640
www.mcfarlandpub.com*

With love and gratitude to Christie,
who's been there every step along the sand

Table of Contents

Acknowledgments   ix
Preface   1

1. Shooting the Curl   5
2. Five Hundred Summer Stories: The Surf Movie and Documentary   24
3. In Hollywood's Hands: The Feature Film Surfing Narrative   144

Conclusion: Zero Summer   207
Chapter Notes   223
Bibliography   226
Index   239

Acknowledgments

My grateful acknowledgments and sincere personal thanks go to Anna Trent Moore and Ron Moore of the Bud Browne Film Archives for sharing Bud's work with me, correcting misconceptions, and so kindly welcoming me to their home just one day after a particularly difficult return trip from Europe. Much gratitude as well to Tommy Stathes of the Bray Animation Project, who graciously offered access to what seems to be the earliest animated treatment of surfing, *Bobby Bumps, Surf Rider*.

I would like to express special gratitude to Sybil and Taylor Steele, to Greg MacGillivray, and to Lori Rick. Grateful acknowledgments go as well to extraordinary surf photographers Todd Glaser and Ted Grambeau, to Jeff Hall of A-Frame, and to Remi D'Urso.

I want again to thank Gary Morris of *Bright Lights Film Journal* for first publishing my thoughts on the surf move and for his continued guidance and support, as well as Bob Cumbow for his kind words in recognizing the worth of this project. I am equally indebted to Michael Mintz and to my colleagues Clare Sibley and Sandra Gorgievski. Sandra will find the results of at least two of her brilliant suggestions in these pages. Much gratitude goes to Gaëlle Chapdelaine of the Université de Toulon library for her steadfast help in running down some awfully skittish documents.

I want to express my warmest personal gratitude to my dear sister Sue and her family, who keep us coming to the beach, and to my wonderful son Liam, who keeps me going out into the surf, that is, when he's not being a first-class filmmaker and my source for expert information on film technique, history, and vocabulary. *Un grand merci* as well to sweet Laure and to everyone's favorite grom James. Thanks to John Leininger for a fun and informative lunch at the Shellback, and to Bob Rich, Kyle Cozine, Gen Collopy, and Paul Snyder, my team on the ground in Manhattan Beach and Kailua. Chloe and Emily, thank you so much for enduring the million surfing movies all over the house, the hours hunched up over the computer, and the thousand yard stare after long days of work.

Thanks to my buddy Rocky Bauer for his cheerful backing and that of the small but hardy Oregon surf community. Finally, a very special thank you to my great friend and ideal reader Lee Zimmerman, who has been such a source of affection and encouragement all the way through this project.

Finally, of course, unlimited love and gratitude to my surfer girl Christie, whose first sweet gift to me many unforgettable years ago was a copy of *Caught Inside*.

Preface

When I first considered writing this book, I naturally wondered what else had been done in the field. Waveriders and those who observe them have been scribbling about this curious occupation for over two centuries. Early curiosity and befuddled admiration would eventually give over to forms of careful historical and technical writing, personal reminiscence, and game attempts to find words for the stoke. The pages would only start stacking up by reams in the last few decades, though, as surfing created its own vibrant subculture and that subculture gradually negotiated its place within or at least at the edge of the larger general culture. Alongside a few notions of history, a tangy vocabulary, a certain attitude and style, a small specialist press, and the occasional song, film has played a central role in the emerging surfing subculture. To begin to understand its place in the surfing universe, the first authority to consult is, as in all things surfing, the indispensable Matt Warshaw, whose monumental *Encyclopedia* is only one of a number of the former *Surfer* editor's vital contributions to our understanding of waves and the people who ride them. Like that of several other fine historians of surfing and surf culture, Warshaw's work finds some room in its many pages for the insider "surf movie" as well as for Hollywood's attempts to fashion cineplex-friendly stories featuring the sport. As surfing in cinema is just an aspect of these much larger generalist treatments, though, one might expect to locate a few specialist full-length works on the subject. There are perhaps four. In 2008 *The Surfer's Journal* produced for Outdoor Life Network an excellent multi-volume *Fifty Years of Surfing on Film* that introduces the major figures, briefly describes and contextualizes their contribution, and furnishes tight excerpts from the movies. Warshaw's own *Surf Movie Tonite!* draws together some cogent remarks and details around the visual pleasures of the surf movie poster. Albie Thoms's book *Surfmovies* ostensibly covers Australian films but in fact takes on the whole surf cinema scene with sometimes astounding factual minutiae. As its title indicates, Thomas Lisanti limits himself to the frothy *Hollywood Surf and Beach Movies: The First Wave, 1959–1969*, but his 446 pages tell you all you could ever want to know about Gidget and her cousins.

Together with occasional stretches in other books and a handful of salient articles and web sites, the *Surfer's Journal* videos and the writings of Warshaw, Thoms, and Lisanti constitute a vital compendium of necessary titles, facts, events, names, and dates. Yet while this material is invaluable, something has too often gone missing in the treatment of the more than 1000 movies and videos generated by the surf community and the entertainment industry since Bud Browne started taping up posters in the fall of 1953. Lisanti could be speaking for others when his preface candidly admits that "this book does not contain in-depth analyses." Which brings us to the point of these pages, for what I hope to provide in the pages to follow is *close critical attention to surf films as films*. While there's certainly a good dose of "history" here as well, the bare facts are less the priority, and in any case the whos, the whats, the wheres, and the whens are largely available in the fine works above, online, and elsewhere. If something has been absent in the treatment of too many surfing movies, though, it is the purely critical dimension. By that I mean taking the time to look with attention at *Gun Ho!* and *Big Wednesday*, at *The Endless Summer* and *Blue Crush*. To focus on these films as films means considering such cinematic constituents as use of space and time, point of view, structure, characterization, narrative pattern, mise-en-scene and editing, metaphor and symbol, framing, cinematography, dialogue or narration, and music or other sound effects. Surfing has extraordinary potential as a primary subject or a significant plot or background element. Even if they have not always served that potential as well as they might have, surfing movies deserve the respect of detailed attention as freestanding aesthetic objects and not simply as signs of their times, historical occurrences, and components of larger traditions.

As I look back on things, there's a certain logic in the way I came to this subject. In the last decade or so, a university career dedicated to research on modern and contemporary literature gradually morphed into a new interest in cinema. From there the idea of studying the surfing film came naturally. I've always loved the genre, and the surf scene is in many ways where I grew up. A fourth-generation Californian, I surfed as a 1960s teenager in Santa Cruz. For purposes of full disclosure, by the way, I don't claim any great surfing chops—those familiar with Santa Cruz will know what I mean when I say my go-to spots were Cowell's and occasionally Pleasure Point, but not Steamer Lane. In college in Southern California a friend and I took the inevitable Baja run. Since then, as grad school, professional life, and family made their demands, I've surfed intermittently, usually in the South Bay, where I've spent part of nearly every summer of my life at my aunt's place just off the Strand in Manhattan Beach, and sometimes in my new home of France, where I remember in particular a wonderful week surfing at a Biarritz camp with my son after watching him pop up for the first time. A great early California memory was Corky Carroll winning a competition at Steamer Lane in 1969. As far as movies are concerned, I didn't catch *Gidget* the first time around, but I do recall the TV series, Frankie and Annette, *The Endless Summer*, the *Big Wednesday* flop, *Point Break*, and dozens of other films in their original runs. When I was a little kid my dad took me along one August evening to Hermosa to see Greg Noll's movies and the man himself. During my college years I remember catching *Five Summer Stories* and arriving too late for a sold-out beach showing of *Free Ride* before tracking it down later in the summer.

The first fruit of my serious interest in the surf movie was an article I wrote a few years ago about the Hollywood entertainment version. When I look back on those remarks today, I realize they were somewhat limited, even if I'm still happy with the analyses of certain films. Concentrating on only a few of the best-known studio narrative releases and, with the exception of Bruce Brown's classic, essentially ignoring the hundreds of movies specially made for the surf faithful, I was necessarily only scratching the surface. Since then it has been an absolute kick to plunge deep into the past and get caught up with what's happening right now, to re-examine the classics and run down the oddities. When I got started I thought I knew a lot about surfing and only now do I realize how little. I have viewed and re-viewed hundreds of films and videos. In the process I've watched zillions of waves, and it's a minor form of empowerment today to be able to look for two seconds at a breaking wave and pretty much know that it's Margaret River or Skeleton Bay or Ala Moana. I've tried to watch films from the surfer's obsessed perspective and from that of the vaguely curious Saturday night entertainment consumer. I've examined movies as part of an evolving genre and part of a filmmaker's oeuvre, as cultural or social signposts, as responses to changing aesthetic norms, and as products in an economic system. Most of all, I've tried to watch each film or video as the individual creative work it is.

As you read, you'll notice that I've chosen not to take a cursory glimpse at an absolute maximum of films and videos but rather to offer detailed attention to a smaller number of the many hundreds that treat surfing cinematically. In all these remarks address about 200 separate works, sometimes glancingly but whenever possible by slowing down to look closely. So many movies in the long surf community tradition started by Bud Browne can be quickly summarized as following the same surfing-plus-comic-filler formula, just as so many Hollywood fictional treatments can be quickly dismissed as cleaving to the growing-up-plus-fateful-challenge pattern. To leave it at that, though, is to shortchange the fertile subject that surfing is and the many creative imaginations that have dealt with its pleasures and meanings. It's time to take the surfing movie and the theatrical release-with-surfing-in-it seriously, spend some time with these films, look at how they function, what they mean. When we do, of course, there are going to be disagreements. You may like *The Golden Breed* while I find it a pallid copy of *The Endless Summer*. You may consider *Point Break* melodramatic tripe, where I locate sensitive pertinence within its Hollywood bombast. As far as I'm concerned that's fine, as long as the conversation continues. The same goes for the choices here. It's impossible to cover everything, and at one point necessary to choose what to leave in and what to leave out. Some readers will no doubt simply consult the index and be shocked that their favorite film of all time is not even covered; I could list a dozen movies or videos right now that I'm sure will evoke this reaction in certain readers. If you feel that strongly, great. Among other things, that means the surf movie is an alive and kicking (out) part of our cultural scene today. In any case, I hope you enjoy the close attention given to the works that are covered in this book. As for the inevitable disagreements, let's enjoy them too, realizing they're all part of a deep down love for surfing and the contradictions of the fascinating subculture that has grown up around this pleasant weekend recreation and utterly life-changing daily obsession.

Surfing in the Movies: A Critical History begins with a chapter providing a brief look at the history of the sport, a preparatory glance at the organizational sweep of the book and an examination of the rich visual and thematic potential of surfing, the beachspace, and the filmmaking act of "shooting the curl." The main body of the book consists of the two major sections which follow. "Five Hundred Summer Stories: The Surf Movie and Documentary" takes as its subject the non-fiction treatment of surfing from its earliest appearances on celluloid through the three decades of communally viewed surfing moves and on to yesterday's Internet-uploaded surf video. While the surf movie's never not about the joy and the delirium, part of its meaning lies in the ways surfing's insouciant pleasures bump up against the pragmatic economic complications of a wider culture of dizzying change. If anything, that's even more the case in the several dozen studio and independently produced narrative films that are the subject of Chapter 3, "In Hollywood's Hands." A brief conclusion, "Zero Summer," consists of a subjective glance back at the best surfing films and videos and a searching look forward to the as-yet unimagined potential of this genre and subject that will always be fundamentally about the stoke but which at its best takes us into other fascinating, and sometimes troubling, areas of feeling and reflection. While it's tough these days to consider any attitude "universal," the undiluted bliss, 800 years old, of the medieval rota "*Sumer is icumen in*" comes pretty close. Even if many of their greatest achievements in fact take place in the winter, at some level surfing and the film genre it has engendered have always been about summer's joyful immersion in the now. As this manuscript emerged, however, its working title "Summer and the Fall" stood as a daily reminder that tension between surfing's otherworldly presentness and a real world's weighty imperatives is inevitable. As I hope to show in the pages to follow, the history of surfing and the surf movie can never be fully detached from history, just as even the most endless of summers can only tell its full story when framed by the other seasons.

~ 1 ~

Shooting the Curl

> Free man, you'll always love the sea,
> Which is your mirror, your soul reflecting
> The unending rise and fall of the waves....
> —Charles Baudelaire, "Man and the Sea"

For the greater part of its long life, a wave is silent and essentially invisible. Sun pours down far offshore, hot-cold tensions engender wind, gusts tug at the ocean's surface. Countless frictions accrete, shaping themselves over vast distances into pulses of pure energy that align with others of their kind. The result is something more sensed than seen, that is, until the wave's push meets the shove-back of the shore. There what had seemed near-abstraction—a barely traced line, a gentle lift—bunches up suddenly into something abundantly physical. When its hidden undercarriage, long accustomed to smooth, unencumbered sea passage, starts to graze the coastal shallows, the wave's story races to its brusque conclusion: energy soundlessly traversing liquid abruptly morphs into a rising, then inevitably tumbling wall of water that is noisy and very visible indeed.

Certain peoples of the South Pacific seem to have always known how to find in those moments of watery transition moments of pure pleasure. Then, in the eighteenth century, others started to notice. Over a good century and a half, the word would very slowly trickle out—until the 1950s when, in a sun-stunned eyeblink, surfing hit America and the world it was learning to dominate with the full weight of modern capitalism, mass culture, and the entertainment machine. Like the wave itself, surfing had been happening for the longest time, but it was essentially silent and invisible—that is, until it was all you could see and hear. The same could be said of the movies that suddenly were providing audiences worldwide with the sights and sounds of surfing. Over a hundred years ago the emerging communication and entertainment medium of cinema began very slowly to catch on to the emerging sport and life choice that was surfing. But for decades few people outside a small cadre of initiated insiders really noticed—that is, again, until it seemed that everybody did.

This book proposes to tell the story of the long relationship between surfing and cinema, one at first timidly discreet, then abruptly public. Shooting the curl began very quietly with such men as Thomas Edison and those French pioneers, the Pathé *frères*, coaxing a few silent, grainy images from bulky cameras aimed at incoming Hawaiian beachboys. For decades surfing occasionally showed up in still photography and even less occasionally on film: in at least two early cartoons, to be sure, but generally in the odd travelogue or newsreel feature for curious landlubbers, as well as in artlessly enthusiastic home movies, some of which have luckily survived. It was the gentlest of swells at best. But then an L.A. schoolteacher spliced together some of his 16 millimeter Hawaiian footage, posted a few handbills, and charged 65 cents for a 45 minute cinematic package of silly humor and what for the time were smoking rides. From the modest beginning of Bud Browne's *Hawaiian Surfing Movie*[1] and its shared tribal pleasure for the small but swelling surf community, the film wave born that 1953 evening would continue a modest but inexorable rise for the rest of the decade. Finally it would break with a full Hollywood splash in the April 1959 hit feature *Gidget*. And when it did, the rest, as they say, is history: the surf-crazy '60s with the Beach Boys on the radio and an endless string of *Beach Party* movies at the drive-in; the oft-imitated but inimitable *The Endless Summer*; the surfing movie and documentary expanding from *Spinning Boards* into *Sipping Jetstreams* and *Riding Giants*, and migrating from the beach town multi-purpose hall to the multiplex and then online; and a requisite two or three big studio productions per decade from *Big Wednesday* in the '70s through today's *Chasing Mavericks* and *The Perfect Wave*.

Like all relationships, the bond between cinema and surfing has had its good moments and bad. Documentary, narrative, or curious hybrid, the surfing movie can sometimes give you the tingles and send you racing to the beach (or YouTube) for more. It can also set you squirming in your seat, laughing at the wrong time, and making for the exit. In its quiet beginnings the documentary as broadly understood was indeed the genre of choice. According to Matt Warshaw's compulsory *Encyclopedia of Surfing*, in fact, "surf movie" doesn't refer to *Gidget* or other movie storytelling at all, but only to often loosely linked collections of surfing action sequences aimed at a niche audience of aficionados.[2] Confidential and very barefoot amateur in their early days, these films would grow and change, eventually reaching out to—and sometimes reaching—larger mainstream audiences; certain of the more ambitious products aim to communicate the raw "surf movie" vibe, while others head into more classically informational documentary territory. In any case, for Warshaw fictional narratives—beginning, of course, with Sandra Dee's saucy tomboy scoring a board and joining the boys on the beach—fall into another, slightly derisive category, "Hollywood and surfing."

To accept this distinction, it seems, is to agree at least in part with the title of the unreleased documentary *Hollywood Don't Surf*: on one hand, the "real" surf flick made for and by surfers, on the other the Tinseltown product with its connotations of illusion and base commercialism. This distinction is too neat not to be suspicious, of course, and as such it makes an instructive starting-point for this book. As we'll see, various versions of this tension will appear and re-appear—often in extremely complex and conflicting ways—throughout the history of surfing and the attempts to commit this intriguing and photogenic activity to celluloid. Within the world of surfing and surfing films, borders separate but are also fluidly, and frequently, crossed. Not coincidentally, the two most recent histories of the sport focus repeatedly upon certain unresolved contradictions in the surfing world. In his history of the sport, the prolific Warshaw states that "the nonsurfing world has shaped and formed the sport more deeply than surfers care to admit."[3] Peter Westwick and Peter Neushul's *The World in the Curl: An Unconventional History of Surfing* (2013) returns with tidal regularity to the similar argument that "surfing's story is that of the modern world."[4] At its heart are the discrepancies between an often carefully cultivated image of the surfer as primitive innocent holding the world at distance, a Thoreau-in-trunks, and what the authors contend is the sport's recurring entanglement with a landlocked world of larger social forces. Unsurprisingly, elements of these same unresolved tensions permeate filmic treatments of the sport.

In 1958, eight years before the 35mm release of *The Endless Summer*, certainly the most iconic of all surfing films, Bruce Brown brought out his first effort, a look at five California surfers wintering on the North Shore of Oahu called *Slippery When Wet*. Sweetly naive, technically clunky, its 72 minutes link dozens of screaming wave sequences with a comic portrayal of the beans-eating sleeping bag lives of typically broke surfers. Fine, but the very first words of the opening credits are "Velzy & Jacobs Surfboards Presents." Sure, Dale Velzy and Hap Jacobs' board shaping empire was a far cry from the later multinational doings of a Billabong, but still. In any case, the participating surfers were recruited expressly for the trip, the "docu-narrative" was staged, and a company picked up the tab. For all its earnest innocence, how not to think of the whole deal as a sales promotion? Such blurred lines, we'll see, will consistently frame the picture of surfing in cinema that follows. And, in a sense, why shouldn't they? Anyone who's ever surfed knows how it pulls you out of work and planning and worries; and how it leads you to the most present of spaces in an alert fusion with the wave's rhythms and even—the imaginative take-off comes easily—the beating heart of the world itself. But if this intensely privileged moment does not take place on the dry land of obligations, it does take place on its edge. To get there the woody needs gas.

Perhaps it's sad, or simply inevitable, that a surfing ethos of marginality and pure connection with the natural world finds itself overlapping with the need to make a living. In filmic representations of surfing, whether insider collections of hot curls and wipeouts, documentaries, or narratives, for the local auditorium or the cineplex, the result has been a cinema of often richly conflicting signals and messages. Even Bud Browne's '50s ur-films—as unstained for-surfers-by-surfers as they come—were from the beginning considered "commercial" by the filmmaker himself.[5] Among other things they demonstrate the cinematic principle that the documentary never simply documents reality, but rather changes that reality by the mere fact of focusing a lens on it. Browne's up-close, artisanal, natural glances at the surfing scene at times feature legendary Waikiki regulars Rabbit Kekai and Scooter Boy Kaopuiki—who, we were told decades later, "loved to *perform* for Browne's camera" and, adds Rabbit, very self-consciously nurtured a "notoriety" that was evidently useful in their day jobs as Waikiki hotel beachboys, the proto-professionals of surfing. Okay, not the star system but from the beginning already edging away from a primal surfing cool one imagines oblivious to things like cameras and image. Line crossing of a different sort occurs frequently in the narrative film as well. Look at, say, *North Shore*, *Blue Juice*, *Surfer, Dude*, or again *Gidget*. All of these movies take pains to glorify a carefree surfer vibe—that is, until have-it-all *dénouements* which somehow force that round peg into the square hole of careers and grown-up expectations. It's not just in the featherweight Twainian fairy tale world of *The Prince and the Surfer* that you can be a cool dude and still marry a princess. The hero of *North Shore* wins a moral victory in the big final competition, but he's also got that place in a prestigious New York art school.

To tell the story of these and other surf films, you have to tell the story of surfing itself. And, as Warshaw, Westwick, and Neushul insist, its history is entwined in turn with nothing less than that of History writ large: the ravages of colonialism, the twentieth century and the new tourism economy for the islands, then the full range of social changes unleashed in that crucial period of the late '50s and early '60s, and later with the subsequent technological mutations and shifts in economic and social model that have marked our dizzying last half century. In 1963, in other words, "Surf City" was as much an outpost on the New Frontier as it was a Jan & Dean hit. It was no coincidence that surfing boomed just as America's kids—and soon those of other countries—were learning to rock around the clock and, shortly thereafter, throw rocks at the cops. They were hitting the beach to practice a sport with no apparent utility, odd codes, and a language completely foreign to their parents, who themselves had done their growing up not in trunks and bikinis but in Depression soup lines and, in many cases, on faraway battlefields. Even the finally safe '50s suburban Gidget was '60s subversive in her own way, intrigued as she was by new patterns of social organization and a timidly emerging feminism.

Like the sport itself, *Gidget*, the three dozen Hollywood narratives it has essentially inspired, and an endless stream of "surf movies" and documentaries have at some level always been about the tension between a marginal, present-centered, hedonistic beach life and the pressure to get a degree and a job. Yet while the competing tugs of August and September remain at some level the thematic framing of the surf film—and the obsession of the Hollywood version—over the decades to come the sport's cinematic representations would go on to view through that lens wider issues in the larger society: changes in gender roles, post-colonial questions of race and ethnicity, the shiny (mis-) representations of increasingly dominant media empires, the alluring traps of big money and fame. The surf movie examines these and other questions, in part because surfing itself has become just another element of that larger society. Unsurprisingly, as surfing boomed in popularity and entered the mall, its counter-cultural edge started to erode, and often from within. Over only the last few decades several hundred wave addicts grew to today's 20 million-strong surfing population worldwide, a handful of sandy surf shops morphed into sportswear conglomerates catering to this group and the countless more who just like the look, and an elaborate global system of competition, sponsorship, and advertising slotted slickly into place. Inevitably the surf film reflecting this changing sport and life option began to put on some serious financial muscle and willingly play its role in what the professionals themselves identify without blushing as the "surf industry."[6] Present from the beginning, the ironies nevertheless sharpened when the loveable surfer myth of a carefree slide in the liquid moment dropped into much more frequent and intimate collision with the star system, heavy prize money, big-time sponsorship, and product placement at its most venal.

While looking closely at certain of the major, and many minor, films inspired by surfing in the last century—including video, there are, amazingly, perhaps a thousand—this history will critically examine these ironies and other complex patterns as they emerge from the story of surfing itself and are reflected in the framing, dialogue, montage, narrative structure, sound tracks, and other elements of filmmaking. It will begin as cinema's relationship with surfing began, that is, with non-fiction—the early witnessing of the pioneers, the pure surf movies, the informational documentaries and travelogues, the more recent video on DVD and the Web. It will then turn to the cinema of narrative fiction, those stories focusing on surfing as sport or obsessive life choice, or at least as significant background informing and directing the film's meaning. While many movies from both broad categories are the formulaic work of indifferent talents, a handful of these films have risen to the level of art, and a number, while flawed, nevertheless find ways to shimmer intermittently with the grace and mystery of the surfing that inspired them. This chapter will prepare the ground by, first, briefly examining the long history of the sport itself. Through its historical record of European "discovery," then tragic decline, revival, exportation, and eventual evolution to worldwide popularity and status as a significant global commercial and media commodity, the surfing story not surprisingly frames the central issues that will animate its reflection on the wide screen. These introductory remarks will conclude with an exploration of the richly symbolic, aesthetic, and thematic opportunities presented to the filmmaker/artist by surfing per se, as act and life option, and by the evocative hybrid beachspace in which it occurs. To be sure, too few filmmakers fully honor the dazzling potential of the subject and the setting. Yet even the more modest talents occasionally ask questions worth asking, and most remain alert at least to certain intriguing suggestions of the space and the act of surfing.

As in any tale worth telling, the story of surfing is structured by conflict. The tensions reflected in most surf films are those at the heart of waveriding itself: proud marginality and the stoke vs. compromise and mainstream acceptance, paddling out or growing up, sliding unnoticed in the 6 a.m. curl or shredding for fame and the big bucks. Even at their most commercial or compromised, however, the motivations of the various players in the surf world tend to remain mixed; the practical need to find an accommodation with the larger society at times dilutes but rarely fully erases the magical appeal of surfing and its empathetic relationship with a raw natural force. Still, the conflict remains between a normative life and an ideal—and idealized—surfing life, and it's not too much to say that versions of it play out in some way or another in virtually every encounter between cinema and waveriding. In the history of representations of the sport that tension is nothing new. As we'll see, it was apparent from the very first instant of the recorded history of surfing.

~ ~ ~ ~ ~

A Strange Diversion

Europeans first glimpsed and noted their impressions of surfing—an activity for which they had no name, obviously—in the latter half of the eighteenth century. What we might consider surfing's proto-history was the indeterminate but doubtless very long period before this in which Pacific Islanders and, most likely, other peoples worldwide took simple daily pleasure in the challenge and thrill of riding incoming waves to shore. While a powerful record exists in the songs, oral tradition, and language of indigenous Hawaiians, the first written traces would only come in the careful scientific and bureaucratic journaling of crew members on the famous exploratory voyages of Captain James Cook. Born in 1728, Cook led two monumental circumnavigations through the then largely unexplored South Pacific, as well as a final voyage that included mapping much of the northern coast of North America and the European "discovery" of Hawaii.

In the surfing community, the first Western record of surfing was for many years considered to date from Cook's final voyage and a crew member's 1777 journal entry describing waveriding in Tahiti, followed by a similar description in 1779, this time at Kealakekua Bay in Hawaii.[7] In fact, at least one other significant earlier eyewitness account exists.[8] Accompanying Cook on his first epic journey, botanist Joseph Banks would achieve impressive research results soon to vault him into the presidency of the young Royal Society. On May 29, 1769, he found himself in Tahiti returning from a frustrated attempt to recover clothes stolen during a night spent on shore:

> In our return to the boat we saw the Indians amuse or exercise themselves in a manner truly surprising. It was in a place where the shore was not guarded by a reef as is usually the case; consequently a high surf fell upon the shore; a more dreadful one I have not often seen: no European boat could have landed in it and I think no European who had by any means got into [it] could possibly have saved his life, as the shore was covered with pebbles and large stones. In the midst of these breakers 10 or 12 Indians were swimming who, whenever a surf broke near them, dived under it with infinite ease, rising up on the other side; but their chief amusement was carried on by the stern of an old canoe; with this before them they swam out as far as the outermost breach, the[n] one or two would get into it and opposing the blunt end to the breaking wave were hurried in with incredible swiftness. Sometimes they were carried almost ashore but generally the wave broke over them before they were half way, in which case the[y] dived and quickly rose on the other side with the canoe in their hands, which was towed out again and the same method repeated. We stood admiring this very wonderful scene for full half an hour, in which time no one of the actors attempted to come ashore but all seemed most highly entertained with their strange diversion.[9]

In language jury-rigged to deal with the completely novel scene before him, Banks's remarks share much with those made by others a decade later: a scientist's sharp eye for detail faced with the unfamiliar, admiration for the skill displayed, and a barely suppressed sense of envy. William Anderson, the ship surgeon observing wave riders in Tahiti in 1777, stresses equally their "most supreme pleasure," as well as similar surprise at the gleefully repeated nature of their play in the breakers.[10] Interestingly, Anderson's first interpretation was that the canoe surfer he sighted was fleeing after stealing something from the ship, an attitude oddly echoing the bitterness a "dissatisfied" Banks felt fretting about stolen property just before happening upon the surfing scene. In such a juxtaposition of disillusionment and suspicion with innocent fact—on, literally, days one and two of surfing's written history—we see the first quickly sketched version of a dichotomy that will recur with remarkable frequency in the two and a half centuries to follow: on one hand the custodians of order, responsibility, discipline, and ownership; on the other lighthearted devotees of pleasure, insouciance, and useless, instinctive absorption in the moment. Arriving from an industrializing Europe in a ship called the *Endeavour*, Cook's men came to map what they considered one of the planet's dark corners, categorize its plants and animals, and take the crucial first steps towards exploiting its residents and expropriating its resources. The locals waved aloha and went surfing.

The first European visitors regularly used terms like utopia and paradise to refer to the South Pacific islands.[11] Such language betrays the bias of Westerners towards exoticizing the indigenous people they would soon exploit, and indeed we do know how the story of their Garden ends. Ironically, it was representatives of cultures striving for certain Enlightenment ideals of social organization and universal human rights who would set in motion these distant peoples' eviction from the very Eden Europeans imagined they inhabited. That certainly was the case in Hawaii, where modern surfing was born and where its diverse fortunes would reflect the sudden radical changes to come in traditional island life. A certain abundance of resources and the leisure time it facilitates are necessary for the regular

1. *Shooting the Curl* 11

"Surf-swimming," from *Sketches of the Life of Bishop Patteson in Melanesia* (1876). From 1855 to 1871 John Coleridge Patteson pursued Anglican missionary activities in the South Pacific. Amongst many cultural observations, he portrayed an activity practiced by both sexes involving the use of "a piece of wood ... called a surf-board," on which participants "are carried along on the apex of the surf at a prodigious rate."

practice of surfing, an amiable formula in the earlier days of these islands with their small populations and relatively easy access to food sources, not to mention warm water and absurdly pleasant weather. According to tradition, surfing had a sacred dimension and everyone surfed, young and old, women and men, commoners and royalty. In the century following Cook's stealth invasion, the arrival of other Europeans and Americans would increasingly disrupt traditional practices. In the process surfers, for centuries at one with their culture and their environment, would become an endangered species.

In "Roll Plymouth Rock" from the flawed masterpiece *Smile*, Beach Boy Brian Wilson links the Western power steaming into the Sandwich Isles with what that power was doing at the same time to the North American Indian population. And indeed, well-practiced in the paving over of indigenous cultures, nineteenth century Americans were equally adept at remaking Hawaii in their Protestant, competitive, mercantile image. From a uniquely commercial perspective, the opportunities were irresistible: a wide range of available resources, booming markets, and relatively simple manipulation or co-optation of a local ruling elite. There was sandalwood until the hills were bare, whale oil until petroleum did in that market, then pineapples and sugar. Even as missionaries targeted the locals, year by year white foreigners wangled more and more land and power for themselves, reducing much of a free population to the status of serfs on their own islands. "There is no document of civilization," wrote Walter Benjamin, "which is not at the same time a document of barbarism."[12]

In the midst of such a century-long nightmare, the decline of surfing per se might seem relatively insignificant if its practice were not so deeply ingrained in the culture and its fortunes thus so representative of the common fate. It's often said that the censorious hand of religion dealt the most serious blow to Hawaiian surfing in the nineteenth century. Westwick and Neushul jostle conventional wisdom, arguing that the real villain was the new pattern of brutal work at sustenance wages imposed upon nearly all of the islands' population. Yet while it is clear that exhausting labor left little time and missionaries did what they could to discourage surfing, if only because of their discomfort with undraped sexes mixing as they traditionally did on the islands' waves, finally worst of all was the nearly total demographic collapse of Hawaiian society. A combination of new microbes and alcohol for organisms accustomed to neither led to an horrific drop of *90 percent* in the native population from beginning to end of the nineteenth century. Finally sealing the deal was the "official" sheen given to the de facto dominance of foreigners over a reeling local population, first in the 1894 establishment of a puppet "Hawaiian Republic," then the humiliation of gunboat annexation in 1898. While the 1892 observation that surfboards could only be found those days in museums[13] was distinct hyperbole, more than a century of Western presence had taken its toll on Hawaiian traditional culture. Notable was the disappearance of the ancient system of religious strictures governing most aspects of daily life and conferring on waveriding a ritualistic, culturally central status. With it vanished much of the sport's link with the profoundly traditional values of an indigenous pre-contact past.

Yet just as it severed those ties, it would be foreign influence that would help reshape Hawaiian surf culture and export it to the rest of the world. For the moneymen found at last their most durably profitable island industry, tourism. As the hotel infrastructure grew to accommodate the affluent elite who discovered Hawaii early in the twentieth century, the beachboy glide-in at Waikiki would come eventually to compete with the swaying grass skirt as an emblem of the tropical paradise's marketability. On the islands the surfing life began its rebound around 1900, in good part due to the efforts of a couple of early surfing proselytizers and prophets, as well as the inspired example of at least one genuine surfing god. It would of course be decades before surfing was implanted elsewhere to any serious degree—in fact, not until the '50s when Pan-Am's regular routes erased overnight the formidable barrier of sheer distance and isolation. But those throngs at Malibu would not have so suddenly materialized were it not for the same enthusiastic campaigners.

Products of the ethnic jumble of early twentieth century Hawaii, surf-smitten recent arrival Alexander Hume Ford, the Irish-origined but locally born George Freeth, and the great Duke Kahanamoku were to mark surfing history, giving the sport a precious boost at home and spreading the word abroad. One of the first regular stand-up riders, Freeth figures in perhaps the sport's most influential early written promotion, a dithyrambic 1907 piece in the *Woman's Home Companion* by the popular Jack London. "A royal sport for the natural kings of earth" is London's windy term for what he witnessed and gamely tried at Waikiki. A blend of manly aesthetics, self-deprecatory humor, and appreciatively precise description of complex physical activities unfamiliar to his readers, London's first-person account introduced both Freeth—tearing past, "carelessly poised, a young god bronzed with sunburn"—and the cheerful Ford. Ford hustles London around, giving him the lowdown on surfing with the fanatical energy of the recently converted—for in fact he had only just arrived that year, taking to the waves instantly and soon riding outer breaks with the best Hawaiians. In 1908 and 1909 he would follow London in writing up his own impassioned version of the joys of surfing in a magazine for children and in an "Outdoor America" feature for the widely read *Colliers*.

It was between those two events that Ford made his most permanent mark on the local scene with his founding of the Outrigger Canoe Club, an omnibus water-sports association considered now the world's first surf club. Recalling an ugly century of foreign domination and forecasting social tensions to come, the haole-dominated Outrigger would soon enter into half-open conflict with the ethnically mixed Hui Nalu Canoe Club, founded shortly after as a more egalitarian, less expensive alternative. As its website proudly proclaims today, the Hui Nalu was co-founded by the young Duke Kahanamoku, swimmer, surfer, and waterman extraordinaire. It is hard to exaggerate Duke's contribution to the revival of Hawaiian surfing and role as unofficial ambassador to a world ignorant of its joys. A wet Jim Thorpe, Kahanamoku broke world sprint swimming records by margins of *three and four seconds*, and ruled the Olympics for years. Such was that domination that one might say he also surfed, though he was clearly the finest surfer of his time.

Offered opportunities to travel for what we would call today public relations, the modest, charismatic Duke performed swimming—and, when the waves cooperated, surfing—exhibitions far afield, famously bringing the sport to a later surf-mad Australia in 1914 and causing a sensation in beach towns on the East and West Coasts of the States. At much the same time, though far less the star than Duke, George Freeth was similarly plying the American seaside. While his first trip to the mainland in 1907, organized by the hyperactive Ford, was to pitch Hawaii as a tourist destination, his surfing demonstrations took on a life of their own. L.A. developers soon made Freeth the first "professional" surfer (followed shortly by Duke), paying him for regular surfing displays in the South Bay and, accessorily, encouraging his activism in almost single-handedly creating the profession of beach lifeguard. While three Hawaiian princes studying in Northern California were "giving interesting exhibitions of surfboard swimming as practiced in their native land"[14] as early as 1885, the more influential contributions of Freeth are generally considered the true birth of surfing on the mainland and certainly of the famous Southern California beach culture.

Unsurprisingly, the Hawaiian surf scene had rebounded quickly due to vestigial cultural roots and ideal climatic and swell conditions, not to mention a growing population of those beachboys catering to the well-heeled clients of the grand new hotels and ocean liners eager for the thrill of waveriding. In California, by contrast, the full flowering of beach culture was still decades off. The small community of early adopters that had the waves to themselves through the '20s and '30s nevertheless did start a number of surfing clubs, one of which organized the Pacific Coast Surfriding Championships in 1928, a competition for what was essentially a group of buddies that would continue until the beginning of the War. Like the individual observed in 1939 from the "Palos Verdes Cliffs" by poet Muriel Rukeyser, surfers were thin in the lineup, but they were there.

A number of forces would conspire to turn that scattered band of briny fanatics into a social phenomenon. The war shipped thousands of servicemen to the islands, while in its aftermath Pan Am, already exploring commercial flights to Honolulu in the '30s, brought thousands more yearly to breathe in the trade winds and outrigger-surf the waves. The tiki craze sent out its first shoots in the 1934 Hollywood opening of Don the Beachcomber and, five years later, the Golden Gate International Exposition's celebration of Polynesian culture. As the state's population soared and economy boomed after the war, a baby boom generation of suburban kids was looking for fun fun fun all summer long. Technical changes in surfboard design had come along and were continuing. Balsa to hollow board; fiberglass, foam, and fixed fins: from the crafted koa and redwood behemoths of early days, boards were becoming lighter, more maneuverable, and more easily available. Modern communication, including the early surf films of Browne and his cohorts, was also getting out the word, and notably the buzz about big wave surfing. In a widely printed 1953 Associated Press still by Honolulu reporter Scoop Tsuzuki, a hairy Makaha breaker dwarfing three surfers was the wave face that launched a thousand trips—not just the Fred Van Dykes off to Hawaii on the next plane to try the big stuff, but many more off to the board shapers just starting to set up shop. By the end of the decade, as Orange County artist Rex Brandt would show in oil with the warm ambers of *Surfriders* (1959), surfing had even become a tasteful, saleable gallery subject.

Any account of the 1950s surf boom must, of course, include *Gidget*. A popular 1957 novel and hit 1959 film, it fictionalizes the real-life adventures of the author and screenwriter's daughter Kathy Kohner, a suburban 15-year-old who discovered the vibrant scene at Malibu in 1956, got in with a group of serious surfers, and soon popped up on the board herself. The novel makes clear that "there was indeed a boom in surfing, but *Gidget* was as much an effect as a cause of it."[15] With accurately described waveriding, summer nicknames, sexual curiosity, casual surf crew rites, and totally bitchen slang, its tartly mouthed first person narrative bespoke an already well-established surfing scene. That was Malibu, sure, but the new California wave culture that emerged there would soon race up and down the coast with the speed of radio waves pumping Dick Dale out of sandy transistors.

When Gidg' frets about the "big jig-saw puzzle"[16] that relations with her parents have become, she's giving sweet voice to generational tensions just starting to roil Western society. Incomprehensible to many adults, surfing played a key role in the developing youth culture then yelling messages of rebellion to their kids. If only because it offered many a compelling alternative to the route traced by Mom and Dad, what was happening at Redondo Beach had its resemblances with what was going down at North Beach. Like most everywhere in those days, the sand was terrain for debate: was surfing a wholesome athletic pursuit or a druggy, dangerous raised middle finger? In '63s "Surfin' Bird," the Trashmen flipped the second word of the title out there loud and clear. But many defended their sullied reputations, like the "Devoted Surfers" who wrote that same year to the *Alfred Hitchcock Hour* to take issue with certain character portrayals in a recent episode and argue that "all surfers are not bums. It isn't fair to put them all in the same category." As long as the quiet swell of surfing remained essentially invisible, either in far-off Hawaii or practiced closer to home by a few colorful eccentrics, everything was apparently fine. But when that wave suddenly hit the home front and kids started paddling out by the thousands, some adults started sounding like the scolding missionaries of the nineteenth century or those earliest European witnesses primed to read pleasure as theft.

In any case, the alternate world proposed by the surfing boom fit the times. And just as Elvis and Dylan burst into kids' lives around the globe, so did surfing. After Hawaii and then California, the next great homeland for world-class surfing would be Australia. As in the States, a few post–Duke outliers became a human wave in the '50s and '60s, a process that would repeat itself on a more modest but still impressive scale from France and Portugal through South Africa, Peru, Japan, and nearly anywhere with a half-decent coastline. In the United States the East Coast soon followed the West, and it's not incongruous that the world's greatest surfer today—most would say, ever—hails from Cocoa Beach, Florida. Kelly Slater's status as the sport's first near–Household Name derives, of course, from his breathtaking talent and longevity, not to mention good looks and a natural, unassuming personality. But even a poster boy of that quality doesn't get invited into the cast of *Baywatch* unless the sport he represents already occupies a critical mass of public attention and favorable media positioning.

Ironically, just as its counter-cultural nature began to appeal broadly to a younger generation, surfing began to put on serious "official" and institutional weight, a process that would only accelerate over the decades to come. It was, of course, not alone in its appropriation by the mainstream: because the Doors' dangerous edge made them popular, Buick planned to pitch station wagons with their music. In nearly every surfing nation, the first organized low-profile professional competitions and rudimentary circuits fell obediently into place at this time, events indissociable from the still-echoing surf music boom, *Beach Party* and its clones, Kansans scoring board shorts and flip-flops from Hang Ten, the founding of *Surfer* magazine, Bruce Brown the darling of New York film critics, and the attention of occasional television producers willing to provide a new revenue source while tapping a growing youth market. The wetsuit arrived, giving the chilliest of waters new accessibility and far more than doubling the range of surfable coastlines. The short board showed up as well, followed in years to come by twin- and tri-fin arrangements, each new step allowing for more aggressive cut-backs and flashier, more camera-friendly moves.

By the '70s, with the professional door forever busted open by some cheeky Aussies, and then the '80s, surfing was consolidating a certain institutional identity. The obsessive avocation of dawn road trips and secret breaks, of rowdy tight-knit crews and a private language, was also the showpiece of a young but ambitious global infrastructure of competition, commercial opportunity, and media exposure. In the decades since, that infrastructure would continue its expansion until even the sport's wildest wildmen, the moon-howlers who ride the big waves, would be coaxed within sight of the corporate boardroom. Peter Ames Carlin's parallel between surfing and the untamed "longing that had called all American adventurers out into the frontier"[17] applies in spades to big wave surfing and its near-mythical juxtaposition of the tiny human form with endless mountains of moving water. In the mid-'90s it would be, somewhat ironically, modern technological innovation that would take a throwback mountain man like Laird Hamilton past impassable frontiers of physics and fear. Where a Greg Noll, gung-ho crazy as he was, could only paddle so fast, the early '90s introduction of the Jet Ski tow-in began to drop foot-strapped maniacs into previously unsurfable storm-born monsters. While big waves had always meant Waimea and Sunset, harrowing new opportunities were showing up in places no one thought to look before, in California, Australia, Spain, Tahiti, and even over forbidding mid-ocean reefs. The sophistication of scientific wave forecasting and of modern communications that had enabled the search for these more primally frightening new breaks—including, of course, the Internet, which would soon document a hairy morning session in real time—would in turn lead to attempts to commercially harness the over-the-top abnormality that takes some people out into them. From helicopters or from cameras immersed in the heavy stuff itself, of course, what great footage. The Big Wave Tour was born. When a big swell hits Dungeons or Peahi, two dozen pre-selected competitors instantly converge, and gear sponsors or cell phone providers serve up the resulting photogenic cocktail of grace and high danger. The streamed video of those dense, deadly rollers is wonderful, but at times it can seem like an infomercial.

Worn as he repeatedly paddled off the map of the known world in the '50s and '60s, Noll's distinctive jailhouse shorts were a casual statement of outlaw defiance but already also a calculated visual marker for the early surf media. It's impossible not to recognize where a baby step towards professionalism like that has led, see the growing daylight between the commodified domestication of the many events sponsored by the thirty-year-old Association of Surfing Professionals (now called 2015 the World Surf League) and the romantic soul of surfing. That soul has never left a single committed surfer's body, but the conflict persists because surfing as activity can't help but exist within an evolving larger social world. In at least one way, though, increasing corporatization has been accompanied by indisputably positive change: a rampant sexism that for decades marred the sport is at last perhaps—perhaps—meeting its match. The route to full gender equality remains very long: listen to Dusty Payne in the 2011 video *Lost Atlas* ragging about girls waiting until "it gets one foot again and they can do their little tailslides." But nearly one in four waveriders today is female, a number edging yearly upward as wildly talented professional role models are at last getting a share of the spotlight. "It was never like that when I was growing up," marvels champion Layne Beachley.[18] In this sense, one imagines, even the old-school generally up in arms about such things might see the good side of a Team Roxy, the Quiksilver-sponsored surf unit that financially supports a number of the most competitive young women surfers.

Surfing's a riven scene, at once seeking out that hidden reef break and turning a spotlight on it while selling the rights. Today even everyday stylistic issues reflect such divisions. The longboard revival that cruised in to stay some twenty years ago was, a board manufacturer makes clear, about a "more graceful, aesthetically pleasing and easier style of surfing."[19] The tone is gracious but the comparative form points to a deep cultural rift: more graceful and aesthetically pleasing, that is, than the relentless shredding and aerials of the competitive ASP/WSL media show and legions of soulless, hyperkinetic consumer kids. In recent years surfing has gone on to join forces in the public imagination, and that of many surfers themselves, with the full range of those kids' "extreme" or "action" sports, like snowboarding, BASE-jumping, skateboarding, free climbing, BMX, and parkour. What better proof of this than Benji Weatherley's genial, empathetic 2008 video *Life as a Movie* that takes some of the world's top surfers, skaters, and snowboarders on the road and, gamely, into the different similarities of each other's disciplines? In the alliance of these sports many see surfing at last renewing with its sadly lost anti-establishment ethos and edge, while others smell the weed, scope the baggy pants or dreads, and cringe at the conformist anti-conformity of the image-obsessed. Others see dollar signs in either or both of the above, savor the lucrative youthful demographic and its savvy, style-aware customer base. In any case, stroll into Becker Surf outlets in Southern California tomorrow, and you'll be struck by an acre or two of the hottest clothing lines—and over there, tucked in the far corner, a few boards. The legendary Phil Becker was the most prolific board maker ever, shaping by hand in Hermosa Beach as of the early '60s and later out of the longest continually run surfboard factory in the world. Billabong bought his company in 2010.

The full story, though, is that the troubled, multinational bought everything but the surfboard business, which the boss and his partners refused to sell and which remains to this day Becker Surfboards in a direct line back to those first hand-planed blanks. One might say that Phil Becker sold out but didn't sell out. The history of surfing is certainly marked by compromises and opportunism, by scolding glances, cultural skirmishes, and hard real world choices that weigh on real people. But then there's lovingly shaping a board with the same cats you've known for years. There's watching from the rise, splashing out through the soup, paddling hard to crest an incoming, floating, talking, and then that darkening blue outside and the sudden turn to shore. Like William Anderson's surfer in 1777, maybe you were stealing or maybe not, but it doesn't matter anyway when the hissing glide begins.

~ ~ ~ ~ ~

Little Eden

The shore, the wave, the human form: it's no surprise that from the early infancy of cinema filmmakers have been drawn to surfing. An alternate way of being, an activity practiced for pure non-utilitarian pleasure in a striking natural décor set literally apart from the pedestrian doings on land, surfing in and of itself offers an immense palette of visual, aesthetic, and symbolic potential. It's remarkable how from the beginning filmmakers sensed that range of possibilities. It was 1895, the year before the famous train arrived in La Ciotat, that *les Frères* Lumière set up their camera on the little *plage* south of town to shoot kids splashing in the waves. In this 34 second trifle they seem already to intuit the rich potential of the subject. There's something strangely hypnotic in *La Mer (Baignade en mer)* ("The Sea, Sea-Bathing"). Ten-year-olds tumble off the tiny planks of a pier into small breakers, stumble and half-ride them back in, repeat the operation. Even in silent grainy black and white one hears and sees the palpable delight as the boys, at once interchangeable and distinctively individual, loop repeatedly out and back.

This is proto-surfing, already the repetition-with-difference of the journey out, the wave-trip back in, and the seaward return presaging that of the surfing cycle. The boys' mini-session echoes too the circular drama of the breakers themselves, always the same and always different, the inward surge, the outward slosh, the ceaseless repeat. Having too much fun, the kids never want off this merry-go-round of shore and sea. Their filmed cycle of insouciant pleasure, though, soon found itself in a telling cinematic clash. In Paris on December 28, 1895, the filmmakers first displayed their revolutionary efforts to a paying audience thrilled by the new medium. The ten short films of that legendary *séance* began, significantly, with *La Sortie de l'usine* ("Leaving the Factory"), slalomed through a varied series of action sequences, and finished with *La Mer*. Placed in the strategic first and last positions, shot similarly mid-distance from fixed positions, the two films oddly recall and evocatively contextualize each other. In the former, massed women in elaborate hats and

"*La Mer*," les Frères Lumière (1895). With their series of brief films shown at *Le Salon Indien du Grand Café* in Paris, the Lumière brothers organized the first projection for paying spectators in the history of cinema. The last of ten, this 30-second clip shows young boys repeatedly jumping off a small pier into the sea at La Ciotat.

heavy full-length dresses emerge tiredly into an early evening light through the rectangular framing of a factory door, before splitting off as individuals in their separate directions. Where the camera here films from outside towards the restrictive interior of the factory, it opens on wide sea and infinite horizon in *La Mer*. Separate individuals and never an amorphous group, half naked, the kids are not closing in on the lens to escape an interior but rather moving away towards the Mediterranean where they repeatedly plunge into their chosen element. Theirs is a carousel of ardently celebrated freedom and joy. In the juxtaposition of the two films, the implication is that their mothers too are on a carousel but one which at most accords them brief instants to themselves before domestic chores imprison. And then tomorrow and so on and on, when their fatiguing circuit will lead them inevitably each day back through that door into the factory's somber interior.

A couple of minutes of film and already a visual and thematic harvest: the protean magic of water, the fluid transfers of sea and shore, human and nature, human and machine, the generations, a socio-economic subtext, even that age-old surfing divide between the reality principle and the pleasure principle. Auguste and Louis Lumière almost certainly knew nothing of surfing, but they were alert to a visual language that could make poetic sense of its world. Pioneer cinéastes still inventing their medium in the first decade of the motion picture, they were not surprisingly drawn to the sheer visual potential of water in motion, the play of depth and surface, its restless, evolving repetitions, the quiet dark fluidity and the sudden visibly noisy white shatterings as it meets the shore. In this they were not alone. From the most mediocre of Sunday seascape painters through Turner or Winslow Homer, artists have taken to that meeting. Its beauty inspires, but even more so the mysterious suggestions present in the intermingling of the elements of earth, water, and, above, the air of an evocatively far horizon.

The eventual worldwide adoption of surfing could never have occurred, of course, had not its necessary prerequisite, swimming, become widespread practice in the Western world. This in turn would not have happened without the fundamental change in attitude towards water and the sea that took place at the end of the eighteenth century—again, just about the time Europeans were first watching those aquatic islanders ride waves to shore. The Romantics in particular found in the sea an image of life's raw mystery and spiritual intensity, qualities they rightly felt were ignored as the Industrial Revolution and an emerging consumer culture began to impose their conditions. It is on the ocean shore after all that Wordsworth rejects that world that is "too much with us"—a world of zombie "getting and spending"—as he yearns instead seaward to affirm the deeper truths of Proteus and Triton. His young contemporary Lord Byron prided himself on an utter ease in the water rare in those days; when he, famously, swam the Hellespont, it was as much a philosophical statement about a necessary immersion in life's currents as it was an act of bravado. Byron commemorates the feat in Canto II of his epic masterpiece *Don Juan*. "A better swimmer you could scarce see ever," he labels his extravagant semi-autobiographical hero five Cantos later, going on to describe him riding waves to shore after a violent shipwreck. "Though faint, emaciated, and stark," writes Byron, "He buoy'd his boyish limbs, and strove to ply / With the quick wave, and gain … / The beach which lay before him."

Many writers have listened in on the unending, rhythmic conversation between the more knowable shore and a sea Thoreau called "a wilderness reaching across the globe, wilder than a Bengal jungle, and fuller of monsters."[20] In "Dover Beach," a signal cry of nineteenth century spiritual confusion, Matthew Arnold hears "the eternal note of sadness" in "the grating roar" and cadence of the incoming waves. For Tennyson "Crossing the Bar" past the rollers' moaning "sound and foam" is an image of the final, inexorable return to death's "boundless deep." In the great conclusion to *A Portrait of the Artist as a Young Man*, Joyce's young alter-ego Stephen Dedalus wades through waves that beckon instead to new possibility. There, his soul "singing wildly to the sea," he strides through the seadrift to "greet the advent of the life that had cried to him" over "the dull gross voice of the world of duties and despair."[21] His contemporary Ernest Hemingway also takes his signature hero to the beach. Near the end of *The Sun Also Rises*, Jake Barnes returns to San Sebastian after his Pamplona (mis-)adventures and plunges into the surf: "I swam out, trying to swim through the rollers, but having to dive sometimes. Then in the quiet water I turned and floated. Floating I saw only the sky, and felt the drop and lift of the swells. I swam back to the surf and coasted in, face down, on a big roller, then turned and swam, trying to keep in the trough and not have a wave break over me."[22] This is a precise description of body-surfing. It's also a narrative and symbolic recapitulation of the ethic of an author aware that we can't hope to know what life means, only how to swim in it. Turning away from the symbolic void of the heavens, he feels the tangible, symbolic "drop and lift" that is life. He accepts the wave's energy, content just to keep ahead of the break on his return to a wounded world. That it was during the filming of *The Sun Also Rises* that the first surfboard made its way to the Basque Coast is fitting.

Filming surfing, addressing the surfing life, the best filmmakers draw intentionally and instinctively on these and a multitude of other meanings as they emerge from the expressive transaction between surfer and wave along that symbolically rich land- and seascape that is the shore. Many, it seems, resort to clichés, melodrama, and a series of predictable formulas. That said, such is the beauty and thematic cargo of the waves that even some of the less distinguished narratives and surf community movies occasionally flare into life. And if nothing else, they get by on the undeniable fact that surfing is an extraordinarily photogenic activity—so much so, wrote Elvis Mitchell in the *New York Times*, "it's hard to believe that color film wasn't invented just to capture it." Edison recognized the power of those visuals a century ago, and the same stupefying wonder he must have felt underlies any shot of surfing even today: no matter how many times we've seen it, there is something basically unbelievable about human beings *standing up* on a tumbling wave, not to mention carving sleek sweeps and tight reverses back up its face. And as the scene developed and widened its social footprint, what was also not to like cinematically about fit, good-looking kids in a dream locale practicing that potentially dangerous sport which, even straight-on from a fixed shore location in black and white, films like a million bucks?

The scene is much more than its very pretty pictures, of course.. As sport, identity definer, and style locus, the surfing the twentieth century brought gradually into visibility and which has become familiar these last decades is a space of, variously, big money competition, reverent communication with the natural world, heavy partying, one-to-one confrontation with appalling physical force, proprietary localism of the ugliest sort, New Age self-discovery. It is a counter-culture and a culture. It can be a way to rebel and a way to grow up, and some live an entire adult life, work and all, somehow rhythmed by the daily wave report. Surfing is the Beach Boys sweet in their striped Kingston Trio short-sleeve button-downs, and it's original rebel-misanthrope Miki Dora dive-bombing kooks and bouncing checks. The Top 40 joyfully told us everybody was learnin' how, but to paddle out as the new guy can be to try entering the most closed of societies. Surfing can seem like an ocean of style, posing, and attitude, but out in the impact zone and beyond the superficial abruptly washes off. Celebrating the utter specificity of place and the instant's fluid, forever-gone evanescence, surfing refuses the modern commercial myth of franchised, reproducible predictability. To choose a short board or long, three fins or one, can be no less than to define different selves and value systems.

Paradoxes—snap-backs and 360s—rule surfing. Another example: recovering what it can from its traumatic history, surfing encourages a deep respect for tradition and ancestral wisdom—a reverence particularly surprising for a sport that seems so much to emblematize modern youth culture and utter devotion to the present instant. Among other things, this deference is signaled by key markers of Hawaiian language and the prevalence of inherited ritual—the shaka, the paddle-out funeral, a ti leaf taken along for the ride—as well as the mandatory Hawaiian pilgrimage that, beyond the evident attraction of the waves, is also an act of respect for the Duke and for the Holy Sand itself. It's not just slick marketing that labels a senior competition category of contemporary pro surfing the Heritage Series. Some of the youthful rebelliousness tapped by surfing thus lies paradoxically in the growing self's willing inscription into what is presented as an ancient lineage, with its incumbent history, codes, and restrictions. Yet, deeply steeped in tradition as it is, at the same time could surfing be more post-modern? Like wind-surfing or hang-gliding, it is central to what philosopher Gilles Deleuze identifies as the "new sports." Unlike traditional sporting activities defined by strict limits of time and space and the inherited hierarchical authority structures imposing them, these pursuits involve fluid entry "into an existing wave," where "there's no longer an origin as a starting point…. The key thing is how to get taken up into the motion of a big wave, a column of rising air, to 'get into something' instead of being the origin of an effort."[23] To such implicit, deconstructive resistance to traditional frames of reference, the organized competition wing of the surfing community pugnaciously responds, of course, every time it saleably transforms those moments of fusion with the natural force that's just passing through into maneuvers of quantifiable value and rigid parcels of time. To which responds in circular turn one of the oldest romantic surfing traditions. Though they probably wouldn't have spoken of resisting attempts to delimit and commodify pure pulses of energy, that's basically what a bunch of pissed-off locals were doing when they pushed a contest judging stand off the cliffs at Santa Cruz's Steamer Lane in 1969.

As Whitman said of his XXL self, surfing contains multitudes—the rich inconsistencies and thematic abundance of the action itself, and of course its evocative environment and physical setting. Think how it has been appropriated for metaphor, from international businessmen "riding the waves of culture," to lovers in a contemporary Chinese novel portrayed as "unfailing surfers" carving a century of paradise "at that turbulent instant," to the digital browsing that has become too much of our daily lives.[24] At the shore, from knee-high kids' stuff to Fukushima, pure fluid energy rears in defiance at sudden, solid resistance. The arriving swell is repetitive pattern and it's endless variety, or as Laird Hamilton says of the big ones in *The Wave*, "it's never the same mountain."[25] Proceeding in stately sequence, breakers seem all ruler-edged order, but of course they are also sites of chaos and fear. There the simple can become "in practice immediately complex," writes Virginia Woolf in

To the Lighthouse, "as the waves shape themselves symmetrically from the cliff top, but to the swimmer among them are divided by steep gulfs, and foaming crests."[26] Wild swings of perspective rule the sand as well, for what place is more one for sun-drenched, thought-free lotus-eating than the beach, yet on that thin strip of dry land the tragic drama of our collective addiction to fossil fuels is already playing out. And even carefree Waikiki lies hard by an ocean's unfathomable mass with the troubling, timeless reach of myth and suggestion that legions of writers and other artists have tapped. The beach, in other words, is just the beach, and it is much more than that. The greatest of the wavewriters, Daniel Duane, recognizes the way the surf scene can encode paradox, locate that sweet spot where the unreflective simple and the deeply complex both somehow find their footing. His brilliant 1996 *Caught Inside: A Surfer's Year on the California Coast* concludes with a subtly telling conversation between the author/narrator and a local painter. Prompting a response the surfing grad student clearly wants to hear, he asks why she's chosen to live there on a cliff overlooking the sea:

"Daily contact with the inhuman vast?"
  She thought about this, sighed as she looked down the block; the ocean had now faded to a black far deeper than that ashore. She shook her head: "Nah."[27]

The shore is a fine line, at once a sandy playground and an environment fertile with suggestion and potential meaning. As for the latter, the beach is perhaps most notably a place of transition and transformation. There land gives over to sea and surface to depth, white water segues into deep blue, and in that season between spring and fall individuals no longer children but not yet adults enact their necessarily open-ended scenarios, seeking their identities, falling in or out of love or conflict, playing, significantly displaying. While Hollywood has erred in so obsessively looking to the process of growing up for the sole thematic interest of surfing, it is nonetheless a real presence in any serious consideration of its meaning and not a surprise that, explicitly or implicitly, surfing films of every stripe have asked questions about personal transitions. Even when its tensions are not the primary interest of films treating the surfing life, the broad concept of maturation often serves as a prism through which to illuminate other issues, reflect social shifts, examine new pressures on the self in a changing world. Despite our best efforts, the adult scene wants us to leave the beach and, with the apparent exception of Kelly Slater, generally gets its way. This tension is interesting, as not only filmmakers have discovered. Gestated perhaps while bunking down with some band members at the Challenger Eastern surfboard factory on the Jersey Shore in the early '70s, Springsteen's "4th of July, Asbury Park (Sandy)" addresses the moment of eviction right from the memorable opening by setting the scene in Little Eden. A place so named, we know, can only mean eventual obligatory exile. The action may take place in early July, but even Bruce connects its tone to the fading summer and that moment when it's time to split this scene for good.[28] Ah Sandy, her name is just right—for what's under the boardwalk, but also for the grains of time that finally rule even this carnival paradise.

These metaphorical terms sing at once of innocence and its loss in the passage to adulthood, a carefree bopping down the beach and the sudden awareness that that life's through. They could as easily be describing the fateful first meetings between shiploads of focused, toiling Europeans and those tolerant, gently present surfers at "infinite ease" with their "strange diversion." Enchanted, some Westerners jumped ship to remain in what they saw as a paradise, but many more would instead offer the bitter apple of industry, disease, and manichean religion, of getting and spending. We know how that story plays out, but there is at least some agreeable irony in the fact that since the islanders taught the world how to listen, the seductive song of the waves has continued to tempt each new generation away from the desk and to the shore. For a good century now cinema has come along to record and, with varying degrees of success, creatively re-frame what happens there on the margin between the fluid promises of the sea and the land's hard certitudes. The story of those hundreds of films, we'll see, is nothing less than that of the surfing that has inspired them, with its complex narrative of pleasure and commerce, dream and reality. It's the story of summer and the fall.

~ 2 ~

Five Hundred Summer Stories
The Surf Movie and Documentary

> Long have you timidly waded holding a plank by the shore,
> Now I will you to be a bold swimmer,
> To jump off in the midst of the sea, rise again, nod to me, shout, and laughingly dash with your hair.
> —Walt Whitman, *Song of Myself*

When Joseph Banks first glimpsed those swimming "Indians" in May of 1769, the promising young botanist struggled for appropriate language to describe how they glided landward on incoming swells. While he could only understand the odd planks they rode to be "the stern of an old canoe," the rest of his remarks are recognizably precise even as they convey a certain rising excitement. Like most of the other Western accounts through the century to follow, Banks's description of this entirely novel scene is marked both by an age-of-science commitment to portray accurately what he saw and by the desire to convey the emotional rush abundantly enjoyed by the surfers themselves and contagiously communicated to the viewer. In a journal entry in faraway Tahiti Enlightenment Reason and Romantic Emotion met just as they were meeting in the larger context of European cultural change. In the countless non-fictional representations of surfing to follow—written descriptions, visual renderings, photos, and, of course, cinema and video—surprisingly little has fundamentally changed. The two poles remain informational, "documentary" communication of the curious realities of this marginal sport and life choice, and a consuming desire to bring the stoke alive and transmit its passionate allure. Theorists have brought their particular language to this contrast, referring to a traditional documentary's "discourse of sobriety" and to its opposite, the "discourse of delirium" dominating in the "surf movie" genre per se, where "a heightened and frequently excessive visual and aural intensity [is] brought to bear on the isolated action of surfing in order to reveal its secrets and meanings."[1] While certain representations do confine themselves to one extreme or other, the real action's usually between these poles, in a hybrid space where excitement may run high but it still fluidly intermingles with currents of information.

As Banks recognized, people who didn't know this unusual scene were intellectually curious about the odd activity and its accompanying subculture—but something was missing without a sense of the primary thrill of surfing and the ancillary kick of watching. In terms of publicity, the most significant early written account was the popular Jack London's first-person plunge into the sport, published in 1907 in the *Woman's Home Companion*. Giving it a try in that muscular pre–Hemingway way of his, London clearly got "surfriding," communicating its "particular physics" in paragraph after paragraph of still fascinatingly accurate detail. Then suddenly he'll break into song to celebrate delight in his own "ecstatic bliss" catching a first wave or in observing "a brown Mercury" whose "heels are winged, and in them is the swiftness of the sea." This blend of objective surfing fact and subjective emotional lift returns again and again, from the later Cook expedition accounts through others as varied as, say, Alfred Métraux's 1941 study of Easter Island or an 1881 English schoolbook illustration depicting a "Polynesian Scene."[2] Drawing on observations from a 1934 research expedition to Easter Island, the ethnologist Métraux precisely describes a few of the dying society's remaining children maneuvering their "*planches*" in the waves. Inspired by their daring and elegance, their joy mingled with "the voluptuousness of danger," the Swiss-American researcher assigned to Honolulu's Bishop Museum then waxes even more poetic, reading in them the island legend of Heru and Patu, who reveal their supernatural origin by defying the largest breakers.[3] The textbook engraving eases a similarly sublime mist over accurately portrayed details of Polynesian life. Near the clearly delineated grass huts and an incoming outrigger, a woman surfer proudly erect on her board throws arms out and head back in evident rapture. Imagine the Victorian schoolboys opening this book. Grass-skirted and topless, a smoking volcano in the distance, this surfer girl's from a different—a thrillingly different—world.

Not surprisingly, the earliest filmmakers turned quickly to the exotic and visually rewarding feast of the surfing. At first of course it was enough for cinema's pioneers simply to project movement on a screen, but soon the sheer novelty of seeing a train pulling into a station or a man watering a lawn no longer did it. The search was on for richer, more visually arresting subject matter to gratify public curiosity about a world made notably smaller by, among other things, advances in steam power and the international telegraph cable. Opening the way for the portrayal of surfing would be, first, the simple but nevertheless interesting spectacle of water in movement as expressed in a number of short sequences of coastal spaces and breaking waves. Towards the turn of the nineteenth century, as the Western world discovered the bracing effects of the sea, it is a short leap from the popular painting sub-genre of the seascape to the brief early clips of waves crashing on shore in Monterey or off the Southern French coast. When the scantily dressed human form in movement enters such scenes in the post–Victorian, pre-contemporary world of the early twentieth century, tensions relevant to the study of surfing immediately insinuate their presence: work and play, restraint and freedom, the stable dry and the protean wet. And once the camera caught actual surfers in movement, there would be no stopping it. In the first decades of the new century, the golden age of anthropology and a time when America saw itself in peripatetic, outdoorsy Teddy Roosevelt, the so-called "scenic," or travelogue documentary, dominated the embryonic cinema marketplace. With its utter novelty, colorful customs, constant action, relatively undraped "natives," waving palm trees, white sand, and hot sun, the Hawaiian surfing previously revealed to a small tourist public seemed made for a wider viewing audience soon to fall under the similarly distant, exotic charms of Robert Flaherty's *Moana* and *Nanook of the North*. As early as 1906 the Thomas Edison Company included clips of surfing at Waikiki in its scenic on the Hawaiian Islands just at the dawn of their tourist revival. The vigorous, entrepreneurial Pathé brothers upped the ante in 1911 to a now unfortunately lost film of 111 minutes entitled *Surfing, le sport national des Illes Hawaii* In the decades to come, newsreels and travelogues would return with regularity to the Waikiki beachboy streaking landward on long wooden boards and exotic outriggers.

The initial cinematic treatments of surfing itself were documentary in nature for the simple reason that their potential audiences knew virtually nothing of the subject. The evident intention of early photographers and filmmakers was to convey excitingly unfamiliar information and sights to avid viewers awakening to the possibilities of the new medium. Bill Nichols speaks correctly about the three "stories" that intertwine in every documentary, "the filmmaker's, the film's, and the audience's."[4] For decades, as the latter's story was one at best of vague, uninformed curiosity, it was normal that the rare features on surfing, usually in newsreels, did little more than focus on soft Waikiki combers as one of the many intriguing pleasures in what was rapidly becoming a tourist wonderland. When surf culture at last took hold on the more media-ready mainland in the 1950s, however, it suddenly achieved the critical mass necessary to alter forever the relationship between surfing and film. Signs of this shift included the pioneering still photography (and occasional filming) of figures like Tom Blake and John Ball, who memorialized on film the more developed Hawaiian scene and the small but growing Southern California surfing milieu. To extend Nichols's terms, lengthening one foot of the tripod inevitably meant readjusting the other two. A burgeoning audience abruptly offered a commercial market not only for filmed surf action but for footage of higher quality, intensity, and variety that in turn could only be shot by those actually familiar with the subject. And that process would only increase the target audience, and so on.

In 1953, showing the *Hawaiian Surfing Movie* he'd tossed together from years of footage shot on vacation, a Southern California Navy vet and schoolteacher named Bud Browne created the surf movie. A surfer who knew the scene and players, Browne offered SoCal's small but growing surfing population what they'd never seen before but knew suddenly they wanted more of. For a vastly male mob of teens and twenty-somethings, the model created by Browne meant lots of great action on soon-to-be mythical Hawaiian (and Californian) breaks accompanied by voice-over narration and music, and punctuated by a bit of surfing history and the odd corny skit; the latter created comic relief, often transitioning in very loosely narrative fashion to the next round of cool wave exploits. In suburban L.A. where it all started, coming together at the Elks Club or high school auditorium was all at once to declare a new personal identity, bond collectively, and have a blast. The celluloid was suddenly not about informing an unaware general audience but about sharing the rush. To be fair, a ration of pedagogy also went down, notably in the form of Hawaiian geography lessons, the recurrence of top surfers' names, and brief analyses of the riders' different styles, the whole contributing sizeably to the subcultural base of knowledge and to the emerging star quality of certain breaks and those who rode them. In an audiovisual landscape so far from today's sound and image surfeit, it's not difficult to imagine the attraction—the sheer *event-ness*—of Browne's films and those of a rising number of friendly rivals in the years to follow. *Gidget* was published in 1957 and already little Francie[5] is tickled about watching surf movies; she furthermore references Warren Miller, whose ski flicks provided their template. Surf movies were a real kick in the 1950s when there was an authentic, if small, subculture but no surfing publications existed, the sport was invisible even in the far fewer than 50 percent of American homes with television, and the tiny handful of Hollywood pictures that had inserted an odd surfing scene did so only for local color and background. All that would change, of course, in 1959. When Kohner's novel hit the silver screen it was in equal measure a reflection of the pop culture surf boom already under way and its single most influential spur. Then, as Jan & Dean and the Wilson brothers filled the jukeboxes, the *Gidget* spin-off *Beach Party* films fumbled maladroitly for story lines to commodify the sport and the scene for a vast new youth market.

For surfers these were abruptly the best of times and the worst of times. Certainly, the wider culture was validating surfing's existence but, as Sam George groused in promotional materials for *Hollywood Don't Surf*, "it was as if *Gidget* had opened the gates to the sacred city and the barbarian hordes swarmed in." The number of surfers rose exponentially, but so did the number of phonies only talking the talk and hangers-on trying to make a buck from the image. Where it all started on the mainland, the emblematic Malibu became a zoo. One response of the surf community was to further the development of its own authentic subculture, seeking refuge within it and distance from the wannabes. For several years a good two dozen other surfer/filmmakers continued Bud Browne's good work in insider surf movies that kept speaking to the faithful in the old way, with those wild rides and whimsical filler interludes. At the same time one of those filmmakers, John Severson, would also give surfers their own welcoming print medium home in the founding of *Surfer*. And then came another of the sons of Bud, the unrelated Bruce Brown, who did nothing less than finally seize the unseizable—the feeling of surfing—in 35mm and share it with the world at large. *The Endless Summer* (1964, 1966) spoke truth to surfers and non-surfers alike, at once reminding the former why they were different and confirming for the latter the sport's arrival as a permanent mainstream cultural phenomenon. Brown's classic ended the first major chapter in surf films, and it enabled everything that came after.

Which, despite never-ending golden age nostalgia for *The Endless Summer*, was a lot. After the sweet attempt of *Gidget* and then the *Beach Party* nonsense, the challenge of bringing surfing into narrative Hollywood filmmaking would be met repeatedly in the decades to follow, with results varying from the occasionally honorable to the often risible. As for the far more numerous non-fiction efforts, the following two decades would vary and enrich the classic formula to the point that the '70s are sometimes considered the surf film's "high period."[6] Using the term, Warshaw points winkingly at the turned-on, authority-allergic, ecologically enlightened direction taken by movies like *Morning of the Earth* and *Pacific Vibrations*. Surfing's always been about getting (naturally?) high and flipping off The Man. After the ho-dad commercial invasion spearheaded by Frankie Avalon and Annette Funicello, the counter-culture offered surfing a rainbow bridge back towards its rebel streak and forward towards subversive communal and environmentalist values—even as other forces such as the burgeoning surfwear industry and mid-'70s creation of the full-blown pro circuit were leading towards serious commercial transactions with the Man. As further subject matter, there was also the radical change in the surfing experience itself with the triumphant introduction of the alert new shortboard and the concurrent shift of surfing power to the Southern Hemisphere. For a core audience of surfers and sympathizers, though, the viewing experience remained fundamentally the same. But building on the example of their forebears with substantially improved technical capacities and, by this point, the need to pay ASCAP licensing fees for music, the new generation quickly turned the old three- to five-grand budget into a memory as hazy as the marine layer. Bruce Brown had shown that breakthrough to a wide general audience was possible, and investments followed suit until a film like *Free Ride* in 1977 would run $70,000. Nothing for a Hollywood release, of course, but something when you're lucky to be playing little art theaters for a week or two. Though it took three six-month runs up and down coasts from California to Australia for *Free Ride* to break even, it eventually grossed half a million dollars, but unless you were Brown you weren't making the real fortune. Though that was never the point, even for Brown.

In any case, as of the early 1980s the viewing experience of surf films—to that point public, sectarian, and rowdy—would, with the exception of surf film festivals or occasional special promotional tours and showings, change radically. The reason, of course, was the arrival of home video; while expensive at first, films became quickly accessible and, thanks to the re-wind, divisibly re-watchable. Starting with *The Endless Summer* itself, certain older movies began appearing on tape, and soon direct at-home video would be the format of choice for new ones. Cost made that decision for most aspiring filmmakers. But as expenses plunged, so did image quality and other production values. In the early days even those movies still shot on 16mm film would lose a great deal in their transfer to videotape, and those filmed directly on ungainly camcorders lacked sharpness, not to mention the slow-motion function. As a new financing system structured around surf brand partnerships began to slot into place, the results remained largely, in not universally, forgettable. After this unpromising start, though, the step-by-step arrival of DVDs, new small digital cameras, pro-quality home computer montage software, and direct online posting would over the last couple of decades lead to greater democratization of the creative process, to an explosion in video production, and to a profusion of technically and artistically worthy films. Today, three decades after the traditional four-walled surf movie closed its doors, such as Taylor Steele, Jack Johnson, Thomas Campbell, or Jack McCoy have more than honored their illustrious ancestors Greenough, Severson, and MacGillivray/Freeman. Like their films, the surf video remains a central component of the surfing scene and each generation's ever-renewing "process of subcultural identity and community formation."[7] If there has been an occasional exception to the new video norm, it has been a very small handful of big budget, wide-release Hollywood forays into surf culture addressing accessorily the hardcore surf community as they primarily target a general audience willing to drop a few bucks to be sold the dream at the megaplex. We're talking high profile films of the last two decades like Stacy Peralta's *Riding Giants*, Dana Brown's *Step Into Liquid*, and his dad Bruce's own attempt to follow the Beach Boys' advice and "Do It Again," *The Endless Summer II*.

The recurrence of the Brown family name is significant for Bruce is as much a father figure to succeeding generations as Bud Browne was to the generation that preceded him. The influence of *The Endless Summer* may not always be explicitly acknowledged, but that theme music's in every ear. And while Brown by no means invented the surf trip as film subject, each time a camera team hits the road with surfers to Costa Rica or Portugal or the Philippines they are walking in the flip-flops of Robert August and Mike Hynson. Today, with the extraordinary surf trip the new normal, "video pro" is a more common job title for professional surfers than WSL contestant, and even those on the circuit double up on the road whenever possible . If surf media since the 1970s have been marked by one thing, it is the globalization of surfing as sport and life choice. For surf movies the very cool travelogue has become the default mode for unsurprising reasons. The well-known breaks have been gridlocked for decades, and coastlines south and north offer beauty, space, and a

Poster, *The Endless Summer*, director Bruce Brown (1964, 1966). In 1964 co-producer Bob Bagley shot (left to right) Bruce Brown, Mike Hynson, and Robert August at Orange County's Salt Creek Beach. A student at the Art Center College of Design in Pasadena, John Van Hamersveld silk-screened the negative, pocketed the $150 fee, and created an icon (Cinema V/Photofest).

bracing sense of possibility. While Hawaii, California, Mexico, and later addition Australia will never be "worn out" as surfing destinations, forms of surf culture have expanded into literally every country with a promising coastline, and the *National Geographic*s of this expansion, *Surfer*, *The Surfer's Journal*, and a few others have not only taken consistent, abundant notice but have frequently arranged trips themselves to provide subject matter for future spreads.

As every few years yield their lot of "new" breaks and fashionable destinations. the explosion in casually improvised Western world youth travel that began in the late '60s has kept breathless pace; the more formal surf tourism of recent years has been its logical continuance for the now flush generation of graying baby boomers. Surf filmmakers have been instrumental in highlighting these new destinations and, in unending spirals of one-upmanship, have continued to boldly go where no surfer has gone before. The same technical advances that brought video into the home have been equally vital, making available to non-professionals radically smaller cameras and production equipment of increasingly professional quality. To the point that today two or three guys who can scrape together the dough for, say, some surf exploration up the western coastline of Canada can film the whole thing with palm-held digital cameras and on-board Go-Pros. If they don't get eaten by bears, they can PC edit the result, and within a couple of weeks be sharing a creditably sharp, exciting record of their adventure on YouTube with, no exaggeration, surfers from around the world.

Like so many aspects of surfing, the emphasis on travel again illustrates the sport's fluid, varying relationship with mainstream culture and the currents of social change that animate it. Up through the early '70s the road that led to the North Shore and elsewhere was in good part an extension of Kerouac's, and even at his most Hollywood the "surf bum" Kahuna spoke of a subversively alternative existence: Peru or Hawaii, "gotta' follow the sun … ride the waves, eat, sleep, not a care in the world." Ironically, when Brown took his surfers to LAX, it was in part to escape the bumper-to-bumper rollers of the Kahuna's home break at what the filmmaker wryly identified as "this secret spot." Yet just as the celebration of Malibu spoiled it, the hordes sent on the road by Brown would eventually do the same with countless Bali's and transform following the sun without a care in the world into one more commercial opportunity. Just as the globalized economy has sent its tentacles into all aspects of our lives, corporate sponsorship is, to the bewilderment of many, now behind a majority of films, even those ostensibly slipping their respectful surf stars into indigenous local customs and rhythms. Surf travel filmmaking may share more than it wishes to admit with the been-there-done-that vision of widely available commodity tourism. One reaction to the normalization of surf travel has been increasingly gonzo over-the-edge, under-the-radar surf/film expeditions to impossible places like Iceland or Kamchatka, even if corporate money's likely to be along even for those rides. Relatively unmediated by previous spreads in *Surfer* and untouched by organized travel offers, this is commando stuff with scraggly roots in the contemporary extreme sports impulse and its implicit attempt to reconnect with a certain rebel marginality.

Like the sport itself, the non-fiction surf film places itself ostensibly on (or beyond) the edge of the land and the broader culture it represents, but its relations to that wider society have always been more than complex. For example, an environmentalist tenor—and, at times, overt engagement and argumentation—pervades most films of the last three or four decades. Since the embarrassingly dated cultural bloopers in Bruce Brown's films, the same can often be said of an apparently grateful openness to the different cultural riches of the indigenous peoples encountered while scouring the world for the next perfect wave. Okay, but the very curiosity about exotic locations harnessed and encouraged in the "search for surf" film formula that began so tentatively in the '50s and accelerated to warp speed in the '90s has led inevitably to wider publicity, the establishment of tourist beachheads, the construction of environment-unfriendly infrastructure, and other forms of host culture dilution and invasion. In 2014 Gregory Thomas is still rightly fretting in *Surfer* about how unhassled wave privacy just ends up going to the highest bidder. On every coast that these legions of empowered young white men have showed up, often accompanied by camera crews, even the best of intentions have not left their destinations untouched. The pattern should be familiar to anyone aware of surfing's history. Westerners applied the mental construct "paradise" to the Pacific Islands they visited, in the process rendering those places something close to the opposite for their original inhabitants. In more recent times authentic admiration for an Hawaiian style and mode of life has led inevitably from affectionate adoption to exploitative co-optation. Since the 1950s at least, a discourse of combat and conquest—"surf safari," "wave hunters"—has articulated the surfing experience. Graft to this the American culture-driven pattern of frontier-pushing and the male myth of daring adventure questing and "discovery," and we are not far from replicating the colonialist pattern.

In gender terms the message is similarly checkered. The first surf filmmaker Bud Browne actually presented women surfers without a snicker or leer, refusing generally to allow his on-shore camerawork to linger on tan curves and bathing suits on-shore. For the most part, though, even as the early movies explore refreshingly alternative (and sometimes subversive) patterns of male behavior and identity, the few women who do appear do so largely as bathing beauties. While an occasional film like *Five Summer Stories* did its part to shift the paradigm back to female surfing accomplishment, the camera eye has far more often focused a possessive, objectifying male gaze, that is, when the films are not simply celebrating a hearty men-without-women camaraderie. On the verge of the '90s an otherwise engaging surf film by Steve Soderberg will still include—literally—off-screen (male chauvinist pig) snorting to "comically" accompany shots of beachside beauties. In example after example the surfline remains a heavily gendered male space, where action and desire overlap and expression turns to sticks, big guns, and quasi-sexual longing for the tube. Surprisingly little has changed in the video era. To be sure, in the context of a Western world feminist discourse essentially normalized since the '80s, filmmakers are less likely than before to aim their lenses at bikinied bottoms and permit themselves the blatantly sexist comment. But, aside from videos like *The Women and the Waves* or *One Winter Story* which specifically address the place of women in surfing, where are the women who make up perhaps 20 percent of the overall surfing population[8] and who have made going concerns of such women-centered surf concerns as La Jolla's Surf Diva or Maui Surfer Girls? While they do figure in significant episodes from occasional videos like *One California Day*, *Litmus*, and *Singlefin: Yellow*, vast stretches of contemporary surf videos remain testosterone-only zones.

Similar incoherencies and fault lines mark the treatment of economic realities and temptations in the surfing movie. The early films were shoestring one-man shows. Hoping to generate enough revenue in the summer to head back to the North Shore the next winter, their creators struggled like their films' subjects, living on Spam and diving for the odd lobster. Resentment at the *Beach Party* commodification of their life choice orients the presentation of surfing in most movies during this period, and it was clearly not just Malibu overcrowding that drove Bruce Brown abroad to prolong what he perceived as a waning summer. Yet while his critical and financial success sharpened appetites and swelled budgets, it was the rapidly professionalizing competitive scene and the entry into the surf gear and related sportswear market of the "Big Three" that most introduced into surfing a divisive tonal split. *L'air du temps* at their back, films of the late '60s and '70s reacted by repeatedly grappling with the lure of cash and then-controversial notion of competition, while aggressively staking out alternative modes of being. The Kahuna only had to react against the square world and not its institutionalized incursion *into his*; in a similar way, the concept of the soul surfer—meaningless when that was the only identity available to a Duke, Rabbit, Buzzy Trent, or Peter Cole—would come into general usage at this time as a response to surfing's abrupt and growing commodification. And that tension's far from gone today if Noa Deane's "Fuck the WSL!" during the Best Movie sequence at the 2014 *Surfer* Poll Awards is any indication, his Instagram apology chalking bad manners up to concern about surfing "becoming a corporate sport."[9]

As top surfers adapted their styles to competitive norms and became paddling billboards, the surf movie and video reacted in a number of ways. While certain movies simply covered the main contests, Billabong for example tweaked the competitive system to come up with videos on its alternative "Challenges" or its more recent web-based XXL big wave and wipeout competitions. With a now imposing past to plumb, the historical documentary became a notable sub-genre, as did the star video biography after the prescient first of the form, a tight 23 minutes on Kelly Slater in 1992. Such concern with the human side of surfing heroes points the way as well to a parallel development, the surf movie "re-branding" of certain professionals, notably by association with soul surfer cred in low-key wave odysseys to developing world destinations like Indonesia and India. Offered modest collaborations in the movie years, corporate sponsors (or, more often, co-sponsors in elaborately assembled production packages) have become the dominant, if not only, players in the video era. A bald, frontal approach to the video as advertising vehicle rather quickly gave way to more subtle tactics and the realization that the less is more and that the laid-back, light-handed association of brand names with cool surfing in beautifully exotic locations might be all it takes. When, as is the case with a Taylor Steele or Jack McCoy, extreme technical prowess meets thoughtful narrative structuring and character revelation, the results can be outstanding. Generally independent but occasionally with limited forms of corporate support, a number of talented filmmakers have turned to the past for inspiration. Andrew Kidman, Thomas Campbell, and others embody a palpable impatience with the monetizing of surfing as well as the limits of a reductively hyperkinetic surfing style drawn from the skateboarding scene and read by many as a bit too heavy on wave attitude and light on brain waves. Accompanying the return of the longboard in the '90s, they cultivate a comfortably ripened aesthetic and a harmonious receptivity to an age-old surfing ethic that still may still have truths to share. Then there's the contemporary use of the Web to crowd-source individually lived and filmed surfing moments. Looking decisively forward in a technical sense, a project like *Innersection* is at once the latest thing and, in its grateful respect for the artisanal instinct and gesture, perhaps as well a homage to those values as they began to reveal themselves in the work of the surf film pioneers some sixty-plus years ago.

Together with the specialist written press, the odd bit of music, and the occasional Hollywood production, the non-fiction surf movie constitutes for most surfers the bulk of the popular cultural experience surrounding the actual paddling out and riding in. The pages to follow will address a small but representative handful of the multiple hundreds of films and videos that exist. It is important to view these works first as the significant surf community expression and bonding experiences they are, and then as manifestations of the intricate and evolving rapport between surfing and the society it alternately rejects or reflects. It is at least as vital, though, to examine them as they have been too rarely viewed, that is, as free-standing creations meriting close critical analysis, as worthy aesthetic objects. It's not enough simply to catalogue the athletes and breaks, evaluate the quality of surfing, and describe the comic or other transitions. Alone, within a particular filmmaker's overall body of work, and as part of a wider cinematic tradition, surfing movies deserve—and can respond to—serious questioning about, among other issues, framing, cinematography, narrative structure, rhythm, the employment of myth and archetype, visual metaphor, narration strategy and tone, and the expressive use of musical soundtracks. Beyond the evident, how do the parts constituting these aesthetic wholes function alone and together, and how might they work subtextually to convey subsidiary themes or cultural meanings? These are movies made with the relatively straightforward goal of sharing with others of the initiated something of the recalled thrill and shared joy of surfing. But as they take us to the sand and out through the soup, are they exploring other thematic terrain as well?

In order to make some sense of a vast, century-long body of work, "Five Hundred Summer Stories" will look closely at a number of the most significant non-fictional treatments of surfing. These remarks will begin with the earliest appearances of surfing on film and in still photography, then follow with the formal birth of the genre in the revolutionary contribution of Bud Browne. After a brief look at Bud's contemporaries and immediate successors, they turn to the exceptional work of Bruce Brown and the only surf film members of the general public are likely to know. With *The Endless Summer* the surf movie would enter what many consider to be its greatest days. Visually, aurally, and thematically freshening the films of the period, the densely interrelated cultural and subcultural "Storms" of the long section to follow were at least three: the shortboard squall, the concurrent political and social tempest of the late '60s and early '70s', and finally the tumultuous mid-decade emergence of the professional circuit. While a small number of high-profile theatrical releases would go on to reach a wider public in the last three decades, that would be it for the traditional surf movie, replaced as of the 1980s by home video. "Small Screens" looks at video which, after growing pains and a deserved initial critical scorn, may at last now be creating some of the finest surfing movies ever. The digitalized creative and viewing experiences are not that of the loudly communal early days. But in a time of technologically democratized filmmaking, streaming and other easy online sharing, and recent attempts to welcome surfers and amateur filmmakers into the process in the form of crowd-sourced films like the *Innersection* series, the surf film's new incarnations continue to play their traditional role. With *Surfer*, *The Surfer's Journal*, and other important physical and online print sources, the surf video remains a vital dry-land rallying point for the surfing subculture.

Whether *Surf Mania*, *Sik Joy*, or *Step Into Liquid*, all the films and videos in question are technically "documentary" in nature, presenting as they do, in John Grierson's classic terms, the "creative treatment of actuality."[10] In practice, of course, there are monumental differences in intent and intended audience between a 70 minute stoke-fest for a '50s zinc oxide crowd and a $2,600,000 Sony production in wide theatrical release recounting to a general public the history of surfing, surf culture, and the special attraction of big waves. These remarks will thus tend to use "documentary" for the relatively few films like *Surfwise* or *The Endless Winter* whose purpose is primarily informational, and "surf movie" or "surf film" for the endlessly multiple versions of the former, those communal celebrations of the stoke. That said, few films communicate the rush of surfing better than *Riding Giants*, and even hardcore action surf films generally take pains between drop-ins and wipeouts to educate curious viewers about the language, geography, personalities, customs, and techniques of the ever changing, new-to-every-generation surf scene. The surf movie primarily celebrates the stoke but also documents a way of life: the surf documentary primarily conveys information about that way of life but also celebrates the stoke. In other words, the lines between such sub-generic distinctions are fuzzy. At once scientifically curious and giddy with the spectacle before them, Joseph Banks and the other early Western witnesses to South Pacific skill and grace on the incoming combers had it right from the beginning. In representing this "strange diversion," the facts about surfing only make sense with the feelings.

~ ~ ~ ~ ~

From Filmed Surf to the Surf Film

The ultimate source of the feelings surfing arouses is the surf itself. That "surf" is both noun and verb highlights the finally subsidiary position of the human participant, reduced to inactivity when the waves don't cooperate and potentially capable of outstanding performance only when they do. How, a Yeats might have asked, can we tell the surfer from the surf? Or, to use completely different terms, "Who gazes at a tennis court?" Asking the question in *Step Into Liquid*, Randy Rarick again underlines the dependence of figure on ground in the act of surfing and in its visual presentation. From *The Angry Sea* through *Momentum* through *Riding Giants*, multiple dozens of surf movies offer visual confirmation, beginning as they do with the simple opening shot of a powerful incoming wave proudly free of human presence. Appropriately, the century-long history of surfing in cinema began with the camera's entranced gaze at the naked surf. Seeking visually arresting raw material for the industry of image production they were forging in the later nineteenth and early twentieth centuries, Thomas Edison, Robert Paul, *les frères* Lumière and Pathé, and others returned with insistence to the endlessly repeated and eternally varied spectacle of water crashing on land. Paul made a particular specialty of the sea and shore interface. The first film ever projected in Britain was his appropriately titled 1896 *Rough Sea at Dover*, a few seconds of heavy breakers side-slamming a jetty. Soon he would draw, twice, on similar storm conditions at Ramsgate, while *A Sea Cave Near Lisbon* (1898) aims the camera subjectively towards onrushing ocean waves surging through a cavern's rocky maw. The legendary Georges Méliès filmed storm waves on the west coast of France, Mark Blow and fellow Australian pioneers the same at Bondi and other beaches. Eventually designing a more portable camera, the Edison team shot storm winter surf in New Jersey before setting their rig up across the bay from Steamer Lane and filming the brief *Surf at Monterey* in

1897. The recurrence of such footage tapped a visceral Romantic attraction to the turbulent exchanges of the seaside. Versions of this fascination sent Winslow Homer and Delacroix to the shore; they helped establish Japanese woodcut master Hokusai ("The Great Wave of Kanagawa") and eighteenth century screenpainting genius Ogata Korin (the delicately powerful "Rough Waves") as iconic figures of Impressionism's *Japoniste* phase.

Place humans at play within the same frame as the breaking wave, and the image becomes interesting in new ways. Hokusai does so with works like "Ocean Waves" and "View of Honmoku" which portray desperately pulling seamen dwarfed on the faces of enormous ocean waves. In a tonally different manner, this is what the Auguste and Louis Lumière did with some of the earliest film, turning their newly invented 35mm *cinématographe* on the Mediterranean for "*Villégiature: Premiers bains*" and "*La Mer (Baignade en mer)*." The latter *actualité*, or brief documentary film, sparks an extended discussion in the introductory chapter of this analysis, but in fact both point expressively towards the rich aesthetic and symbolic potential of filmed surfing. In the first sequence, frolicking adults splash off and climb back on a platform bobbing in the swells; the second features youngsters doing much the same, plunging from a tiny pier into waist-high breakers before remounting and repeating the process. Contextualized by the imperatives of the Industrial Revolution and the filmmakers' well-known choice of busy factory and barreling locomotive as parallel subject matter, their subjects leave the regimentations and segmentations of modern life to return with ceaseless circularity to the amniotic preformal oneness suggested by the sea, like Cézanne's and Picasso's bathers from the same period, at once completely elsewhere and intensely present. Their actions group-determined and distinctively individual, they proceed out and back, on and off in tirelessly repeated cycles of pleasure that foreshadow the addictive repetitions of surfing and soon-to-arrive society of leisure, while mirroring the eternally repeated patterns of the tides and waves that make it possible. When H.J. Miles shot *Panorama of Ocean Beach and Cliff House* in San Francisco in September 1903, he insisted upon an intriguingly different kind of circularity. Long at more than a minute, the actuality applies recent technical advances allowing the camera to turn on its tripod hub and pan fluidly across a beachside scene; filming subjectively from the beach's center, he begins with the surfline and returns with orbital inevitability to it. As the shot lingers for nearly a

"Ocean Waves," Katsushika Hokusai (1833). Drawn from *Oceans of Wisdom*, this woodblock print is considered a classic example of Japanese *ukiyo-e*, or "images of an ephemeral and floating world."

third of its length over half-dressed kids dashing in and out of small waves, its persistence and their instinctive immersion in the fluid instant symbolically rebuke the stiff squad of adults fully clad in their wool suits and inhibitions.

While numerous actualities by other early filmmakers drew similarly on the inherent drama and spectacle of the shore, for the purposes of these remarks the most historically significant remain the Edison company's 1906 *Surf Board Riders, Waikiki, Honolulu, Hawaiian Islands* and *Surf Scenes* from the same location. The first films of surfers in action, the one minute sequences count among the two dozen or so clips that famed Edison technician Robert Bonine prepared for an Hawaii "scenic"; such rudimentary travelogues would go on to be immense successes with a public encouraged for nearly two decades by *National Geographic* and hungry for images of exotic locales and practices that, even in the era of grand liners, remained largely inaccessible to most. In a competitive professional environment responsive to such curiosity during a period generally considered the high point[11] of Western colonial expansion, dark, physically robust, undraped "natives" coasting in while standing on warm Pacific rollers were attractively, even titillatingly exotic. Which was the point, of course, for an energetic American empire that eight years earlier had illegally seized Hawaii and was already pitching its new possession as a hedonistic tourist wonderland. Silent like the other footage of the time, both sequences seem to have been shot at present-day Canoes, where Jack London experienced the breakthrough surfing moment with Ford and Freeth famously memorialized in the *Women's Home Companion*. Like the London piece, the films implicitly entwine three thematic strands, the relaxed holiday lure of Hawaii, the recovery of surfing there after the dire nineteenth century, and the sheer thrill and spectacle of the human form in dynamic concert with the wave's natural force.

Composed of two successive shots aimed directly seaward from a fixed beach location, *Surf Board Riders* portrays about ten surfers 50 meters offshore advancing towards the camera on mild two foot Waikiki combers; occasionally dismounting or gently wiping out, some enter the frame while others are included or excluded by a discreet right to left pan. *Surf Scenes* is a much busier shot from shore slowly taking in a crowd of several dozen tourists and locals playing in the same soft surf; fully bathing-costumed, what looks like a well-heeled tourist couple stands out in the foreground as they stroll with arm-in-arm intimacy through chest-deep water. Panning left, the shot features two heavy outriggers barreling in, as well as a prone surfer threading the needle. The craft of the latter sequence is interesting for its careful spatial orientation, establishment of the land/sea margin as playspace, and dramatic conclusion with the gliding surfcraft fluidly linking the outside break and shore. What you notice about *Surf Board Riders*, by contrast, is its extremely simple point-and-shoot nature. With this rudimentary minute of film, Bonine may be unwittingly illustrating a truth about the surf movie to come. When the subject being filmed—human beings standing on collapsing walls of water, after all!—is so inherently riveting, perhaps little other technique is needed. In any case, in the latter half of the century, the vast majority of surf filmmakers go on to confirm something like this point; while the search would from the beginning be on to find new ways to communicate the rush of surfing (see next paragraph), the ultra-simple tripod arrangement from shore has remained the bread-and-butter shot. With it what becomes interesting then is context and cast, the quality (or size) of the waves and, vitally, the performance of individual surfers. The visuals of Taylor Steele's first film *Momentum* aren't a great deal more complex than Bonine's, but the guy is filming a 20-year-old named Kelly Slater.

In the decades to follow, the cinema business would grow at a vertiginous rate, in the process responding to and encouraging a similarly burgeoning Hawaiian tourist industry; at the same time, Duke, George Freeth, and others would do the good work of surf evangelism, in a kind of reverse colonialization multiplying mainland U.S. and Australian converts and establishing the Hawaiian sport permanently on their faraway beaches. While a booming Hollywood as of the '20s would occasionally slip surfing into its entertainment mix, usually in the form of local color (a subject discussed at length elsewhere in this analysis), newsreel features and extended travelogues in the United States and Australia would gravitate with some regularity to Waikiki rollers. Such coverage complemented the popular magazine stills rapidly establishing the Hawaiian beachboy as an image with an iconic value nearly equal to that of the be-leied hula dancer. As early as 1911 Pathé-Frères *scénique* would devote 100 minutes to *Le Surfing: Sport national des îles Hawaii*. While the film is now lost, it almost certainly focused on the reliable Oahu tourist beach and its ready-made cast of available surfers. In 1931, for example, British Pathé News features what they called *Water Sportites*, a lightly captioned 80 second look from shore at incoming outriggers and, from the canoes themselves, at a handful of standup riders, including a couple of women. In 1926 prolific producer and director Robert C. Bruce was also there with *Sons of the Surf*, a featurette that builds interestingly on the simple approach early documentarists took to this strange, photogenic activity. Seven minutes long, Bruce's silent "scenic novelty" alternates fairly long shots of surfing action with text panels. The latter offer a mini-course in islands waveography: the "great breakers ... retain their form after dashing over the outer coral reef and rush the last two miles to the beach at the rate of forty miles per hour." Early on Bruce offers a two minute sequence composed of nine shots from the same shore perspective: the less experienced work the foreground while a couple of seasoned surfers comfortably ride three footers in the distance. Text panels then introduce two of the most skilled riders, William and David Kahanamoku, and David's dog Spot. Then comes the build-up about "the real sport ... out where the big ones are running."

The remainder of the film takes us out there, where the shooting comes, suddenly, from an outrigger obligingly rowed through and with the waves by locals to provide a number of mobile perspectives: below the breaking wave line as the regal Kahanamoku brothers arrive, off the shoulder as the roller passes and lifts the boat, and most notably a series of tracking shots across the same wave in movement from the surf-riding outrigger. In the vintage *Snapshots at the Seashore* (1903), British innovator Cecil Hepworth had bobbed through breaking surf on some sort of craft to put his viewers subjectively "in the thick of the excitement."[12] Bruce does the same here, following the stable shore perspective with the dynamic embarked camera in a progression like that pursued by later surf filmmakers always looking for money shots closer and closer to the curl. Yet, as remarkable as Bruce's enthusiastic presentation of waveriding is, it's finally lodged within a pattern of intention marking his film's subject less as a true surfing feature than as tourist promotion. The opening text insists on the uniqueness ("nowhere in the world") of a very clearly identified "Waikiki Beach on the island of Oahu." Then cut to the classic image of Diamond Head, tropical breezes fairly sighing, footage establishing not only the location but the tourism slant of what's to follow. In Bruce's shots from the onrushing outrigger that same iconic image will preside relentlessly over the surfers' racing glide in the foreground, at times to the point of allowing the board riders themselves to slip out of the frame. Though the two surfers are from that celebrated family, in the context of 1920s America and a mass-market entertainment product the fact that they were exotically dark-skinned "foreign" males may have implicitly required a certain image makeover. Bruce accordingly takes pains to domesticize his presentation of the two brothers, devoting a mini-"chapter" to David petting Spot and cutesily calling attention more than once to the pooch's all–American name in the accompanying text.

A comparison with photos of a closely similar scene is instructive. Nine years later *National Geographic* would publish a series of action shots by Thomas Edward Blake of "Waves and Thrills at Waikiki." Snapped from Blake's paddleboard, several adopt the same in-wave perspective as Bruce, off to the left of groups of three to five solo and tandem surfers with the emblematic peak in the background. In most of them Diamond Head is extraneous, either partially presented or notably absent, with attention directed instead to progressive phases of surfing technique: the start of the "pop up," stabilization in the standing position, the launching or completion of tandem positioning, etc. One photo with the classic Diamond Head silhouette, a shot of Amelia Earhart skimming by in an outrigger, is included to accompany the aviatrix's article "My Flight from Hawaii" in the same issue. The other shows two standing "surfmen" and a prone third either dropping in on the pair or wiping out. The selection of this photo seems aesthetically determined for much of the somberly toned peak is obscured by a rising cloud of brilliantly white foam and mist that, strikingly, takes the inverted form of the mountain behind it. Publication in *National Geographic* partially explains the studiedly neutral presentation here of what might elsewhere have been considered somewhat compromising physical proximity between the Hawaiian men and their Anglo women partners, as well as the careful, dispassionate attention to details of surfing technique and the specifications of board construction in the accompanying captions. As similar as the film and spread are, their agendas are clearly not, a difference that perhaps most of all stems from the fact that Tom Blake was a surfer. And not just any, for Blake is now considered the near-equal of Duke Kahanamoku for the totality of his enormous contribution to the development and popularization of the sport.

Born in the Midwest in 1902, a Blake on the cusp of adulthood met Kahanamoku at a newsreel projection of the Antwerp Olympics and more or less dropped everything to move to Hawaii, where he plunged himself into surfing and local culture with a voracious dedication that would eventually lead to his entry, exceptional for a haole, into the Hui Nalu surf club. Carrying the message much of his life from Hawaii to the mainland, Blake has inspired surfers since with a sweeping Whitmanian idealism. A top swimmer, he revolutionized board design with his lighter hollow paddleboards and surfboards, as well as the first board fin and primitive leash. Blake's innovation and historical importance extend to his work as a photographer. With a camera bought from Duke himself and a first-ever hand-crafted water housing, he began taking in-water shots in the early 1930s, a decade that would be marked, among others, by the *National Geographic* piece, the first surfing book ever, *Hawaiian Surfboard*, and magazine pieces and a second book on surfboard design and technique. Surfers recording images of other surfers and sharing them with a wider public have since, of course, become the norm for surf photography and filmmaking. It was utterly new at the time, but soon, just as Blake's initial interest in Hawaii had been sparked by a Waikiki newsreel viewed as a kid, others toying with the idea would be enabled by his pioneering example.

In Southern California in 1931 a USC-trained dentistry student named John Ball, already surfing for a couple of years, caught a photo by Blake in the *Los Angeles Times*. It would inspire him to turn his own early experiments with photography resolutely towards the young SoCal surfing scene. With Waikiki the newsreels had tapped into a certain cultural curiosity and appetite for the striking visual image; "Doc" Ball was prescient enough to recognize these attractions in his own backyard, where a few dozen individuals were knocking together an equally fascinating subculture with borrowed or homemade material, empty waves, and beat-up jalopies to get there. Eventually upgrading to a Series D Graflex camera and fashioning his own waterproof camera casings, Ball documented the surfing but also the preparation, the getting there, the hanging out. It was a scene he knew intimately as a founding member of one of the early California attempts to organize the sport socially, the Palos Verdes Surf Club. He took nearly a thousand black and white shots that have remained the gold standard for early surf photography, inspiring such greats as Don James, who began shooting as well in the '30s, and close buddy Leroy Grannis, who would launch a second career as photographer and publisher nearly three decades later. Ball's work showed up in *Look*, *Life*, the *Los Angeles Times*, the *Encylopædia Britannica*, and, recalling Blake's piece while recognizing the new geographical reach of surfing, in a 1944 *National Geographic* spread called "Surf-Boarders Capture California."

Returning after war service like many of his generation starved for the intense normalcy of the beach, he brought this and other work together with a few shots from other photographers in the famous *California Surfriders* in 1946. If you want some sense of how it was back in the day, this is the place to look. Ball's eye for eloquent framing and expressive detail will seem familiar to anyone who has seen the early surf films. In ten chapters moving south from Northern California's Pedro Bay to Windansea, the shots vary eloquently from "standard" shore shots to close in-water framing, from ukulele camp fires and cars parked on the beach to wide angle shots of surf spilling across a bay or off a point. Some of the waves are zero-break winter stuff impressive in size for California and all the more so without a wetsuit in sight. There's Pete Peterson, Tom Blake, Mary Ann Morrissey standing tall at Palos Verdes, Doc Paskowitz at San Onofre, and a certain "Bud Brown" bringing it on his "paddlewacker." Describing the action on these "fringing giants," an emerging surf lingo tussles with well-behaved '30s reminders that "Poise and Confidence Are Prime Factors in Surfboarding."[13] Doc Ball's importance to the history of the surf movie would have been secured by his photography alone, for his stills communicate an insider's affectionate understanding of the rapidly evolving surf culture and capture it on film with immediacy and freshness. Ball furthermore understood that slices of that life were all the better if communally shared. He frequently used his photos to create posters announcing that, as historian Gary Lynch tells it, his surf club was "holding a hula luau. Hawaiian music, food, drink, female companionship, and of course the newest surfing photographic images to leave the darkroom were the rewards if one attended the event." Subtracting the less frequent "female companionship," this already sounds like countless surf film nights to come.

Like fellow surfer photographers Jon Larronde and Don James, Ball clearly knew where things were heading technically, for by the late '30s he was complementing his still photography with 16mm footage of surf action by pals like Grannis and Hoppy Swarts as well as their hi-jinks on shore; in addition to the initial aerial views of surfing, he would also take the first-ever 8mm color films of the sport. While Doc treated this footage as home movies to be shared with friends, in the 1950s some would find its way as far as Australia for screening at a lifesaving club. Ball was a photographer of the first order and influential waterman in his own right as the modern surfing scene picked up subcultural speed and glided with increasing insistence into mainstream Western culture. With technical means improving and a potential audience expanding, Ball drew on Blake's example as a photographer to document with trenchant near-obsession not just the new surfing but the curious social world growing up around it; at the same time he looked provocatively towards the technical and aesthetic horizon with his film work. On p. 53 of Doc's *California Surfriders*, Bud Browne advances towards the camera on a sizeable right at Palos Verdes, left arm raised as though announcing his arrival. While flamboyant gesture was not his style, he and the new surf movie genre he would coax into existence were indeed on their way. In the early 1950s Browne's fervent personal interests and life of thoughtful adventure began to entwine with more public strands of sport, culture, art, media, and technical advances. When they did, he responded by taking his *Hawaiian Surfing Movie* over to a Southern California middle school auditorium and charging 65 cents for admission. After that evening in the fall of 1953 the surfing world would never be the same.

~ ~ ~ ~ ~

Santa Monica, Fall 1953

A lifelong love of the water, a series of personal choices, and some happenstance set Bud Browne up in front of the crowd that first night with a projector and a few scraps of music. As it might not have been only a short time before, Southern California was ready for him the year wire services everywhere picked up the famous photo of huge Makaha point surf, just a few weeks following Rock Hudson's broken shoulder surfing at Laguna Beach, and just a year after Hanna-Barbera's Tom and Jerry rode the waves of Hawaii. The pop cultural prow of the nation and in many ways the Western world, California was leading the way both with its expanding mainland surfing subculture and with the mainstream culture's awareness of its existence. A sign of the two, only four years later the novel *Gidget* would make the *New York Times* Bestseller List. The filmmaker who responded to an evident desire for images of surfing action (while in the process sharpening appetites for more of the same) was at once the perfect guy for the job and an unlikely candidate. A few years younger than Ball and Blake, Browne was born in Boston in 1912 and moved to L.A. at 19 to attend college. There he displayed piscatorial swimming ability that would lead to captaincy of the USC swim team and near qualification for the Olympic Games. Following the Tom Blake '30s SoCal model, it was then on to beach lifeguarding and a panoply of ocean activities including abalone diving and surfing. As we have seen, Browne got far enough into the local surfing scene to figure among the *California Surfriders*. But to Bud just as important as starting surfing in 1938 was the "profound effect" of his first trip to Hawaii, with its life-changing new sounds and smells, its still calm and uncrowded landscape.[14] Thus began a deep affection for the South Pacific that would lead to long stretches in Hawaii and, including a pivotal journey farther south in 1940, ten trips to a Tahiti that may actually have been a truer love.[15]

Even before his wartime Navy stint as a water skills instructor, Bud had been shooting photos and some 8mm hobby film. After the war he invested in a 16mm rig, shooting Hawaiian surfing in color regularly during the summers and other breaks from his new job as a schoolteacher. He knew the old guys, including Tom Blake and Duke—with whom he developed a true friendship—as well as most of the younger local generation and the odd early California transplant like Walter Hoffman. Some formal editing coursework at USC film school was a sign that Browne was starting to take film seriously. Then came one of those offhand suggestions that change a life. Dave Heiser was a Santa Monica teacher and surfer who, not incidentally, had nine years earlier completed a lifeguard course with later surfing legend and Browne friend Buzzy Trent, soon to carve out a big wave rep on the North Shore. Chatting with Browne at Waikiki about his filmmaking in the summer of 1953, Heiser suggested that John Adams Junior High School where he was a P.E. teacher, might be a good venue should Bud wish to share his footage with an audience.[16] Splicing together some of his better sequences and encouraged by the reaction of friends to earlier informal showings, he gave it a try. As much as one could call it that in the early days, a profession was born,[17] which Browne almost immediately considered as such. Even though he showed *Hawaiian Surfing Movie* only a couple of times that year, the reaction was positive enough that Browne soon quit his day job as a teacher to head each winter to the North Shore and gather film for the next summer's showings.

As of 1957, with the movies of Greg Noll, John Severson, Bruce Brown, and soon many others, Browne's films would not be alone on the limited California coastal "market." For him and for the dozens of early surf movie successors, things went more or less as they did at the historic Santa Monica evening. The pattern might vary according to whom the filmmaker might convince to come along and help, but in general it was very much a one man show. Having shot and edited the film, Browne made posters by hand, stuck them up in likely beachside locations (where most would immediately disappear, such was the hunger for surfing images), sold tickets himself at the door, coached a projectionist to start and stop as needed, flipped a soundtrack

Locked In, director Bud Browne (1964): Buzzy Trent at Waimea Bay. Wave king and court jester, Browne's close friend was one of the first Californians to take on the North Shore (Bud Browne Film Archives, Anna Moore).

tape recorder on and off for musical accompaniment, provided a live narration himself, and dealt with the inevitable glitches. Then start again the next day, and the next year. You had to be a highly energetic, canny showman to pull it off, especially given the rambunctious impatience of a young, highly male audience loudly bonding over images of the new, marginal sport that was becoming central to many of their energetically developing identities. Part of Bud's mystery was that he was all of this while always remaining the measured, deliberate introvert remembered by his friends. To complete the paradoxes, on one hand he presented a conservative, tight-laced persona; on the other, in those days when the Beats were theorizing a counter-culture to bongo drums, Browne actually gave up a safe job, dropping out to live small and off the land, and to follow his passion into the then very alternative cultural reaches of this new sport and life choice.

Like his colleague competitors, Browne shot in the winter, edited in the spring, and showed in the summer, at first along the California coast and later, responding to demand, in Hawaii, Australia, and elsewhere. From 1954 through 1956 he followed *Hawaiian Surfing Movie* yearly with films similarly blunt of label, *Hawaiian Holiday* and a new *Hawaiian Surfing Movie*, before taking his titles up a notch with *Trek to Makaha*. The earliest films stuck to the gentle breaks of Waikiki, where top beachboys like Rabbit Kekai, Blackout Whaley, and Scooter Boy Kaopuiki confirmed their reputations as the original hot-doggers. Guiding finless boards with a dropped foot, they did headstands and danced up and back at Queens or Public Baths, showing off for Brown's ever-present camera in a symbiotic exchange for "notoriety." As the title of the fourth movie indicates, he began to film the big waves on the North Shore in the mid-'50s after the huge influx of California transplants like Buzzy Trent, Peter Cole, and Greg Noll, but the mutuality of the filmmaker/surfer rapport remained the same. In *Fifty Years of Surfing on Film* Cole recalls that "it was very important to get into the movies and everyone would hang around Bud" to do so. Over the decades to follow, even when payment and contracts entered the picture, that win-win relationship has not changed.

Another thing that has not significantly changed is the formula Browne established in those original films. From the beginning his movies, generally running between 45 and 75 minutes, were at their simplest composed of several minute surfing sequences often focusing on one break and a particular surfer or small group, occasional transitional comic bits (like idle surfers riding cows or even elaborate skits), a touch of surfing history, and what would soon become a favorite, the wipeout anthology. To this he added narration identifying the performers and casually providing lessons in wave forms, technique, etc.; delivered live by Browne in the early films, the voiceover was a work-in-progress that varied according to circumstance. The last element was music, in this case selections drawn from Bud's record collection and transferred to a reel-to-reel recorder, which was the state of the recording art in the early '50s. He remembered favoring guitar, but it could be Hawaiian music or "whatever fit."[18] For decades these have remained the nearly invariable components of the "surf movie," and while a number of filmmakers and videographers have gone to more sophisticated narrative structuring and other variations, the Browne formula remains even today instantly recognizable and familiar. For that matter it was already familiar to some when Bud made his first film in 1953, the surf movie being a younger cousin of the ski films of pioneer Warren Miller. In 1950 the California skier and surfer put his model in place and set the pace of a film a year. As a description of a later Miller opus put it, "all the elements that fans had come to rely on year after year are there: extreme skiing, exotic locations, silly sequences, and hokey but earnest narration."[19] The surfing versions of these elements were certainly present in Browne's first films, but unfortunately it's impossible today to examine their exact arrangement, for the movies no longer exist as such. In those early years Browne showed the physical film he shot, making no prints, often re-using material and changing things on the fly according to audience feedback. As late as 1958 in *Surf Down Under* an audience nearly rioted because he had included too much local color and too little surfing action, to which he reacted with an all-night re-edit for the next evening's projection. The result is that the early films exist now only in bits and pieces in later compilations and in spools stored by category in the Bud Browne Film Archives in Pismo Beach, California.

The title of the fourth movie, *Trek to Makaha*, speaks to the direction Browne's work would take, and with it the artisanal surf film "industry" soon to draw upon his example. Leaving Honolulu to set up his camera on the northwest coast of Oahu, Browne brought action footage of extraordinary Hawaiian waves to the American mainland (and, soon, Australia) for the first time. In a world in which such moving images were simply unavailable elsewhere, imagine the stoke of Makaha point surf for a roomful of guys who at best knew Malibu or had glimpsed a grainy still photo or two of the heavy islands juice. Often considered the first "big wave," Makaha would soon lead to consciousness of other iconic breaks like Sunset and Waimea and, in a different mythic register, Pipeline. In faraway Oddfellows Halls and multi-purpose rooms, the surf film model as created by Bud Browne was about turning the syllables of those places and the names of the people who rode them into legend. At the same time it was also about travelling in search of new places and new legends. Today, from the weekend romance of a drive up the coast to the pilgrimage to the classic spot to the full-on expedition to exotic and challenging locales, the journey is central to the surfing experience and the surfing imagination. Before *Surfer* and other specialist publications would play their indispensable role in incarnating that imagination, cinema got the show on the road with this first modest "trek," followed only two years later by Browne's globe-crossing hunt for *Surf Down Under*. When the model passed to his successors and to theirs, the homey early surfaris up to North Shore recalled by Rabbit Kekai went on to become open-ended geographical and cultural adventures, ethereal dream structures for spiritual exploration, ambitious commercial projects spotlighting the best gear and the biggest names against colorfully unfamiliar backgrounds. Bud's *Trek* is the first step towards the *Search for Surf* and *The Endless Summer*, the *Billabong Odyssey* and *Chasing Mavericks*, the projection of today into *This Time Tomorrow* and even the interior quest for *The Innermost Limits of Pure Fun*.

Every expedition demands its expeditionary corps, and, with the obvious exception of Duke and perhaps Tom Blake, Browne's surfers earned the sport's first stars. Once he started filming the heavier action at Makaha or the North Shore, his cast was composed largely of big wave-stalking California transplants like Ricky Grigg, Peter Cole, Buzzy Trent, and the young Greg Noll, along with Phil Edwards or John Peck and their more delicate artistry, and a George Downing or Buffalo Keaulana to represent the local dignitaries. In most of his films, Browne also blended into the mix takes of many of the same performers at Trestles, Santa Cruz, Rincon, Malibu, and other California hot spots. In the portrayal of what he referred to as "my surfers,"[20] he drew the intentionally thin line that most later filmmakers would walk. On one hand Browne's surfers were larger-than-life heroes. Introducing "Master of Waimea" Pat Curren in *Cavalcade of Surf*, a drumrolling voiceover impels you in near-rhyme to "feast your eyes on a suicide ride." On the other, these guys are just goofballs in their 20s caught tandem surfing in drag or acting out elaborately corny pranks. In one, from *Spinning Boards*, a surfer tries trapping thieves by sleeping with his board tied to his ankle. When a sneaky grom (played by future great, and father of great, Billy Hamilton) makes off with it in a jalopy, he makes off with the owner as well, slapstick towing him down the road. Versions of this blend of action hero and dunce will play out in countless surf films to follow. It is a response, it seems, to the schizophrenic surfing self-image at once as the locus of over-sized, mythical acts and as a no-pretension zone of slacker messing around, Laird Hamilton meets Jeff Spicoli. In his friend Buzzy Trent, Browne found the perfect embodiment of these two attitudes. With the drill sergeant chin and poured concrete body, the former USC fullback charged as hard as anyone at monster Waimea and Makaha. Hard to believe, but he was maybe even better on land, as Browne astutely recognized, interviewing him in several films about challenging the world's biggest waves. Charisma to burn, Buzzy somehow communicates in sentence after sentence inflated self-dramatization and a self-deprecation that drags it all hilariously back to earth.

Browne made twelve surf movies from 1953 to 1964 and completed two more after 1973. In between he justified his reputation as the premier in-water cameraman of his day with work on other projects. What's done today with Go-Pro and other easily accessible technology was a struggle for early photographers like Blake and Ball, not to mention those using the motion picture technology of the period. Browne's clever solution to shooting in the breaking wave involved a makeshift rubber bag glued to a ring tightened around the lens; unlike a cumbersome hard casing, it allowed him both to tuck the Bell & Howell or Bolex tightly between his legs during wipeouts and rewind it easily through the flexible fabric. As their brilliant surf movie careers took off, Greg MacGillivray and Jim Freeman called on Bud for the popular 16mm *Waves of Change* (1970, re-released in 35mm the next year as *The Sunshine Sea*). Browne brought his daring curl-close camera angles and graceful underwater shooting to such intimidating breaks as the Wedge and Pipeline. He was back to do a sizeable share of such shooting in the pair's multi-versioned '70s classic *Five Summer Stories*. The precursor to immersion camera artists like Dan Merkel and Jack McCoy, a Browne at over–60 also shot second unit water footage for John Milius's ambitious Hollywood surfing feature *Big Wednesday* (1978).

Browne's impressive body of personal work included the first international surf movie. Following up in 1957 on the previous year's visit by California lifeguard-surfers whose easy style on new balsa boards revolutionized Australian surfing, Bud used the long ocean liner passage to edit footage for, among other things, his next feature, *The Big Surf*. With the encouragement of the indefatigable Bob Evans, who would a few years later become the first commercial surf filmmaker down under, he showed it and other work to SRO crowds at a half dozen surf clubs. The locals went wild for footage of the Makaha International, the day's competition gold standard, and hot new mainland talents including Phil Edwards. Browne used his spare time to film the Aussie scene in his usual preparation for the next year's production, erring, as noted above. with too much surf carnival and too little surf. He wouldn't make that mistake again, emphasizing state-of-the-art wave technique in an extended focus on emerging ace Edwards, the eponymous *Cat on a Hot Foam Board* (1959).

In the year of *Gidget,* Browne's hep-cat title suggested counter-cultural cool while referencing the latest advance in board design. It bounced off the title of the Tennessee Williams Pulitzer Prize-winning play and high profile 1958 film as so many subsequent surf movies and videos would with similar cultural signifiers (*Gone with the Wave, Some Like It Wet, Have Board Will Travel, Tubular Swells, Going My Wave, Hawaii Nine-0,* etc.) The recurrence of such titling suggests something of the uneasy truce between surfing and the mainstream, where tweaking the instantly recognizable common reference both embraces the familiar and pushes it away. In any case, one concrete concession to social norms on the part of Browne was his decision to pay Edwards and the other star of the film, Dewey Weber. All the pair got for their performances in his film was airfare from the mainland to Honolulu and a very occasional share of the take, but doing so was significant as a first step towards today's profession of video pro.

The classic Browne method is clearly on display in a series of films from the 1960s. Featuring a young Mike Doyle, most of the regulars, and the usual brew of action and distraction, *Surf Happy* and *Spinning Boards* (1960, 1961) provided beach communities, if not the wider society, with an authentic alternative to *Gidget* and what Doyle labeled its "silly, adolescent, and superficial" take on surfing.[21] That superficiality would, of course, be cranked up several notches when the *Beach Party* movies started their invasion of the adolescent consciousness in August of 1963. Through it all Browne kept serving the faithful, turning out from 1962 to 1964 *Cavalcade of Surf, Gun Ho!,* and *Locked In!* Like *Spinning Boards,* the three were marked by an important innovation, what a poster for the latter discreetly advertises as "sound track with multiple voices & effects." Bringing in John Weiser and the ever-articulate Peter Cole for recorded narration, while including on-screen interviews and indeed the odd sound effect, the taciturn Browne got himself off the live-narration hook. This allowed him to widen significantly the reach of his films, sending copies off to the East Coast, Australia, South Africa, and elsewhere in a not-negligible contribution to the sport's emerging globalization. As for the content of these later movies, the only changes to the time-honored formula are a slightly amped-up attention to the particulars of surfing style and somewhat greater emphasis upon the historical dimension of the sport. Both seem like understandable reactions to the phony image of surfers perpetuated by the overheating surf music and Hollywood co-optation machines.

With a whiff of irony, the title *Cavalcade of Surf* again plays off a mainstream media product, the suburbs-familiar *Gillette Cavalcade of Sports* with its Friday night boxing extravaganzas. While a big wave *mano a mano* does conclude the movie (reinforcing a Browne formula honored by many later filmmakers), its emphasis throughout is much more upon a careful anatomy of stylistic nuance in a much less mainstream sport. A brief intro to the "functional" form/hotdogging tension and an invitation to analyze the styles of the "better surfers" like Doyle, Weber, Edwards, and LJ Richards help to unify what is structurally a smorgasbord, with ragged leaps from small to big wave and abrupt shifts from Hawaii to California and back again. Master of ceremonies Cole leads the narration, taking us through a representative sample of surfers in action before directing attention to big Makaha survival tips with a verbose Trent as star witness and killer rides by Doyle and Mike Stange. With the same occasional slo-mo as elsewhere, it's then on to a two-part seminar on the bodysurfing subtleties of a Mickey Munoz somehow holding it together at the Wedge, or Buffalo looking better than most of the stand-up riders at Makaha. A savory chapter on California surfing history as of 1927 enlists terrific footage by Doc Ball and John Larronde, including poignant film of board innovator Bob Simmons before his accidental death. The vintage shots of loading up or the jeep slogging though mud offer an engaging look at the off-wave surfing life back in the day. Browne himself shot abundant footage of the everyday doings that contextualize surfing artistry, more often inserting it for comic effect than for its purely documentary value. One presumes he heavily favored hot surfing action for fear of alienating rowdy, demanding audiences, in the process leaving a lot of board stowing and grocery runs on the cutting room floor. More fascinating and pertinent today than Bud perhaps ever imagined, much remains tantalizingly spooled up in the archives. What generally made it through the editing process, though, was the big wave finale. A classic figure since, here it concludes a swelling music buildup comprising Aussie bombora derring-do, Grigg testifying how Waimea can "psyche me out," and narration teetering between epic and mock epic. The seemingly surprised lone survivor of an initial trio with Peter Cole and Byron Keough, Pat Curren masters "one of the biggest waves ever ridden." That his "suicide ride" will also appear in Bruce Brown's *Surf Crazy* is a reminder that, once Bud's competitors got going, there was more than one camera trained on Waimea and consort. Of course, before today's forest of tripods no gesture slides by unrecorded.

As its title might suggest, the last images of *Gun Ho!* also go big, with chopper shots, expensively and daringly innovative at the time, of late February 1963 Waimea meatgrinding Edwards, Trent, Stange, and Noll, and a sublime tube at "the newest and deadliest challenge," Pipeline, by its then-master Butch Van Artsdalen. Much of the rest guides viewers through the different artistries of eleven "All-Stars": Dewey Weber's nimble dance, newcomer John Peck's delicate inventiveness close to the curl, Van Artsdalen's switchfoot magic, etc. Whether comparing the carving turns of Rusty Miller and Midget Farrelly, or the particularities of "peak" and "wall" breaks, such lingerings on pedagogy were especially welcome in surfing's early days, and they do offer a kind of structure for what is mostly a happy jumble of recurring crowd pleasers. We're treated to the contest scenes at Makaha, Ocean Beach, and Huntington Beach (including the still popular if irreverently presented tandem trials, not to mention the H.B. post-party "surf stomp"); good old "el spontaneo" head dips; reiterated curiosity about that odd Santa Cruz seven foot board sighted in Browne's previous film; the hoary saw about getting up early to catch a wave at gridlocked Malibu. For the sublime there's always a wave of the year and, for the ridiculous, cardboard sliding down "the mighty California Alps." The gags are for the most part pleasant, almost-funny fillers, an example being the "fin" circling a surfer and sawing through his board. Which doesn't mean they can't be insufferable, like stout Hevs McClelland in *Locked In*, torturously stringing out the weary hamming as "Super Surfer." The best stuff is either the kind of bone dry throwaway ribbing Bruce Brown was perfecting at the same period (waxing the front half of his board, "Peck the optimist prepares for some toes over") or, again, the priceless Trent. Buzzy waxes deconstructively eloquent about impact zone danger before a chalkboard displayed, lollipop and tongue-in-cheek, by a bikinied babe.

Seen within the whole of the treatment of women in Browne's films, the girl in question performs less as the sexist ornament she might appear than as an ironic take on the reduction of women to attractive decor. From the work of his earliest colleagues through, literally, last month's videos, the surf film industry has far more often than not been depressingly retrograde in its presentation of women in the beachspace. With a few notable exceptions, women surfers are invisible or, when present, treated patronizingly and/or given the heavy one over by male filmmaker-narrators. Shot almost exclusively for their curves, the non-surfers occasionally play the role of nurturing care-giver but much more often that of eye-candy—and the implicit warriors' reward for all that alpha-male performance. What's refreshing about Browne's films is that even in the gender-conventional '50s and early '60s he lingers little on bathing beauties (though he does include some wet tee-shirt action later in *Going Surfin'*). More importantly, perhaps, he presents women surfers without leering or diminishing their performance. To the contrary: Linda Benson "has it when it comes to nerves," and Candy and Marge Calhoun are simply allowed to show their stuff wake-boarding alongside Phil Edwards without raised eyebrows or additional comment. That "up and coming" Joyce Hoffman's "the only girl to have ridden Pipeline" and Candy Calhoun among the first at the Wedge are just statements of fact; when a pelican attacks the latter outside, Cole's narration emphasizes her spunky response instead of the scene's teenage male humor potential. Bud clearly wants to show how good these young women are. Benson's terrifically mobile and physical at Makaha in *Cavalcade*. In *Gun Ho!* how cool is Candy as she transforms a Rincon wipeout into an extended body surfing demonstration?

When his last movie *Surfing the 50's* was released on VHS in 1994, Browne featured subjects like "Waimea, First Time" and "Huge Makaha Surf." Prominently third in this list of nine is "Women Pioneers": choosing "women" over "girls" and associating them with the male-driven American frontier myth, Browne crystallizes something of the progressive attitude towards gender that marks his films. Although one might better just speak of an instinctive sense of fairness when discussing this director who, with one notable exception (the end of *Surfing the 50's*), seems to have resolutely avoided the political or polemical in his films. In 1963, for example, a major Huntington Beach oil spill goes completely unexamined, and even when he returned to making films during the hyper-socially aware early '70s Browne's politics are a trace element next to the rich veins running through concurrent films by John Severson and MacGillivray/Freeman. For eight years between 1964's *Locked In!* and *Going Surfin'* (1973), Browne took his talents to other films rather than his own projects due to a series of circumstances including one particularly wave-poor Hawaii winter with little good footage and a failed collaboration with Bruce Brown. Following the traditional formula, *Locked In!* had had some very good moments, including features on the silky beauty of Joey Cabell's surfing, an explosive 15-year-old named Jeff Hakman, and a brief but fascinating pro's eye view, shot with an extra-long lens from the opposite side of the Bay, of trying to find the right lineups at Waimea. Browne's contact down under Bob Evans revealed in *Surfing World* that his new 70 minute film was the result of over 100 hours of shooting. As in other surf movies of the time, there's a short skateboard chapter, but one in retrospect that seems particularly pertinent. Spotlighting members of the Santa Monica team and their "stunts borrowed from surfing," the commentary looks beyond the still rather staid moves to stress wide-open potential: "It makes us wonder what new tricks will be performed in the future." Does it ever, especially when Browne's shooting on the border of Dogtown only a decade before it became ground zero in the skate stylistic explosion.

A couple of years before that explosion, Browne would be back on the scene with *Going Surfin'*, a film that despite his 61 years remains the same kind of innocent, carefree jumble as the younger work. He released the 92 minute movie in 1973 and, vaguely along the model of *Five Summer Stories*, tinkered with different versions over time, eventually putting out a *New Going Surfin'* in 1977. The routine blend's at work, but due to technological progress the colors are warmer and richer, and the image unrecognizably sharper. The daring angles of underwater and in-curl photography also show a clear evolution in quality. Backed by the narration of Hevs McClelland (and, for the sequel, Greg MacGillivray), Browne uses a loose journey motif to tie together 50s footage—by then totally vintage—of Noll, Edwards, and the crew in California and on the North Shore—old chestnut gags, a wipeout compendium, and the new generation doing its thing on the day's short boards. Browne is very alert in particular to the changes in material driving the new surfing. Hot contemporary performances come from guys like a now grownup, and talkative, Hakman and Gerry Lopez, back-lit and ultra slow motion at Pipeline in the opening images, and slipping a hand-held camera deep into the mother of all barrels for a few subjective seconds. David Nuuhiwa takes a fish out at Rocky Point, and Reno Abellira rides a six-foot Brewer single-fin in a beautifully back-lit sequence. Another memorable stretch finds Mike Purpus and hyperactive Larry Bertlemann in Ventura for a session highlighting the reactiveness of Ben Aipa's so-called "swallowtail" board. Going with his times, Browne included a hot skateboard sequence at the Toilet Bowl, a hairy legend of a storm drain in Century City. Bud's earlier soundtracks had used what he had

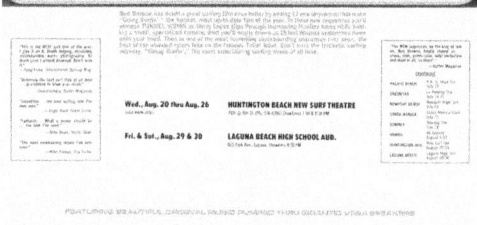

Poster, *Going Surfin'*, director Bud Browne (1975). The original 1973 film came out again in 1975 "with great new sequences!" Like Rick Griffin, Jim Evans brought together underground cartooning, album art, and film poster design. Here Evans represents Gerry Lopez with a handheld camera at Pipeline (Bud Browne Film Archives, Anna Moore).

around, favoring a melodic guitar-based sound such as that of The Fireballs, and when he released his '60s films on tape, he turned to surf music revivalists like The Packards and The Surf Raiders. Here guitars again dominate in a soundtrack that includes the playful fly-in-amber twangs, enthusiasm, and surf lingo lyrics of the commissioned title song by Rick Henn of The Sunrays, a talented, semi-successful early surf music group created and managed by no other than Brian Wilson's father.

In 1994, well into the video era, Bud would put the finishing touches on a career that started it all *41 years* previously. *Going Surfin'* is generally considered his last movie and *Surfing the 50's* just a greatest hits coda. This is not entirely fair for, while Browne himself considered the latter "of value as an historical record of an important time in the early years of surfing,"²² in fact it functions as an extremely pleasant and coherently organized cinematic whole. *Surfing the 50's* offers viewers the chance to see footage from his films of that period that for the most part only the raucous few present at the original screenings have ever been able to see, and it does so while placing that crucial decade within a meaningful cultural, historical, and, finally, political and moral context. Browne got the faithful Peter Cole and John Kelly to compose and deliver the pithy narrative for a montage of historical film excerpts and his own footage, some pristine, much showing scratchy signs of projector wear. While the normal surf movie elements are present, the structure, built on successive layers of history and geography, is much tighter than in any of Browne's other films. He gets things started with an historical survey of Hawaiian beginnings up through George Downing and the first big wave challenges, breaking this up nicely with an entertainment pause for some winter Makaha madness, before continuing on with Duke's surf missionary work and the early days in Australia and California. From there history transitions to geography on a tour of early West Coast spots like San Onofre in the '30s and '40s (a delicious portrait), the Malibu Dora owned, and Steamer Lane (where the shaper of that first short board finally gets a name). Then it's back to Hawaii for the rest of the movie, with stops at screamingly fast Laniakea (named, incidentally, by Browne), Haleiwa, '57 Waimea with Noll and company, and Makaha for the first championships and a lot of hairy point surf. The whole gang's there, including Linda Benson ripping like Dewey Weber and Donald Takayama making it look easy. To break things up we get to see the crew sliding in mud, scarfing 72 ounce steaks in an hour, riding catamarans with Woody Brown and Duke, enduring wipeouts a go-go, and staring down waves with a machete. Browne needed music to back all this so he put an ad in *Surfer* for contributions. Endearingly, he received three dozen tapes from musicians or groups offering their material for free; the 23 selections he used bring a breezy, retro folk lilt to the film.

For Browne collaborating with John Kelly meant dealing with his old friend's ardent environmentalism and engagement in the cause of Hawaiian sovereignty and reparations. Whatever his feelings, Bud's instinct was always towards a certain reticence, but he graciously let John have the last word. After an opening referencing the "many cultural contributions made by native Hawaiians," Kelly's concluding remarks link generous respect for that embattled culture with gratitude to Hawaiians who continue to "help us all conserve our surf environment." This is a perfect capstone for Browne's work. Even if his cinema shied away by temperament from direct engagement, he certainly shared Kelly's sentiments and love for the islands and the islanders who changed his life. The remarks furthermore add an appropriate touch of gravitas to the finale of a remarkable career and to a last film whose very subject is, paradoxically, at the heart of a surfing life often associated with blithe youth: a living reverence for and deep sense of continuity with the past. In words that would go on to epitomize the significant retro movement in surfing and the surf film in the 1990s and oughts, John Kelly argued that it was vital "to keep the good past alive as we face the future." Bud embodied that continuity in his life and work, linking successive generations with his singlehanded creation of one of the most important elements of surf culture and establishing an aesthetic model still recognizable and even serviceable more than six decades later. Those who knew the filmmaker, though, might consider Kelly's words the testament to an even more important kind of continuity: Browne's profound sense of friendship and personal loyalty. Peter Cole and John Kelly were there in Bud's little place in Costa Mesa the final day of editing *Surfing the 50's*. On what turned out to be their last day together, the three great watermen, the youngest 63, would celebrate by bodysurfing the Wedge.

~ ~ ~ ~ ~

Team of Rivals

When Browne screened his first surf film, he was alone; four decades later as his last debuted, Taylor Steele's *Momentum* was making a sensation in an entirely different world with a kid named Slater. In order to keep the critical focus tightly on Browne's sizeable achievement, a certain amount of narrative tidying up marks the above look at his dozen-plus films over this long period. In fact, of course, the filmmaker's full story is a messier affair, one intricately entwined with that of a surfing that would undergo immense, unending mutation, the constantly changing film genre Browne created to reflect that sport and life, and the generations of filmmakers his work directly and indirectly inspired. To back up nearly to the beginning of that larger tale is necessarily to recognize how far from alone Browne was in his development of the surf movie As early as 1957 and 1958 other surfers began to pick up cameras themselves and pick up on Bud by taking the self-edited, -titled, and -advertised results on the road to coastal audiences ready for more. When *Gidget* brought surfing to every small town, those audiences further swelled with a widening base of practicing surfers, not to mention the numerous hangers-on and merely curious. By the middle of the 1960s a good three dozen other surf filmmakers had taken a crack at serving this audience. Building on Browne's prototype, they put together their own two-reel 16mm spectaculars of action, comedy, and live narration, in some cases one-off efforts, in others annual contributions to more-or-less long personal series. Yet even with the big screen, the surf music flare-up, and Kansans in huaraches, the hard-core surfing community in California, where most films originated, was still small: everyone knew each other, shot the same surfers (often at the same time), and saw each other's films. Much the same could be said of Australia, where Bud Browne, Bruce Brown, and others toured, and where a fledging surf movie scene was establishing itself around the early example of Bob Evans. If the spirit in these hotbeds was perhaps not of full collaboration, it was one of collaborative competition.

Remembering shooting Bruce Brown the year before the director of *The Endless Summer* made his own first film and ribbing Bud for his seriousness, Greg Noll spoke in *Fifty Years of Surfing on Film* of "humorous competition, friendly competition, 'cause these guys are … your buddies." As both a frequent subject of Browne's lens and the second commercial surf moviemaker in the market Bud created, he should know about this. Such was Noll's passionate youthful obsession with surfing (as well as an entrepreneurial spirit that exists to this day) that he wanted to get involved in as many aspects of the sport as possible. The emblematic big wave rider of the late '50s and '60s, Noll also found time to run one of the most successful board shaping businesses of the period, get a short-lived early surf magazine and surf cartoon collection off the ground, and make surfing movies. Participating in the instrumental 1956 Australia Olympics trip with other California lifeguards, who would reshape Aussie surfing by leaving their new Malibu boards and know-how behind, Noll shot some film of surfing and the curiously martial lifesaving carnivals with a Bell & Howell obtained from Warren Miller. Heading down a path cleared by Browne, he linked up this material with some other California and Hawaii footage he'd been assembling to release a simple self-narrated film in 1957 called *Search for Surf*. Playing on the quest motif (and perhaps the soap opera *Search for Tomorrow*, a '50s TV institution), the catchy, alliterative title pleased Noll so much he recycled it for four subsequent yearly editions. These were essentially promotional films made, as he also said, "to help the boards along." For a guy never shy on the product placement, they certainly didn't hurt as Noll Surfboards rode the move from balsa to foam and moved from a garage sideline to a Hermosa Beach factory turning out 200 boards a week by the mid–'60s. But with the auditoriums and posters and the rest, Noll never really liked "all the bullshit of making surf movies." As he said, again from *Fifty Years*, "I can't think of a worse business." The results of his efforts are an absolutely unassuming take on Browne's model, with simply shot surfing scenes, on-shore hanging out, and a few mostly lame comic pauses. Next to Browne's increasingly skilled photography, the Bull had the finesse of his nickname in the filmmaker china shop. The image in Noll's film is sometimes shaky and often dim and muddily colored. The later movies have some underwhelming in-water filming, but the non-tech savvy Noll mostly just points and shoots.

What makes the films interesting, even invaluable, is what he shoots. For Noll's contemporary audiences, the main deal was the surfing, of which he served healthy doses. In addition to a regular paddleboard feature back when that was an essential adjunct to the surfing life, most of the classic SoCal breaks appear, including a big Redondo Breakwater and endless Malibu rollers with affable Chubby Mitchell, tricky Miki Dora, and Tubesteak Tracy. Every year there was a then extremely exotic (but soon familiar) Mexico junket to unexplored breaks, and of course Hawaii, with the Browne-familiar team at Makaha and the North Shore, and even some inter-islands exploration. With certain notable exceptions, particularly at Makaha and Waimea, the general impression of the surfing is one more of quantity than quality, but the audiences thought it was a kick, if this author's memory as a pre-teen of a Hermosa Beach Noll film screening is accurate. Today what's striking, though, is their generous portrait of that early generation of surfers driving around and killing time between sessions. The near-equal of Doc Ball's photographic commemoration of an era in *California Surfriders*, Noll's films gives us the mattress-bearing jalopy apartment, old country Haleiwa, and Pat Curren stealing a duck for dinner. In fact, food's a recurring motif here for these active young men getting by on pennies but eating massively when the opportunity—a luau invite, a spaghetti eating face-off, an "all you can eat" night —presented itself. The pranking too is endless, in part as a playful riposte to the cultural labeling of surfers as possibly

Poster, *Search for Surf*, director Greg Noll. The Bull keeping it simple year to year: same title, new footage from 1957 to 1961.

reprobate oddballs. A teenager named Rick Griffin drew (and occasionally misspelled) the credits and intermission graphics; *Mad* magazine-inflected and proto-psychedelic, they add to the sweet homemade feel of the whole while pointing towards a near-future when surfing would find a place in the late '60s youth subculture. Griffin went on to draw the Murphy character for the new *Surfer* magazine and eventually do high-level logo, concert, album, and surf film work out of post–Summer of Love San Francisco.

Noll willingly put his wife Beverly and others behind the camera so he could surf in his own films, but there's less than you'd expect, especially on the big waves for which he is best remembered. In fact, while Greg was part of the first crazy paddle out at Waimea Bay in 1957, it was Bud Browne who filmed the scene, as well as another classic Noll ride at Outside Pipeline. As Peter Cole remembers things in *50 Years*, he spent more time filming than surfing for a while; when he gave up on the movies and rejoined the line-up, the nickname the Bull fell into place, and "we got a lot less big waves." A self-confessed "fun hog"[23] on the waves and off, Noll was a favorite of the countless other surfers who took to the camera at this time. Already by 1958 John Severson was barnstorming the first of a series of illustrious films, as was eventual legend Bruce Brown. Around 1960, the year Severson started *Surfer*, Walt Phillips and Grant Rohloff were into their own roughly annual cycles, producing, respectively, seven and ten surf films. As others like Dale Davis, Jim Freeman, and Greg MacGillivray began to gear up along the California coast, Bob Evans was filming fellow Aussies during Midget Farrelly's successful assault on the Makaha International Surfing Championships; the 1962 result, the rough-hewn but historic *Surf Trek to Hawaii*, was the first of Evans's dozen or so efforts and a spur to successors like Paul Witzig and Alby Falzon. In addition to the top surfers they "shared" and the stimulation of viewing each other's work, it's important to stress how interwoven the lives and careers of these people were. Just a brief sample: Rohloff worked on Severson's first film and appeared in at least one of Noll's, as Phillips and Severson did in Brown's, that is, when they weren't making their own movies and founding *Surfer* or its 1962 rival *Surfing Illustrated*. After meeting the California contingent in 1956 and receiving the high-prestige gift of Noll's Malibu board, Evans invited Browne to Australia, promoted his later films, and, inspired by Severson, launched one of the first Australian surf magazines. Witzig was psyched by Evans's screening of Browne in Sydney; he sought out Bruce Brown during a stopover in Hawaii, in turn inviting him to Australia. Occurring shortly after Severson's first trip south with his films, the resulting journey would lead to Witzig's representation of Brown on the subcontinent, a Bolex to shoot footage for the American's next movie, and eventually his own filmmaking career.

Certainly part of the reason such a creative flurry of "pure" surf films took place at this time was simply because they were perceived as such: in the rapidly growing and changing subculture, the films of Browne and Rohloff and Freeman were the surfer-produced real thing and not the ersatz beach rip-offs Hollywood began churning out to capitalize on the *Gidget* effect. Their purpose was, as Nick Carroll neatly summarizes, to "explain surfing and surfers to themselves."[24] This communal function took place, of course, communally, in the "fairly crazed ritual gathering" of surf movie night.[25] According to personal interest and sometimes pure chance during a shoot, individuals found their own dosage of the elements composing the consensual model: again, as established by Browne and quickly ratified and enhanced by his successors, a good handful of surfing action sequences, comic relief, surfer lifestyle bits, a touch of local color, and soon an occasional glance at an alternative sports scene interesting to viewers (skateboarding, skiing, skydiving, etc.) While over time some filmmakers began to adopt plot-like structures, notably in their use of the journey motif, most surf movies of the '60s and even later simply string events along with a pearls-on-a-necklace picaresque randomness. Such as it is, the organizing force remains the narrator's voice, at first live but soon recorded, inviting us to "take a trip up to Rincon" and then "look in on the North Shore." The often-dumb non-surfing content casually dropped into this action mix by our host responded to a reality of surfing, that even the shortest surf trip can mean lots of downtime getting there or waiting for waves to show. In part this filler material accurately simulated that waiting period and the largely innocent (only hints of sexual fantasy and a drop or two of booze) ways a bunch of good-natured young guys with too much energy and too little dough might try to fill it.

Because they were casually thrown together and re-edited, often uncopied and nonchalantly stored, many films of this period exist only as distant memories or luckily conserved handbills. Anecdotes from back in the day confirm what the extant films evidence, that indeed there was a surf movie mold. To get a sense of how the younger generation shooting just down the beach from Bud Browne conformed to it or personally diverged, it's instructive to take a look at the work of a representative filmmaker whose output can still be viewed today. It's unsurprising that Walt Phillips saw to the digitalization of four of his films for, never short on ego or energy, he has always been known as one of the most enterprising, media-savvy figures of the early period. After making several movies for the circuit, he put CBS experience to work hosting a Southern California TV show dedicated to surfing and creating a syndicated program on the subject; he also founded a short-lived alternative surf magazine that seems not to have endeared him to the *Surfer* crowd. Like virtually all of the first film guys struggling to get quality footage and then get it around to the masses, Phillips could handle himself on the waves. That is, until the day in the late '50s when it's said that a bad wipeout convinced him his real future lay on the other side of the camera. The Phillips who surfs occasionally in his own movies and at least one of Bruce Brown's is a leg-spread charger and not a smoothy. He's the same kind of stylist in films, efficiently more than elegantly splicing stretches of strong big and small wave surfing together with the compulsory lame humor to form a generally satisfying package for the high school auditorium or veterans' hall.

From 1959 through 1963 *Sunset Surf Craze, Surf Mania, Psyche Out,* and *Once Upon a Wave* spilled out according to the typical shoot-edit-show rhythm; he would later add three films to this run. Phillips hung with the successive crews that ruled the North Shore in those days and took miles of great color big wave footage, to which he added shots at three or four favorite California spots and an occasional bop down to Mexico. The surfing is first rate, with most of the big names of the time, George Downing, Del Cannon, Pat Curren. The impressive Peter Cole was a particular star—on the wave but also alongside the projector. Like Fred Van Dyke for John Severson's first film, Cole did the mainland touring and live narration for *Sunset Surf Craze* when Phillips couldn't get away from his day job. The tallest guy in the lineup, he also mugged it up as Frankenstein's stiff-gaited monster in a recurring comic number in the first movie. Humor's far from Phillips's strength, though, and this like most of the comedy interludes has a pro-forma quality. In *Surf Mania* a young Robert August will do anything to have some Mexican waves to himself, so he gleefully sets off a cherry bomb that, we see, wipes out his travelling companions in their beachside camp. Okay but, appearing out of nowhere, the gag could have used at least a little preparation, and certainly a more thoughtful follow-up, for immediately afterwards another surfer inexplicably joins August in the waves. In the taped narration added later to his films, Phillips also just misses the mark. He's an amiable enough host, but there's a flagrant contrast with the master of narration Bruce Brown and his warm, instinctive blend of guileless fun, intelligent continuity and pacing, and dose of self-reflexive irony.

The films get better as they go along, in part because the proportion of comic stuff goes down. Phillips concentrates on the filming of surfing action, nicely varying wide frame full speed shots—one after another after another—with occasional tight focus slo-mo. At times it seems like the "performing"—he repeats variants of the word a wearying dozen times in *Psyche Out*—keeps coming in a undirected flow, only cut by dizzying jumps from Rincon to Santa Cruz to Sunset, and back again. *Psyche Out* gets under way with what looks like a promising framing device, a tyke walking on the shore and dreaming of one day being a surfer like the big boys (the title referring apparently to the way the kid feels, not intimidated but something more like our contemporary expression "psyched up"; it also clearly plays on the 1960 Hitchcock classic). Unfortunately, while he does drift back occasionally to the phrase, Phillips drops the conceit of the young fellow's dreams. Too bad, for as Brown and others were starting to find out, some plausible pseudo-narrative connections between the endless surfing scenes can sometimes do the job better than simple filler. Taking us herky-jerky to the name breaks, though, Phillips does manage one thing with a certain flair: he gives his early surfing audiences much needed lessons in geography. It's important to insist upon the information-bearing dimension of the early films. En route to show the surfing, Phillips will patiently pass through cane fields leading to the North Shore, pausing for vistas that allow the viewer who'd never been to the islands—most, certainly in those days—to make some geographic sense of things. In this there's a certain respect for the Californian's Hawaiian hosts as well. It's one thing to be told Ala Moana is the first "engineered" wave; it's another to see it from the hilly distance, as we do in *Surf Mania*, as part of a complex, evolving economic and ecological space, with the dredged-out yacht harbor and breakwater clearly contextualizing the famous break they brought into being. In *Once Upon a Wave* Phillips similarly gratifies understandable curiosity about how these famous places relate to each other spacially as he takes some distance and widens the visual field while following Greg Noll out through the Waimea shore break.

Filmmakers like Phillips acted as an interface between the relatively small number of individuals who essentially dropped everything to live for surfing and a vastly more numerous audience seeking their own forms of escape and excitement through the filmed adventures they provided. With a few notable exceptions, those committed surfers were male like their overwhelmingly masculine audiences. As discussed above, the form of the surfing movie with its invariable blend of heavy action and light comedy spoke to the split personality of surfing, its sense of oversized accomplishment warring with cool dismissal of the overly serious. Viewed from another angle, that blend addresses as well the America of the 1950s and 1960s and its conflicting, profoundly mutating sense of masculine gender norms. That period, of course, begins in the confident moral certitudes of the wartime generation and ends in the uncomfortable questioning of their children. One way to comprehend more fully the masculine surfing world of high waves and hi-jinks portrayed by Browne and the cohort of filmmakers that accompanied him is to apply two different conceptual frameworks, one oriented towards the past and the inertial forces of culturally defined traditional masculinity, the second looking forward towards cultural revolt and change as reflected in a changing sense of male identity. The Beach Boys would soon wonder how things would be "When I Grow Up (To Be a Man)." Always relevant, of course, such questioning was particularly pertinent during the '50s and '60s when the maturing masculine self was torn so fully between stolidly traditional norms and the possibility of radical change.

The first conceptual framework views the combination of heroic and wacky extremes apparent in early surf films as reflections of a form of conventional American masculinity forged mid-twentieth century by depression and war. While the setting's admittedly the pastoral North Shore and not wartime Okinawa, the group of young men living off the land, going forth resolutely to fight daily battles, and letting go in their down time is, in its way, a Band of Brothers. In Hemingway's world and terms they're "men without women" living on a certain edge, cranky with society but comfortable in their small crew, inarticulate and seemingly unemotional before danger, finding meaning in individual acts of physical courage, in codes and ritual, and when it's all over as unafraid of the ridiculous as they were of the mountainous challenge. The figure from popular culture who perhaps offers the clearest understanding of the man-child in question is the filmmaker Howard Hawks, he of *The Big Sleep* and *The Big Sky*, *Bringing Up Baby* and *Gentlemen Prefer Blondes*. From the mid–20s through 1970, the full range of genres that Hawks explored can be boiled down, as Peter Wollen argues, "to two basic types: the adventure drama and the crazy comedy."[26] This sounds familiar.

A brief summary of Wollen's perceptive analysis follows. In an existence given "pungency" by danger, Hawks's heroes take pride in their expertise but don't expect external praise, for the doing's enough. They exclude themselves intentionally from society, cut off "physically by dense forest, sea, snow or desert" in a self-sufficient male-only group that in turn imposes its own exclusivity through the test of guts or skill. Outsiders, they turn others into outsiders. While they do crazy things, they "see the ordinary world as being 'crazy' in a much more fundamental sense." A threat to the elite group, the banal crowd takes it in mockery and other forms of retaliation. Women are a similar threat to the group's cohesiveness, but they can in exceptional circumstances—by performing "minor feats of valour"—achieve admittance, though never as full members of the crew. To this heroic model Hawks then adds its comic pendant, a counter-reality of regressive farce. His comedies explore the shadowy underside of the "retrograde" all-male group through the theme of reversion towards the infantile or primitive. When back within the reach of normative society, figures who in the dramas dominate the natural, the feminine, and the conventional find themselves the butts of comic social and sexual humiliation. Multiple parallels between Hawks's conceptions of heroism and the way surfing is represented in the early films are evident; so too are the echoes in the comic stretches of Browne and company, which often explicitly highlight the regression to childlike behavior, yearning but frustrated desire, and Mr. Hulot-like humiliation at the hands of technology or business interests. A true *auteur*, Hawks returned with near obsession to certain recurrent narrative premises and character types that, while particular to his unique creative vision, nevertheless recall important American cultural patterns, and notably a certain kind of masculinity with roots deep in the frontier myth. Pushing beyond civilization's edge to the Californian and Hawaiian coasts, there where the wide-open adventure myth opposes the closed domestic space, those guys on the waves live in a similar male-only club of intense physical challenge, actions louder than words, coolness under pressure, and crazy spare time.

Yet, while this reading gestures back towards embedded traditional behavior, it's equally possible to see the cinematically portrayed '50s surfing life as progressive and forward-looking. These were the years of Sloan Wilson's *The Man in the Gray Flannel Suit* and John Marquand's *Point of No Return*, with their critiques of a deadening American business culture and pointless suburban aspiration. In the conceptual framework suggested by these and other works, surfing becomes a form of symbolic masculine revolt against the suburban breadwinner "trap" presaging '60s hedonism and other forms of countercultural change. Arguments such as that in Barbara Ehrenreich's 1983 *The Hearts of Men: American Dreams and the Flight from Commitment* insist upon the dark restraints accompanying American male gender-based advantages—bills, the little lady, a permanent job, kids, the demanding lawn—and the various ways men felt tempted to slip those chains. For these "gray-flannel dissidents"[27] alternate models would soon present themselves. As the subtitle of Ehrenreich's book might suggest, the *On the Road* Beat model, with its critique of the rat maze of work and consumption, was certainly one, but so too was the temptation of the at-first-blush conservative *Playboy* example espoused by Hugh Hefner. Worlds apart stylistically and politically, both nevertheless suggested forms of autonomy and freedom essentially unavailable to the suburban husband, king of the yard that he may be.

In the same way *Search for Surf* is about much more than finding waves, of course, and from the beginning surfing movies have stressed the open-ended pursuit, the impulse towards the wild and instinctive, the romance of jobless poverty, the implied availability of nubile forms, the easy swing between the highly individual and casually communal, the idle (i.e., non-surfing) day filled with pranks and other kid stuff. In these ways certainly, it is easy to see the link between such implicit rebellion and the more explicit forms to come in later years. Which raises the question whether the surfing life as sketched out in *Gun Ho!* or *Surf Fever* or *Once Upon a Wave* is a rugged masculine frontier holdover or the precursor of new ways of being. The answer would seem to be both, for the two visions overlap in their prizing of instinct and personal freedom, their itchy discomfort with mainstream society, and their problematic attitudes towards women, especially as embodied in what they saw as conventional domestic womanhood. The surf boom came just as American society, tired of war and depression, was ensconcing itself firmly in the housing tracts and daily commute, but also the moment that, not coincidentally, Hef was crafting the first of his glossy monthly dreams of escape and Allen Ginsberg was writing *Howl!* in a Berkeley cafe. The obedient/rebellious child of this world, surfing learned from its pipe-smoking vet father but also from its suavely disreputable uncle and from its wild freak half-brother sneaking up to the window at midnight.

~ ~ ~ ~ ~

Endless, Perfect

In the '60s the surf movie boomed just as the sport did. The great figure linking the first wave propelled by Bud Browne with surfing's intense mediatization a decade later was, of course, that different, unrelated Brown, Bruce. If non-surfers know one surf film today, it is *The Endless Summer*. With one of those perfect titles that would live on as a cliché in its own right, it is indisputably the best film ever made on surfing. The year was 1966, a moment when most Americans under 20 could name-check the breaks in "Surfin' USA" and where pseudo-surfing had been busily hijacking the sport's image. Culturally, the sweet peace-and-love haze was just drifting in, soon to be cut by tear gas and bullets as things turned ugly. *The Endless Summer* managed to hearken back to simpler times and values while incarnating the best of the '60s in its vision of personal freedom, mobile curiosity, and the joyfully chosen, not socially ordained vocation. It's completely of its time and, if Amazon sales today and user comments regularly breaking towards "Classic!" are any indication, of lasting appeal. Perhaps most remarkably, *The Endless Summer* pulled off the very tricky feat of appealing massively to surfers and nonsurfers alike.

As widely known and beloved as Brown's masterpiece is, not that many outside the venerably aged within the surf community are familiar with his other films. In fact, *The Endless Summer* was the sixth. Born in the Bay Area, Brown grew up in Southern California and started surfing at a number of Orange County beaches. After high school he enlisted in the Navy, managing to get posted in Honolulu where he spent as much time as possible in the waves at Ala Moana and started tinkering with an 8mm camera. Back lifeguarding in SoCal in 1957, Brown got an intriguing proposition from Dale Velzy, a buddy and, with Hobie Alter and Greg Noll one of the leading board manufacturers: how about a cool five grand to finance a winter on Oahu's North Shore with a handful of surfers, and turn out a promotional film for Velzy? Brown didn't have to be asked twice. He brought a 16mm camera and instructional guide to making movies, rounded up five top local riders, put them up for a couple of months in Hawaii, and filmed on a wide variety of breaks and wave conditions. Then back for some speed editing and hauling the result around to the inevitable multi-purpose halls. Fun for a 20-year-old, but more than that. "I made a dollar," said Brown. "I figured, heck, I got a career."[28]

Like the four movies that followed it, *Slippery When Wet* is a relatively slight effort with a certain charm. These films deserve attention less for their limited qualities than for the way they bring together in admittedly rudimentary form elements of what would become Brown's signature style: great surfing, exotic travel, engagingly dumb humor cut by Brown's verbal wit, the master's already irresistible voice-over, and a loose narrative line. As he recalls, "instead of the standard newsreel approach, I decided I wanted to tell a story." Soon-to-be classic, the organized surfing pilgrimage to Hawaii that he proposed in *Slippery When Wet* was "pretty exotic" in 1958. Just how much is evident in the dream of one of the film's surfers when the trip idea first comes up: a pair of lovely wahines feeding him grapes as they fan with palm fronds. The unsurprising reality to which he wakes is, instead, the shoestring budget that is already clearly part of the surfer image. This was a year before Cliff Robertson's Kahuna would bounce off the notion of the ski bum to immortalize the "surf bum," but Brown and his audience were evidently conversant with Frederick Kohner's novel and the slang it drew on: Gidget's the all-purpose name for a couple of girls his surfers run into. Simple and innocent as Brown's first film is, its materials are, notably, already alloyed—a real surfing life and its public and pop cultural image, a rootsy surfari thrown together by broke surfers and the deal to stage one for a promotional film.

The economic imperative's one thing, though, and Brown's evident passion for surfing is another. As in all his movies, he's unafraid to reveal a lushly romantic soul. Perhaps too unafraid here, as Brown sheepishly remembers his son Dana's remark in the video commentary to the re-issued film: "It's one thing to tell a story but you didn't have to start at the dawn of mankind!" The opening is positively biblical. "In the beginning there was the sun, nothing but the sun"—then poetically grainy color images of winds, seas, foamy turmoil, "endless breakers," and finally "civilization" with—very quick leap—its surfers ready "to conquer these walls of water." This kind of lyrical stops-pulling is not uncommon in the surfing movie; in fact, a decade later it would become the norm in such whole earth, hippie-scented efforts as Severson's *Pacific Vibrations* or Alby Falzon's *Morning of the Earth*. Here the effect's a slightly bathetic clash when we exit those epochal changes to discover a sleepy Dale Velzy checking the roadside mail box. The Hawaiian photos he and Del Cannon discover set what plot there is in motion. Cannon recruits some surfers who, straight off the DC8, settle into a comically impoverished island existence of sight gags like bunking down on bare mattress springs or a fridge full of canned pork and beans.

The raison d'être of all this is naturally the waves. After a bit of earlier surfing in California we get some nice sequences from Public Baths and Yokahama Bay, then some hairier stuff at Makaha and Sunset. The Makaha session comes only after one of Brown's typically cornball humor interludes. Bored waiting for no-show waves, the guys crash on the beach until Kemp Aaberg returns cleverly from the store with a box of detergent called … *Surf*! A little chanting over the magic bubbles they produce in the lazy shorewash—you can guess the swell that follows. Surfers know a surf trip means lots of waiting; this kind of filler material simulated that downtime and some of the ways a bunch of idle boneheads might fill it. In the surf movie of those days those ways are insistently innocent. One thing they do include is the substitute action sequence for when the waves are flat, a recurring surf movie figure. Here it's goofing around riding a cow on the side of the road and a trip sloshing through epic mud up to Waimea Falls for the soon-to-be-classic 85-foot drop into the water below.

Slippery When Wet is silent except for Brown's easygoing, deadpan narration and an original soundtrack by Bud Shank. Brown ran jazzman Shank down in a club in Hermosa Beach and out of the blue asked about scoring the film. The resulting recording—the first original soundtrack created specially for a surf movie—came about as the combo jammed live to a cut of the film projected on a record company office wall, spontaneously varying the tempo and tone according to the images. Brown is still understandably proud to have convinced musicians of that caliber to contribute to his little movie, and for $250 at that. The fit comes off as a miscalculation, however. With its nervous flute line, the score is a bit jumpy and "urban" for a cool surfing film. It's a very '50s soundtrack from a time when jazz was still— but just barely—a signifier for an edgy, alternative state of mind. Shank handled the third film as well, but by Brown's second effort guitars are not surprisingly slipping into the blend. With its melodica-flavored acoustic and electric guitar, the track by The Sandals for *The Endless Summer* is perfect for its lazy sunniness. Hawaii's there in the mix, but as important is the way the warm surf guitar of the Ventures gives over to the incoming folk-rock tone of that year's "California Dreamin'." In the mid-'60s this was starting to sound like times that were a-changing.

The next year Brown was back with *Surf Crazy*. While offering more of the same, including a look-in at Velzy & Jacobs Surfboards, its 71 minutes take an essential step towards the peripatetic *Endless Summer:* leading a surfari south of the border, Brown moves for the first time beyond the relative comfort zone of California and, by this point, Hawaii. Even in 1959 certain spots were getting crowded, and the search was on. Brown starts with a quick medley of surfing shots, namechecking fine riders on breaks from Rincon and Huntington Beach to Sunset. Then his warm, conversational voiceover extends a personal invitation: "Let's look in on three California surfers about to depart on a trip to Mexico." Just where we find out from a very low-tech road map with a hand directing a pointer all the way south to Acapulco. The three are soon joined by a fourth, a Brown regular named Little John Richards. Waking after a wild party, LJ turns up mysteriously along the side of a dusty road wrapped in a serape, topped by an immense sombrero, and under a huge saguaro cactus. And the clichés are off and careening through "Old Mexico": the Aztec Two-Step; women washing clothes on a river bank or, rather, "a local laundromat in operation"; sheer gringo delight at the exchange rate and a fistful of "Spanish pesos" (?!). This is only a hint of Brown's tin-ear on such matters, as his later movies and notably *The Endless Summer*(s) would confirm.

Touring with these films could be discouraging—one time only a half dozen viewers showed up in a huge hall—but more often the opposite, like at a jammed Santa Monica Civic Auditorium where the big wave shots had people screaming. Along the way Brown learned what worked and what didn't. What did was that Oahu monster surf, as well as lists, like the Big Five breakers of the year or the Terrible Ten of wipeouts. Both find their way into the second part of films and generally the last fifteen minutes. Indeed, after a pre-intermission largely devoted to Mexico and the fresh tingle of first-rate surfers on previously unsurfed, if middling, breaks, "let's visit our newest state" for some surefire thrills. A touch of local color and a few gags later, we're at Sunset for the "biggest waves of '59–'60!" Then a comic relief saimin eating contest, and the ante's upped again. It's January 17, 1960, at Waimea Bay—this is history, says the tersely announced date (that also brought Bud Browne out for the same scene in *Spinning Boards*). "This is maybe the biggest wave ever ridden!" Brown comments, tension rising in his voice, "Watch the size of it!" Two top surfers go down but Pat Curren hangs in, and with that rush for the spectator to take home, it's a summary "Thank you for coming. I hope you all enjoyed *Surf Crazy*."

Brown's originally live commentaries eventually made it to tape, but the vibe is always in-person and interactive. The talkily introduced that-about-wraps-this-part-up intermission is obligatory, for the filmmaker/host had to change reels. All along Brown varies tones and plays with the spectator. He returns to bits he knows will get a laugh, like the good old demolished surfboard: blown out of a convertible, dropped from an overpass, smashed by a passing car, etc. There's finding a bra in the guys' laundry and running gags like the grinning molasses-slow goof called Lightnin' or the bottle-rocket scientist diligently trying to send up little balsa models "at Canaveral." The mock technical names Brown gives to flub-ups are also part of the fun, like, one of many, a "clever Reverse Enchilada Sit-down Pull-out." But while he knows that his boisterous, largely male audience wants to clown around, they mostly want to see the best surfers in action. Brown will then deftly shift out of corndog yuks to become serious and informative. He consistently identifies the surfers—not just his excellent bunch but the pantheon of the day—often expertly guiding the viewer towards what's best in the action. You come to appreciate what is different and better about a Phil Edwards's smooth mastery. Brown can sometimes be at his most effective when he simply engineers moments of quiet wonder. As the sun's dropping low and beautiful, he'll offer an understated oral subtitle to what we're seeing: simply " Rincon, best swell of the year, Joey Cabell...." Then 30 seconds of the latter's delicate work in the curl, often in backlit slow motion, accompanied by an expressive, lyrical silence.

Brown's viewers loved being taken along on the trip. A difference with the Bud Browne and Greg Noll films is that the earlier ones *show us* Hawaii and Australia, whereas Brown *takes us* there and elsewhere on consciously organized journeys. In other words, the audience is invited not just to view surfing in exotic locales but to participate vicariously in the mechanics of getting there and getting around—the flight, trooping in from the airport, the housing arrangements, dealing with the locals, etc. To understand this distinction is to understand much of Brown's appeal throughout, and particularly in *The Endless Summer*. Back in 1960 only 2 percent of Americans had ever taken an international flight, but the period was also the time Jackie Kennedy was admired for speaking and dressing French and her husband created the Peace Corps. Not only a Cold War tool, the latter signified a nascent curiosity for things international after war and a decade and a half hunkering in the suburbs. Certainly, one vicarious frisson of the first James Bond films from this same period was Pan Am touching down, all sophistication, in Istanbul or Rio. That Brown was often ham-handed in his dealings with cultural difference doesn't change the fundamental appeal of the journey at a time when Kerouac had gone on the road and young Americans were first heading off in large numbers to backpack across Europe and the world. Brown's recurrent *invitations au voyage* were particularly appropriate for a target group of American surfers already drawn from the dispiriting geometry of the housing tract to the excitingly marginal physical and emotional space of the shore and the surf. In 1962 the Beach Boys recognized the attraction of the "Surfin' Safari," framing surfing as a journey into the dangerous and wild. Brown would double down on this appeal, grafting an openness to and discovery of radically new sights and ways of life to the inherent adventure-quest of driving the coast and looking for where it's breaking. As we have seen, in this he was not alone, for in addition to the trek and search motifs in Noll and Browne Australia's Bob Evans would soon be clattering along the Pacific Highway with surfers like Nat Young and Midget Farrelly in *The Young Wave Hunters* (1964). The narrative thrust of that journey meant an unbroken succession of fine waves, usually deserted beaches, and serendipitous meetings with Bob McTavish at Noosa Heads and surf tourist Joey Cabell at Angourie.

The hunger for mobility is apparent in the titles of Brown's 1961–2 films *Barefoot Adventure* and *Surfing Hollow Days*. While the first limits its journeying to various sites in California and Hawaii, the second takes Brown's viewers farther afield than they'd gone before, to Australia, New Zealand, Fiji, back east to Florida, and of course the usual suspects of California and Oahu. For the 2000 re-issue of *Barefoot Adventure* the audio commentary apparently couldn't be found, so Brown improvised a contemporary voiceover that, while occasionally taking some comic distance on the film across half a century, hits all the right notes. Notably, he continues the cheery inclusiveness of the imperative "let's," as in "Let's drop in on a friend at Cape Canaveral" or "Let's head back to Hawaii." Again, he's asking us along. The organized adventure this time gets under way when Del Cannon sights an ad for cheap islands airfare. Most of the film features the big waves there, with Brown's mobile camera slipping back to Newport's Wedge for bodysurfing body-slams or Santa Cruz for some kayak waveriding. The comic interludes include "toe-wrestling" and the ubiquitous Cannon—the Laurence Olivier of surf movies, according to Dana Brown—when he breaks into a surf shop to make his own board. Like Lucy and Ethel baking bread, he cooks up a batch of foam that's soon oozing all over his bare toes. The sight gag pay-off is the culprit tracked down in the street with enormous foam blocks for feet. Riding that slim comic conceit an instant, Brown also shows his audience where a blank—the starting point for surfboard shaping—comes from. For often, and here even at his wackiest, Brown can take pains to inform his viewer about surfing. Aware that many in his audience know less about the sport than they'd admit, he'll conscientiously define goofy-footer, closing out, or the curl, explain why a certain wave is vicious or that Waikiki is actually composed of six different breaks. Perhaps it was respect that led more experienced watermen to accept Brown's dispensation of what they might consider rudimentary information: even back in the day the guy had maximum pioneer cred. Brown not only rode and filmed but *named* such legendary spots as Velzyland and the famed Pipeline.

His next film, *Surfing Hollow Days*, is more frequently revived than the other early movies, and with reason. By this point the mature Brown method is firmly in place. The humor's still there but he's cut back on the full-blown adolescent skits. The one exception is a gag about a ho-dad who buys a "Like-Real Instant Surfing Kit," a bit of very slack theater that nevertheless addresses growing concern in the surfing community about mainstream image-theft. Decades later in the re-done *Barefoot Adventure* narration Brown would deadpan, "It's hard to believe these guys weren't professional actors. One thing about these old surfing films: at least they weren't corny." Having learned his craft and his audience's expectations over several years, the filmmaker who's no longer 20 seems less willing to distract from increasingly refined surfing footage, including some top in- and under-water shooting. The first part is devoted to a six week trip to Australia with the day's finest daredevil artist Phil Edwards, already a star as Bud Browne's *Cat on a Hot Foam Board* (1959); the trip would include a stop in "a little country called New Zealand" on the way back. Brown loosely structures the post-intermission sequences around another jaunt, this time east to highlight for the first time surfing in Florida. Peppered into the relaxed guidance of these narratives are regular drop-ins back to the inevitable California and Hawaii, as well a handsome alternate sports episode on snow skiing in New Zealand. Much as he will do in *The Endless Summer*, Brown delicately balances different interests and appeals: the novelty of a stiffly ritualized surf carnival down under and the initial international spotlight on the Byron Bay tubes; lots of cool shots back home at Trestles or Santa Barbara's Sand Bar; local Florida color and a first look at that virtually unknown surf scene; the sheer talent of Edwards, evident but nevertheless discreetly anatomized by Brown; and the film's big scoop, the latter's first ride ever of the mythical Pipeline, not to mention the folksy story of how the Brown bunch named it.

Brown's mobile focus draws an implicit parallel between distant novelty and scenes familiar to many in his barefoot audiences: the "hollow day" as faraway vacation and as daily escape to the wave's hollow. "People are choking and coughing from the smog in L.A.," he levels, but "if you stay on the freeway … you get to Rincon." One message Brown will refine in his masterpiece to come is becoming clear: the trip to foreign parts is a physical passage into a distant, unexpected world of life-affirming differences and challenges; it's also a state of mind, a place you're heading anytime you take the board out of the garage. Maladroit as these early films can be, they always communicate the heart-truth of surfing, that the place you most want to inhabit is the present moment. Shuffling back and forth between here and the distant there, Brown presents the kick of watching Edwards on those first unknown Australian waves as tinglingly fresh but also implicitly as a way to re-value the familiar and accessible. To long, affectionate takes of a quiet sunset session, the narration of this film that travels halfway around the world quietly reminds us that "the most joyous times surfing" can be just catching a few gentle waves with friends. "The end of all our exploring," T.S. Eliot wrote, "Will be to arrive where we started / And know the place for the first time." After *Surfing Hollow Days*—a film that already has much the same vibe—*The Endless Summer* would take viewers worldwide on such a journey of exploration, one that would mark the history both of surfing and of cinema. From the beginning Brown seems to have known he was on to something. But from lugging his fourth film around in the summer of 1962 until he was dubbed the "Fellini of the Foam" by Peter Bart of the *New York Times*, four years would pass.

Like the other early surf moviemakers, Brown was locked into the wearing yearly cycle of producing two reels of showable material in order to scrape together enough so he could do the same thing the next year. While his films were by this point events on the beach circuit, Brown could tell that things were changing. The Bud Browne business model was nearing its end; at the same time, while increasingly surf-aware, the civilians were getting a skewed pop-cultural impression of the sport. Already by 1961 the King was rear-projection "surfing" in *Blue Hawaii*, every hair in place, and a new Gidget was cast in *Gidget Goes Hawaiian*, the next in what was suddenly a profitable product line. Looking both to keep it real in the face of such ersatz stuff and freshen things up by introducing a new surfing scene even farther afield, Brown considered taking some surfers to distant South Africa. When the travel agent came back with the counter-intuitive news that a round-the-world ticket cost only fifty bucks more than the round trip in question, something clicked. Why not take those surfers around the world? Why not follow them as they followed the warm summer weather? Certainly somewhere in these early reflections lay as well the notion of eventually bringing the result to a larger mainstream audience. If nothing else, only that wider audience could reimburse the kind of cash such a project demanded.

In the interim Brown needed time and every penny he could scrape together. So he quickly cut and pasted a greatest-hits compilation of sequences from the first four films called *Waterlogged*, wringing what he could from it on the beach circuit in '63. That same year he hit the road with two young surfers for several months of filming throughout the Southern Hemisphere. In 1964 Brown created an edited whole from the wanderers' surfing footage and the exotic scenes they encountered, intermixed as usual with usable material from other Californian and Hawaiian surfers. According to the old pattern, Brown barnstormed the now titled *The Endless Summer* in California and Hawaii, providing and in the process refining an engaging live narration. The first time Brown and his assistant / film projector/producer Paul Allen showed it there was a dead silence of thirty seconds following the closing credits—and then an explosion of applause. The always warm reaction Brown received was wild this time, telling the by now veteran 26-year-old filmmaker this could be big. It'd better be, for Brown had sunk fifty grand into the film, in other words, everything the other movies had made and more.

Brown decided to record the narration as well as a sound track largely drawn from the San Clemente group The Sandells, whom he'd come to know during the editing of *The*

Endless Summer and whose band name would eventually morph into The Sandals. Allen was then dispatched to show the film around to movie execs who liked it personally but felt that it would only do business on the coasts. Brown's improbable, in hindsight brilliant, response was to take it as far from salt water as possible, to a single venue in Wichita, Kansas, where, despite a raging blizzard in January 1965, lines snaked every night around the corner. When the first week sold out, the run extended for a second, with the same results. The industry guys always know better, of course, so even with that proof, a three-minute cut, other tight re-editing, and a clean blown-up 35mm print, the New Yorkers weren't biting. So Brown and Allen finally just opened it themselves as they'd done in the sticks, and the result in sophisticated Gotham was a similar sell-out. This time, not just good word of mouth but reviews over the moon, including glowing accounts from the *Times* and the day's ultimate cinema kingmaker, Pauline Kael of the *New Yorker*. Eventual worldwide distribution by Columbia followed, with the film bringing in over $30 million and forging its still undisputed reputation as *the* surf film.

Hollywood had been *Beach Party*-ing since the early '60s, with surfing as two-dimensional décor for its safe, parent-friendly repackaging of an emerging youth culture. While 1964's *Ride the Wild Surf* produced some terrific early big wave footage as background, its romantic entanglements and close-up action still stink of production executive tampering. The paddle-outs and rear projections are astonishingly creaky, even by the time's standards. Heads bobbing rhythmically, heavy James Mitchum glowers as the handsome watermen heroes chat casually while coasting down 20 footers. Only a couple of years later Brown would call into question such blatantly phony treatment of surfing—the scene, the athletics, the meaning. His new film would be shaped by a slim, seductive narrative conceit: two real surfers follow the summer around the world and really ride the wild surf they find on route. After Tinseltown's early commercial forays into the beach scene, he offered a different kind of product, one that felt, in fact, so much like a non-product that he had to go through the above contortions to land a distributor.

Yet while Brown's film did do business, that never seemed like the point. It had the vibe of joyful projection in the back of a surf shop for the zinc-oxide crowd—like Brown's early work, only with the door wider open. The rest of us, kooks and all, were not only let in but let in on the secret. In large part, what gave the film its wide appeal to a non-surfing audience was the fact that *The Endless Summer* felt more than anything like a movie for surfers by surfers. In reality there's a sizeable chunk of fairly elementary pedagogy in the film; the first eleven minutes alone are a veritable surfing primer for those unfamiliar with the moves and the lingo. Yet experienced surfers loved and have always loved the movie. Walking the line between their insider pleasures and wide commercial appeal, Brown notably resisted industry demands to bikini-fy the poster or write in beach blanket love interest. Though it contained proportionately fewer minutes of pure waveriding than his earlier movies, it was always about the surfing. It was also about good-natured adventure travel, affectionate engagement with a beautiful and varied natural world, and sheer curiosity. The combination was right for the times. It looks forward to the late '60s in its implicit belief in global community, and even beyond in its shifting post-modern blend of local and global identities; at the same time *The Endless Summer* embodies a nostalgic search for lost perfection and sunny refuge from the ugliness of Vietnam and assassination. Bringing Pop Art day-glo fluorescence to the timeless serenity of August, Hynson, and Brown standing with their boards at Salt Creek, the famous silkscreen poster by John Van Hamersveld looks similarly fore and aft.

That three surfers figure on this poster for a film about two guys travelling the world points to the importance of Brown as a character in his own movie. Crafted in earlier films over summer after summer of live narration, the gentle force holding things together is his witty charm and friendly, engaging voice. Surfing sold the tickets, but Brown is the man. Warm and companionable, his voiceover instructs, exaggerates, inspires, and entertains, shifting easily from informative to goofy to quietly lyrical. Writer, director, cameraman, occasional surfer for his own lens, Brown is most of all that voice, and as in the other films it is the only one we'll hear for 95 minutes. Yet before his first pronounced words about the varied meanings of summer to different people, Brown already speaks with a perfectly modulated visual language. As the credits of *The Endless Summer* roll to the languid twangs of The Sandals' distinctive theme, a sunset's warm orange glow profiles two surfers floating just outside. A board-loaded beater clatters off towards the beach, followed by the foreground closeup of a profiled tail and fin, the same orange and the sun's molten disk gliding past on the horizon in a simple but striking time-lapse shot. The film's terms are already there in Brown's brief triptych: the summer of that glow and music, a representative pair of surfers ready to go, the journey and the hint of endless geographical sweep and possibility. And then it's off into the film's rollicking first chapter, where Brown toasts the pleasures of summer, tickling and educating his audience through a sequence of tubes, nosewalks, and wipeouts in Hawaii and California. But what if you could surf like this all year round, he wonders, what if you could follow the summer around the world? Strangely enough, turns out that two California surfers have been planning just such a trip. After one of those cornball interludes that Brown somehow pulls off—the tousled Americans reading *Shark Attack* and *Malaria Manual*—he sends them east from LAX to, successively, Senegal, Ghana, Liberia, South Africa, Australia, New Zealand, Tahiti, and the North Shore of Oahu. As exotic as the catalogue from "Surfin' U.S.A." was, this was suddenly something else. Watching the film, you feel even now the stoke—and the apprehension—of paddling out in waters that had never seen a surfboard.

One of the many pleasures of the film is striking up a casual acquaintance with its easygoing 19-year-old protagonists, Mike Hynson and—he of the name too good not to be true—Robert August. Brown, who knew everyone in the small Southern California surf elite, could have chosen a Phil Edwards and Mike Doyle, but then he would have made a different film. Sponsored by local boardmakers, Hynson and August were classy surfers but virtual unknowns outside their small circle; all surf and no name, they abruptly reversed the superficial Elvis and Frankie Avalon star formula. The former blond, the latter dark, one a regular-footer, the other a goofyfooter, both cute and anonymous, they were perfect blank slates on which to trace late-Sixties dreams of mobility and freedom.[29] Though we never hear them speak, they gamely negotiate with their Senegalese taxi driver, cast mildly lascivious glances at Australian bikinis, feign boredom as they supposedly sit for hours thumbing a ride in South Africa. And surf like gods. The non-wave action's woodenly staged yet at some fundamental level it rings true: it's clear these three young fellows headed off with little real preparation into very unfamiliar geographical and cultural settings and were making things up as they went along. If the surprises and culture shocks enacted in the film don't always feel like real experience, they do feel like believable versions. All along too there's Brown's impish humor and fresh narration highlighting the novelty and the gee-whiz curiosity of these innocents abroad trying to cope.

Capital letters in the opening credits note, touchingly, that the shirtless travelogue to follow was "Filmed in ACTUAL LOCATIONS AROUND THE WORLD," and one apparently unironic visual is the little animated map with a toy plane hopscotching across the globe. The sequences to come will find the trio surprised by prices and a massive tourist hotel in Senegal, then gamely and good-naturedly interacting with baffled locals, with their age-old fishing practices and traditional tribal organization along the West African coast. Brown rightly underlines the scary charge of surfing even the best formed waves in such forbiddingly unfamiliar waters. Then it's off to South Africa for much-needed geography lessons and a long hitched ride up the Indian Ocean coast with its hundreds of miles of prime, unsurfed waves. From there the team did some (unused) filming in India, preferring to push on to Australia. Waiting is the primary theme down under due to the relative lack of good surf in summer, bad luck that Brown turns into narrative opportunity. Not only do semi-regular shut-outs ring true with surfers, they also allow some time to hang with the locals. One such is Paul Witzig, supposedly happened upon, but in fact Brown's Aussie impresario and later filmmaker in his own right. Witzig lends the film some excellent too-bad-you-missed-it winter Bells Beach sequences he shot featuring a young, fearsomely talented Nat Young. As our pair of travellers moves on through New Zealand and Tahiti, getting sweet rides on surf where there shouldn't be any, getting skunked when they expect action, Brown intercuts his familiar "letter from back home" drop-ins at the Wedge, Rincon, or Sunset. The stop in Japan that followed yielded 30 minutes of good film that time constraints kept out of the final product. As, it seems, every filmmaker of the time had to do, Brown then brings things to an end in Hawaii's endless summer.

Accompanying the duo's on-site adventures with regularly interspersed "memories" of other surfing moments from Hawaii and California let Brown use good material gathered over the years while drawing an audience-friendly thematic parallel between the daily surfing adventure and this exotic version. The systematic recourse to such narrative pauses also suggests, however, that discoveries in distant climes can really be judged only by reference to a known American reality. And indeed, in the West African part of their journey—its most savory, troubling chapters—August and Hynson struggle in vain to persuade a taxi driver to strap their boards to the top of the car; as he heads off, planks jutting out of the trunk, Brown wonders how this would play on U.S. freeways. When it comes to ethnicity in what was then called the Third World, though, Brown's innocents have apparently learned little from their own country's past and notably its recent history of racial strife from Little Rock and Birmingham through Watts and beyond. The above incident comes just after these queries: "Would they find surf? Would they catch malaria? Would they be speared by a native?" The ensuing voiceover uses the word "primitive" at least five times. When the guys paddle out alongside a dugout of Ghanaian fishermen, they hear "something like 'Oomgawa mungy wango'.... Mike smiled and said, 'Yeah man, hang ten!' They thought that was great. They went stroking out, chanting, 'Hang ten, hang ten.'" If such can be imagined, an even more *Tintin in the Congo* moment occurs later near Durban. Wracked in fact by (totally unmentioned) apartheid, Brown's South Africa is apparently populated only by matey white surfers. The film makes much of the way they travel and surf in compact bands, but nothing, say, about how such tight protective grouping might speak to their

The Endless Summer, director Bruce Brown (1964, 1966). In Durban, South Africa, Mike Hynson and Robert August "ride the Zulu rickshaw down the promenade" (Bruce Brown Films/Photofest).

sensed vulnerability as a minuscule minority in an overwhelmingly black society three years into Nelson Mandela's life sentence. In any case, in their sharky waters the appearance of dolphins is apparently a good sign, for "sharks and porpoises have yet to integrate."

Delivering such lines with a wink has made Brown a very easy target for an aware viewer like Daniel Duane, who rightly highlights the embarrassing "1960s colonial stupidity" of "two healthy, wealthy Western boys on an unparalleled journey of cultural imperialism—the whole world as their amusing theme park."[30] Duane's not alone in such sentiments.[31] Perhaps, though, because Brown is a still powerful icon, a part of every surfer's collective past, and seemingly a great guy, and because those were different times, the tendency is to let it slide. To his credit, Matt Warshaw clearly underlines these and other howlers from *The Endless Summer*, but Brown could easily have figured under the rubric "Racism and Surfing" in *The Encyclopedia of Surfing*. An earlier version of these remarks takes an indulgent stance towards this aspect of *The Endless Summer*, a regrettable position today since the man already had a record: *Surfing Hollow Days* was filmed in 1962 and released in 1963, the years, respectively, of violent opposition to James Meredith's enrollment at Ole Miss and the Medgar Evers murder. On the beach circuit Brown would point out nightly that New Zealand had black sand on its west coast and white sand on its east. "Segregation!" he'd then quip. It does seem creepy that his film's narrator would use a shameful injustice central to his own American society as a facile punchline. Years after *The Endless Summer*, Brown offered an inside look at the creation of the film in a feature directed by his son Dana. We hear the names of the local contacts and the inside story of the famous Cape St. Francis sequence, but no word about the blithely overlooked reality of apartheid.

The blind spots of American cultural empowerment and prosperous exceptionalism so apparent in *The Endless Summer* illustrate how easily surfing's don't-give-a-shit cool can veer into ugly apoliticism. They are also a reminder that, indeed, the film did show up on just *that* side of the massive shifts in consciousness announced in the Haight-Ashbury or the Pentagon Papers. The Sixties vibe of *The Endless Summer* certainly exists, but it's elsewhere, in a free, mobile open-endedness and a fresh, if naively inchoate—and paradoxical, given the racial text and subtext elsewhere—dream of universal community. By their very nature, Walter Salles writes, road movies "challenge the culture of conformity" if only because they are "about experience ... about the journey." Combine that formula with tentatively searching out, then surfing tinglingly unfamiliar waters, and, for all the fun, we are probably talking about the something serious that Salles identifies as a "form of resistance" to convention and the status quo. The sheer rush of surfing, the unadulterated in-the-moment uselessness of the thing, is a large part of its meaning. Brown furthermore makes it clear that around the world others were simultaneously waking to the significance of subversively pure experience in the rhythmed unpredictability of wave sets. And willing to share these heightened, intensely personal moments across different cultures and histories, the heartening opposite of the foul localism that would come to mar the surfing life. Despite the orchestrating hand of the director, it is moving to watch Hynson and August bond with local informants, little micro-coteries, neophytes who try their boards, and a South African who goes 2000 miles out of his way to drive them from spot to spot.

That guy, by the way, leads them on a hunch to isolated, magic Cape St. Francis where our pair stumbles across miles of dunes and onto "what every surfer dreams of finding ... a perfect wave." While in fact things didn't exactly happen that way,[32] it's true that Brown and his surfers did come upon those flawless pipes totally by chance. Such is the vigor of the resulting images and the power of the notion of the perfect wave that the perceived subject of the film almost instantly changed. A lucid viewing of *The Endless Summer* makes it clear that the movie is about the adventures of two surfers as they follow the summer around the globe—a pursuit perhaps, but not quite a quest. Yet query nearly anyone who knows the film—including professionals and, for that matter, the Brown organization itself—and they will refer to it as some variant on "the search for the perfect wave."[33] In fact, the term "perfect wave" is not used until the *fiftieth* minute and then only because of the serendipitous discovery of this prime, and fickle, break on a particularly exceptional day. Why then do we persist in seeing it as a Grail-like quest? The answer may lie in the meaning of those lucky surfers' discovery as perceived by a confused society itself in search of an elusive, missing something. Just a year later *The Graduate* would crystallize the comically depressive message that all the suburban business world out there could offer the new generation was a future in 'Plastics!'" The truth of *The Endless Summer* is elsewhere entirely, in the communicated intensity of authentic experience and a living present moment. If something's worth seeking out in a plastic world, it's that. Watching Mike Hynson niched effortlessly in the curl on a matchless right—still on the same wave, Brown says, as he runs out of film, changes the reel, and starts shooting again[34]—it's understandable why the desultory international bopping around leading to this moment would suddenly and retroactively take on the form of a quest. And one, the film title coaches, that remains as endless as every summer moment it celebrates is fleeting. Over long sequences, tubes for once exactly the right metaphor, Brown's narration insists on the "hundreds of years" that razor-traced perfection went unridden and "the thousands of waves that have gone to waste since." Not waste as in unproductive, but as Eliot would have it: "Ridiculous the waste sad time / Stretching before and after." What comes in between is what counts, the "quick now, here, now always," the afternoon of redemptively pure presentness where the quest's ending is always its new beginning.

~ ~ ~ ~ ~

Riders on the Storm(s)

In the history of surfing in cinema, there is clearly a before- and an after- *The Endless Summer*. For the first time a wide general audience discovered what Noll called "the real deal,"[35] the essence of this new life choice that was no long just a fad. When we look back at the best surf movies of the decade or so that followed—many of the genre's most memorable achievements—it's clear that he set an example that was both challenging and liberating. Brown's protagonists wore suits and neat haircuts. With the Haight and Jackson State and the bombing of Cambodia, that couldn't last, but his film's message of freedom, footloose curiosity, unhassled immersion in the natural world, and at least the promise of new cultural encounters spoke stirringly to the filmmakers who would take the surf movie in different directions in response to changing realities within and outside the sport from the late 1960s through the early 1980s. Hynson and August rode the stately nine foot boards of the time, but the film had been in wide release less than a year before Bob McTavish and George Greenough essentially designed the first modern short surfboards. During the same period revolutionary re-thinking was hitting the larger Western culture, with freedom the word scrawled on what could in both domains easily seem like a newly blank slate. In 1976 the expatriate writer and composer Paul Bowles spoke for more than himself in contending that "when you've cut yourself off from the life you've been living and you haven't yet established another life, you're free.... If you don't know where you're going, you're even freer." The cool open-endedness of Brown's wryly curated journey was an era's.

The bracing off-shore breeze of freedom and possibility in *The Endless Summer* thus corresponded perfectly to a late-'60s Western world soon stirred by similar gusts and to a surfing world shaken by the shortboard storm front and, a few years later, buffeted by the sport's modernization. The film showed that one could speak meaningfully to a broad general audience about the joys and mysteries of surfing without resorting to clichéd Hollywood dumbing down and, vitally, without alienating a touchy surfing hard core. The result would be an exciting renaissance for the surfing movie. Heady changing times on shore and in the surfline, technological advances, and some exceptional talents transformed the genre, with more innovative presentations of ever hotter surfing and a more complex interrogation of the meaning of the surf life and its relation to a larger world of mass culture, commercial pressures, environmental challenges, and social ferment. Between Brown and home video's virtual extinction of the communal surf film experience in the mid–1980s, such filmmakers as Australians Paul Witzig, Albert Falzon, and Santa Barbara Queenslander George Greenough, and Southern Californians John Severson, Jim Freeman, Greg MacGillivray, Hal Jepsen, Steve Soderberg, and Bill Delaney would create film experiences that at minimum were honorably entertaining and responsive to their time, and which rose at times beyond memorable to the level of art. Though even the most successful never broke through to general audiences to the degree Brown did, "Top Ten" and other lists in generalist magazines and websites have demonstrated their staying power in the collective surfing imagination and even within the larger culture. Notable in all this was the sudden, radically southern shift of surfing innovation and prestige during this period. The new boards came from the Southern Hemisphere, the best surfers were suddenly from Australia and South Africa, and, when it was time for the sport to go pro, that impetus came from down under as well. All along the top filmmakers were there to record these moments. The remarks to follow will accordingly begin with the cinematic reply to the revolution of the shortboard in the surfing hotbed of Australia in the '60s. From there we will turn to the developing response from California filmmakers to the seismic cultural shifts with which the new surfing seemed such a natural partner, before finally treating the commercial revolution of professionalism and sponsorship incited by other exceptional talents from the Southern Hemisphere.

What the best of the Australian and Californian filmmakers did was freshen, modernize, and personalize the Bruce Brown model, which, it must be said, was not so much a model as a state of mind and a manner: a deeply felt sense of surfing's meaning and potential, an openness to the zeitgeist, and an authentic empathy for the full range of viewers, whether the truly initiated and only casually curious. The best did not try to imitate Brown, as the brief counter-example of Southern California filmmaker Dale Davis might help to demonstrate. Davis turned formal Brooks Institute training into five full-length films from 1963 through 1973. His 1964 release *Strictly Hot* exemplifies his early work. Even by the day's standards short at 48 minutes, it brings together talents like Mike Doyle, Johnny Fain, Miki Dora, and Mike Hynson hopscotching classically from Malibu to Sunset to Ventura. Davis innovated by recording his chatty, upbeat narration rather than delivering it live each night. For the traditional pauses in the non-stop wave action, he introduces the obligatory humorous touch less by familiar sight gags or daffy antics than by playing in his commentary with spoken accents, swinging with bewildering confidence from flamboyant country twang ("Look a' him, he's a ridin' backwards!") to thick Boris Karloff echoes straight from the crypt; the indulgent might perhaps grant that the latter were funny for American 15-year-olds in 1964, the year both *The Munsters* and *The Addams Family* began haunting the small-screen. The surfing's well-shot and there is a tingly moment for today's viewers when the narrator alertly points out someone at Haleiwa with a *six-foot board*, but overall this is pleasant if unexceptional stuff dated by a nearly insufferable narration. Then four years later *The Endless Summer* was the new reality, and all that juvenile corn's gone from the voiceover, replaced by overbearing insistence on the by now fully recognizable trope of the quest without end.

The Golden Breed (1968) asserts its Bruce Brown inheritance in the opening minutes as Davis intones his definition of the breed in question over excessively familiar images of a blood orange sunset backlighting two silhouetted guys with boards. This group of exceptional individuals is "always in search of a *perfect* ride," we hear. "It's an *endless* search." The italicized words and their close cousins will reappear in varying combinations throughout a narration that veers towards solemnity as the earlier one tripped into giddiness. Though familiar from other films as well, chapters on surfing terminology and related alternative sports recall the 1966 classic, and its instrumental musical theme is so clone-perfect one looks for The Sandals in the credits. To be sure, instead of a pair of representative individuals, Davis features a "breed," and indeed, as his opening credits make clear, he's got the day's Who's Who of surfing in his film. His substitute for a costly world tour is a relatively fruitless trip to Mexico and the inevitable California-Hawaii shuttle, but make no mistake, his film's about the tribe's "endless quest" "for the ride of their dreams." Independent of the obvious resemblances with *The Endless Summer*, *The Golden Breed* presents surfing that is unsurprisingly intense given the crew Davis assembled, with some big wave drops shot very effectively from helicopter, a rarity in those days (and the occasion of a scary accident when the director fell while shooting). The film's abundant cast includes "newcomer" Eddie Aikau; with retrospective poignancy, the legendary waterman who would perish at sea in 1978 frets on camera about those, especially with families, who bet their lives in big waves. The movie's weaknesses include factual problems, like incorrectly labeling Waimea the statistically most dangerous wave when it was already becoming clear that Pipeline had that honor, or defining the word Banzai as "kill," as well as certain moments of rhetorical excess: agreed, Billy Hamilton can lay on the body English, but, honestly, "you can't tell the difference between him and the board"? Playing loose with facts, exaggerating, mythifying, hammering away at his theme, Davis mars able, enthusiastic filmmaking by straining so insistently for the public-popular and surfer-approved dual effect that Bruce Brown pulled off with effortless cool. The glorious notion of the quest for perfection only sneaks up on you in *The Endless Summer*; it's not a program announced from minute one.

Thunder Down Under

A contemporary who could even more easily have fallen into the trap of imitation, but didn't, is Australian Paul Witzig, who actually shot some footage of groms Rodney Sumpter and Nat Young for *The Endless Summer*, and worked for a stretch as Brown's Australian agent. The surfer and one-time architecture student was one of the most exceptional of the period's filmmakers less for his often limited technique than for the responsive way he chronicled the radical changes in surfing in the late 1960s. Witzig listened to his own instinct and the pulse of his own abruptly very different times in six full-length movies, three of which witness in remarkable sequence the most intense period of change the sport has known. In *The Hot Generation* (1967), *Evolution* (1969), and *Sea of Joy* (1971) Witzig makes up for his technical limitations as a filmmaker by his bang-on selection of subject matter and perhaps even more by his unerring personnel choices. Not only on the spot when the shortboard revolution was occurring but alert to what it meant, he documents better than any other filmmaker—and nearly in real time—the thrilling quantum leaps in surfing performance achieved down under by the alliance of the freeing new boards and spectacular talent. Central to the shortboard story, which by rights includes other innovators like Peter Drouyn and Dick Brewer, were kneeboard maestro George Greenough and shaper/surf champ Bob McTavish. The two teamed up on the Sunshine Coast in 1967 to re-think fin shape and progressively reduce board length, thickness, and weight in an attempt to heighten mobility on the breaking wave and venture into its most critical areas. Their primary partner in design was the hard-driving Young, the intensely physical yet still graceful regularfooter who had already dominated the World Championships in 1966 on a thinner than usual nine-foot board and who was taking on star status, complete with early sponsorship deals. Following a cast of characters that changes little from film to film, the three movies usher us along quietly, if sometimes maladroitly, through an earlier era and then smack-dab into the revolutionary ferment cooked up by these guys; it's expressed spectacularly in the waves and then roughly paralleled on shore in a world of paisley dresses, long hair, and easy weed. In all this, by the way, Witzig certainly couldn't go incognito, for his surf scribe and brilliant photographer brother John famously penned an incendiary 1967 piece in *Surfer* titled (by editor John Severson) "We're Tops Now." Not surprisingly, his bro's California-dissing and anointment of the new Australian elite got American trunks in a bunch; in retrospect, though, John Witzig was only speaking truth to power.

The Australians did take charge of surfing at this time, first through their sizeable contributions to the shortboard insurgence and then with their brash arrival on the North Shore in the mid-'70s. Tonally, though, during much of *The Hot Generation* you'd never know change was afoot. This is largely because Witzig entrusted the narration to John Thompson. Even if the Sydney DJ's stuffy upper-crust manner—"The scenery was *superb!*"—may have been intended as ironic, it still runs in jarringly different circles than the film's Who-inspired title. Also, speaking of archaic touches, what about the early scene where a skindiving Russell Hughes, sighting a shark just hanging out, calls in a specialist to off it with a bang stick? Once the nine-footer is dragged to the surface, Hughes actually punches the nose repeatedly before letting its dead form twist off to the bottom. The legendary Australian touchiness about sharks in coastal waters has to be taken into consideration, but this is very weird, period, and all the odder in a film whose title song—generic, but struggling for period relevance—seems to want to pit today's hot generation off against a corrupt civilization that has it all wrong. Where the film surpasses its tone-deafness to live up to its title is the surfing, at Australian locales like Noosa and Byron Bay, during a sweep along the French Basque Coast, and finally in Hawaii. The boards are still long, but the enhancement of turning capacity by the

Poster, *The Hot Generation*, director Paul Witzig (1967): Reigning World Champ Nat Young and Co. changing surfing. Two years later Wayne Lynch would abruptly signal the next phase in the sport's *Evolution*.

experimental "vee-bottom" design and thinner rails is evident in some scenes. Nat Young and Ted Spencer impressively slice and carve, but try to keep your eyes off the incredibly nimble switchfooter Kevin Brennan in some of the early scenes. You can't not regret that wild potential heroin-snuffed at 26 when you watch him gavotte across the board or casually tuck himself into the crystal green pocket at Burleigh Heads.

The closing chapters of *The Hot Generation* take place on Maui. The New Crew's there, Nat, McTavish, and Greenough, as well as their islands counterpart in innovation, Dick Brewer. Things were moving so fast at this time that one can practically see the changes taking place on the screen. Nat "gets the feeling of his new vee-bottom board," the narrator notes, and Reno Abellira rides "a new board shaped by Dick Brewer and finished only hours earlier." These three guys together with McTavish and a Greenough shooting tube footage for his own film from his futurist kneeboard may look like they're riding waves, but in fact they're busy splicing strands of surfing DNA into new forms. Young in particular limns the shape of things to come, driving up to carom off the wave's roof, or dropping back in from the crest after pulling a "floater" years before such a maneuver even had a name. The Honolua Bay sessions may conclude Witzig's 75 minute film, but in hindsight they seem more like a teaser for the next and for the next phase in surfing history. *Evolution*, the following film's promotional materials claim with perfect justification, "shook the established surfing world to its foundations when it was released."[36] And it did this despite repetitiveness, little variety in camera work, unremarkable music, and slack editing. Like its predecessor (and successor), the movie does begin with one of its best touches, the introduction of the film's surfing cast first in action then freeze-framed at a critical wave instant as their respective names appear on screen. Not only a respectful gesture, the shift from slashing action to freeze-frame and back to movement also highlights the sheer radicality of the moves. Beyond this intro, though, little else in the form and manner of *Evolution* recalls the earlier movie. Most obviously there's zero spoken narration, just spare visual signposting ("Autumn in Victoria," "Guéthary") for vast expanses of surfing, the likes of which no one had ever seen before. That surfing is the thing and not the storytelling or aesthetic choices, though one is tempted to be generous and suggest that, as it will for Greenough and Alby Falzon, breaking with traditional form can work when your subject is the sudden free flowering of the new.

While *Evolution* should probably have been called *Revolution*, the two words anyone really remembers from the film are Wayne Lynch. Beyond the odd bit of irritating double exposure, there's little craft, mostly just wave-riding filmed straight-on from fixed shore locations. The filming, though, is of Lynch, and, to be fair, the nearly as incisive Nat Young, plus the excellent Ted Spencer, Reno Abellira, and others. Looking at that line-up, one would expect the 17-year-old to play Robin to Young's Batman, but in fact the goofyfooter steals the show. Even today, after Slater and the New School supposedly changed the world, the radical turns Lynch rips up and down sheer left walls are breathtaking. When he made his first appearance 2½ minutes in, contemporary audiences apparently went bonkers and didn't stop for the next hour. *Evolution* passes half its time in Australia and half on a mellow shuttle through France, Morocco for the first time in a surf film, and Puerto Rico for the World Championships. Sensational as it is, the smoother harnessing of power of Young at the heavy *La Barre* and Peter Drouyn on the Australian west coast only highlights the snap turn difference of Lynch, with his low center of gravity, ravenous wave attacks, and bounces off the crest and back again into the action. Meant to amp up the excitement, Witzig's periodic double exposures distract from the real thrill of just looking. His more effective artistic decisions were to juxtapose the World and Australian Championships, and then to accompany the latter with a "Boléro," which was perhaps inspired by Albie Thoms's similar use of the celebrated music in a 1967 experimental film and which comes as a relief after the banal progressive jazz improvisation of the rest. Despite sharp work by Young, Hughes, and Midget Farrelly in Puerto Rico, it's the show on the lefts and rights of the Margaret River Australian championships that makes it mindblowingly clear the surfing balance of power has shifted. Accompanying the long sequence, and unpretentious despite what one might think, Ravel's smooth melodic build adds just the right touch of graceful drama.

For the soundtracks of *Evolution* and 1971's *Sea of Joy*, Witzig responded in a recent interview that he was consciously trying to "break away a bit from the traditional surfing sound." For the period piece that is the latter, the result was unexceptional instrumental psychedelia. The earlier vibe of flannel shirts and Marrakesh Express djellabas is multiplied exponentially in *Sea of Joy*, as are the laid-back chapter headings providing a grinning shrug of vague direction for the similarly narration-free flow. Two such are "The Pipe of Peace," where reef break meets reefer break, and "Our Brother John" signaling a welcome post–Brown social awareness for the film's voyagers in apartheid-infected South Africa. Beyond a moment like the latter, though, it can seem at times that the cast is just dressed for 1971 and smoking the requisite joint, with little attempt beyond juxtaposition to investigate the potentially intriguing relationship between the changing social scene and the radically new surfing. Witzig is far more focused in the surfing and will leave that interesting cultural work to Falzon, Greenough, Severson, and others.

In addition to Africa, *Sea of Joy* drops into Hawaii and Mauritius (three years before it would become the cryptic *Forgotten Island of Santosha* in another film). It also features the home breaks of a Nat Young newly out of the competition circuit and back to the land, and, again, the boy wonder. Even if he was only widely "discovered" in the previous movie, it's now Wayne's World, with Lynch's number one spot in the credits intros, and a lead-off chapter dubbed a nerd-cool "Wayne at Home." Yet while his surfing's every bit as much on fire, the news is that it's no longer quite the same news: albeit with a touch less flair and assurance, everyone on screen is more or less surfing like that, and Young at times even catches the eye more. In three films and four short years Paul Witzig takes us from the exploratory early tinkering with technology and attitude of a few outliers through the sudden shortboard paradigm shift and new reality. If he doesn't seriously interrogate links between that new questioning spirit and manner and the social and stylistic upheavals of the period in the way others soon will, he does at least place them side by side. As filmmaking it's rudimentary stuff with the occasional flare of inspiration. About the creative process that led to the centerpiece *Evolution*, Young did say that the Pipe of Peace played a substantial role: "It's a miracle the thing came out as well as it did."[37] It did, if nothing else because Witzig had exactly the right subject and exactly the right poster boy at exactly the right time.

And where were the Yanks while the Aussies were up to all this? The answer: after a visiting group of Californians graciously showed up in 1956 with the lighter balsa "Malibu board" that essentially revolutionized Australian surfing, they were still standing on the nose and sitting on their laurels. Nat Young's San Diego World Championships victory in

1966 should have knocked them off, but didn't. For this situation to change, it would take another long Australian trip, though this time it would be the Aussies giving the lessons. This story is told in one of the weirdest surf movies ever, a short-lived 1969 20th Century–Fox release that is all the same oddly compelling for its clumsily appropriate bipartite structure and, most of all, for its accidental timeliness. *The Fantastic Plastic Machine* borrows the closing two words of its very of-the-period title from the name Bob McTavish gave to the first really short surfboard, invented during that short stretch of intense innovation with Young and Greenough. Aiming for an *Endless Summer* feel but with an oddly Hollywood orchestral soundtrack, filmmakers Eric and Lowell Blum followed a cocky, "outasite" bunch from the Windansea Surf Club hopscotching down through the South Pacific to a late 1967 face-off with a group of top Australians. Only there does the film find out what it really wants to be about.

The wan, derivative travelogue south finally gets interesting when the competition starts. The Aussies, riding their more alert new vee-bottom boards, work the curl even on the day's mushy waves, dominating the Americans, their battleships, and their suddenly antiquated fixation with the nose. At this point, making it up as they went, the smitten Blums impetuously dropped the Windansea band to throw in with McTavish, Greenough, and Young, non-participants in the competition but clearly the new surfing's power trio; the rest of the film repeatedly celebrates their high-performance shortboard and kneeboard slashes and cutbacks. If the thematic point of all this is rupture, the two-headed monster that is *FPM* certainly makes it. To top things off, should confiding the voiceover to TV's *Dennis the Menace*, Jay North, not be bizarre enough, the filmmakers abruptly transferred it to Young. whose interspersed free-form remarks convincingly frame the new surfing style in the pseudo-philosophical terms of the day. Speaking with the appropriate accent to discuss such a phenomenon in the late '60s, Young makes it clear that days of political and social revolution and the advent of the shortboard have more in common than mere simultaneity. The new board, he says in terms echoing the discourse of those years of self-actualization, "brings the surfer closer than ever before to the full expression of his personality."

While the U.S. surf establishment needed some lag-time to break with the past's restrictive schemas and get to that place, one Californian who always knew about the full expression of personality was the restlessly creative Santa Barbara techie who collaborated with McTavish and Young on those first shortboards. Images of George Greenough are instantly recognizable to, now, generations of surfers: knees prayerfully dropped, hydrodynamically perfect, banking hard, tucked as deep as one can into the tube. Such was his instinctive wave reading and studied sense of the physics involved that Greenough inspired traditional surfers when he took his specially designed flexible kneeboards into previously inaccessible wave areas and even gave the low-born surf mat its *lettres de noblesse*. Escaping the crowded SoCal scene for the open air and creative ferment of Queensland, he came up with the delicate modern "dolphin" (or "high aspect ratio") fin. The tireless tinkering and curiosity that would lead Greenough into, say, experimenting with carbon fiber before anyone else led as well into the surf film, another way for this generous perfectionist to explore the urgent space of the curl. *The Innermost Limits of Pure Fun* (1970) is one of the signal achievements of surf filmmaking. It is at once entirely idiosyncratic and an accurate mirror held to up to a radically changing world—that of surfing and, more pertinently than Witzig, that of a wider society in restless mutation. As Denny Aaberg and other members of the group Farm would attest, surfing's Edison was an unsurprisingly "quick study" in the making of his one full-length film. Using the group's period-perfect soundtrack, alternately bluesy, devotional, and alt-funny ("V-12 Cadillac"), Greenough laid down a series of images that explore the full potential of one of the genre's most intriguing and appropriate titles.

A six word enigmatic hint, it cheerily enfolds suggestions of the mind-expanding, limit-testing subjective inner quest with unadulterated fun, surfing's ultimate (non-)goal. This is a very 1970 program, the credits' flower-child graphics make clear, while remaining as old as that "most supreme pleasure" surfing has always been about. As he would show as well when shooting so brilliantly for others—including *Big Wednesday*, *Five Summer Stories*, and *Blackrock*—no one gets as "innermost" into the curl and the wave's living dynamics as Greenough. The film's real subject, it seems, is point of view, which he delivers low on his board, a heavy camera jury-strapped to film over his right shoulder, and decades before Go-Pro. To filmmakers, photographers, and writers the subjective "feel" of surfing is *the* prey, but it is elusive. Going radically less-is-more, Frederick Kohner may come as close as anyone in the closing chapter of *Gidget*: "The only sound in the vast moving green was the hissing of the board over the water." Similarly discreet and attentive to the subjective impression, Greenough takes us with the filmed image to this mobile meeting of outward and inward, time and the eternal present. In that paradoxical place, he said in the beautiful documentary *Crystal Voyager*, "a few seconds in real time ... goes on for hours," but "the only reality is what's happening right then."[38]

The Innermost Limits of Pure Fun is narration-free plunge into sensation. With minimalist signposting and the ramshackle homemade vibe a clear aesthetic choice, Greenough's 64 minutes lead, in a simple three-part structure, from Australia to the States then back south. Along the way, "objective" land-based shots feature surfers like McTavish, Chris Brock (still another shortboard visionary), Baddy Treloar, and himself on kneeboard or air mattress. But the magic of Greenough's final montage is the fluid, continuous shuttle from the land-based perspective to critically positioned slow motion immersion takes as a rider approaches, and then—the real money shots—to enthralling subjective footage shot from deep within the curl, just as the crest begins to rain. Then start again, in varying order, and again and again. Inside the gorgeous green tunnel with the subjective lens of Greenough's heavy, back-strapped 35mm rig pointed variously forwards and back, or (when this was still very fresh) buoyed as the wave's mass lifts and the surfer being filmed drops glidingly off, the viewer is inserted into a wet, copacetic cooperative reality of kaleidoscopically shifting perspectives. The empathetic effect over time is to meld the third and the first person, and even the second as the passing surfer occasionally pops a little glance at the camera. Greenough multiplies the effect by shuffling through other perspective shifts as well. He'll sight the tube we'll enter or have entered through the viewfinder of his editing machine, off the far end of a dirt road or, evocatively, from a small plane chartered to view a series of breaks from above; there the macro patterns of curving blue-to-white water transformations echo retinally the same forms and color blends at the micro-level of deep immersion in the wave. Taking his dolphin fin into dolphin-torn seas and his 60 percent water body deep within the living curl, he suggests themes of Romantic interconnection, homespun environmentalism, and the fluid dialectic between interior and exterior space that chime with the profane mysticisms of the late 1960s.

A contemporary political subtext is also present. Not that long before Wayne Lynch would duck Australia's Vietnam-era draft, Greenough and the bunch venture past RAAF prohibited entry signs, make a raid to what can only be the off-limits Ranch, and visit an abandoned tanker's rotting hulk. In the politically fraught year after Crosby, Stills & Nash's "Long Time Gone," the title of the much celebrated closing chapter "Coming of the Dawn" may gesture towards the light to follow the darkest hours. That said, the interest was often other for surfing audiences who went wild watching the ten minute tour de force. Following an alfresco feast of magic mushrooms for his on-camera surfers—a self-reflexive nod to the largely high viewers—Greenough streams color saturated hyper-slow motion sequences from deep within the barrel that were simply unlike anything proposed before in the surf movie. Action painting with water and light, a soaked Jackson Pollock, he's not just recording the mobile liquid medium but is part of it, water flowing aft in blacks and greys, lens droplets with a life of their own, the curved roof tightening in and the aquamarine tunnel contracting like a camera's aperture to a morning light pinprick before the wipeout upset and swirl. In that era of concert light shows, it's not surprising that Pink Floyd fell hard for Greenough's work; the group offered him their hypnotically experimental 1971 "Echoes" for his short film of the same name. Greenough continued his tubular investigations in other short works and in the absorbing 1973 documentary *Crystal Voyager*, which included the 23-minute "Echoes" and the 133 feet of film shot deep within one particularly epic tube at Lennox Head. Greenough is a modest, unassuming spokesman for a body of work that includes exciting technical and design advances in a number of areas, fresh ways to investigate and navigate the wave, and a cinema opening up new perspectives and possibilities of perception. He is a creative, introspective filmmaker who at some level deserves serious comparison with a brilliant video artist like Bill Viola, as obsessional in his relationship with water, fluidly "sculpting time" with the "camera ... the second eye that 're-teaches us how to see' and addresses the world beyond, or beneath, appearances."

Such was the impact of *Innermost Limits* and the centrality of Greenough to the transformations of Australian surfing that it's no surprise two of the most important figures in Aussie surf media would collaborate with him on *Crystal Voyager*. Among other things co-founders of the green-alt surf monthly *Tracks*, David Elfick and Alby Falzon shared with Greenough himself the intriguing task of bringing to the screen some sense of the Californian's burgeoning creative imagination and multiple talents. As fully achieved as the result is, Greenough's tinkering, theorizing mad scientist brilliantly setting off the musical and tubular magic of "Echoes," the two will always be best known for *Morning of the Earth*. The title of the 1972 film draws from Nehru's expressed wonder during his first experience of Bali, but one also hears "Coming of the Dawn." *Morning of the Earth* shares with Greenough's film its sense of a new day in the surfspace, where from land and sea radically fresh possibilities of existence and expression seemed to be fusing. Famously saying that "just by going surfing we're supporting the revolution,"[39] Nat Young and cohort furthered the radical remaking of surfing in their eco-instinctive image while dropping conspicuously off the social and economic grid for a few years. *Morning* catches their vibe, immersing the viewer in an often surreal flood of color, period music, and ethereal union with the wave. Few films are so much of their day, and the early '70s were intense to the point of extreme self-caricature. Yet despite occasional bellbottoms-in-amber moments, Alby Falzon's film still largely deserves its cult status, not only as a beloved icon from a bygone era but for the timelessness of its generously romantic commitment and the before-its-time quality of the surfing. In a commentary on the film's reissue Falzon said he wanted to make "a really beautiful, positive film about the world." From these vapory aspirations and an experimental cinematic bent signaled by the introductory citation from avant-garde giant Jonas Mekas, he fashioned a surprisingly tight aesthetic whole that retains its lush beauty and ability to inspire will never tipping into complete hippy absurdity. Falzon managed this, somewhat ironically, by spending what at time was considered a pile of cash. Experienced as a photographer/designer for the godfather of Aussie surf films Bob Evans (to whom *Morning* is dedicated), he and David Elfick secured a then-hefty twenty grand subsidy from the Australian Film Development Corporation. While remaining always in the service of a flagrantly sincere countercultural environmentalist vision, the money shows throughout in the technical values of the camerawork, the post-production treatment of the image, the exotic locations, and the palpable sense of patience.

Morning of the Earth begins with the morning of the earth, Falzon's wildly ambitious and partially achieved attempt to evoke the processes of creation and the nostalgic return to primal innocence. This trenchantly Romantic theme is so embedded in surfing that Bruce Brown attempts the same thing in his first film, just as Greg MacGillivray and Jim Freeman will in *Five Summer Stories*. A pre-credits sequence of swirling waves, molten solar effects, and trippy, color-drenched solarized footage unfolds to a hymn-like sound track which melds into the Tim Buckley-influenced title song. Then that title in Summer of Love "shagadelic" font, and the gloss: "A fantasy of surfers living in three unspoiled lands & playing in natures oceans" (sic). The 73 minutes to come will follow the unidentified Nat Young, Michael Peterson, Terry Fitzgerald, and others as they unequivocally demonstrate again that the new shortboard balance of surfing power had indeed shifted radically south. The smooth, powerful sweeps up the wave face of this incisive, dynamic surfing constitute a huge step forward towards today's best action. The effect at the time can't be overstated. Stirred gently into the flow of surfing immersion are quiet country soul land scenes of whole-earthy farming and homecrafts that draw surfboard shaping and surfboard riding into serene parallel with the simple life of a return to the earth. Plus the odd bit of weed corresponding perfectly to the film's stoner buzz, which is softy genial and never acid-scary, even given the screaming energy of much of the surfing.

The film's three unannounced chapters conduct the surfers from Australia to Bali and—some things never change—on to the North Shore. Against the down homey background of Young's own hideaway farm, the Australian scenes include a prolonged, hypnotic series of Byron Bay rights, nearly all filmed straight on from the mid-distance, one surfer per shot. Falzon will then announce the Bali section with a formal shift, offering views of local women transporting produce on their heads, the ocean in the distance, and then Rusty Miller and 14-year-old Steve Cooney accompanied by grinning locals to the water's edge. Filming them as they approach, Falzon frames the scene as revelation, which indeed it was, for they were among the first Westerners to sight the break of Uluwatu that has since taken on mythic status. Falzon's empathy as a filmmaker shows here. He knows how the endless succession of identically shot Gold Coast rights had mesmerized viewer retinas. So when his surfers venture out to the movie's first left-handers and he shoots them from farther off, bringing into view a wider sweep of that great wave in action, the effect is discovery-fresh. After a interspersed series of piquant glimpses into the life rhythms of the indigenous population of fishermen and sustenance farmers, this sequence eventually draws to a close. And then a new change in water color and the near-perfect right at Rocky Point to signal the Hawaiian phase of the adventure.

This is next generation Bruce Brown for a different world. Brown's narration, of course, plays a vital role in the meaning and feel of *The Endless Summer*. Here, as in Witzig's *Evolution* and Greenough's work, not a word is spoken. In a film about yielding to natural flow and process, the lack of narration identifies the silencing of an articulate, directive intelligence as a value. Before the new Cape St. Francis that is Uluwatu, there's no chatter but a dumbstruck silence. In any case, what these guys are doing can easily remain unspoken, for the viewer has internalized the voyage m.o. of the earlier film and the "search for surf" pattern implicit in surfing since at least Greg Noll's repeated use of the same film title in the '50s. Against a visual background of trance-like repetition and softly mystical color shading, Falzon's itinerants are not in neat suits but in baggy local trousers or saris and traditional conical hats. They can never not be white guys with, compared to their Balinese hosts, all the money and mobility in the world, but the tone and pattern of their "colonial odyssey" suggest an alternative desire to "reoccupy" what David Adams calls "'the god-shaped vacuum' that exists in modern secular society."[40] The Westerners interact respectfully, the lack of verbal commentary further suggesting appreciative observation rather than judgment or distance. To a fault at one point, in fact. In one of the remarkable sequences from *Morning of the Earth*, Falzon's empathy across cultures extends to a grueling episode of cock-fighting. As locals exchange wads of grubby bills, he takes us to, and beyond, the limits of cultural sensitivity: not only does he present a long stretch of the combat, but he does so in highly aestheticized slow motion, distastefully transforming the toxicity into lush feathery surges of regal male animal pride. The

A film by Albert Falzon

"We are the measure of all things.
And the beauty of our creation, of our art
is proportional to the beauty of ourselves
of our souls" Jonas Mekas

Poster, *Morning of the Earth*, directors David Elfick, Alby Falzon (1972). Drawing the title from Nehru's stunned reaction to Bali, evoking the single ocean that once covered the earth, quoting the godfather of the New American Cinema, Falzon and Elfick signal the film's lushly Romantic theme and underground aesthetic. Inset: Rusty Miller and Steve Cooney heading out the first time at Uluwatu.

effect is jarring, and not just for the hint of repressed sexual rage under the surface of this men-only film. *The Deer Hunter*, we know now, was also locking and loading just over the horizon. Watching these shots today, one feels the nightmare of gut-churning South East Asian violence jostling for space with a sunny dream of universal community.

What *Morning of the Earth* lacks in narration's labeling and direction, it certainty tries to make up in music. The soundtrack, considered cult in many circles and high in the Australian charts for months, accompanies every moment of film with overgrown instrumentals and country-infused flower children lyricism. Varying in tone from mysterious Cistercian devotional to full-on amp shaking guitar to down home twangs, the tunes are essential to the film's tidal sweeps of rhythm and tone, and at times ravishing, as in the flute-based enchantment accompanying the Uluwatu revelation. Unfortunately, when the songs include lyrics the latter often turn out distractingly prosaic. As well-intentioned as they are, most of the sung lyrics in the film are baldly lacking in verbal depth and subtlety. Under the potent spell of the images, one is tempted to let their clumsy straightforwardness slide, but, like the irritating "adrenaline flashes" inserted, it seems, to communicate the visceral rush of surfing, they too often laboriously highlight meaning already richly implicit in the visuals and certain moments in the instrumental mix. The work of minor composers and performers, the songs for the most part have a dated, tie-died naïveté, straining to evoke the best music of the period but, to be honest, lyrically unable in their plainness and sheer obviousness to stand beside it. G. Wayne Thomas and the crew can sound convincingly like *The White Album*, Country Joe, or The Grateful Dead, but the resemblance drops away quickly when, again, one concentrates on the words. If the montage manages to make something of the flimsy wording, it's by efficiently coordinating particular phrases and instrumental riffs with the filmed image, like the first land interlude, for example, which finds the surfers at Young's farm to a song about stripping back to the simple life. Evident a mile off, but okay in context. The hit single from the soundtrack was "Open Up Your Heart." By the end of the film's exciting, warmly enchanting journey Falzon has perhaps earned the right to underline his message with its sincere, trite injunction. We're still a very long way from Cream and "Tales of Brave Ulysses," though.

Throughout *Morning*, Falzon shows his stuff best by the careful visual design that underlies the loose-limbed hippy feel and sound of the film. We seem to be floating along between dynamic rides and maundering back-to-the-earth simplicity, and suddenly Falzon's cinematic craft will quietly catch the eye. Two moments among many stand out. After the unhurried, unannounced lead-up at last reveals the waves at Uluwatu to the surfers picking their way towards the shore, Falzon offers long shots from a relatively low vantage point of big incoming surf with rollers stacking up behind. We see no one paddling out, but as one particularly sizeable left breaks, the head and then the body of Cooney backside on the next wave emerge magically from the froth topping the preceding wall. The effect is striking, the surfer materializing like the wonder of the encounter with a pristinely unsurfed wave. Then, later in the same Indonesia chapter, a non-surfing interval presents two returning Balinese fishermen carrying their small outrigger up the beach as well as two others with a large shark dangling from a slat balanced on their shoulders. We're mercifully spared the obligatory narratorial quip about sharks, and more importantly offered a quietly meaningful statement in articulate visual language. Juxtaposed with the fishermen is a shot of two of the surfers, boards under their arms, returning across a low wooden tidal bridge at the end of a session. The way the varied horizontals—outrigger, slat, boards, bridge—echo each other is unobtrusively careful film craftsmanship: with his judicious eye and camera Falzon draws into expressive parallel the pairs of watermen, so different and so similar, making their daily journeys to the sea and back.

Morning brought in ten times its cost, its iconic status as Australia's great surf movie later confirmed by inclusion in the list of 50 indispensable films selected for preservation by the Kodak/Atlab National Film and Sound Archive Cinema Collection. Should confirmation be needed of the perennial charms of what's been called "a surf classic ... a cultural statement, a call to arms,"[41] Andrew Kidman provided it in *Spirit of Akasha*, a soulfully soundtracked tribute on the occasion of its fortieth anniversary bringing together surfers like Stephanie Gilmore and Mick Fanning, and the same romantic generosity. Despite the flaws—a dated over-seriousness, the gimmicky milli-second flashes, again the slim lyrics diluting an atmospherically charged musical background—Falzon's movie bears its sacred weight with sincerity and style. Putting it all into what he considered his one pure surfing film, he reveals the religious experience in a Michael Peterson one with the curl at Noosa Heads, and in Gerry Lopez almost tenderly taking that signature drop and glide at Pipe. *Whole Earth Catalog* meets involvement surfing, *Morning of the Earth* is a 1972 film oriented hazily backward towards the Summer of Love and crisply forward towards surfing's future. As the already inimitable Lopez writes those few lines in the early chapters of his book of legends, Falzon slips in the tellingly aromatic outdoors tableau of a mellow group tending a huge bong balanced on a surfboard. If it wasn't already clear how tightly entwined the stories of two worlds in creative ferment were, Falzon dovetails them once again with his sly visual pun on the name of that famous North Shore break.

Winds of Change

Back home in the birthplace of the surfing movie, that relationship between revolutionary dealings on land and on the shoreline was slightly different in nature, and not only because the effects of the faraway shortboard uprising would take some time to arrive. As it was for the Australian surf film, though, the off-shore breeze of freedom was apparently just what was needed to refresh and energize the genre in Southern California. In addition to his single-handed creation of the sport's central publication *Surfer*, Bruce Brown's contemporary John Severson had been turning out surf films in the late '50s and early '60s at the standard pace. After a pause dedicated to the magazine and, clearly, some serious rethinking, he brought out *Pacific Vibrations* in 1970. Turned on, tuned in, dropped out, and as of its very particular times as it could be, it was a belovedly trippy classic from day one, and certainly an influence upon *Morning of the Earth* and, also from 1972, fellow Californians Greg MacGillivray and Jim Freeman's *Five Summer Stories*, perhaps the only film to nudge *The Endless Summer* occasionally off rung one of the surf film ladder. With the revolutionary counter-cultural static of the period an erratic soundtrack to all these films, for the Californians in particular the conditions of that transitional early '70s creative microclimate included a grab-bag of interrelated factors: the perverse stimulation of Vietnam's ugly tensions and an increasingly caricatural Nixon White House (including the Western version next door to John Severson's place and irritatingly closing down at least one prime San Clemente break); fresh environmentalist stirrings coalescing in 1970 in the first Earth

Day and the creation of the EPA; the self-assertive model of the New Hollywood, with its itchy questioning of studio power and narrative or genre conventions; and a qualitative surge in film technology assuring crystalline slow motion and high performance sound. When it at last made its way north, add to this another "revolution," that of the short board, and stir vigorously.

While it drew on the models and creative experience of the first surf films—Bud Browne did much of the in-water shooting for *Five Summer Stories*—the new wave broke differently, picturing the surfing experience not simply as primo wave action and a few laughs on the sand. Counter-cultural change calmly imbues the films of Falzon, Greenough, and, to a lesser degree, Witzig. Closer to the action, with the Summer of Love and Richard Nixon both California creations, it's not surprising that political and cultural tension are a more explicit, and often thornier, presence in Severson and company. Only a couple of years after the last Beach Party movie, the shore and surf line became a place, variously, of creative expression, self-discovery, social satire, altered consciousness, ironic political statement, fusion with natural forces. It was about atmospheric, lush surf sessions, and getting grinningly back to the land, a huge oil spill off Santa Barbara and a nuclear power plant opening above San Onofre. It was about getting pissed off at cops in black shoes on the beach, "No Surfing" signs, gagging on PCH fast food, and development disfiguring the coast. Counter-cultural as the films felt, though, the implicit challenge of *The Endless Summer* general audience breakthrough no doubt made itself felt. Ambition translated into better equipment and into larger creative teams added to costs, and the new higher profile of the sport and its representations put surf films on the radar of record companies requiring licensing fees. The latter meant upward pressure on budgets, sure, but for some great soundtracks in an era of great music. A certain dissonance arises, though, every time a discussion brushes surfing up against money. In this case, a very slight one, for figures like the $24,000 budget of *Five Summer Stories* are laughably small for money that well spent, that is, if exceptional surfing beautifully filmed, an offbeat point of view, and a positive environmentalist vision appeal to you. Where incoherencies loom a bit larger are in the old surfing bugaboos of gender and cultural imperialism. After a shaky start, MacGillivray and Freeman eventually showed the way in featuring hot surfers who happen to be women, but elsewhere, even in the Age of Aquarius, it was still a man's world. As for questions of race and ethnicity, maybe Bruce Brown's worry about getting speared by natives was gone, but surfers were still almost always white dudes. When they hit the road with a camera on missions of "discovery," the celluloid flags they planted at "new" spots just showed the way for the next wave of surf colonists.

Such tensions are unsurprising, for history advances by fits and starts, and even what seem later to be the most evident progressive truths rarely follow a smooth arc to their normalization. The Equal Rights Amendment first went before Congress in 1972 but finally fell short of ratification; and things are such that, try as they may, white males visiting the developing world still can't shake the Captain Cook lineage. Just as they enrich and stand apart from it, surfing and its representations reflect their society. The surf movies of the 1970s thus inadvertently mirror certain social fractures even as they position themselves resolutely at the far, resistant edge of what they present as a dispiritingly dysfunctional Western culture. Starting off the decade, *Pacific Vibrations* is a good example. It has its occasional blind spots, but the film as a whole is an immersion, both luxuriant and thoughtful, in the hopeful transformations of its excessive, historically important era. Severson takes us to beaches where, he makes clear, the prudish, wasteful, money-grubbing American body politic could use some morning glass, a nice buzz, and a little communion with nature. *Pacific Vibrations* was John Severson's last film in part because, as he has said, the business model in the still pre-video world was making it too expensive to "play and experiment"[42]; just as much, it seems, it was because he always had other things to do. The dedication of Drew Kampion's *Stoked!: A History of Surf Culture* is "For John Severson: who started it all." The vagueness of "it" is appropriate for Severson was truly surf culture's Renaissance Man: fine surfer, seminal thinker, one of the earliest filmmakers, an acclaimed artist and writer, an articulate public voice for the environment and the surfing life, and, of course, the creator, publisher, and first editor of what would become the sport's monthly holy book, *Surfer*. Shaun Tomson has written that *Surfer* "is not just a magazine, but is the framework for a surfing existence, a collection of reference points for an obsession."

Like Bruce Brown, Orange County's Severson got a lucky posting in Hawaii for military service, not to mention the juicy plum of Army Surf Team membership. There he combined daily surfing, friendship with the line-up regulars, local knowledge, some cash picked up from his painting, and a precocious fascination with film to produce the 8mm *Surf* in 1958. Then in yearly order he turned a little "surf film hobby"[43] into *Surf Safari*, *Surf Fever*, *Big Wednesday*, *Going My Wave*, *The Angry Sea*, and *Surf Classics*. After some success in Hawaii, Severson worked out a profit-sharing deal with Fred Van Dyke to tour *Surf* in California in his place; later, like the other early filmmakers, he took his own work up and down the Coast providing live narration and music brought up at each push of the recorder on-button. Produced as single prints, the movies have unfortunately not survived except in little snippets here and there: Severson said in an interview at the Library of Congress that they're "ripples in a pond—slowing disappearing." Luckily we have Severson's own memories of those early days in his savory photo book/memoir *John Severson's Surf* (2014).[44] The first film, in color like its successors, contained film of the legendary Makaha of mid–January 1958, as well as footage from Waimea, Yokahama Bay, and a smattering of California classics. In addition to giving the Beach Boys a memorable song title, *Surf Safari* laid its own varied musical score (jazz and mariachi to Wagner) over the adventures of a group heading from the Lompoc area to Point Conception where, Severson contends, his surfers "discovered" the Ranch; sticking with the potpourri style of the period, the film also included look-ins at Sunset, Waimea, the best South Bay and Orange County spots, etc. *Big Wednesday* played on fascination with the great swell, structured as it was upon progression, a selection of waves rising in size day after day, from the ten foot Ala Moana barrel ending the first reel until the mythical moment at Waimea Bay in question. After the uninventive bluntness of the first films' labels, the concise poetry of the latter's title clearly lodged in the imagination of at least one Malibu beach rat. Sixteen years later John Milius would purchase the title from Severson for his today better-known 1978 film, incorporating its implicit whiff of mythic challenge into what he would help establish as the classic structure of the narrative surf film with its ritual final challenge. In *The Angry Sea* Severson's first use of recorded narration made more than explicit this sense of the brute natural force of the wave as the waterman's nearly existential testing ground. "Man's attempts to conquer the sea, if only for a moment, are met with angry resistance," intones the portentous introductory voiceover. "Our film deals with the surfer's efforts to use the power of the sea and conquer the angry elements."

A half-decade later, that "angry" would become "pacific." In the '60s, wrote Kampion, "the past was dying, the future was incubating."[45] Artistic, introspective while active, at the subculture's heart through his work with *Surfer*, Severson like the times radically shifted focus in his last film from an earlier discourse of domination ("conquer") or pragmatic "use" to one of generous submission to natural rhythms. Yet, while Severson is correct to describe *Pacific Vibrations* as "an environmental surf film celebrating the beauty of the ocean and our relationship, and at the same time, making the viewer aware that we needed to take care of this resource," the cinematic experience is far more intentionally jarring than the poised summary suggests. Psychedelic lower-case credits roll over a backdrop of "solarized" drift, slow motion cut-backs, and a gliding seabird, and abruptly *Pacific Vibrations* hits like a Winterland light show. There's cranking Steve Miller, and not the *Peter Gunn*-themed jazz of *The Angry Sea*, then a staccato series of retinal image flashes—skull, news shots, Rick Griffin's cartooned Murphy, hirsute unknowns, headlines—juxtaposes shattered cultural shards with the liquid flow of gorgeously shot surfing. After this there's a good stretch with no narration, just a kaleidoscopic sweep of little vignettes whose commingling is the message. First an interviewed blonde arrival from Ohio who thinks surfers are cool; then an evolutionary sequence of body- and mattress-surfing, belly- and knee-boarding, some sweet short board action; then a cute post-gremmy prototype who identifies wave riding as a far-out way to catch nature's flow. Implicitly responding to the film's amphetamine strobe kick-off, the gentle, sun-warmed cool needs no narration to underline its stance vis-à-vis a messed-up mainstream in the year of Kent State. When the kid earnestly recounts how his parents hold surfing in hostage for homework and good grades, we can't miss its alignment against the other power structures imposing their authority.

Severson's method throughout is juxtaposition, a hamburger joint duking it out with a chill restaurant called "The Good Earth." When his voiceover intervenes, it's to introduce a young Bill Hamilton whose harmonica-accompanied Oahu road trip and creative doings with Jock Sutherland at a formidable Honolua Bay set up California cops cracking down on demonstrators and—always there in a pinch—Miki Dora frothing about a "barbaristic" (sic) America speeding towards a nervous breakdown. With those pigs on the beach, it's no surprise Hamilton split for the North Shore. But then where? "Well, there's about a thousand islands out there in the Pacific," he muses. Pointing towards surfing's and the surf film's post–*Endless Summer* near-obsession with travel, he and Severson nevertheless miss the irony in the flower child exile quest for liberty leading to the very place the earlier Westerners first imported their disease, bad religion, and profit motive. From here the fun house tour continues, with surfing a distorted mirror in which to view the larger culture. Corky Carroll may tell us that winning those U.S. titles was beyond an ego trip, but the Sousa military parade musical accompaniment says something else about surf competitions. A mini-chapter takes us to Big Surf, the artificial wave park in Tempe with "the first genuine artificial wave," perhaps the only quiet laugh in a film whose comic touch is not its strong suit. Then there's Rolf Aurness treasuring every real wave's complete uniqueness, and fine shots of his ethereal surfing in drug-porn solarized color and the psychedelic "delay" effect Severson pioneered. And then oil wells on the Coast, pollution and an evocation of the erasure of a legendary break in the creation of Dana Point Harbor, for Southern Californians still the primal surfing-wound-that-never-heals. Following the same structure, Jock Sutherland's smooth power sweeps and a set of earthy Hawaiian up-country scenes frame footage of Honolulu high-rise hotels and broad suburban butts learning the hula.

For many viewers, one of the most memorable sequences begins with the psychedelic decoration of a magical mystery tour bus right out of Ken Kesey by visionary artist Rick Griffin *(Surfer* and innumerable concert and surf film posters, including *Pacific Vibrations* and *Five Summer Stories)*. After a Waimea adrenaline rush, things calm down as the clackety bus makes the trip metaphor literal on a subversive spin to the already restricted-access Ranch for a copacetic back-lit session of pristine little rights. Severson had included some shots at Hollister Ranch's hidden point breaks in *Surf Safari* and *Big Wednesday*; here the visual and aural effects he brings together are simply magical. In that Central Coast cold, scarves of kelp suspended in the bog-dark clarity of wave fronts decorate perfect pipes and echo the long locks of Griffin in the pocket and out of time. The film's high point, the privileged domain we're invited into is an enchanted refuge standing for all that must be protected; it is the still point of the turning world, or rather one whirling out of control. Filmed with a lightweight water-housed Beaulieu camera, the image is rich, textured, and color-drenched. As big a part of the scene's, and the film's, success is the music. A few minutes after Cream's "Tales of Brave Ulysses" evocatively frames a killer Pipeline session, "Wooden Ships" by Crosby, Stills, and Nash sounds like it was written expressly to accompany the mystical perfection of these human-scale tubes ridden in tranquil fusion by Griffin and crew. Though MacGillivray and Freeman will still use the Beach Boys to charming effect, these tunes, the title song (tweaked into Hendrix-meets-Iron Butterfly by great studio musicians Jim Keltner and Randy Nauert), and others by artists like Ry Cooder and Leo Kottke announce to a new generation fresh tonal and lyrical possibilities for the surf movie. It was time. While sun-warmed surf guitar may even now generate a certain nostalgic affection, for film soundtracks to work they have to sound like the soundtracks of their young viewers' lives. That was true in the days of Dick Dale or the Sandals, and it's true of the rap laid down over a Volcom video or yesterday's home-shot YouTube posting.

With *Pacific Vibrations* Severson caught the ear, eye, and pulse of a particular generation. After the mainstream co-optation and early commodification of surf culture in the 1960s, he re-connects with the marginality of surfing in the terms of the day: the surf life as alternative to the buying and selling, the Cold War paranoia, the oil spills and official lies. A sterile earlier debate had classed surfers either as reprobate biker hoods in trunks or as energetic, if slightly wild, practitioners of a healthful outdoor sport—with the norm the suburban family and good job, the former group excluding itself, the latter putting on the tie after some youthful wild oats. As represented by Severson and other filmmakers of the '70s, surfing was a wholly different way of being and living. Vividly imagined and ardently portrayed—if, like many counter-cultural initiatives, vaguely thought through—its alternative model of our intimate human connection with a living universe drew unconsciously on a long Romantic tradition combining irritation and affectionate immersion. In the same poem Wordsworth lashes out at the "getting and spending" of blind, unmoved beings "out of tune" with their environment, and communicates the resuscitating thrill of sighting Proteus and Triton just out past the breakers. In recent decades the surf movie has followed youth culture down various paths and notably towards the kick-ass edginess of extreme and alternative sports; but the Romantic environmentalist breeze has never failed to blow. At times it has done so explicitly, as when, well before *Pacific Vibrations*, Severson includes the image of an dead oil-soaked gull in *Surf Fever*, but that commitment remains close to the surface in nearly every surf film, from the rustic North Shore frontiers to the touchy reaction about crowding in the surfline and on coast highway. If the genre in its totality can in any way be said to be "political," it is through an engagement, no less strong because generally implicit, to respect and protect the natural world that is the sport's and the life's very medium.

An irony of the *Pacific Vibrations* story is that the film dubbed "Woodstock on a Wave"[46] was the subject of a certain amount of studio executive attention. Approached by MGM as early as 1961 for a general release surf film, Severson toyed with the proposed "improvements," then chucked what they produced as "stinking of Hollywoodism." A decade later a first version of *Pacific Vibrations* would take form without narration, with scenes radically free associating to a musical thread. But, the big triumph of *The Endless Summer* fresh in memory and a film called *Woodstock* in the pipeline, the search for a distributor led to an eager Warner Bros. production team and, once again, suggested "improvements." That too would finally go nowhere for a clearly ambivalent Severson, though changes including a dose of narration remained in the film the *auteur* at last opened independently in Southern California. In an ultimate irony, American International Pictures—the *Beach Party* geniuses—signed on to distribute the movie nationally, which they did ineptly and, it turned out, unsuccessfully.

Pacific Vibrations thus became a "lost classic, the favorite surf film of one of today's best surf filmmakers, Mark Jeremias (*One California Day*), and a big reason up there with the founding of *Surfer* for Severson's recognized icon status. It also remains, among other things, an example of the increasingly inevitable tensions between a "pure" surfing vision and the need to finance projects responding at minimum to heightened core audience expectations—which essentially meant, in circular economic reasoning, having to appeal to wider mainstream audiences. Bud Browne could do it all himself and the sheer novelty of the surf film for his small audience was enough for the little homemade machine to work; two decades later to make a good surf film in a more institutionally entrenched surf scene meant going farther afield with sophisticated equipment, top professional talent, music rights, and the rest. Bruce Brown's fifty grand risk-it-all throw of the dice came up sevens, but Severson was prescient in getting out because of the cost factor. A decade later the traditional surf movie as binding communal experience would be essentially dead, killed by expense and buried by video.

In the short term, though, filmmakers were hanging in there, and some, like Severson, were producing films that even a decade and half into a new century still stand as landmark surf cinema experiences. This they pulled off, paradoxically, not by aiming for timelessness but by unashamedly reflecting their times. Two years after *Pacific Vibrations*, Greg MacGillivray and Jim Freeman would make *Five Summer Stories*, a movie equally of its day but one turned somehow more towards questions of the '70s than answers of the late '60s. Our reading of *Five Summer Stories* is conditioned by its reappearance in new yearly incarnations through 1979 and the impression it gave of alert evolution with the concerns of its times. Yet from the beginning of the Freeman-MacGillivray collaboration hints of a slightly different attitude—a certain playful, deconstructive irony, in particular—peek out through the requisite easygoing environmentalism and earnest distance from the uptight suits. As early as 1967 in the pair's first dual effort, *Free and Easy*, the sincere, vague romanticism we associate with those days is already cut by a bracingly "pre-contemporary" self-reflexiveness and wised-up awareness of image and media.

After having followed their own first full-length surf movies, shot separately by age 19, with other films and shorts, Orange County's Freeman and MacGillivray met and set off on a decade of exceptional artistic collaboration that would be cut tragically short by Freeman's death in a 1976 helicopter crash. Hard-working, creative, state-of-the-art technically, they made three full length surf movies in a stretch otherwise occupied by several short subjects, extensive TV and Hollywood work, and their first IMAX effort (thus beginning an exemplary second career for MacGillivray that would lead to the National Film Registry, Oscar nominations, and undisputed dominance in the giant screen 15/70 format). The talent's on show from the opening credits of *Free and Easy*, where lovely soft rights and lefts roll serenely towards and through the in-water camerawork, gently unscrolling a backdrop that, with a splash of sun and seabirds, quietly exemplifies the title. The "Strawberry Fields Forever" laid over this may be an elevator-music instrumental, but Lennon's melody is so exceptional that lyrics kick unconsciously in: John's also inviting us. From here Freeman and MacGillivray weave the sunny assonance of their film's title consistently into their shared narration, spare but affable and tugging insistently at zeitgeist-friendly emotions. The free and easy surfer, we're told a half dozen different ways, "is no one's puppet because he lives the way he chooses."

The times are there largely in this attitude if not in a more active environmentalist stance that will be apparent in the pair's later films. A year after *The Endless Summer*, this is still a very classically formulated surf movie, with non-stop California-Hawaii shuttling; the predictable blend of neatly formed little curlers, North Shore behemoths, and the inevitable Wedge; a featured surfer (David Nuuhiwa); some scouting around for hidden breaks (Maui); wacky down-time antics; a touch of surf history; and the straightforward intermission and conclusion sign-offs. MacGillivray shot from the water, at times innovatively attaching a camera to the board, and Freeman from the shore; the duo shared the narration as well. As *Free and Easy* was filmed and then shown, the shortboard tsunami hitting Australia had not yet arrived in the Northern Hemisphere. That the movie came along just before helps explain the ample, soon-to-be-dated focus on the "far ahead of his time" Nuuhiwa's silky noseriding and the failure to read the full significance of Nat Young's dominance in the 1966 World Championships. Where the film peeks chronologically forward, though, is in its frisky hints of meta-cinematic self-consciousness. Hovering about in the 1960s, the reflections upon the meanings of media by such as Susan Sontag and Marshall McLuhan would storm the general culture in the decade to follow. When Freeman and MacGillivray take viewers to what they label on-screen as "The Super Spectacular Banzai Pipeline," they insert "Bam!" and "Boom! captions to the theme of the *Batman* TV series. Camping-up the experience, as might have said Sontag, they both playfully highlight its extreme nature and view it from a cool, ironic perspective.

In an increasingly media-savvy American cultural landscape, such an off-center stance would come to seem normal, but in the surf movie it was something new. Earlier filmmakers had a hoot at the expense of elderly civilians and poked fun at their surfing subjects by putting funny accents in their mouths or dubbing wipeout flyers "Junior Birdmen!" *Free and Easy* differs by directing explicit attention to the act of filmmaking, at once immersing viewers in the process and partially distancing them from the result. Hanalei Bay is "the setting for many Hollywood movies, like *Mutiny on the Bounty, South Pacific ... Free and Easy*." Playing with the occasional scripted conflicts their dual narration afforded, Freeman points out "my partner Greg" in the water and the "new game, to try and run over the water cameraman." A few minutes after mentioning the loss of a $600 camera in a wipeout, he recounts asking Billy Hamilton not to look at the new one, which naturally he does. The post-intermission return begins with a shot first down the business end of a long telephoto lens, then one wheeling to show the cameraman behind it; in the jump cut that follows, the sun's white hot disk visually echoes the lens opening the sequence. The non-surf hi-jinks include "The Great Race," a highly stylized North Shore jalopy derby no doubt inspired by the '65 slapstick comedy of the same name, announced on-screen in the vintage carnival font later associated with Monty Python, and commented by a sport-coated announcer in trunks from the *ABCD Wide Weird World of Sports*. By the time a board blows off the top of a car, it's less that surf film chestnut than a kind of take on the inevitable gag. In MacGillivray and Freeman, part of the game is presenting information while playing with the presentation, in the process implicitly questioning the rapport between the thing and its representation. Beyond the mammoth issue of a post–World War II mass entertainment culture selling "reality," this questioning speaks to the life choice of surfers, for whom a sense of cool is at once intensely linked to personal image and style and somehow beyond them, and where the best perspective on things is on the far edge of standard culture looking occasionally back at it, and at yourself on it, with wry bemusement.

Greg MacGillivray filming for *The Sweet Ride* (1968) with 45-pound Arriflex rig. Robert August (left) and Herbie Fletcher at Rights-and-Lefts (Hollister Ranch). Already legendary for their water camerawork a half decade before *Five Summer Stories*, MacGillivray/Freeman were signed by 20th Century–Fox to shoot the first 35mm Cinemascope surfing footage (MacGillivray Freeman Films).

The next film *Waves of Change* (1970) less frequently tinkers with questions of image and representation, but does bring "The Great Race" back for round two, luxuriating to the point of self-conscious caricature in the cultivated "mess-off" image of the surfers in their old clunkers, and, to thunderous canned applause. awarding victory to surfing Dadaist Miki Dora. *Waves* follows the *Free and Easy* formulaic blend, with a bit more travel (Portugal and the Basque Coast, with its sublime Hossegor beachbreak) and some proto-snowboarding by Mike Doyle thrown in, as well as a more clearly enunciated back-to-the-land Romanticism. Wordsworth sang the "spousal verse" of humankind and the universe; here "the ultimate message of surfing is the wedding of nature and man" (imagery that will re-appear in more graphic form in *Five Summer Stories*, with the tube dubbed "The Tunnel of Love" and Gerry Lopez "definitely sexual" in his excursions there). Supporting this luxuriantly Romantic vision is densely hued photography, tight editing, and dreamy slow-motion immersion shooting. In the second part of the film Freeman and MacGillivray exploit the expressive qualities of the soundtrack particularly well, with long surfing sequences to the languorous San Francisco psychedelia of "White Bird" and the melodic high-energy rush of "Ride My See-Saw." The full panel of top surfers appears, including Nat Young, Keith Paull, Gerry Lopez, Bill Hamilton, and David Nuuhiwa. About the latter's surfing, the narration speaks again of "man in harmony with his environment." Interestingly, this comes just after we've been told that "the ocean is his personal property." Elsewhere similar good intentions spill over into similar unintended irony. Antiquated shots of Waikiki labeled "Paradise Found, 1942" are juxtaposed with those of the contemporary tourist nightmare, "Paradise Lost, Today." Shift your perspective back a couple of centuries, though, and 1942 Honolulu may not be as Edenic as it's imagined.

Waves of Change was blown up to 35mm, re-edited, and re-titled *The Sunshine Sea* for a short-lived major theatrical release in 1971. Appealing to a general audience, the latter title puts a warm smiley face on the ecological awareness present in a film that in any case did not pertinently address those other, shortboard waves of change then rocking the surfing world. With a look back on the work of MacGillivray and Freeman, this film and its predecessor *Free and Easy* seem like the intermittently successful marshaling of varied creative forces that would only fully come together in masterful deployment in 1972's *Five Summer Stories*. Their private code for the latter during production was "the last surfing movie," a bit of verbal play which turned out personally true for the filmmakers, which perhaps also indicated something of the mature, measuring distance the pair had on its own project, and which in retrospect highlights its place as the ultimate surf film experience for more than a few from that generation. The last surfing movie also lasted in an unusual way, brought back as it was in annually revised versions through 1979. Always on the breaking edge of technology, conscious of the quality of their soundtrack as much as of the filmed image, MacGillivray and Freeman insisted on the best venues possible, where they installed their own stereo systems with appreciably better sound quality than even a *2001: A Space Odyssey* in Super Panavision 70 might muster at the time. After its raucous launch at the Santa Monica Civic Auditorium, such were the critical response and word of mouth that *Stories* would go on to play even very upscale theaters, sometimes for runs of several weeks.

In constant revision, there is thus no one prototypal *Five Summer Stories*, but rather a fluidly adaptive artistic response to the surfing/society crux over the course of several years (and even up through 1995 when, for the DVD release, MacGillivray once again updated the film). This, it seems clear, is a part of its meaning. Like the earlier incarnations, the final version (the subject of the discussion below) unsurprisingly honors the basic surf movie contract to feature the best surfers and surfing at a wide range of legendary breaks. Like the pair's earlier work, but in spades, it embodies an extravagantly Romantic environmentalist ethic—following the example of Brown and like Falzon, nothing less than the birth of the world is enacted once again—but one more clearly politicized and steeled at moments into cynical anger. That MacGillivray signs letters today "Yours in a healthy ocean" is consistent with this commitment. As the title indicates, the method of the film is episodic, bopping from laid-back North Shore country living to Mr. Pipeline Gerry Lopez, from features on top individual stylists ("Different Drummers" like Barry Kanaiaupuni, switchfooter Angie Reno, and speedmeister Terry Fitzgerald) to a different kind of stylist on a different kind of board, the "Magic Rolling" sort, in a sensational look at cutting-edge skateboarding. With, again in the surf movie, the death of Killer Dana as evidence for the prosecution, one chapter asks derisively, "Is Surfing Closed Out?" Nearly two decades later the heartening response is perhaps not, as the Hanalei harbor plans were eventually scuttled and a once off-limits Salt Creek is now a protected Beach Park. The next chapter and its paranoiac fantasy send-up of Nixon-era paranoiac political ugliness go on, though, to make one thing perfectly clear: the threat to abuse commercial and institutional power always looms.

In a world tainted by bad politics and crowded by developers, the emotional heart of all this is stirringly simple. Elizabeth Bishop got it in "Pleasure Seas": "The sea is delight. The sea means *room*." Freeman and MacGillivray bring these truths home in scene after gorgeously filmed, color-soaked scene, including stunning in-wave shots. To give an idea, what MacGillivray, as good as they get, didn't shoot in the water, Bud Browne and George Greenough did. A particularly stunning sequence blends cartoonist John Lamb's colorful, freaky surfboard-dolphin, with a series of deeply immersed shots as surfers glide past, including one whose way is traced by a dolphin's last second dive. The rich visual compendium includes graceful slow motion skiing and soaring, and a cottony cloud that, in an accelerated image paced like that of the slow motion surfing, billows into the form of a breaking wave. The challenge of such visual delight and its subliminal message of interconnection is that it demands an aural complement of equal quality. Tough as it may seem, in the grandiose visual experience that is *Five Summer Stories*, music more than holds up its end of the artistic bargain. The previous images, for example, roll to the rich, melodic rollicking of Brian Wilson's "Cool, Cool Water." Much of the remaining score is brilliant, expressly written work from the Laguna Beach band Honk. With its silky percussive buildup, delicate melodic line, and adrenaline guitar punctuation, "Pipeline Sequence" has an iconic resonance only equaled by the Sandals' famous theme: for the Gerry Lopez featured, it's the perfect music of beauty, guts, and smooth, otherworldly confidence. Never quite to achieve the career they deserved, the underrated Honk ranges expressively throughout the film from a playful cornpone twang through ear-grabbing guitar to a textured, sophisticated jazz flow that could be predicting the Yellowjackets of a decade later. To this musical foundation the filmmakers added some classic Beach Boys, like the self-consciously retro "Surfin'" to introduce the movie and its nostalgic subtext, then later during a mini-chapter of black and white historical footage. Even better is the lesser known Brian Wilson that would find its final home in *Smile*, sublime bits like "Surf's Up" behind a commentary on courting an "intimate relationship with Mother Ocean," or the buoyant "Water" flowing into the sequence above, with its other water games and, more largely, the alternate sports already gliding into philosophical alliance with the surfing mindset.

Five Summer Stories is eminently countercultural in the 1972 hippy sense, but it may be more lastingly subversive than that. Even the quickest math based on the paragraphs above will show that there are more than five summer stories in *Five Summer Stories*. A neat quintet was the plan when things got under way in 1970, but as photography started new ideas kept coming and with them the fractions: stories 2, 2½, 2¾, 3, *Five Summer Stories Plus Four*, and so forth. The result is less form than free-form, a tentative, adaptive approach perhaps right for a blurrily shaded decade marked fully neither by the bold primary colors of the radical, self-righteous '60' nor those of the differently radical, self-righteous Reagan-Thatcher '80s. That was the decade *Saturday Night Live* first stepped out of prime time to make arch comedy by improvisatorially dismantling not so much contemporary realities as the media-mediated language and images that have essentially taken their place. Said the show's creator Lorne Michaels, "the 1970s, I realize now, were a time when things were both coming undone and being put together in a different way." How, though, was far from clear. Another film from a time of revolutionary questioning, *Morning of the Earth* is nevertheless marked by an oddly resolute assurance—getting back to the garden, as Joni Mitchell advised, is very simply and emphatically where it's at. While certainly leaning in this same direction, *Five Summer Stories*, by contrast, creates an alert, inquisitive, and unfinished narrative space where no one story, or five, or more, can tell the whole truth. In narrative terms the five of our fingers or perfect senses also suggests classic dramatic structure with complications leading reliably to comic or tragic resolution. Here not only is the number announced in the title called throughout into question; the succeeding modifier "summer" further suggests the unresolved temporary, while "stories" connotes the inherent instability of the varying version and of fiction itself. Freeman and MacGillivray's multiplying partial stories furthermore kept spilling out in revised later variants responding to necessarily mutating realities. All this to say that *FSS* has a surprisingly post-modern indeterminacy, one perhaps consistent with the stealth avant-garde interrogation about media, image, and identity already present in the pair's earlier films.

The fluid structure of piecemeal assembly and its resulting juxtapositions offer multiplied possibilities of shaded meaning that are particularly interesting when the film treats such hot-button surfing issues as ethnically driven Hawaiian localism, competition, and gender. The understandable resentment of native Hawaiian surfers, for example, rises hotly to the surface in a brief head-shot interview: " I want all the haoles to go home," declares a local named Black. with a menace oddly heightened by an ice cream cone. "I've been surfing all my life with my brothers, and I want to keep it that way." Point well taken, but MacGillivray and Freeman frame these sentiments with vignettes concerning David Nuuhiwa and Billy Hamilton, respectively an Hawaiian then walking the nose in California and a Golden Stater shaping and surfing in "the mellowest place on the planet," the North Shore. This implicit nudge towards questioning identity and the delicate issue of proprietary localism then re-occurs in "Story 1⅜," a brief survey of surfing history which could not not include the Duke who took the surfing gospel ecumenically from the islands to beaches around the world—which would in turn send faraway surfers to Hawaii to open up breaks that the locals themselves had never even tried. The question to whom waves "belong" is a complicated one when, as the film earlier informs us, the title of Mr. Pipeline could go to mainlander Butch Van Artsdalen just as to its then-current holder, Hawaiian Gerry Lopez. Leading up to the Pipeline sequence, by the way, the narration again addresses the "Hawaiian Paradise" metaphor but perhaps this time (unlike *Waves of Change*) with a degree of irony. Ten years earlier, we're told, a surfer went to this Paradise where he "discovered" the Pipeline and named it. In a sense he did, for no Hawaiians were daring to surf there until Bruce Brown filmed Phil Edwards doing the impossible; on the other hand the discourse is undeniably that of the colonialist explorer. That the unidentified surfer is the filmmaker who would send legions off to "discover" untold numbers of paradisiacal beaches further muddles the touchy question of wave ownership.

With similar complexity *Five Summer Stories* also addresses the schizophrenic relationship between surfing and competition. Until they were discouraged by missionaries, competition and gambling on the results were from the earliest days part of the Hawaiian surfing scene. It's unsurprising that the meeting of vigorous young people and challenging physical activity would lead to competition: already 1500 years and half a globe away it was Beowulf "who took on Breca / in a swimming match on the open sea, / risking the water just to prove that you could win."[47] Accompanying the revival of the sport in the early twentieth century were a spattering of contests in California, Australia, and Hawaii, leading at last to the Makaha International in 1954, followed by the gradual emergence of scattered championships and informal circuits before competition got globally serious in the mid '70s. Surfers, though, have always been conflicted on the question, wondering if institutionalized competitive structures don't demean or at least distract from the unmediated relationship with nature—by turns, harmonious and challengingly adversarial—that should characterize surfing. Some top riders like Phil Edwards and Nat Young nurtured the famous "soul surfer" mythos by saying no at times to the commercial opportunities contests offered, while a few took a full-scale plunge into competition and far more staked out a kind of uneasy compromise. In an Australian TV interview the year that *Five Summer Stories* first appeared, John Severson summed up the lack of easy answers, succinctly examining the tension in "asking the surfer to perform in a certain way to win something, yet ... the whole idea behind surfing is freedom." But "if it can be handled in a certain free manner," he hesitated, "I think the pro circuit has great possibilities."

In their work Freeman and MacGillivray embody some of these ambiguities, moving from the sanguine observation in the first film that "part of the lives of free and easy surfers is the contest" through harmless carnival-music mockery of a tandem competition in *Waves of Change* to an affectionate short subject on the first contest-phobic North Shore "Expression Session." By the next year, in a counter-culture atmosphere marked by the assumed stench of nearly any kind of financial exchange, their opposition to the surf contest had more clearly hardened. Yet as the pair's collage method would later hint, things were perhaps not quite that simple. Story 2¾ follows a cleverly cut sequence on skateboarding stressing the technical prowess and animal delight in this still uncorrupted young cousin of surfing. By contrast, when "Contest Weight" then weighs in, competition comes off as the heavy institutional uncle, surfing's embarrassing "commercial side" that "has nothing to do with surfers riding waves." Linked visually to the Mayor of Squaresville Pat Boone and to football at its most conservato-militaristic, surf contests are presented as bogus rip-offs with organizers and the business community the only winners. That's some Surf City that has you essentially surfing for the Chamber of Commerce, until skewed judging of game attempts in absurd blown-out afternoon chop finally comes up with the lucky soul—the derision starts to get sticky—who "gets to be called" U.S. Champion. With its lugubrious rhythms and theme of the burdens we unnecessarily heap on ourselves, the Beatles' "Carry That Weight" is the ideal accompaniment. Though here again the film's structure refuses the simple answer. Immediately following is Story 3, added in 1974 and subsequent editions, and entitled "Women in Motion." Suddenly we move from Weight to Motion, from pitiful staggering in slosh for meaningless points to graceful takeoffs and sweeps up the face of scorching waves by Linda Benson and Lynne Boyer and Margo Godfrey Oberg. Interestingly, the attitude towards competition immediately changes. It's now a sign of worth and point of pride that Joyce Hoffman was 1965 World Champion, that Godfrey took the laurels in 1968 in Puerto Rico. Apparently, the surf contest means something different when it's about validating the achievement of women scrapping for unpatronizing appraisal on their own merits and a rightful place in surfing's traditionally sexist hierarchy.

While the position of women in surfing, following changes in the larger society, has vastly improved in recent years, gender has always been a prickly issue. The early surf film offered an accurate reflection of the limited range of roles available to women in the '50s and '60s: though female surfers do pop up on screen occasionally to remind us that such an entity exists—a Linda Benson in *Sunset Surf Craze*, Joey Hamasaki in *Barefoot Adventure* Candy Calhoun in *Gun Ho!*—the predominant identity options remain decorative ornament, supportive presence, and object of desire and the male gaze. This is ironic, of course, in light of surfing history, with gender equality on the wave the norm in pre-missionary Hawaii. Given the post–War cheerleader/suburban housewife model that Gidget has such a time resisting, though, it's unsurprising that few girls at the time were invited to or even willing to mix it up with the boys in the impact zone. Despite Gidget's example, Annette Funicello in the *Beach Party* films was more about keeping Frankie's paws off her than paddling out. In terms of gender the social loosening up of the '60s had relatively little impact at first for the predicament of women passed behind concerns about other forms of liberation—Stokely Carmichael's famous 1966 remark that the only position for women in the Student Non-Violent Coordinating Committee was "prone" (sic) did not mean on a surfboard. Only in the early '70s, with the ERA's initial passage through Congress, the publication of *Ms.*, and Roe v. Wade would wide awareness of traditional gender inequalities take hold. In Severson's *Pacific Vibrations*, swept by winds of change as it was, the only women not primarily serving as eye-candy are serving lunch. When you think about their presentation, "Tales of Brave Ulysses" then sounds different, with its referenced narrative of Sirens tempting their heroes and Penelopes yearning for their return. Things, though, would change dramatically with "Women in Motion," a bracing sequence of beautifully shot surfing moments starring the best women surfers and notably uncluttered by the typical obsession with looks or juvenile attempts at sexist humor.

It took a while getting there. Top female surfers do appear in *Free and Easy*—which is progress—but always as a "blonde Joyce Hoffman" or a Mimi Munro at the Huntington Pier who "holds on to her surfboard and her bathing suit." Girls, goes the narration, "soak up the beautiful heat and stoke the boys." In *The Sunshine Sea* they enjoy surfing, that is—wink—"when they're not adjusting their sun shields." A brilliant surfer and one of the first full-time women pros, Jericho Poppler was and is an articulate, media-savvy representative of the sport, women's interests, and larger social and environmental concerns. Here, though, when she's given the pulpit to argue that most people don't take women surfers seriously, the sequence as cut emphasizes only comically ditzy nervousness. The Poppler surfing shots are great and it's probably all just good fun between friends, but the damage is done. A later sequence then takes us to the North Shore for a glance at the surfing life at its laid-back ideal, with slow-motion nestling in the curl, beautiful people, and perfect sunsets there where everyone's come for the right reasons, "to be near the ocean, to surf, to be free." That Laird Hamilton's mother highlights these motivations gives them substantial retrospective cool, but JoAnn Zerfas is simply labeled "Housewife" here, and this in scenes where women only get their pretty toes wet. Each flashing adorable grins, three successive shots of Keith Paull, Barry Kanaiaupuni, and Mike Tabeling are respectfully labeled with the surfers' names and their states of origin. Then comes one of a lovely girl whose bikinied breasts frame the dog sitting in front of her. The picture's label: no identity and no origin for the babe, just the comic caption "Dog, Hawaii." And all along the soundtrack's "White Bird" glides luxuriantly on, the bird at issue a she, the lyrics' message the constraint of gilded cages and the imperative of free flight, and little sense that they might apply to anything but these guys riding the wave of liberating self-expression.

Reflecting a new '70s awareness of gender issues, the shift from this kind of stuff to the evolved presentation of women in *Five Summer Stories* is notable. The musical introduction of "Women in Motion" moves meaningfully from the warm nostalgia of the Beach Boys' "Do It Again" to Neil Young's "Cowgirl in the Sand," with its implied female appropriation of the traditional male role. Women need action as much as their brothers, not only Charlotte Brontë maintained. For the first time in the surf film since Gidget began insisting on the same thing, MacGillivray and Freeman gave ample, respectful attention to the action, "style, punch, and bite" of an early Marge Calhoun and the more recent stars. Soulful artisans and power surfers on sizeable breakers, these are also articulate proponents of a different contribution to the sport: a manner perhaps more "relaxed and stylish" than the men's and, particularly appropriate to the period, less gratuitously aggressive and more drawn to the "positive force" of the wave. Juxtaposition then radiates its meanings as Story 3¼, a profile of Shaun Tomson, goes on to use the same language field to describe the refined young South African regularfooter whose slight shifts in stance allowed him a new, nimble subtlety even deep in the pocket. If Tomson went to battle it was only with himself, this "soft man who has proven himself in the hard world of professional surfing." Facing off the traditionally "feminine" and "masculine" adjectives in this way and within this context, the filmmakers state without stating the evident truth that women's liberation also liberates men.

STRONG OFF-SHORES

Pacific Vibrations and *Five Summer Stories*, "the last surfing movies" of Severson and MacGillivray/Freeman, address very explicitly the interface between the era's overheated social questioning and surfing as a coolly alternate life choice. In that crux what goes curiously missing is the shortboard revolution, the celebration of which had clearly energized Witzig, Greenough, and Falzon. The shortboard explosion happened in another hemisphere, the echo took time to make its way north, and when it did it fell on the ears of Californians accustomed to considering surf culture, if not surfing, their invention. Which may explain why a film provocatively called *Waves of Change*, produced during the three years following the McTavish-Greenough design whirlwind, failed to deliver fully on its title promise and "was dated upon arrival."[48] While the new surfing in the form of Rolf Aurness, Jock Sutherland, Jeff Hakman, and others is very visible in *Pacific Vibrations*, and all over *Five Summer Stories*, in their generous flurry of interest in wider social issues proper to their time and a parallel eco-earthy surfing ethic, neither film specifically explores the very radical changes occurring on the wave. Those changes and more would be the subject of the next—and, under the pressure of video, last—phase of the surf movie. Films from the 1970s from Californians like Hal Jepsen, Steve Soderberg, and Bill Delaney are all about surfing's decade-long extreme makeover: the now globalized, ever-multiplying possibilities of the shortboard, the abrupt creation—again Aussie-inspired—of a professional circuit after a couple of particularly dramatic winters on the North Shore, and surfing's increasing identification with a parallel "extreme sports" style and attitude.

According to *Surfer*, Jepsen's *The Cosmic Children* (1970) "was the first New Wave shortboard surf movie, establishing itself as the 'Momentum' of its era."[49] While this seems off—*Evolution* deserves that honor—the remark does point to the radical shock that an explicit focus on the new surfing import could communicate to oddly parochial Americans still gazing at the navel of Orange and Los Angeles Counties. From 1970 through 1981 the Southern Californian would amply demonstrate that the heroic era of the classic communal surfing movie had a few good days left, firing up theaters and auditoriums with his endless enthusiasm about surfing's transformations and its abiding charms. The colorful Jepsen walked the early '70s talk, dropping a post–National Guard business degree and real estate opportunities for a Topanga shack and a tenuous shoot-and-show existence. Good enough on the board to go out at Sunset and Pipeline, he fell in with a group of surfers who did the films' heavy lifting, guys like Barry Kanaiaupuni, Larry Bertlemann, J Riddle, and particularly a Jeff Hakman in his sizzling prime. The first of Jepsen's four full-length surfing films remains his best known. *The Cosmic Children* is often linked with *Pacific Vibrations* and *Morning of the Earth*, though one wonders if that's not largely a function of the release date and its total trip of a title. Granted, the hippy scene's there, notably in a post-titles beach party that should be required viewing for cultural historians. But while Severson and Falzon, as well as MacGillivray and Freeman, were hyper-alert to the interface between the surf scene and a normative culture's hazy turmoil, Jepsen finally just can't keep his eyes off the waves. It's no news that surfing movies are about surfing, but some are really only about that. In this Jepsen's films hearken back to the simpler age of the first surf flicks, when just showing impressive waves and riders was enough to set a multi-purpose room on fire. A group of surfers associated with Natural Progression boards, he and his Topanga buddies recall the surf-then-party-hearty vibe of those early crews getting by on the North Shore. While the DVD cover for the first film may feature a timely tied-dyed globe swimming in space and psychedelic wave swirls, the real message's on the back. "*The Cosmic Children*," writes Steve Pezman, "fulfills the most important criteria of a good surf movie—it righteously stokes you to get up early the next morning and go surfing."

That's was Jepsen was about, even if he could occasionally fret about Honolulu highrises or ironize concerning "Ronnie" and his jaunty assurance that we have oil supplies for centuries. There's certainly no heady mysticism in his definition of Cosmic Children as those "who feel the juice of powerful waves." In his approach to one of the most exciting moments in the sport's history, though, the New and the Wave in Jepsen's "New Wave shortboard surf movie are in the new high performance wave action and not Jepsen's aesthetic approach, relying as it does on largely shore-based camerawork and the time-honored bouncing ball structure, Malibu to Haleiwa to a Baja road trip, etc. With his 16 mm Beaulieu Jepsen did shoot with a wider than normal camera angle that contextualizes maneuvers better within the length of the breaking wave than an overly tight focus, but what counts in his work is what he shot. As Ira Opper said, he "had an uncanny ability to show up at the right place at the right time,"[50] the result being a number of particularly memorable sequences, including Rory Russell slo-mo at Pipeline and Hakman and Kanaiaupuni at the top of their game ripping cut-backs up the face at Sunset and at a big winter Honolua Bay. Beavertails dangling, back-lit, a hushed Hollister Ranch session with Topanga buds George Trapton, Dave Hilton, and J Riddle catches some of the place's stolen magic but unfortunately not to the degree that Severson did in *Pacific Vibrations*. The villain: an f-stop problem or something of the like that gave the image throughout the film a persistent murkiness. Such is the quality of the small wave shredding and intense maneuverability on the bigger waves captured by Jepsen that the film has retained a weighty reputation despite the truly distracting nature of its muddy photography. For this the soundtrack no doubt was a help. Jepsen was known for his liberal hand, rights be damned, in helping himself to the music he needed. The Dave Brubeck Quartet's "Take Five" is surprisingly right to establish a summery atmosphere in the opening sequence; later we get Cream's "White Room" behind some tasty Velzyland and, just before intermission, the sinister crank of "Gimme Shelter" over unbelievable drops into very heavy Pipeline.

A Sea for Yourself (1973) and *Super Session* (1975) are in fact better films and not only because Jepsen had solved the shadowy image problem. If anything, the shortboard exploits in the former are even hotter, with regulars Hakman and Kanaiaupuni, an extended focus on the ineffable Gerry Lopez, and a Peter Townend on his first trip to California who would slip right into Jepsen's Malibu gang. Smatterings of small wave Ventura

Poster, *A Sea for Yourself*, director Hal Jepsen (1973): Still cosmic after all these years.

County and San Diego blend nicely with the bigger Hawaiian challenges, including a roaring Sunset with Reno Abellira, Angie Reno, and the charging, blond-mopped Terry Fitzgerald's deep bottom turns. The title *A Sea for Yourself* provides its loose thematic thread: in addition to punning praise for primary over secondary experience (see for yourself!), we hear the recurrent plea for a little elbow room in an increasingly jammed-up surfing scene. As always, while Jepsen may show us a PCH crowded with freaks and cars, his concern is the surfline. The search for space will lead twice to the road, for a relatively flat chapter on Peru and a sublime sequence on France's Atlantic Coast. After a cut-rate September 1971 flight to Germany and a 30 hour drive, Jepsen and Hakman hit Biarritz to pitch *The Cosmic Children*. On the way they came upon the idyllic waves of Hossegor, where Jepsen shot Hakman and Mike Miller, a visiting Yank, in some glorious tubes. Unidentified in the narration, the surf breaks of *La Nord* and *La Gravière* had appeared already in *Evolution* and *Waves of Change*, but for the French and their then-embryonic surf culture *A Sea for Yourself* was what truly amped up the attention both at home and abroad.[51] Unsurprisingly, given such a fickle sandbar wave even during a good fall swell, the French stay led as well to trips to the more reliable (and now extinct) *La Barre* as well as to free time. The narrator self-deflatingly refers to the way surf movies can make a new place seem "like a paradise if you haven't been there"—and then he does just that, taking Hakman and Miller to eat *gateau basque* at a charming centuries' old mill during a pause before another ethereal session. By the way, that off time also allowed Hakman to kindle a friendship with *surfeur* Jean-Louis Bianco and a love for the French way of life that would come into play a decade later when he would take part in the founding of Quiksilver Europe in St. Jean de Luz.

The sheer beauty of the French interlude has a broad general appeal, as does Jepsen's easily comprehensible quest for a little room on the wave. Back in the States a few years later, though, he would release a film more clearly directed to a specialist audience. By 1975 the shortboard revolution was historical fact, and Jepsen, an early leader in paying surfers appearance fees, clearly felt it was time to get down a bit technically. The structure of *Super Session* is simple and efficient: a set of nuts-and-bolts synch-sound interviews with five surfers "recognized as consistently the hottest," followed by close to a dozen notable "sessions" (one of the Expression Sessions, the WISA Championships, North Shore Winter '75, a "Body Session," etc.) When you listen to these brief exchanges, you wonder why the format's not used more often in the surf movie. It's fascinating to hear these guys talk serious shop, whether it be Bertlemann, Kanaiaupuni, Russell, Hakman, or some "Gerry" with no last name. Product placing his Lightning Bolt in the frame, Russell runs through when a 6'6" or a 7'8" fits the bill and what pairing up with Lopez has done for him; Hakman takes you through the impossible list of board characteristics needed for Sunset's peaks where you have to cover a lot of water, jockey for position, drop in late, and be able to move straight up and down the wave—which explains his 20 boards a season search for the right blend. Lopez leads a regular seminar on weather and tide conditions at Pipeline, why you actually don't want a glassy day and can do better without a straight west swell. Each set of responses illuminates the succeeding sequences of the same surfer at both full speed and slow-motion. The arcane technical details are fun, chewy stuff delivered by experts who've thought a lot about these things but whose wave performances then illustrate just how magical the putting together of the details remains. A quietly sincere Lopez captures this perfectly when he sums up making the wave that made his name: "All it is … is just taking off in the right place, pulling into the section, and just holding your edge." A little embarrassed perhaps by the double "just," he grins shyly before a winning, "It's a cakewalk." When Gerry spits out of the Pipe, rising to upright with that distinctive shoulder slump, you recognize just how much it isn't.

The super sessions that follow lead off with a look down under, Jepsen's spare but precise narration neatly distinguishing subtle differences in the high-performance Aussie aggressiveness of Nat Young, Peter Townend, and Michael Peterson. "Lightning Bolt Sessions" features sponsor awareness and a handful of top riders tearing up well-groomed Velzyland, but the highlight is Rory Russell on crowds, a recurring issue with Jepsen: "Sometimes you have to be an asshole." A big Malibu swell shows just such a logjam with, "count 'em," 13 scrambling for a little section to call their own, and a recurring cartoon called "Karma" that highlights how fast that can go bad on a wave. The crowds are less hairy, the waves more, in the big winter surf of Oahu, with a ripping Townend and Shaun Tomson. Another surfer meriting a mention there is Becky Benson, outstanding on big Haleiwa and "fast becoming the top woman surfer." Jepsen's relationship with the women's surf scene is typical of the period: obliviousness, some dawning awareness, and then the sudden realization that there is a women's surf scene. The first film is all-male, the second accords brief film time to Blanche Benson; in addition to featuring her sister, the third offers a "session," complete with female narration, to the Women's International Surfing Association Championship. Margo Godfrey Oberg takes half the Hang Ten three grand purse, a figure less than a third that of the men in the Smirnoff competition later in the film. This goes uncommented, but at least there's some righteous indignation that the women have to share the waves with macho Malibu weekenders. Lest we transform Jepsen into a feminist hero, though, know that as late as 1981 in his next and last complete surfing film, *We Got Surf*, there's a bathing beauty contest followed by coverage of a punishing Backdoors Pipeline that elicits a cheerful "Check the boobs and get some tubes!"

That last film is a smorgasbord with good longboard footage collected along the way and film shot by friends (including the best in-water shooting in Jepsen's movies). The one memorable stretch is towards the end with, first, the big February '81 California swell that set off the rarely breaking Supertubes south of Point Mugu. Jepsen's probably right that that sensational barreling just off the rocks was "never before seen on film"—and with a nice bonus, a 15-year-old named Tom Curren. The final shots at Waimea Bay include the prophecy a decade before the tow-in revolution that short boards will one day be carving these immense wave faces. Such interest in the technical evolution of the sport is pure Jepsen, whose curiosity also extended in a serious way to the very short boards of skateboarding. In 1978 he released a full-length skateboarding feature, *Spinning Wheels* (1978) and did shooting for the classic *Skateboard Madness* (1980). His surf films included an impressive parallel surf/skate sequence with "Rubberman" Bertlemann, as well as interludes with young riders like Stacy Peralta, Tony Alva, and Jay Adams back before awareness of Dogtown and that first revolutionary styling in empty pools would enter the general culture. Peralta later drew on Jepsen footage for *Dogtown and Z-Boys*, as well as selections from his surfing archives for *Riding Giants*.

As Jan and Dean's 1964 "Sidewalk Surfin'" made clear, surfing and skateboarding have been from the early days close cousins,[52] and filmmakers from Bud Browne on frequently inserted skateboarding chapters. With Jepsen it became increasingly clear that the radicalization of style in the shortboard revolution had its counterpart in the '72 introduction of the polyurethane wheel, and that both activities were accelerating down roughly parallel routes towards more critical maneuvers and an increasingly kick-ass rebel attitude. Like Jepsen fellow Southern Californian Steve Soderberg also made room for skating in his surf films, notably featuring an unidentified 14-year-old Tony Hawk in his second. Even if less hooked than Jepsen, Soderberg regularly featured skateboarding as part of a panel of amusements—free-form skiing and snowboarding, motocross, what we've come to call extreme sports—appealing to an energetic young male audience and harnessing an attitude of similarly playful, off-center unruliness. As always, such other material also provided a necessary visual break from miles of surfing footage. Having grown up in Manhattan Beach, where he shot his first 8mm film from the pier, Soderberg would make three very agreeable full-length films between 1975 and 1987. Where Jepsen caught first-hand the sound and fury of the shortboard revolution, his younger contemporary had a front-door seat at another noisy insurrection, that period in the 1970s when the Aussies and South Africans famously "busted down the door," took charge of North Shore waves, and effectively willed the contemporary system of professional surfing into existence. Soderberg made the first of seven winter trips to Oahu in that fateful big swell season of 1974–75, when Shaun Tomson, Ian Cairns, Rabbit Bartholomew, Mark Richards, *et al.* began tearing up waves with an aggressiveness matched only by their desire to hustle a sport already shaken by new board possibilities into a new phase. They were phenomenally successful. Amongst other things, in a few years a stodgy slate of uncoordinated, badly run, and poorly-funded competitions would morph into an increasingly sophisticated pro circuit responsive to new realities of media exposure, sponsorship, showmanship, and financial reward. Even as a skateboarding elite began to emerge, the hottest surfers were by 1976 traversing the planet in the nascent world pro tour. It wasn't, and still isn't, the equivalent of professional golf, but by the early '80s the top ten surfers could approach a decent living and there was something left to go around for a few of the others as well. The conflict between soul surfer and pro hotdogger will never fully disappear; as it finally worked out, though, the tour, under the auspices of the new ASP as of 1982, was largely welcomed by fans and the surfers themselves.

The title of Soderberg's first film, *A Matter of Style*, implicitly recognizes the new manner that would power surfing forward towards different realities. Released in 1975 and reissued with additional material in 1980, it includes among numerous style profiles a look at young phenom Tomson, with his tiny board, wide stance, precision in the pocket, and gutsy backside control at Pipeline. From the start his role as a "major influence of the North Shore" is apparent, alongside that of the Australians "whose legendary go-for-it attitude altered the face of wave-riding." Even in 1980 Soderberg couldn't be expected to see the full significance of what went down in those years, but he comes close. The then-artisanal pro surfing scene, the narration runs, was "approaching a crossroads where it may take off or collapse." Now we know which one. At this crucial shake-down period, it's a real pleasure to spend time with this cheerful, well-informed guide, whose sense of surfing's essence, dry comic timing, and alert feeling for the apt phrase often pleasantly recall Bruce Brown, even if Brown never said a word about competition and came from a different planet. "Surfing's more than an escape," the narrator notes in passing. "It's something worth escaping to." The father of *The Endless Summer* wouldn't disagree. Or, describing the indescribable as we watch Lopez finesse Pipeline, Soderberg observes, "he not only makes the wave, but he makes it look better." In this offhand SoCal manner, simple as can be, there's personality, truth, and craft. While never sounding like anything more than a friendly guy met in a surf shop, he twice employs the rhetorical device of antistasis, quietly nudging the viewer towards reflection, refreshed attention to the image, and a gentle surfing tingle.

Soderberg manages to communicate both a tolerant openness to radical change and the grateful savoring of a Honolua Bay session with no "slash and destroy" in sight, a delight in pure fun and an informed understanding of pro surfing's imperatives and advantages. Closing the first film with the image of a cute grommet, he yokes the temptation of childlike regression with the inevitability of growth and change. In 1983, several winter Hawaii trips later, *Ocean Fever* would appear with a similar wide-angle focus. Enjoying some consecutive 360's and Todd Martin's "full body flips" a decade before the New School and Kelly Slater, he notes how top competitive surfers have reached "an almost gymnastic or acrobatic approach to surfing." As he will do in all three films, Soderberg takes you grippingly through the heats of the Pipe Masters—and then turns with matching enthusiasm to the zestful non-competitiveness of those two puppy dogs Mark Liddell and Buttons Kaluhiokalani (whose cavorting at Off the Wall more than deserves the Greatest Hits treatment it receives in the 2006 compilation *Ultimate Sessions*). Peter Townend will swear on camera you need a big ego to be a champion, before commenting on his own exceptional performance on monster Waimea with quiet, self-effacing modesty. It's not that Soderberg can't decide between two surfing extremes—it's more that he loves the life and wants to communicate all its facets. There's room for yesterday's Mike Purpus playing the old fart and taking a pie in the face, and for a right-then Jeff Parker ripping the kind of state-of-the-art breakdancing that got him a role in the "Thriller" music video. Parker, by the way, is credited as the impetus for the film's most memorable sequence, the first celluloid appearance of the gnarly Todos Santos break Killers. With its California-close easy exoticism, the Baja run is a classic figure in surf movies; here the journey to a rocky outcrop just off Ensenada is played for *Gilligan's Island* laughs and at the same time alluringly pitched as a mystery for a small, curious crew to solve: "What was on the other side of the island?" The revelatory answer: a tasty overhead right and a great session, followed by two days of flat conditions, requisite surf movie filler, and a wave sacrifice. That actually works!—first for scary closeout ugliness which only Parker dares for one successful white knuckler, and finally hefty, beautifully structured curls illuminated by top surfing by David Barr and others, including some prophetic aerials.

Soderberg was on the road again in *Ticket to Ride* (1987), first for a Mexican jaunt that doesn't go much of anywhere and later for a circuit through the South Seas where striking surfing and memorably bizarre moments battle with disjointed storytelling and lame transitions. Surfers like Max Medeiros, Buttons Kaluhiokalani, and Ronnie Burns in tow, a certain "thrill of discovery" is there in the cultural observations and mixed bag of waves offered by French Polynesia, Tonga, Samoa, the Cook Islands, and Fiji, and this despite slack pacing and a lack of narrative drama. The surfing does get very interesting, though, when badass wave warrior Johnny-Boy Gomes joins the group, tearing a pumping Cook Islands lefthander and leading the charge in the crystalline juice of Cloudbreak and Restaurants. Uncommented irony surfaces as well, with the narrator blithely noting the corporate sponsorship of certain surfers and the $100/day rates at the new Tavarua surf resort against a reverent background discourse of paradise in "waters where surfing originated 1000 years ago." Shooting in and under these waters, cameraman Paul Prewitt offers brilliant, color-imbibed moments up close to the action. *Ticket to Ride* is finally an uneven film, though, one whose real takeaways might just be its incidentals. Fijian fishermen spear a four foot shark in two feet of water, then flip it on shore for some highly distasteful goofing around by the surf crew. A deadly sea snake playfully invades this Eden in another short scene, and in French Polynesia Soderberg plus four grand in material pitch over the gunwale when a sneak wave surprises the team's skiff.

With the last in 1987, these three films more or less run out the clock on the old-fashioned communal surf movie. In the process, Soderberg takes us from one radical twist in surfing history almost to the next, from the sudden precipitation of efforts to create a pro tour in the mid '70s until just before the New School opened its doors in the '90s. As testaments to the changing times and the ratcheting up of surfing's near obsession with novel destination travel, his genially casual films are remembered fondly but, it must be said, without the fervor reserved for one by his contemporary Bill Delaney. Released in 1977, then refreshed the next year and 1983, *Free Ride* is a rare touchstone movie. Just as *Evolution* did for the shortboard seismic shift and *Momentum* would for the hardcore antics of the next generation, it marks a key moment forever in the collective surfing imagination. Like the other two, *Free Ride* pulls this off by giving a clearly identifiable incarnation to the historic instant. If Wayne Lynch and Nat Young *are* the alert new boards in 1969 and Shane Dorian and Kelly Slater the new moves in 1992, here Shaun Thompson and Wayne Bartholomew personify the Southern Hemisphere surf culture cyclone that hit the North Shore in 1974–6. While it's over the top to argue that *Free Ride* "did for professional surfing what [*The Endless Summer*] did for surfing's romantic face,"[53] it did put attractive faces on this new turn for the sizeable, wildly enthusiastic beach town audiences it brought in and for their successors who still refer to the *Free Ride* generation.

Soderberg covered the largely Aussie Hawaiian invasion and emerging pro circuit in *A Matter of Style*. Santa Barbaran Delaney brought more resolute attention to it, however, and furnished even more intense surfing footage. In Bartholomew, Tomson, Mark Richards, and Peter Townend, the sheer talent was available. Delaney took its presentation a notch up by engaging gutsy *Surfer* photographer Dan Merkel, who pushed the immersion shot heritage of Greenough, Bud Browne, and others still closer to the action in still bigger tubes. To the entrancing guitar-honed piano of Pablo Cruise's "Zero to Sixty in Five," his opening credits underwater sequence of ghostly board shapes gliding overhead has a rare, nearly abstract beauty. Captured at hundreds of frames per second, Merkel's intimate 16mm water footage of Tomson's radical wide-stance maneuvers *within* the barrel at Off the Wall easily made the cut of Ira Opper's *Ultimate Sessions*; so did Delaney's land-based filming of the famous "backside attack" of epic Pipeline by supposedly disadvantaged regularfooters Tomson, Bartholomew, and Richards. *Free Ride* complements the excellent adventures of this bunch in Hawaii with top sessions from Queensland and Indonesia, as well as interviews of the principals and archival footage of, among other things, a young Rabbit Bartholomew earning his nickname on a dirt soccer pitch and Tomson endlessly hanging five at ten. About his barrels, the latter explains that "a lot of the tube-riding that's going on now is just a straight line trim. But I try to break that straight line trim and maneuver because I feel that's what surfing's all about … not just standing there and posing." Like, say, Gerry Lopez? Polite and earnest as Tomson always is, this could nevertheless be taken as gratuitous icon-busting. Which is what that '76 winter was about, though not everyone was a well-mannered as the South African star. Bartholomew notably penned his inflammatory (if politely worded) "Bustin' Down the Door" piece in *Surfer*, joining Ian Cairns in a "We're Number One" campaign recalling John Witzig's claim of Aussie predominance a decade earlier. When he returned to the North Shore for the next winter season, Rabbit would pay for his perceived arrogance, wave-hogging, and big-talking occupation of the media stage with busted teeth.

"I'm known as some sort of hustler in the water," Bartholomew admits in *Free Ride*, before adding that he actually considers himself a "casual and artful" surfer. It's tempting to see this as part of a good cop-bad cop communication strategy crafted for a rapidly professionalizing scene equally open to the pitch of the so-called Bronzed Aussies, the Peter Townend-led trio peddling a clean-cut image, and to Muhammad Ali-inspired trashtalk. In 1976 International Professional Surfers came into being, urged along by this rabid bunch towards TV and sponsoring money becoming available for leisure sports willing to take themselves seriously; the association loosely coordinated for the first time a series of often amateurishly run competitions worldwide into the circuit that over the years would become today's sophisticated and eventually lucrative ASP/WSL Tour. In some of the most interesting non-surfing sequences in Delaney's film, the founders of that first early organization, Randy Rarick and Fred Hemmings, appear on-camera like slightly uncomfortable sales directors touting what they see as their prime product, Shaun Tomson. Hemmings lays it on: handsome, articulate, the athletic real deal next to some of the "yo-yos" in more publicized sports, he's "a superstud of the sports world." Voicing the intelligently written narration the year before his appearance in *Big Wednesday*, Jan-Michael Vincent insists on the competitive juices flooding the surfers featured in the film, in particular those weaned on a highly competitive Australian club system. South African Tomson was the icing on a cake of Australian talent that filmmakers couldn't get enough of in the '70s. *In Search of Tubular Swells* identifies its subject very clearly as the "radical performance" of guys like Bartholomew, Ian Cairns, Mark Richards, as well a couple of Hawaiian greats like Rory Russell and Gerry Lopez on breaks at Burleigh Heads, Bells, the North Shore, and, for the first time in a film, G-Land. Over a varied, thoughtfully chosen soundtrack, the 1976 film from Dick Hoole and Jack McCoy is just a narration-linked series of sessions, but it is beautifully shot from land and (by McCoy) sea, and another reminder why, once they got their way about competition in 1976, Australians (and one South African) would win the men's World Pro Tour for its first *seven years* of existence.

Compared to what was to come, that early tour was pretty simple stuff, but the machine was humming. There was colorful, highly visual action to catch on screen and monthly on the page, stars to create and expose, products from emerging sportswear companies to advertise, contests and surfers to sponsor—and, soon, home videos as well. In a very short time the underlying cultural shift to the go-go greed-is-good '80s would make the anti-contest bias of *Pacific Vibrations* or *Five Summer Stories* seem quaint. Yet ambivalence to surfing's dalliance with commerce remained, and still remains, visible just there under a flashier new surface. Not outright resistance, as in that of the hard-core self-styled soul surfer, but ambivalence. This is implicit in *Tubular Swells*, with its implied inability to choose between the flashy débuts of pro surfing and the whispered drop-it-all seduction of Indonesia's hidden magic. Beyond, of course, the top performances by guys like Mark

Poster/cover art, *Storm Riders*, directors David Lourie, Jack McCoy, Dick Hoole (1982). Portrayed, from left: Gerry Lopez (moustache), Rabbit Bartholomew, Mark Richards, Wayne Lynch, friendly dolphin.

Richards and Wayne Lynch, this is the real subject as well of *Storm Riders*, another McCoy co-effort, released in 1981 and one of the last of the old-fashioned surf movies. Before he would turn to video himself later in the decade, Australian Jack McCoy made the film in collaboration with David Lourie and Dick Hoole. With only a pro-forma nip up to Hawaii and no mention of California, it again prominently features surfing's new frontier of Australia, Africa, and, in spades, Southeast Asia. *Storm Riders* begins and ends down under, with a heavy early focus on the aggressive Aussie spirit, "the richest contests in the world," and drop-bys at the Surf Classic at a mammoth '81 Bells Beach, Stubbies at the Gold Coast's Burleigh Heads, and the OM-Bali Pro. Then it abruptly wheels farther afield, for "free surfing" at South Africa's Jeffreys Bay, in Oahu, Java, and finally back to Australia but this time to the deserted southern coast.

Coming about one-third of the way into the film's 72 minutes, the storytelling change of direction in itself gives *Storm Riders* a schizophrenic feel; the same effect comes from the delicate dance between a production "in association with Rip Curl Wetsuits" and the naive "pure adventure" look of the colorfully idealized movie poster. The first part of the film really is all modern competition and prizes. Right up front there's pride in the fact that "Australians have dominated the sport" for a decade, a product of the surf life saving associations and the "million competitions" a representative Mark Richards remembers before dominating the pro tour. The Stubbies contest, the narrator boasts over images of crowds and bikinied curves, "has got it all," and the first trip abroad, to Bali, is not incidentally for a contest dominated by two Aussie goofy-footers. Perhaps the peerless left of Uluwatu goes unidentified because everyone recognizes it. Given the mixed feelings the film will over time communicate, it may also be a deliberate choice not to be too specific: the sacred Balinese break of *Morning of the Earth* was first surfed under distinctly less mercantile auspices than this product-sponsored competition's creepy co-optation of traditional rituals and "welcoming" locals. In any case, the first twenty-five minutes past, the remainder of *Storm Riders* suddenly cleaves to the spirit of revered ancestors like *Morning* and *Endless Summer*. Referring occasionally to an artisanal on-screen map, we're off, as a Brown might have been, to "the Dark Continent" (!) for a brief look at Shaun Tomson alone on big, beautiful Jeffreys Bay. This is just an appetizer, though, for as quickly we're back with surfing pro Joe Engel in Queensland only, it seems, so that his pal Thornton Fallander can drag him away to his new hangout, Bali, for some prime, uncluttered lefts and, even better, to an unnamed "remote island near Malaysia." Speaking of schizophrenic, Fallander is presented in the narration as a free surfer, but in fact he was sponsored by Billabong and the pair convinced the company to foot the bill for the trip.[54] Along with the sights (including cockfighting that specifically recalls *Morning of the Earth*) and an "impossible day" of perfect waves a conch-throw away from the surfers' grass hut accommodations, the pair link up with some Japanese pros also "taking a break from competition." When at last Fallander makes his way back to his "new found Asian paradise," it's unsurprisingly to a place with "no judges or score cards."

To the Doors' "Riders on the Storm" and a consistently great rock-based soundtrack, the emphasis upon soul surfing continues. The required Hawaiian junket follows, but you feel the filmmakers left their hearts in a rustic, freer Southeast Asia. While the North Shore's "the place to make it or break it as a surf star," the Gerry Lopez they follow becomes more interesting when he laboriously makes his way 15 hours from the nearest airstrip to Java's

Grajagan for a yearly stay at the pioneering surf camp. The huts are on stilts, "crowds haven't been invented yet," and Lopez so wires the left-breaking tubes that the neon color enhancement of some rides is just distraction. *Storm Riders* then draws to a conclusion with a look at two more "inveterate travellers." Their four wheel drive loaded with 15 boards, Wayne Lynch and Maurice Cole explore the wild frontier coast of South Australia, with its "isolated beaches and reefs no one before had surfed." The latter is a bit disingenuous, for Lynch himself combed the Cactus area more than a decade earlier during the filming of *Evolution*. But who cares with surfing of this quality? Impressive as Cole is, Lynch's tight driving angles up the wave and dashing drops are still the bomb, even if the real takeaway shots of the whole film are not of his extraordinary surfing. Riding the same reef breaks for a fortnight, Cole and Lynch were progressively befriended by a pod of dolphins, who dazzle with some spectacular bodysurfing and who at last follow them into the shallows. The film that began as all competitive juice thus ends with Australia's '81 national champ and a twice-retired competitive legend alone on the lost southern coast leaning over shallow water playing fetch with attentive mammals to the strains of "Cool Change" by the Little River Band. That one of them is Lynch is particularly savory. Juggling an era-marking stretch of stunning competitive dominance with a mystique of thoughtful distance on the whole surf industry scene, Wayne Lynch fascinated then as he fascinates now. No one could better embody the rich ambivalence of *Storm Riders* and, it seems, a prolific Jack McCoy, who would focus a similar double vision on surfing in other movies and in several outstanding videos in the last three decades.

By McCoy, Soderberg, and others there would be a few more films of the old sort as the '80s wore on, but escalating costs, redoubled ASCAP vigilance following the 1976 Copyright Act, and, of course, the invention and widespread adoption of home video would inexorably get the better of your father's surf movie. It was a good run, though. Hardworking and creative, Bud Browne got it all started for waves of rowdy surfers eager to prolong the stoke, connect with others of their kind, and affirm their own identities. Along with an emerging specialist press, the odd song, and a constantly enriched vocabulary, his model as followed by countless others would constitute the dry side of surf culture for decades. Much of that production remains, honestly, less memorable as films per se than as moments of collective nostalgia for each rising generation. Over time there were new stars and new breaks, and more and more nosing off the beaten track of California and Oahu until *The Endless Summer* game changer. For good or ill the whole world was now surfing's playground. Consecration, challenge, inspiration, Brown's film launched two decades of unprecedented creativity and quality in the surf movie. It wasn't just the technological advances, the invitation to the open road, and each individual talent's competitive addition to the evolving tradition. It was also the era. In their watery sandbox a number of particularly talented and committed filmmakers succeeded in reflecting a whole wider world of questioning and intense socio-political ferment, and a modern surfing's rapidly mutating microcosm. Sometimes directly, sometimes ironically, the surfing movie paddled questions of gender, ethnicity, commerce, and the different forms of imperialism into its more evident preoccupation with the successful colonization of the curl.

The winds of social change blew hard through a surfing world preoccupied as well by its own parallel gusts. In this sense *Storm Riders* is a good title with which to bring this chapter to a close. Against the tempestuous public backdrop of the late '60s and '70s, surfing itself was buffeted by at least two major storm fronts, the blustery arrival of the nimbler new boards and their Australian masters, and, a decade later, the clamorous insistence of the latter upon the creation of a modern economic and competitive infrastructure. Did the fall's storm season mean that the endless summer had in fact come to an end? Not necessarily, if we're to believe McCoy and many others who, while simultaneously admitting the contemporary economic and media realities of the surf scene, never cease also to believe in the wave as a place of personal expression and unfettered freedom. In her analysis of the famous John Van Hamersveld-designed *Endless Summer* poster, Lili Anolik chooses different metaphorical terms to address the dual nature of surfing. Inspecting the horizon-cut sun against which the three surfers stand, she suggests that the time of day is left deliberately ambiguous. "Early or late?" she wonders. "Just after the beginning or coming up on the end?" Symbolically, both, for the life timelessly linked to a tradition of non-utilitarian pleasure that Brown introduced to global audiences is also a sport alert to changing social mores and pragmatically responsive to economic pressures. Who would know that better than Bruce Brown, whose idealistic invitation to follow your sunburned nose wherever it led brought in more than $30 million, not counting DVD sales and branded merchandise from beer to that tank top on Justin Bieber.

~ ~ ~ ~ ~

Step Into Multiplex

When the old two-reel four-wall surfing movie splashed off into the sunset, the surf world waved nostalgically and flipped on the VCR. Ironically, it was only at this moment that its most emblematic figure would stage a comeback. Seconded by son Dana, Brown at last acceded to decades of offers with *The Endless Summer II* (1994), a New Line Cinema release. Costing $3.4 million (in constant dollars, fourteen times what the original ran), the sequel opened in 302 theaters in the States alone. In the years since, as the energy and creativity of the traditional surf movie flowed into tape, DVDs, and the Internet, a duo of surf documentaries would join *The Endless Summer II* as semi-ambitious general audience releases and moderate critical and financial successes. In 2003 Dana Brown returned with *Step Into Liquid*, followed the next year by Stacy Peralta's *Riding Giants*. With Brown's 1966 original (and, generously, perhaps *Five Summer Stories* for Yanks and *Morning of the Earth* for Aussies), the three are important among other things as the only non-fiction surfing movies a general viewing public might reasonably be familiar with. Indeed, a sizeable challenge facing these filmmakers was to walk the delicate line between the lightweight entertainment demands of that date night audience and the more hard core exigencies of the surfing community. In accepting this challenge they have not been alone, for other affectionately produced "specialist-generalist" efforts like *A Deeper Shade of Blue* (2011) and *Down the Barrel* (2007) have also appeared in recent years. Despite the evident quality of both, as well as the prolific Jack McCoy's energetic promotion of the former video in live theater settings, and the latter's high-profile ESPN billboarding of Kelly Slater, neither reached the wider public to the degree that Peralta and the Brown dynasty have.

That the three did manage to manage to enter the general entertainment market is a sign of the extent to which surfing has at last a significant, fully absorbed part of Western leisure culture. As such it is a plausible subject for the occasional film, with, accordingly, basic moves, language, and "feel" demanding far less simplification and explaining than in earlier days. No longer just one-in-a-million shots like *The Endless Summer*, these movies were now thoughtfully considered projects mounted with reasonable hopes of commercial success. By the '90s surfing was past its fad and rebel days and fully operational as a signifier for two key strains of youth culture, laid-back cool and the wilder teen-age energy associated with skateboarding and the mushrooming extreme sports scene. The transition to modern professionalism was complete with the anointment of the sport's first category-transcending and Pamela Anderson-dating media star, Kelly Slater. As the champ's sponsor Aussie-originated Quiksilver demonstrated with a 1995 U.S. profit north of $10 million, the early surf gear suppliers were now international conglomerates successfully pedaling summer fashions and wave dreams to far more than the surfing population. All along, the Hollywood storytelling machine was certainly taking notice as witnessed by the modest but steady stream of surf-oriented scripts that has found its way onto the big screen in recent decades.

In this context, it seemed like a good business decision to make a follow-up to a fondly remembered movie which as a bonus had been nurturing a new audience on videotape since the early date of 1984. Brown might differ about whether it was a wise professional choice, the ultimate DIY guy faced daily with a travelling circus of technicians and studio types who kept forgetting he'd negotiated complete control of the project: "A lot of my ideas, they were like 'You dumb fuck, you don't know what you're talking about. We know what we're doing.'"[55] Thanks largely to affably picaresque narrative pacing and Brown's droll narration, the film comes off with something of the original's light-footed, improvisatory feel. It certainly is a sequel. "When I made my last surf film in 1964, there were only four countries in the world where people surfed," he underlines, later placing the obligatory packing scene of the two leads under the altar-like domination of the famous 1966 poster. To call *Endless Summer II*, as Joe Brown of the *Washington Post* does, "an endless bummer, an amateurish two-hour infomercial for the 1964 16mm original" is to miss the point, though. Viewers going to see a film with that title seek the pleasure of the expected; they want their favorite uncle to tell some new stories but in the way they've always known and loved. Brown obliges, for one thing structuring his film as before. A similar range of appetizers—wipeouts, different surfers and styles, oddities, Waimea shorebreak, icy Alaska surfing—opens the palate for the main course, the tale of two guys living "the ultimate dream ... to follow the surf and the summer around the world." The adjective echoes *Gidget* and the earlier Brown who'd used nearly the same wording then to set the conceit in motion. Only now, thirty years of water under the bridge, even if the sweep of the journey is roughly the same the array of new (and old) destinations will highlight how much the scene has changed—that is, while all the while insisting that the surfing heart still fundamentally beats the same way. The later films by Dana Brown and Peralta will be marked by a similar split, a changing world that can't be ignored but can be lit by a soft, nostalgic, somewhat idealized glow.

To incarnate the story, Brown picked twenty-one-year-old blond SoCal shortboarder Pat O'Connell and longboarding dark-haired college grad Robert "Wingnut" Weaver. Their stylistic differences are apparent, even if the filmmaker chose to develop in surprisingly little depth the varying cultural meanings and philosophies associated with the two kinds of board-riding, adding not a great deal more than that "now a perfect wave depends on the kind of board you use." Here Brown misses a thematic opening as well as the opportunity to add a few traits to his protagonists' two-dimensional characterizations: O'Connell's never much more than a hyperactively upbeat giggler, nor Wingnut more than cool and measured. They are extraordinarily talented surfers, though, as we will see in a journey crafted largely to reference the history of surfing and its legends since 1964. One way to do this is the narrative pretence that you can save dough on such a trip by staying with friends. You should have such an address book. Starting at the beginning in more ways than one, a nip down to Costa Rica sends the pair to Robert August's vacation home; later it's on to see Tommy Curren in France, the same John Whitmore who squired August and Hynson around South Africa, a Shaun Tomson still owning Jeffreys Bay, Tom Carroll and a very young Kelly Slater at Tavarua, Nat Young playing wildman in Australia, ineffable Gerry Lopez at (the appropriately named) G-Land, and finally the Laird Hamilton tow-in crew at Peahi. Brown wants to juxtapose such now mythical breaks with the stars themselves, even if some are getting a bit long in the tooth. Wingnut and Pat are gee-whiz proxies for the viewer, getting to mix it up with these guys, surfing like we wish we could, and checking out the foreign scenes that Brown furnishes with little vignettes like a run-in with African lions or a Costa Rican rodeo. To think that all these places were firing back in 1964 when Brown first told the story of his famous journey, but who knew? We do now, and *The Endless Summer II* presents these extraordinary sites memorably to a general audience more than likely to be unaware of their existence. Pat's playful contemporary styling is nicely complemented by Wingnut's imaginative retro doings, sliding casually out of cool daddio reverse take-offs and surprising everyone by making Cloudbreak a longboard playground. Mike Hoover's cinematography is top quality and Jack McCoy's underwater shooting silent magic. For the multiplex audience, unfamiliar with more recent surfing movies or each month's lot of luxuriant photos in *Surfer*, the effect of such images on the big screens is overpowering, as even the film's less-than-positive reviews confirmed.[56]

Weaver is most transparently a stand-in for the audience when, again to the *Lawrence of Arabia* theme, he "crosses the dunes" for his virgin look at Cape St. Francis—and its dozens of luxury residences fronting a once-isolated, once-perfect break now eroded into sections by changing sandbars. Even as he communicates the reality of time's work, Brown deftly activates the collective surfing unconscious to solicit a nostalgic yearning for the ideal alive in virtually every viewer of *The Endless Summer*. At one point or another we've all made that walk. He knows what potent stuff he has in that first film, finds ways to evoke it and stir up the resulting emotions. With parallel archival footage, August and Whitmore's appearances are the obvious route, but Brown also takes us there by subtler echoes and mannerisms. On a blown-out Basque Coast day with Curren, "Tommy didn't say it, but you knew what he was thinking: 'You shoulda' been here yesterday.'" Familiar with that running gag from thirty years earlier, of course we do. Just before the French episode, the film makes a detour: "Let's check what's happening on the North Shore of Hawaii." Brown could easily have taken us there with the trip mechanism he employs to visit every other site, but this one time he chose the creaky old surf movie transition used to slip parenthetical material into Mike and Robert's trip. Tonally too, his narration is as familiar as the Sandals theme that occasionally punctuates it. Warm, amiable, slightly bemused, he still goes for and gets the gentle laugh, often blending quiet verbal flair and the sight gag. Man in surf with baby daughter hanging on neck fits general category of "people with lumps on their backs," and facing a sign indicating Shark's Bay we're drily informed that it won't be crowded there. All along Brown's narration feeds the running joke of the eternally stoked Pat positive that the wave he just rode was the greatest ever. One of the funniest storytelling touches is silent: an Eiffel Tower establishing shot of Paris with the caption "Somewhere in France."

At other times the whole enterprise shows its age. In part this is because Brown does, like when he uses the adjective "gangbusters," or compares the fastidious Robert to Felix Unger, a long day with Young to the Bataan Death March, and some nerd in the soup to Monsieur Hulot. This is not a call to dumb down the surf film, but for 1994 isn't Jacques Tati an overly dated generational reference? Also at times he projects an old school know-it-all authority persona, with big pronouncements about the "most dangerous animal" or "most deserted place on earth," or how, searching for your perfect wave, if "you went to every spot in every country where people now surf and stayed one day you'd be gone *for 50 years*." Where the film's most stuck in the past, though, is in what reviewer Marjorie Baumgarten identifies as Brown's "insulting" "cultural crudity." The same filmmaker who fretted about becoming dinner in Africa could reasonably be expected to show a touch more international savoir faire this time around. But in the *1990s* his guys just can't get over the toplessness on European beaches, and when they look back at the sand from the waves they only see the "zoomers" (?!) pointing back at them. Menus they don't understand get a clueless going over as do the snails—*essence de cliché* in garlic butter—they haplessly end up with. A Fijian kava ceremony, an important act of welcome and social cohesion, becomes an occasion for sweatsock jokes. Hooking up with Tomson and the "only Zulu surfer" (it might be interesting to ask why) offered Brown the opportunity to make some kind of subtle gesture towards the apartheid past he'd ignored three decades before. Instead, the surfer is just Walter with no last name until the credits (Ngcobo); when Wingnut and Pat say goodbye to the newest of their "close friends," they patronizingly leave the "surfer dude" posing with frozen scarecrow discomfort in their used stuff.

Brown's cultural blinkers diminish a pleasant and beautifully shot travelogue bringing the top surfers of the previous three decades to wonderful destinations made possible, in a very real sense, by his own crucial '60s pioneering. The eye-opening spectacle and exotic locations appealed to casual viewers and surfers alike. Beyond the trip down memory lane, both groups even got access to a couple of minor surf community "scoops." Robert Weaver's adherence to the longboard ethos very publically confirmed the return to grace of the log under way since the mid–'80s; the film's easy embrace of both styles also helped open the way for the ride-anything movement to which later videos by guys like Thomas Campbell and Andrew Kidman would pay tribute. Even more historic is the encounter between Brown's crew and that of Laird Hamilton. Thanks to Brown, we get a front-row seat for what Gerry Lopez calls Laird's "new act." Gerry articulates his real surprise not by superlatives but by searching precision: "What they do is him and his buddies, they're just as crazy as he is, they get in this little zodiac and they take a water-ski rope and they tow each other into *waves that are too big to paddle into*.... Stop and consider that for a moment." Of course, since then the exploits of Hamilton and company have become familiar even to the lay viewer. This, though, was a first privileged glimpse at history in the making back when there was no word for tow-in surfing and the very idea could elicit incredulity from one of the world's most accomplished watermen.

Thirty years on Brown was again there at a turning point in surfing history. So was the co-screenwriter and co-editor of the film, his son Dana who would strike out on his own nine years later (albeit with Dad an executive producer and occasional on-screen interviewee). Without the sequel boost of the 1994 film—but also without its imposed formal limitations—*Step Into Liquid* (2003) surprised as the greater critical and box office success to the point that it was called, with a certain irony, "a perfect companion piece to *The Endless Summer*."[57] The opening seconds are packed with messages that condition the rest: a welcoming "Aloha" over limpid blue flow, a hairy drop down a huge wave face to the captions "no special effects ... no stuntmen ... no stereotypes," and finally Laird's vaulting slow-motion pull-out and graceful drop back to the water's surface. The narrator's voice is a little more gravelly than Bruce's but warmed by the same late afternoon sun: "I'm Dana Brown. I'm a surfer. This film isn't about a lifestyle; it's about a life." That's it. Like his father Brown shows little interest in competition or the surf industry; he admits that this 2000-year-old pastime has become a multi-billion dollar lifestyle business but only to sweep the notion away and re-focus on the surfing life. Or rather on the surfing life sentence. According to Rabbit Kekai—with cred back to the days of the Duke—"you can't never leave." A succession of other surfers will follow: young, old, men, women, brothers, eeny-weeny wahines, driven eccentrics, driven experts, and, major surprise, Kelly Slater. Viewed and interviewed in their marvellous and strange habitats worldwide, all will insist in their own idiosyncratic terms on the fellowship of the stoke and "that time in every surfer's life," at once personal and globally shared, "when he knows he'll always be a surfer."

Perhaps because Brown wanted speech to combat the stereotype of surfer inarticulateness, *Step Into Liquid* brims with such testimonials. Yet while they avoid the dudespeak trap, they do at times stray dangerously close to sentimentality. The nature of the ecstatic surfing experience is at some level beyond words, as—admittedly with words—a surfer recognizes after a legendary day with his crew tow-in surfing the monstrous mid-ocean Cortes Bank: "You don't even have to say anything to each other." The retreat from language is welcome when one too many New Age-scented disquisition turns to "the unifying force in the universe" or when well-intentioned feel-good generosity tips into the maudlin. Affirms Keala Kennelly, for example, following in the verbal footsteps of Phil Edwards and serving up the saccharine with a slightly embarrassed crinkle, "the best surfer in the world is the one having the most fun." Moving fluidly around the world, transitioning from one fascinating or stirring or unlikely vignette to another, Brown combines such talking-head interview copy with his own gently directive narration and filmed surfing sequences of rare beauty and power. To be fair, some of the testimonials do liven things up, such as when, à la Rabbit, Slater compares surfing to hooking up with the mafia ("you're not getting out") or a sweet Gerry Lopez reports, wonderfully, about Pipeline, "You thinkin', I'm gonna' die. Most times you don't." In general, though, the search for language to describe surfing in the on-camera remarks contributes less to Brown's celebration of the obsession than the fine action cinematography by such as Don King and Jack McCoy and the eye-opening range of carefully chosen, warmly narrated human interest stories illustrating the many forms the surfing life can take. Animated by Dana's utter knowledge of and affection for that world, *Step Into Liquid* resembles Bruce's films in the success of its deft dual appeal to the general public and an exigent surfing audience.

Brown's intelligent writing and amiable presence manage to hold together a sprawling collection of material. A brief credits preamble hints at surfing's multiple nature and sets a tone of friendly sincerity. Then, bookended by the visually impressive feats of Hamilton's "strapped crew" on the biggest waves in the world, five to seven minute chapters take the viewer to places like the Malloys' ancestral Ireland, the scene of heavy Donegal tow-in surfing and an inspiring surf camp for Catholic and Protestant kids; the Great Lakes where two-footers tickle the blue-lipped, hardcore locals; Vietnam thirty years after the war when veteran Jim Knost returns with his future-longboard wizard son to the "Da Nang Surf Club"; and the Northern California of a seriously obsessed cat named Dale Webster who's gone out over *nine thousand consecutive days* and is (somewhat grimly, it seems) aiming for ten. Brown gives this mixed bag coherence in different ways. At times it's through lively contrasts of color and aura like the abrupt shift from the brown greys of mild heartland rollers to the dangerous sublimities of Pipeline; at others resemblance does the trick, as when the Malloy brothers hand off the ancestry theme to the extended August clan of Blackie's son Robert, his son Sam, spiritual descendant Robert Weaver, and a couple of the old-timers who started it all and can still get down. A laidback session at August's Costa Rican retreat recalls *The Endless Summer II* and, of course, Brown's own history of family transmission.

Where Brown pleasantly distinguishes himself from the previous generation is a more contemporary sense of difference that takes him comfortably into such areas as gender and handicap. Presenting the story of a paralyzed former top prospect, he steers largely (if not fully) clear of sentimentality; the camera's introduction of Jesse Billauer's punky honesty in tightly framed portrait close-up and the direct talk about his injury tend to orient our

Step Into Liquid, **director Dana Brown (2003): Keala Kennelly bringing it in Tahiti (Top Secret Productions/Photofest).**

subsequent emotional response more towards curious empathy than towards pity. Women surfers also figure non-patronizingly in *Step Into Liquid*, which remains even in the early twenty-first century something of an accomplishment for the surfing movie or video. A sequence in which Layne Beachley, Rochelle Ballard, and Keala Kennelly measure themselves against Teahupoo and other redoubtable Tahitian barrels stresses raw achievement first while never denying the difference of gender and the special stylistic contribution of what Beachley identifies as more casual estrogen-based style. McCoy's water camera loves these surfers not just for the retrograde babe factor but for their tight muscularity in the barrel, guts in the nasty wipeout, and sheer watery ease. One of the most breathtakingly lovely underwater shots in surf movies occurs about 48 minutes in when, filmed in slow-motion from just off the razor-wire reef, two of the women duck-dive a heavy incoming steamroller. Ballard's voiceover addresses the moment when, escaping the constraining straight lines of competition, you again "come into rhythm with the ocean." At that instant the two lissome forms on their boards catch the beat to paddle back up freely through endless nuances of blue.

Brown nimbly inserts just enough basic surfing history and terminology to bring the non-specialist gallery along while telling stories even the monthly devourer of *Surfer* will find fresh and interesting. Like the Galveston gang milking supertanker wakes, a sequence ushered in by a nice verbal and visual segue: Tahiti's lush paradise to paradise as an interior state, a shot of a South Seas whale advancing right to left cut to a Texan tanker charging the opposite way. These are Dana's kind of guys, pioneers carving out a gimongus surfing buzz in unpromising conditions. His serviceable if generic soundtrack perks up here with a bouncy "Johnny Kool." Then it's on to the even more wacko Mavericks Crew. Interrupted briefly by the Vietnam episode, the film's final thirty-plus minutes will for the most part cleave to the surf movie formula of the big stuff for last as they elaborate the latest in tow-in surfing. The engrossing latest includes Hamilton restlessly finding new ways to pull off absurd drops on absurd waves, in this case a hybrid hydrofoil board that skims the surfer a meter above the otherwise unridable superchop of unfathomable Peahi slabs. The narrative motor is the meeting in Maui of the pale, mob-nicknamed Mavericks bunch and Hamilton's tow-in teammates. At first the jokey American male insult-affection comes off forced until some real complicity seems to build in jumbo Hawaii challenges or just playing in the unspoiled waters of Rapa Nui. The set piece that brings things to a close is one of the first organized campaigns at a full-scale Cortes Bank. With its nightmare logistics and combination of fearsome size and utter mid-ocean isolation, the expected unexpected occurs when, paddling for a closer look, the already unsettlingly young-looking boat captain gets caught by the angry side of an imposing wave face. He survives, but 110 miles off the coast you really don't want to lose the guy who drives the boat. Such nerve-jangling visual detail jacks up the suspense and the sobriety. "You *have* to make it," says a somberly out of character Brad Gerlach. They do in a series of intense rides on waves so mountainous—one measures in at 66 feet—you hardly notice the unfortunate string-heavy, Disney-inflected "magical" instrumental over the session's final waves.

Merging tow teams from Hawaii and Santa Cruz, Brown makes literal his film's insistence on the shared, interwoven nature of the stoke surfers first discover for themselves. While he does devote considerable attention to the strapped crews, his method generally is breadth and variety, the result being an affectionate if somewhat diffuse sense of Planet

Surf in all its diversity. In *Riding Giants*, the third general audience non-fiction surfing feature of this period, the emphasis is much more upon narrative intensity and focus. Stacy Peralta's subject is the early history and recent development of big wave riding. Haven't we just been there in *The Endless Summer II* and *Step Into Liquid*, not to mention videos like Tim Bonython's short but intense *Biggest Wednesday* (1999) and the professionally elaborated and paced *Billabong Odyssey* (2003)? Well, yes, the subject is back, and for that matter so is Laird Hamilton, as cartoonishly handsome and buff as ever. The thing about *Riding Giants*, though, it that for all this the film doesn't feel repetitive, it feels definitive. When, aided by Quiksilver, Sony brought the movie out in 2004, critics seemed to agree, as suggested by a *93 percent* positive rating on the review site rottentomatoes.com, numbers nearly doubling those for *ESII* and outdoing the already popular *Step Into Liquid*. Showing his stuff in the first skateboard videos and, later, his pop culture masterpiece *Dogtown and Z-Boys*, Peralta is a brilliant documentary storyteller. He was part of the '70s Dogtown crew that trashed the old skateboarding paradigm and designed its successor, but as he says in the 2001 documentary he only really came into his own behind the scene and the camera. On the *Riding Giants* official site Peralta states simply that he "wanted to see a film like this." No throwaway remark, it signals the empathy driving this taut, highly effective blend of pedagogy, visual and emotional stimulation, textured human interest, and clean narrative pacing.

With the fear factor of big wave surfing's dynamite visuals, equally fascinating to surfers and non-surfers, it's no surprise that Waimea and company have served as the nearly obligatory closing chapter in countless movies and occasionally stepped forward as their primary subject. Cinematically, though, the oversized characters who ride them are at least as important as the waves themselves, an awareness Peralta affirms in his film's tight three-part structure. Introduced by an amusing potted-history of surfing, complete with priceless footage from the early ukulele wildman days, chapters of roughly equal length star, in order, Waimea Bay frontier scout Greg Noll, the lesser-known Jeff Clark who somehow braved Mavericks *alone* for 15 years, and Hamilton, for over two decades now off some outer reef in a class by himself. On-screen interviews of the principals and others offer insight into the odd extremes of motivation needed to be the first guy to take off at Jaws or Mavericks. Accenting as well their faulty normalcy—Laird a sad kid looking for a father, Jeff pleading with a childhood friend to paddle out with him the first time—the personal angle has the perhaps unsurprising effect of lending the characters more stature when on the wave. Peralta's narrative strategy is to bring them to life on screen, wheeling regularly from tight focus to wide angle, the emblematic individual serving as lens through which to view the larger historical picture. From the opening image, a silent black screen exploding like a cannon shot into a mammoth being of white water, image and sound combine repeatedly in *Riding Giants* to personify that indescribable incoming force as a mortal enemy. But like Ali with Frazier, that enemy also plays the role of partner and collaborator. With a melodramatic flourish only permitted by the scope of his exploits, Hamilton refers to the dragons their slayer needs in order to exist; Noll actually characterizes his Waimea as a coy maid, though his boorish insistence on the analogy does wear after a bit.

Look through the perfectly rendered teen trash surface of *Dogtown* and you'll recognize Peralta's acute sense of the Historical Moment: in the seeming randomness of his intentionally twitchy storytelling, what coalesces around a band of deftly sketched individuals is a carefully crafted story of the sudden emergence of something radically new in sport and culture. Even if John Severson says he could have gone further in his search for material,[58] Peralta draws on a impressive collection of filmed archives from figures like Noll himself, Bud Browne, Grant Rohloff, Bruce Brown, and Hal Jepsen. Artfully fusing this material with interviews and more contemporary footage from Jack McCoy and others, Peralta follows through on Noll, Clark, and Hamilton to do for big wave surfing what he did for skateboarding, seizing the critical moments when the paradigm shifts and things are never again quite the same. Given voice by Peralta, those instants speak eloquently both to the wider surfing scene and to the general culture it rejects and reflects. When in October 1957 a 19-year-old had had enough and led eight other guys out to a 20 foot Waimea everyone agreed was unridable, surfing had its first North Shore Moment, one only equaled later by Noll's solo runs on huge Makaha and 2nd Reef Pipeline, both recounted in the film, and by Phil Edwards's impulsive decision to risk Pipeline. Just as the gray '50s were drawing to their close, the cameras of Bud Browne and Bruce Brown were there to record these moments.

In his book *Waves of Resistance* Isaiah Helekunihi Walker is certainly right to lament the exclusion of concurrent native Hawaiian surfers like Kealoha Kaio from this narrative and from the larger story of the North Shore's "discovery." That said, with the sheer foreboding nature of the place underlined by Dickie Cross's tragic death in 1943, the fact is that no one went out at Waimea before Noll and company. Making their way, significantly, into the contemporary medium of film, these haole exploits abruptly proved the impossible was possible, and very visibly so. Thanks in large part to surf movie nights back in California the Shore's constellation of world class breaks went mythic just as pre-production *Gidget* was gearing up to focus a generation's attention on the surfline. In conversation kids who'd never been to Hawaii wielded the words Sunset and Makaha and Waimea like totems, as they did the names of the emerging stars who rode them. With his tightly edited archival footage and on-camera greats from back in the day, Penn's sharp narration, and the writerly precision and infectious enthusiasm of Warshaw, Pezman, and Sam George, Peralta catches the flair and hunger of Noll in his jailhouse shorts: more than just guts, the Bull had a knack for spin-off self-promotion already indicating one direction surfing would take. "Surfing needed Greg Noll," says George. It was a good decision to give the bluff, meaty patriarch of today so much screen time, for the young stud who changed surfing is still flexing there in his humorous profanity and supersized presence.

Skimming past the shortboard revolution and its new standards of performance, Peralta then takes us to the sharky cold just south of San Francisco for the most absorbing of the three chapters. Framed by reference to grizzlies and mountain men, this is again a story of the rustic pioneering and "mythic individualism"[59] at the heart of American cultural imagining. Clark managed to internalize the rush of surfing Mavericks by himself for a decade and half, at last convincing others to join him. But such was the aura of Hawaii that they couldn't get their minds around the fact that this *thing* out the back door was Waimea's equivalent and maybe more. Like a Brueghel painting, where the significant detail is concealed off-center in the daily jumble, a fully firing Mavericks appears in the distant background of a weathered home movie clip effectively inserted at the start of the episode; this becomes the DVD moment you watch repeatedly, trying to get inside the head of the high school freshman who scoped it over Mom's shoulder and, like Noll, would finally say today's the day. What makes the Mavericks section particularly riveting cinema is its empathetic focus on the various stages of the process once one finally does commit to monster surf. Peralta understands and gratifies the natural curiosity of the vast majority of viewers who can only imagine. Want to know about the body's wipeout "McTwists" or what happens when a sneak set sends you paddling, literally, for your life? Taut segments titled "The Line Up," "Caught Inside the Break," "The Take Off," and "The Leash" break the experience down with compellingly edited multi-perspective footage and sober black and white commentary by the Mavericks crew, the whole screwed increasingly tighter by the unthinkable notion of Clark surfing Mavericks alone. All this leads to Mark Foo's death the very day the Hawaiian elite gave the wave legitimacy just by showing up. Even here, beyond the emotion, the sequence of events gets more of the same process analysis as these fearless men and women look unwaveringly at the reasons behind their fears.

Shifting emphasis from the familiar islands to the essentially unheard-of destination, the tale of a Mavericks where the elite flies in just when it goes off reflects something of the geographical reach that's marked the search for surf so extensively in recent decades; it also speaks to the globalization that's put us all in airport lounges. At Teahupoo in faraway Tahiti (where *The Endless Summer* had affirmed there were no serious waves), the film's last episode will serve up some of the most spectacular surfing footage ever shot. The dual subject is Laird Hamilton and the tow-in revolution with which he is synonymous. While Hamilton's doings will be familiar to many viewers of *Riding Giants*, the exceptional volume of technological, human, and visual detail filling in this historical account sets its clearly orchestrated presentation off from their much less elaborate equivalents in *Step Into Liquid* and *The Endless Summer II*. Yet as absorbing as the central tow-in narrative is, the most interesting moments come just before, when little (but already strapping) Laird chooses a father, and just after, when that former lost child does the stuff of gods. Completed with period shots, interlaced commentary by Laird and Bill Hamilton traces the Hollywood narrative arc of the insistent kid who transforms his mother into a newlywed, a guy on the beach into his father, and personal trauma into art. Hamilton finds a canvas his size in Peahi, the fearsome Hawaiian outer reef break also known as Jaws where he, Derrick Doerner, and Dave Kalama keep pushing back the limits of tow-in surfing. Notably with an on-camera jet-ski rescue, Peralta again turns to gripping, detailed pedagogy, marshaling insider testimony, heart-in-mouth footage, and cranking guitar and percussion to communicate some fraction of what goes down in those mountains of white water. Throughout, Laird is so much in another category that the reverent hagiographic tone is no problem. Alert to the building impetus of dramatic structure, Peralta chose Teahupoo as the appropriate final page. With an immense sculpted tube and serrated reef just under the surface, the Tahitian left is extraordinarily powerful and dangerous, an XXL Pipeline with an even finer point of film perspective off its huge shoulder. A few terrifying sample wipeouts lead to a ride by Laird in October 2000 that, to give an idea, has been viewed over three million times since on YouTube; dropping into a wave even Doerner thought unridable, he holds in the barrel, steadying with his *right* hand, disappears in a detonation of foam, spits explosively out, up, and off. "What could be heavier?" Matt Warshaw marvels. Aesthetically stunning and white knuckly even in repeated slow motion, this is a ride that changes perceptions of what's possible on a wave.

The three human stories of *Riding Giants* represent dozens more. Only after viewing the film does the subtlety of the title become clear, where the obvious sense, "Riding" as gerund, flips to read as participle: "Giants" thus as epic waves and, simultaneously, the giants who ride them. Like a Necker cube illusion, meaning shifts unstably between the two senses to identify the knotted central relationship in surfing, that between the wave and the individual. The rest is secondary—surfing as business, style, attitude marker, livelihood, etc. In the film's core presentation of three surfers and the waves which they made and which made them, *Riding Giants* shares much with Dana Brown's invitation to *Step Into Liquid* and Bruce's to stop time again in an *Endless Summer*. First of all about that central relationship between man and wave, the three devote significant energy to surfing's simpler past and to its emotional roots cultivated in odd patches of sand; each addresses the future but only in living continuity with the past. Peralta makes the latter clear, for example, by filtering the state-of-the-art tow-in saga through soulful single-fin vet Gerry Lopez and by following Hamilton's future-enabling run with the grounded conversation he had a week after with the beloved '60s stylist who is his father. With the exception of throwback-cheerful Pat O'Connell and a Taj Burrow obeying an artist's soul in Western Australia, the flash and slash contemporary style's largely absent in the three movies; to any ostentatious degree so is professionalism.

There's an irony, of course, in industry-sponsored major studio productions taking the rootsy approach, and, yes, we see the media helicopters swarming when Laird does Peahi and remember that Noll was often all about business. But Peralta and the Browns know what kind of stories they want to tell and their hybrid theater audiences want to hear. In their focus on a time-honored surfing spirit and a future still anchored to a long tradition of free immersion in the present flow, they are channeling the palpable "One God, One Country, One Fin" impatience that put bumper stickers on Highway One in the '90s and relief in the voice of Australian novelist Tim Winton, happy that surfing seems to be outgrowing "its youth-cult boundaries" and finding "room for more articulate voices."[60] A significant proportion of the surfing community does find today's hyperactive, aggressive style somewhat thin nourishment; it's perceived by many as show-offy and disrespectfully self-involved, then there's the other familiar beefs about the competitive tail wagging the surfing dog and the corporate hijacking of surf style. As we will see, *Riding Giants*, *Step Into Liquid*, and *The Endless Summer II* are exceptions for their time since the main body of surfing movies as of the mid–'80s have appeared on the small screen in tape, DVD, and eventually online formats. But even if the technology, viewing context, and financing have changed radically in the last thirty-five years, the tension implicit in these films' nostalgia-tinted presentation of surfing abides as a constant in the sport and its cinematic representations. *Step Into Liquid* features surfing Stakhanovite Dale Webster as he wheels about on the board to offer thanks to the wave he's riding. His gesture's theatrical, but its meaning is one as old as Tom Blake or the Duke, that it's always better not to turn your back on the past.

~ ~ ~ ~ ~

Small Screens, New Scenes

In the mid–1980s, roughly a decade after the initial availability of the Betamax and VHS formats, the surfing movie found its way into the home video cassette. Writing in

Surfer in 1985, Kevin Naughton asked if "Video Killed the Surf Movie," but it might be more precise to ask how it changed the viewing experience. From beach town howling boos or boisterous jubilation, surf movie night now assembled at most a few buds sharing a nice bud. Given skyrocketing costs for films shot on increasingly far-flung beaches and held by their audiences to always steeper technical norms, the old business model built on taking film canisters physically around to a relatively small specialist audience couldn't stand up (whereas a small number of surf-oriented features targeting general audiences have remained viable projects). That writing had long been all over the wall when Michael Tomson's Gotcha put up $400,000 to underwrite one of the very last, *Surfers: The Movie* (1990). Even with its great contemporary soundtrack, good stoke-insistent interviews, and first on-screen appearance of Miki Dora in decades, that was an unsustainable amount. Given the targeted *à la carte* nature of video sales for cassettes whose price had already significantly dropped by the early '90s, surf filmmakers could reach a large swathe of their audience or more precise segments directly without the heavy infrastructure of venue costs and film treatment and projection. Next to traditional 16mm film, shooting videotape directly cost next to nothing. Of the inevitable trade-offs, the most notable was the hollow "soap opera effect" generated by the camcorders of the day. Unsurprisingly, numerous discriminating filmmakers took the high road of shooting more expensive celluloid and transferring the result to videotape.

The surf movie story is just part of a much bigger one, of course, that of the constantly accelerating changes in information and entertainment technology driving certain aspects of contemporary Western culture. The cool cassette became a clunky pain when the DVD came along, even as Internet streaming and the Cloud have made the once sleek disc a relic. From ungainly cameras incapable of slow-mo or water shooting, video production has followed the same breathless technological evolution digitally towards heightened mobility, a sharply enhanced image, and widely available editing software of professional quality. Today, given some talent behind it, your *phone* can make a perfectly creditable short subject with a warm, crisp image that can show online the same day—add to this the Go-Pro embarked camera and no longer futurist drone-based aerial filming, and you're very much in business. One particularly important development in surf movie history has been the technology-wrought democratization of film production. Even early video sharply reduced the cost and time investment of traditional 16mm; today it is easier than it's ever been to create something that looks a lot like a surf movie. Whether it's bustin' down creative and not just technological doors is another question, but the numbers certainly seem to reflect that relative ease. From Bud Browne's *Hawaiian Surfing Movies* in 1953 through 1990, on average about eight surf movies or documentaries a year came out. Since then new films available on videotape, DVD, and online streaming have very conservatively averaged six or seven times that, much of that total number coming in the last decade or so of high performance digital cameras and widespread Internet use—and this not including a raft of earlier films digitalized for sale today, non-professional efforts encouraged and diffused by professional platforms like Go-Pro or Taylor Steele's *Innersection*, glorified home movies on YouTube, etc. In other words, there's a lot of filmed wave-riding out there, and a good bit of it's online where Internet surfing now means more than just metaphorically riding a search engine.

Not surprisingly, given the relative ease of production and customization, the surf video scene is vast and fragmented. While never forgetting that their primary goal is to celebrate the stoke, videos today give surfing lessons (*110% Surfing Techniques, Volume 1*), attack the commercial eco-toxicity of the sport (*Manufacturing Stoke*), cross imposing international borders to bring surfing to Iranian women (*Into the Sea*), offer models for one's golden years (*Surfing for Life*), fire awareness about a vital environmental problem (*Minds in the Water*), call attention to gender issues across a male-dominated sport (*The Women and the Waves*), and introduce a strange and intense surfing family (*Surfwise*). With the star system implicit since the start of the surf boom (and even before) and solidly institutionalized during the pro surfing '80s, the video biography quickly found its market, from the first on Kelly Slater (already him!) in 1991 through such as *Searching for Tom Curren* and *Occy: The Occumentary*, the three, like most other bios, unsurprisingly corporate-sponsored. With surfing's move towards the commerce and image mainstream, as well as the sheer accumulation of the passing decades' repertory of colorful events and characters, videographers have turned as well to the historical documentary. A mark of surfing's growing cultural importance, the documentary often has the commercial advantage of general audience television sales, especially when the story told converges in pertinent ways with that of the larger society. Amongst the dozens of videos documenting various facets of surfing's annals, three from the first decade of the new century—*Bustin' Down the Door*, *Bra Boys*, and *The Endless Winter*—illustrate something of the variety of theme and approach of this subgenre that has demonstrated a certain crossover appeal.

The most recent, in fact, debuted in 2012 as three separately shown episodes on the United Kingdom's Channel 4. *The Endless Winter* is appropriately subtitled *A Very British Surf Movie*, for part of the abundant charm of this history of sceptred isle surfing is the way it gently rebounds off the standard clichés. Finishing a short feature on Cornishman Mitch Corbett, Matt Crocker and James Dean realized that little note had been taken of surfing's arrival and evolution in Britain. Echoing their title's inspiration, after months of research they sent a pair of young pros, Corbett and Mark Harris, on a road trip. This one was from Cornwall to Scotland for a look at this colorful history and the hardcore oddballs who, encouraged by magazines and the occasional South African lifeguard, braved the stares, grumpy weather, interminable wait for swells, icy water, and lack of equipment to establish an authentic if very quirky surf culture. The film is studded with interviews of older local figures by Corbett and Harris and punctuated by their surfing of each place they stop; it includes intentionally "aged," jumpy historical footage and little Terry Gilliam-esque animated vignettes that semi-comically fill in the details while taking the mickey out of British prudery, eccentricity, and stiff-upper-lipishness. The authoritative BBC edge of sports journalist Ned Boulting's narration accentuates a playful tension between Albion's chilly waves, filmed in color but under such cloud cover they often seem black and white, and the incoming news of sunny aloha and California cool.

In a less sentimentalized and more geographically vivid way, *The Endless Winter* does for British surfing what *Waveriders*, with its seemingly nondescript but in fact apt title, had done for that of the Emerald Isle. Such is the historical subject matter of the latter—notably, the saga of George Freeth and the Naughton-Peterson chronicles—that the most interesting parts of the 2008 film don't even take place in what Kelly Slater grinningly calls Ireland's "cold paradise." By contrast, their storytelling extremely empathetic to non–Brits unfamiliar with the lay of the land, Dean and Crocker patiently show viewers around so that by the end they have a real sense of the geography involved. It will surprise more than a few to see the high quality of spots like Porthleven and Thurso East or the Cribbar when it breaks, and what about the harrowing cliff face slab in Northern Scotland that concludes the movie? Along the way, an episode on the Swinging '60s party central "surf camp" Skewjack is sly fun, especially if you like a good venereal disease joke. On the negative side, the Severn Bore river wave chapter goes on way too long and concludes with uselessly unfilmmable nighttime action. Harris and Corbett are fine surfers but thinly developed characters and indifferent interviewers; while they have some genuine matey moments and can distinguish between a pasty and a pork pie, the poor guys are required to make lame "conversational" transitions between destinations: a dozen versions of "it must have been such a buzz to discover these waves back in the day." It's too bad for an otherwise skillfully choreographed narrative that these dudes, who know their surfing from the top down, spend too much time nodding appreciatively and too little sharing their own sense of the wave opportunities encountered along their eye-opening coast.

While similar in its bridging of the general and specialist audience gap, the 2007 *Bra Boys* could not be more tonally different. Captain James Cook plays a role in both films, but less here as accidental British "surf explorer" than as the figure who wrote the first page of Australia's colonial history in blood at Botany Bay. Nurtured by a past of social exclusion and injustice, that tradition of violence fit well into the '90s tribal beach subculture of a once-disadvantaged Sydney suburb just down the road, Maroubra Beach. *Bra Boys* tells the itchy story of the founding and evolution of the eponymous gang linked by hard-charging surfing, ferocious localism, and an addiction to brutality. To a sober, authority-lending Russell Crowe narration, brief historical chapters alternate with videotape of fistfights and disgusting beatings;

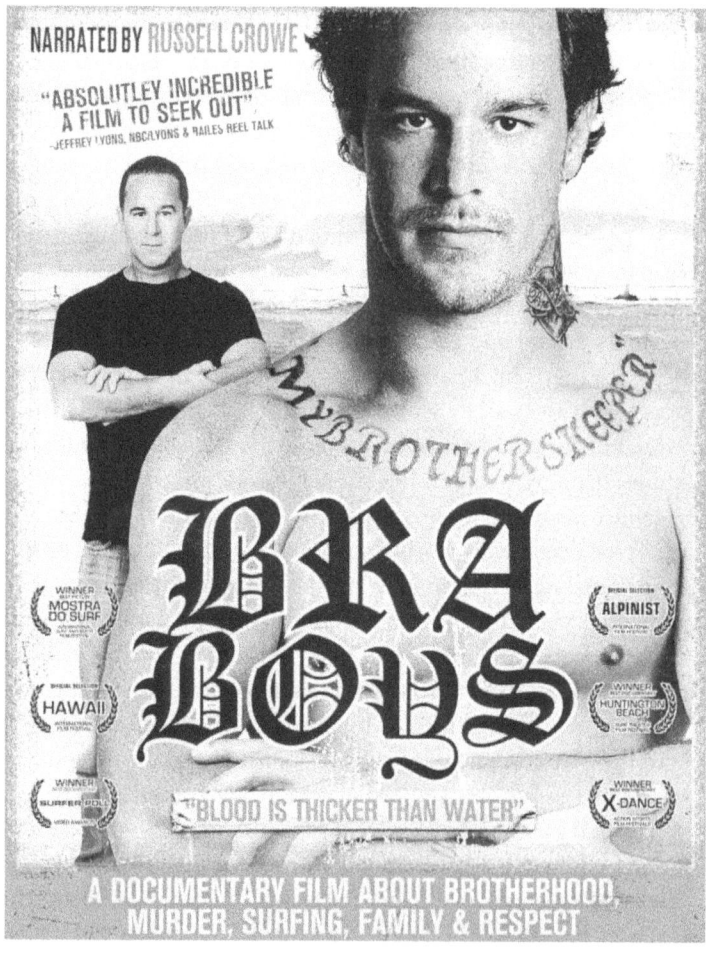

Cover art, *Bra Boys*, director Sunny Abberton (2007). Pictured: Sunny Abberton (background), Koby Abberton. Spilled blood, thicker than water…

contemporary interviews and commentary come from, among others, gang members, cops, and names like Kelly Slater and Laird Hamilton. The film's dueling strength and weakness are its co-direction by Sunny Abberton, Bra Boy legend and patriarch of its founding clan. In what Slater calls "the most localized surf community I've encountered," otherwise unattainable access does make for a storytelling of fascinating density and detail as we watch a band of little flip-off artists take control of the shore. To punk graphics and edgy cuts, we get their story as they mix it up with a troop of off-duty cops, follow the trial and eventual acquittal of two of their lot for murder, and surf a pair of absolutely unsurfable breaks. But when two grom moms smile sanguinely that they have "no issues whatsoever" with their boys hooking up with this bunch, you have to remember that Sunny's on the other side of the camera.

In his version, the Bra Boys certainly aren't angels—they've just pulling together as family against wave theft, anti-surfer profiling, police harassment, and a generally unfair society. "You never knew when it was gonna' go down": for guys Cheyne Horan calls "nothing but trouble," can this only be the defensive reaction it's spun as? And how much weight to give to the portrayal as peacemakers following the Cronulla race riots of 2005 of a group known for the virulent localism identified as a big part of the problem?[61] Tantalizing you forward with planted hints and then notably drawn-out suspense concerning the murder trial—including heartstrings shots just before the verdict of defendant Jai as a child—*Bra Boys* has a seductive grip that distracts from critical judgement. In its pre-video and -TV theatrical release, the film was immensely popular down under, racking up the biggest scores ever for a documentary. According to Kelly Jean Butler's pertinent analysis, Abberton and clan self-servingly participate in a national questioning of historical identity by merging the scrappy Aussie "battler" myth of the disadvantaged with the "white victim narrative." Surfing is central to this core tale of adversity and triumph. The top surfer of this band of serious wave killers, Koby Abberton is the heavily tattooed hub of the film. Playing off sentiments like Derek Hynds's claim that we as surfers "had to battle to hold our head above water in society," even awaiting trial as accessory to murder he mans up to continue a pro surfing career portrayed as vital to his family's well-being. On his home break he beats none other than Slater, though the threatening notes on the latter's car didn't hurt. When Koby leads the charge to appropriate a previously unsurfed headland off their turf, they call it, revealingly, Ours. "Pushing social boundaries is the same as pushing boundaries in surfing," claims one of the group. In the conclusion, Koby's good angel says that "the beach belongs to everyone." Then a different one unironically adds that those showing up should realize "there might be a whole history and a culture spanning for generations there and that should be respected." Like the clinical expression "pushing social boundaries," this sounds like a delicate way to say spoiling for a fight. On the other hand, you have to wonder about the badass cred of a band of brothers that today markets its own line of clothes.

While so different in feeling, the genial *Endless Winter* and defensively twitchy *Bra Boys* have essentially the same simple narrative structure: establish the situation today for the audience, then wheel back to the start to show how we got to this point. The same can be said of *Bustin' Down the Door* (2008), which again focuses on Aussie chargers with a chip on their shoulder but this time in their history-making war on the shore with the rest of the surfing world. Treated elsewhere in these pages, notably in remarks concerning *A Matter of Style* and *Free Ride*, the story's again that of Mark Richards, Rabbit Bartholomew,

Shaun Tomson, and Ian Cairns, who brought their Australian and South African competitive natures, personal issues, and sense of the changing zeitgeist to the North Shore for several consecutive winters in the mid-'70s. To bust into the small existing competitive scene (and encourage its growth), various members of this talented group surfed Pipe backside, courted photographers, brought exciting new mobility to time spent in the curl, and took a celebrated beating for playing the Ali/Joe Namath in-your-face PR game. While the film eludes the contribution of islanders like Larry Bertlemann and Buttons Kaluhiokalani in its never-questioned assumption that radical shortboard surfing was a uniquely Australian invention,[62] the sheer noisiness of its Southern Hemisphere proponents did indisputably urge surfing along a new path in the mid-'70s.

The film begins on the Gold Coast at the 2007 awards night of the ASP professional circuit, the creation of which, it rightly insists, was at very least rapidly accelerated by the antics thirty years earlier of the four hellmen of the surfing apocalypse—Bartholomew, Cairns, Richards, Tomson—re-assembled that evening for a special achievement award. *Bustin' Down the Door* then carefully introduces these and the other major players, slipping classically but gracefully between archival personal and surfing footage and contemporary interviews. As the story takes each one north to grander ambitions, the scope widens to an historical and contemporary portrait of the symbolic value of Hawaiian surfing and the initially more courtly spirit into which they come into conflict. Balanced and intelligent, the video manages a fully empathetic understanding of what drove the audacious new arrivals while generously communicating why the more traditional islanders were not having it. Since then times have changed, things have mellowed. In this indispensable record of one of surfing's most important chapters, though, the history's legible even today in the expressions and style of these fifty-year-olds. Shirtless in his board-bristling garage, Eddie Rothman communicates a taciturn crocodile menace that illustrates better than any period photo what the "Black Shorts" who taught Rabbit a lesson were like. Blond and charismatic, Bartholomew can still tip into brashness, while Richards is marked by the self-effacement that bought him slack from the Hawaiians. Tomson's middle-aged speech and appearance convey another form of the refined subtlety he brought decades earlier to Off the Wall. Big wave wrangler Cairns still looks like a rough chunk chipped from a testosterone mine.

Each was an agent of change, yes, but first a great surfer, as the miles of period footage and subsequent contests confirm, and interspersed testimonials from today's stars underline. With its high dosage of world class action, *Bustin'* resembles the documentaries discussed above in the way it lit up surf festivals, specialist audiences, and awards ceremonies worldwide, all the while very clearly working informational, historical terrain and not that of the pure wave-after-wave surf movie. While the permeability of dividing lines between such distinctions is evident, the vast majority of videos these last decade do fall into a more direct line of descent back to the relatively simple and predictable concerns of the traditional surf movie. Most obviously, this means above all else communicating the stoke of the best surfing at the best locations. As it already did to the four-wall surf movie, this central imperative often, if by no means always, extends to travelling far afield to find fresh and exotic spots, at first generally to Indonesia and other equatorial meccas, then later north to rugged cold water challenges. Along the way, of course, if you can share the human dimension and cultural context surrounding the action, all the better. Yet if the ends of most surf videos remain roughly the same, the aesthetic means can vary widely. At one pole is what Albie Thoms identifies as the "brash 'slash and burn'"[63] mode popularized overnight by Taylor Steele in *Momentum* (1992). Introducing to a mass audience the innovative, radical intensities of the so-called New School, its grainy, no-frills videotape shooting of high performance surfing against a charging soundtrack of pissed-off neo-punk hit hard and unapologetically. The MTV Generation loved it and, predictably, *Momentum* spawned a host of imitators so that even today, if you can't think of anything else to do, the surf video default mode is not far from the rudimentary structure and jackhammer energy of Steele's early '90s formula. The percussive rhythm of such films is the racing pulse of the contemporary hyperactive snap-back and aerial style; in it for the rush, they're in no way about questioning the glossy big-bucks nature of the scene today. But some, perhaps most, of the very best videos of the last two decades are. Far across a wide range of variations to the other end of the scale stand films that combine smooth tracks across the wave with elegantly crafted narrative lines, soundtracks of musical and lyrical complexity, lushly poetic cinematography, and thoughtful reflections on the spirit and meaning of it all. It's noteworthy that, in the course of one of the most remarkable careers in surf videography, Steele has created outstanding films at both ends of this spectrum.

To make some sense of this vast, complex field, the necessarily cursory survey to follow will focus on a couple of such major figures and a smattering of other videos, most of high quality—often recognized by *Surfer* Poll Awards, Top Ten lists, etc.—and all in some way representative of key moments or recent trends in the cinematic treatment of surfing. The dates given for individual videos refer when possible to first public showings and not to VHS, DVD, or streaming release. Before, though, it's important to discuss briefly that blurred boundary between video and theater release as well as the new norms of film financing in the video era. In fact, most professionally produced films intended for diffusion in recorded form or on Internet have had short publicity runs in selected theaters, renewing for a brief stretch at least the tradition of active, sometimes rambunctious public viewing; a good number also appear in the dozens of surf film festivals worldwide, from higher profile festivities like those in New York and Anglet, through homier affairs such as Perth's North Beach Film Festival or Hermosa's Beach Shorts. What we'll refer to as videos, then, are films primarily available for individual sales and viewing. They're to be distinguished from the three general theater releases from the last two decades. *Riding Giants*, *Step Into Liquid*, and *Endless Summer II* went on of course to exist as DVDs after their initial more public careers.

As far as surf video financing is concerned, the norm since the mid–1980s has increasingly become some form of corporate sponsorship. While product placement and embedded advertising existed at least as early as Bruce Brown's first films, and Greg Noll's were essentially ads for his boardmaking concerns, surf movies were traditionally independent productions if not one man shows. Unsurprisingly, with the institutionalization of the pro tour and explosive growth of surf-related sportswear companies like Billabong, Quiksilver, and Rip Curl in the 1970s and '80s, sponsors showed themselves increasingly eager to participate in high-visibility surf culture projects. *Storm Riders* and *Surfers: The Movie* were not alone in drawing seed production money from such sources. But when video hit, it did so from the very beginning under largely commercial auspices. Significantly, Quiksilver funded one of the first direct-for-video films *The Performers* in 1984, and Astrodeck followed in 1985 with *Wave Warriors* (plus sequels). While some of the best videos remain independent, even fully DIY productions, most have at least some kind of commercial tie-in, if not a blatantly corporate identity. Guaranteed relative artistic freedom and offered access to a surfwear company's publicity budget, it's understandable that film producers strike limited financial arrangements or finally just throw in with the companies. While there are certainly egregious examples of the surf movie as billboard (see below), aesthetic compromise is far from inevitable. A genially creative indie who nevertheless inked a sponsorship deal with Reef, Cyrus Sutton (*Stoked and Broke*) sees the lines "getting blurred as surf companies embrace the lifestyle aspect of surfing and fund more and more artists. It all comes back to each artist calibrating their internal compass and not letting the affiliation with companies affect the quality of their work."[64] Two decades back Billabong put up cash for *Sik Joy*, but what's on screen and what viewers remember very fondly is a Jack McCoy film, in other words offbeat musical choices, whimsical narrative touches, gorgeous shots from the water, and heartrendingly beautiful tropical surfing.

McCoy was right in there at the start of the video era as the uncredited creative director and credited cinematographer and water shot specialist of *The Performers*. That film and another big production four years later, *Filthy Habits*, take the corporate-sponsored video in two very different directions. Financed by Quiksilver, *The Performers* is a well-shot, not uninteresting stand-alone surf movie carefully humanizing the brand's surf team, and thus the brand. *Filthy Habits* is a well-shot, slickly packaged and targeted 50 minute ad for Billabong. The former follows its title's lead, painting a series of mini-portraits of such surfers as Wes Laine, Marvin Foster, and, straight from McCoy's *Kong's Island*, Chappy Jennings, Rabbit Bartholomew, and Kong himself, Gary Elkerton. Before a five minute montage of uniquely Hawaiian surfing brilliance, each gets a couple of personalizing offstage land shots, a chance to show off his quiver, and a kind of computer printout graphic with the performer's name, age, residence, favorite surfer, music, food, etc. Straight from *American Graffiti*, the clever voiceover takes the form of surf-oriented radio show chatter that links the chapters and furnishes additional info about the surfers and the scene. As Rabbit cruises to the beach, his car radio crackles on intermittently with the wave report and the particularities of that '83–'84 North Shore winter deprived of competition by a dispute between the ASP and local organizers. Saving the best for last, the video closes with Elkerton's and then Bartholomew's performances. Shot on 16mm, often in slow motion with, McCoy's specialty, lovely 50-shades-of-blue underwater camerawork of boards passing overhead and waves silently steamrolling through, the cinematography's buffed up nicely by a solid soundtrack that includes Pink Floyd and Talking Heads. With its lugubrious rhythms, "Another Brick in the Wall" seems a surprising choice to open a surf movie until its plea for freedom kicks in over the slow-motion collapse of walls of water.

An annoyed adult voice echoing ironically in its title, *Filthy Habits* taps into the same limitless fund of teenage anger and angst as Pink Floyd. Unfortunately, the bad attitude the film excretes feels like it was calculated by those very adults to appeal to the kids. It's understandable the video's fans of a certain age still remember the Billabong stable of young Sunny Garcia, Mark Occhilupo, and others as they rip Grajagan and lots of the North Shore to a hardcore soundtrack by Social Distortion and the Johnnys. "The ripshredslashburnair sensory overload surf movie extravaganza that is status quo these days"[65] recognized in *TransWorld Surf* in 2011 had its birth in these days, with such a video and even more so a few years later in Taylor Steele's take-no-prisoners *Momentum*. But what Jarrod Tallman fondly identifies in *Filthy Habits* as "bringing it back to the basics; A+ surfing cut to kick-ass music"⁶⁶ is also cut by a half-dozen on-screen Billabong poster pauses, the company's omnipresent tee-shirts, and even a shouldercam focus on a surfer's brand-name covered buns. The product pitching would pass, though, if the cool didn't feel so manufactured. Surfwear competitor Gotcha had been mining a dirty punk advertising seam for some time, and the year *Filthy Habits* came out their ad copy famously snarled, "If you don't surf, don't start." So just after the titles done up in an intentional trash graphic style, Richie Collins comes on for a series of mugshots completed by the following message in rough manual typewriter font: "I said to the guy: Hey? you shouldn't even be out here. You should be on the beach watching me surf." As far as the soundtrack's concerned, it's sufficiently "alternative" to fence out the nerds, but if the ear you thought was cool doesn't recognize Dream Syndicate right off, don't worry, it will when you see the on-screen label conveniently accompanying each song. The calculated message of all this is that most people won't get it but you the viewer do. The movie ends with bad boy graphics edgily glowing in the same marginal visual style only with a comforting inclusiveness: "You know the feeling." To some degree surf culture has always been about keeping most people out while reinforcing a sense of community within. But when you feel that tension's so palpably orchestrated around an ad agency table? Significantly, *Filthy Habits* lists no director for it's not so much a film as another Billabong product.

Complementing their massive investment in contest sponsorship, the major surfwear and gear companies have consistently maintained a video presence. Notwithstanding productions like *Filthy Habits* and the Gorilla Grip product placement extravaganza, the *Hawaii Nine-0* series, the realization hit early that a more sophisticated soft sell stance was probably the one to take. That's been the case in most of the many dozens of corporately underwritten videos since, including Ripcurl's Derek Hynd-developed '90s *The Search* series which subsumes its sales agenda nicely in the well-shot chronicles of the team's top surfers scouring the world for pristine breaks and a fondly remembered film on Tom Curren. Another conspicuously good and very early example is *Kelly Slater in Black and White*, after the Jack McCoy *et al.* short *A Day in the Life of Wayne Lynch* one of the first star bio features and the earliest on video. They chose the right guy. For the express purpose of introducing Quiksilver's newly signed wunderkind to the world, Richard Woolcott (today's Volcom CEO) tailed the 18-year-old in 1990 and '91. Woolcott alternates black and white footage of Slater's sweet dry land artlessness when asked playfully dumb questions with his subject's simply filmed but wildly radical surfing, most notably at Fiji's Cloudbreak and a perfect Lower Trestles during the 11-time world champ's first big contest win. Beyond its sizeable commercial value at the time and historic weight today, the film has unintentional rough edges and the offbeat simplicity and charm of the early surfing movies. Slater has been omnipresent in well over a hundred videos since, whether with the *Young Guns*, heading *Down the Barrel*, or just *Letting Go*.

Since then production values have generally kept pace with increased budgets and technological advances; if anything, with all the resources available, one challenge has been not to get too slick. Early this century, a Billabong that had clearly learned something en route plunked down three million dollars to spin the buzz from the company's own yearly XXL big wave prize into an 85 minute film called *Billabong Odyssey* (2003). The sponsor's certainly present in the title, and the company decision to bankroll a commando team to stalk the world's biggest waves at known and new sites was understandably dismissed by some observers as big-money "pseudo-adventure."[67] That said, for the dough and hugely mobilized infrastructure, *Billabong Odyssey* finally takes a modest, sincere tack in telling its engrossing story, one regularly spilling forth ornery surfing sequences and peopled by a salty cast of individualistic tow-in team players, from hardcore straight-arrow Ken Bradshaw to Santa Cruz bad boy "Flea" Virostko. The decision to bring that mix together for a preparatory safety and procedures bootcamp makes for a slight *Dirty Dozen* edge while providing some information transmission interesting even for an insider public. Aside from the jawdropping surfing, including a drive off a Jaws cliff so hairy it looks like CGI, this is a movie for curious people who like to see how things work—big waves, tow-in collaboration, safety drills, weather patterns, getting logistics in place. Implicit all along, the Billabong outdoor lifestyle message is the stronger for its understatement.

On screen the manipulative executive mentality behind *Filthy Habits* was already history by the early '90s, if we can judge by Billabong's decision to hand the keys to Jack McCoy for a series of promotional videos. In short order McCoy turned out cult classics like *Bunyip Dreaming* (1990) and *The Green Iguana* (1992), alert documentaries on the elite alt-competitive Billabong Challenge, and an award-winning, if visually uneven, look at the roller coaster existence of the top surfer in the brand's stable, Mark Occhilupo. Collaboration of this sort has its artistic dangers, of course. Yet as no less than Robert Flaherty showed, drawing inspiration for *Nanook* while on another job and filming *Louisiana Story* for Standard Oil—or for that matter whole earth purist Alby Falzon doing promotional films for Island Records—some filmmakers keep a good portion of their soul. In *The Green Iguana* the eponymous animated reptile sneaks into the frame much more than the sponsor's shadow. Jay DiMartino exaggerates a bit when saying the film's "back country feel gave the impression that we were one of the inner circle on a surf trip to the Aussie Outback," but it does have a friendly oddball tone that recalls earlier generations of surf movie eccentrics. It's not just the millisecond "adrenaline flash" wink in the titles that recalls *Morning of the Earth*.

For this filmmaker who made the leap elegantly to video and on to Internet streaming,[68] what also recalls the earlier days is an attention to craft. The Yank-gone-Aussie McCoy, after all, got his first break thanks to Jim Freeman and Greg MacGillivray, and you can feel it in his obsessive attention to underwater image quality and montage that expressively varies the rhythm of the viewing experience. As in most of McCoy's work in the '80s, Occy is the star, ripping Kirra backside with Luke Egan and others to Sublime's "We're Only Gonna' Die for Our Arrogance." Paced precisely to that tubing right as it screams across the frame, this musical choice is spot on, as is "Head Above Water" (Hunters & Collectors) for a brief wipeout compilation. With, respectively, a spacy hot-dog manner and hammy enthusiasm, Occhilupo and Peter King are also camera-magnets on shore in a series of little skit-lets that riff along like post-modern takes on the male group goofing off of the earliest surf movies. Intentionally rusty animation and jerkily speeded-up camerawork add to the whimsical homemade appeal. From time to time McCoy punctuates these brief pauses in the surfing action with on-screen text blurbs highlighting a politico-environmentalist message familiar to surf movie viewers. "The surfer who is sick of sewage," one reads, "is not sick." In the DVD re-issue of *The Green Iguana*, McCoy includes an elaborate animated plea from a talking globe Mother Earth for an end to the hostilities. Once

I was "covered in forests and full of life, and then you got civilized.... The more you began to think for yourselves, the less you thought about me."

A popular, prolific filmmaker and frequent contributor to other projects, McCoy is a central figure in the wider surfing community. Between 2001 and 2005 he organized an annual mobile surf film festival that took such acclaimed videos as *The September Sessions*, *Sprout*, and his own whimsical *Free as a Dog* on a series of tours that grew from an original ten Australian dates to 156 in thirteen countries. Here, as throughout McCoy's films, one hears the now familiar divided heart of surfing. On one hand, his film fest's another Billabong deal; on the other, McCoy convincingly communicates the meaning and pleasure of recreating something like the good old Browne-to-Brown days of the communal surfing movie when, as he says on his site, the tribe could share the stoke "in the true tradition of the surfing film experience where the person who makes the film meets and greets the audience." Among other things, we can associate nostalgia of this sort with a very loose video movement or school sharply aware that, as Skip Frye says in the opening of *One California Day*, "we've got to look to the past to prepare for the future." This consciously cultivated dual orientation has led to some of the most vital and artistically interesting examples of video craft. In part at least a militant reaction against the "shredfest" ethos heralded by *Filthy Habits* and given a series of adrenaline shots by *Momentum* and company, a sympathetic feel for the spiritual undercurrent of surfing and its tolerant, bygone simplicity shades many films in recent decades.[69] In the work of video artists like Thomas Campbell, Andrew Kidman, Mark Jeremias, Jason Baffa, and Jack Johnson, such sentiments animate a wholesale re-thinking of the life and the sport. In fact, what has that last word even come to mean in today's overheated, mediatized competition environment? Directed in collaboration with Jon Frank and Mark Sutherland as The Val Dusty Experiment, Kidman's under-the-radar classic *Litmus* (1996) begins with a quotation from Nat Young: "I wish that when they asked us: What is surfing?' I would have said it's a spiritual activity, and not just a sport, because that's what put us on the wrong track." Inviting Young along for the ride, Kidman declares an allegiance he would definitively confirm more than a decade later in *Spirit of Akasha*, a homage to Australian ur-monument *Morning of the Earth*, for which he came on board only when icon Alby Falzon conferred his blessing.

For the most part the image in *Litmus* is a somber soft focus near black-and-white that registers visually as parchment darkened by age. With no narration, shaggy free association organizes a sequence of chapters on individual surfers both in the waves and reflecting idiosyncratically on their relationship with them. Largely by Kidman's own group, the moody, introspective soundtrack resonates bluesily and jazzily back towards a time before an aggressively athletic surfing m.o. found its match in seething punk and rap. The filmmaker chooses ride clusters from surfers like Joel Fitzgerald, Derek Hynd, and Tom Curren that tend towards distinctive, elegant lines in flow with the wave. If you think all this evokes another era, you're right. As Hynd, spindly yet graceful, traverses from trough to crest in silky slow-motion, Kidman transposes footage of Nat Young from '71 and Terry Fitzgerald at J-Bay in 1978; in *Spirit of Akasha* he does the same, laying Michael Peterson's famous *Morning* Kirra run over an ethereal session by Stephanie Gilmore. A kind of magical realism, the uncanny echo effect is haunting even if, wrote Faulkner in terms one guesses Kidman might second, "the past is never dead. It's not even past." Beautifully served by the Woody Guthrie–like challenge of Kevin Baker, whose gentle power concludes a soundtrack alternating driving urgency and delicate italicization, *Litmus* is a poetic reflection upon yesterday and today, transmission, and what is retained or lost along the way. One of the most affecting episodes concerns Joel Fitzgerald surfing waves to fiddle and bodhran off an Ireland his family left and going on with admiration for his legend of a father. In his awed understatement, Terry Fitzgerald, along with such as Young and Peterson, were "just takin' it on." Which presumably refers to the way those hellmen wrested surfing abruptly into its modern phase while seeming not to give a shit.

Kidman is certainly drawn to that charmed Australian parenthesis when short board high performance at sea and getting back to the land could mean roughly the same thing. But *Litmus* is less about idealizing a particular time or style of surfing than approving an attitude. It's in the generous imperfection and loose spontaneity of the filmmaking; it's in that pure self-emptying fullness when Miki Dora locks into a tall right for 58 seconds of what Hynd admires as "silent delirium." The surfers who people the film are each in their individual ways what Matt Warshaw identifies as the "pragmatic soul surfer,"[70] true champions or conventional successes, on one hand, but never not at some level also quirky dropouts uncomfortable with the whole crowded package presented them. Wayne Lynch, Tom Curren, Mark Occhilupo, the Fitzgeralds, Hynd, Nat, obviously Dora: part of their charm is their issues with norms and official patterns, how they set their own terms, kept their counsel, negotiated separate peaces. More than the careerists and show-offs, isn't it they who most belong on the literal and symbolic margin of the surfing space? Kidman's at home there as well, continuing his exploration of porous generational borders in *Glass Love* (2005) and *Akasha*, slipping aesthetic confines from film to music to shaping to print to photography, working with equal ease individually or collaboratively. Maybe some of the off-plumb freshness of *Litmus* comes from its creator's jumble of different aesthetic perspectives. Artists are not always their best critics, but the third-person text on Kidman's site is justified in signaling how a "moving familiarity" combines in his work with "an unfamiliar meditative 'otherness.'"

If such an eclectic artist can be said to have a counterpart, it is Thomas Campbell, similarly slippery of category, surfer, skater, filmmaker, photographer, sculptor, painter, author, record label owner, clothing designer, countercultural sensibility, re-thinker of skate and surf culture. An improvisatory DIY non-trajectory eventually moved the OC native to the job list above in the Santa Cruz backcountry via the New York alternative art scene, skateboard magazines, and what not. "There's a kind of eclecticism that wasn't visible 20 years ago," says Tim Winton, clearly thinking of Campbell, Kidman, songwriter-filmmaker Jack Johnson, and others. "It's not just in what craft surfers are riding, but in the ways that surfers express themselves."[71] In the three full-length films which have emerged from a flurry of other artistic endeavors, Campbell has given softspoken voice to a happy, tolerant, grateful vision of surfing. While the films are indisputably about *The Present*—the title of the third—it would be disingenuous not to recognize the good dose of life-affirming movie vibe Campbell draws from the past. *The Seedling*, speaking of which, is nothing less than a 1999 paean to the single fin, with animation by Mr. Longboard Joel Tudor, and vet Skip Frye and Kassia Meador in residence on the nose. Five years later *Sprout* would extend Campbell's interest in surfcraft and opposition to board length segregation by embracing the "many different ways we have to access our ocean existence, using whatever shape or size equipment it might take to have a more connected ride." Connected's the word, with the wave, alternative surf modes, the self and others, a tradition. As for *The Seedling*, the organicism of the title evokes leaves of grass, the log you ride, and something young with roots. "Relationships are like plants," says one of Campbell's go-to longboard guys, Devon Howard. "If you don't water them, they wilt."[72] Underlining this point in a *NY Times* piece by Lisa Eisner, Campbell believes "the only way to get the films to surfers is to take the films to them," which for him means touring in the old-fashioned way. His DVD sales are fine, out over 50,000 for these largely self-financed efforts filmed in expensive 16mm, but for a viewing experience your living room is certainly not the same as the local community center with the man himself and maybe a live band.

For Campbell doing it the old way is not timid refusal of today but an affirmative widening of creative options for a surfing, he said in an interview with Jonathan Feldman, that's been "flattened out, commercialized, and run through these big corporate machines that really don't have any style." In *Sprout* style is content, the romantic enactment of a fervent belief in unfiltered primary experience: once the blood pumping in surfing's rebel heart, now some insipid fluid diluted by posing, image, commodification, and false sectarian debate. The film feels handmade because it is, shot deliberately on real film for analog's potential in capturing emotional depth; to Campbell, the physicality of the medium and a certain permanence are, as for bronze, part of its aesthetic.[73] Funky graffiti graphic style drives the artisanal titles and connective illustrations, as well as a series of "guerrilla art" decoration sessions of an abandoned chicken house during that classic old movie moment when the surf's flat. When it's up, Campbell favors well-groomed point break molehills, where longboards in particular are at home. The way the rides go on forever has a philosophical content here, gracefully stretching the present moment and enforcing a contrast with the hormone-heavy freneticism of the contemporary aerial style on its blown-out shorebreaks. The chill atmospherics of a jazz-happy soundtrack fit a storytelling pace that never drags but is intentionally unhurried. The whole thing's very anti-*Momentum*.

The episodes of *Sprout* bop along with a randomness appropriate to a movie whose theme is whatever gets you through the wave: Sri Lanka with Dan Malloy carving and Belinda Baggs and the balletic Alex Knost navigating "the nasal passage"; a long visit to Noosa Heads, Tom Wegener, his sprouting family, trees, and paulownia wood boards, the Shins on audio; bodysurf and bodyboard delirium with Mark Cunningham (in Speedos) and Mike Stewart (Greenough-filming the tube); Tyler Hatzikian shaping and surfing in El Segundo; skits, gags, cartoons, three masters "sliding their brains out in Central America"; "a multi-dimensional Sprout trip to the East Indies"; other stuff. Eggs, fish, "ridiculously fun" mats, unlikely fin combos, "and the bonzer" all show up, under the zen supervision of stylists like Joel Tudor and Rob Machado. Between pressing snowboard and yoga obligations, Gerry Lopez delivers a flame red '70s singlefin Pipeline hot rod that's no museum piece in the closing Indonesia sessions.

In all about ten summer stories, they are marked by the no rush-just fun mentality of easygoing surf movie predecessors reaching back a half century. Appreciative meta-cinematic touches make it clear where to find some real style, again with the jazz we've hardly heard since Bud Shank in *Slippery When Wet*. Then jazz was a marker for edgy; maybe it is again today, like riding logs, to Devon Howard a "punk rock move" at 14 if there ever was one.[74] The ambient art, like the *Search for Surf*-style titles and surf wagon deco prominently displayed as the last image in the film, says Rick Griffin; an anti-W poster and a few minutes about white people stealing California and surfing recall Severson and MacGillivray-Freeman. Starting stupid and then getting a laugh, a punny shaka-fest stars Chris Malloy is a tribute to the old comic relief filler skit. Along the way, chromatic values suggesting aged film stock and the emotional shading it can lend run a narrow range from b/w through colors resting largely within the darker *Litmus* spectrum. Occasionally, though, the action can go to brighter split- and four-screen formats set up by a filmmaker who clearly gets a kick out of the lively '60s visual aesthetic of *Expo 67* and *The Thomas Crowne Affair*. Our host Campbell's affectless nerd-cool narration is very buttoned-down, with a not-of-this-decade verbal precision and a few retro tics for the fun of it. Dane Peterson prepares not just any snack but one that's "cheap and easily accessible for surfers on the go." And when Campbell's surfers go, they go to "Ceylon"

Cover art, *Sprout*, director Thomas Campbell (2004). Water mountains and mole-hills, logs and nasal passages, single fins of every stripe ... and the bonzer.

and the "East Indies," places that are vibrantly alive even as the names he uses exist only in memory.

As it does for Kidman, the fun swarm of little stylistic details looks gratefully back even if both artists are very now in, among other things, the way they let girls into the surf party. Which shouldn't be any big deal in the 21st century but is because most videos remain guy-only affairs to a remarkable degree. One cool touch in Campbell's contemporareity is the no sweat way Belinda Baggs, Ashley Lloyd, Kassia Meador, and other "ladysliders" just show up on 9+ foot machines and help push back in their relaxed ways against the confining boundaries of surfing, not to mention the selling out and showing off. On everything from a Rasta-guided surf mat through every fish and single fin known to man through a wooden 12 footer, *Sprout* gently militates for the erasure of borders, slowing down to look and listen, and simpler values from that past that, while no doubt idealized, can seem sweetly self-evident when framed by Campbell: "We as surfers, no matter what devices we access with, are so ridiculously lucky to have the lives that we have." Not surprisingly, Campbell's three films have been produced by Woodshed Films, itself a sprout from the Moonshine Conspiracy, an artists' collective associated with the Malloy surfing clan and Jack Johnson. In his collaborations with this bunch, Johnson has also shown that the best surfing movies are *about something* and not simply compilations of insane rides. While providing more than their share of the latter, *Thicker Than Water* and *The September Sessions* share with the films of Campbell and Kidman the belief that the intense inhabitancy of the present instant that is surfing is also part of a meaningful continuum with the past. Released in 1999 and 2000 (just as almost-pro surfer Johnson was multi-tasking his way into another new career as internationally renowned singer-songwriter), the films speak to each other in interesting ways about family ties, inheritance, friendship, aging, and life/career tensions. Johnson shot and directed both films, the first in collaboration with the elder of the Malloy brothers surf triumvirate Chris and his cousin Emmett Malloy, the second alone with Emmett along for the editing work. Johnson expressively scored both films, often with quickly generated "scratch track" versions of his own acoustic compositions but also with eclectic choices, from a chain-gang chant to a Tahitian choir to a composition derived from a Native American peyote song. While Johnson and Chris Malloy are by their abundant talent and connections card-carrying surfing insiders, the patiently communicated sense of human warmth in the films seems to speak of lessons learned from the frenetic, individualistic competition scene and the certain distance they've all taken on it.

Everyone knows what's *Thicker Than Water*, and this is a film made by two cousins, by that form of family not born into but chosen, close friends, and by sons brought early to the foam by surfing fathers. The post-title sequence features a tow-headed grom (neighbor John John Florence) catching a shorebreak right while Johnson's voiceover reminisces about knowing from early childhood where his dad stowed his boards and how he always felt like a surfer. Then an abrupt cut to the adult charging slow motion out of a big right's frothy curl, the crowded water bristling with cameras. Between those two images lies a life, the little simplicities of childhood and the professional complications and bigger challenges of adulthood lent a meaningful continuity by surfing. *Thicker Than Water* follows a varying band of surfer friends (including Dan Malloy, Brad Gerlach, Rob Machado, Conan Hayes, and Kelly Slater) from the ethereal waves of India's Andaman Island chain back home to Hawaii, then on to Australia, Ireland, and finally Raimana Van Bastolaer's Tahiti. In water and out, Johnson shoots the world-class surfing patiently, often sticking with rides to their conclusions, mixing in discreet touches of appropriate local color and boat tedium. As it does, say, when a young Tahitian's leap from a rock echoes Slater's in the previous scene, Malloy's editing sets up questions and meanings. There's no narration, only occasional snatches of dialogue and off-camera reflections by the participants that gently weave a thematic tissue: the thread of surfing knitting together past and present, family members, groups of friends. The phrase "all my friends" appears at least twice, and the piquant intervention by (unidentified) surf photo legend Leroy Grannis is that of an emblematic patriarch, recollecting the transition from redwood to balsa and a surfing community where "we were like a family." Appropriately, the present-instant intensity of the Teahupoo look-alike session ending the film sends searching feelers back to "when we were kids ... we never would have dreamed of something like this."

Cinema itself comes in for some credit in the film's dealings with the links forged by surfing, whether across the generations, a lifespan, or the differences between individuals. "I remember mimicking the guys from the movies we saw at Hollywood Theater," goes a reminiscence. "A surf movie would come out and everyone would pile into the theater and be screaming." Assuming its place in that historical line, *Thicker Than Water* closes with a companionable "thanks for watching" that pleasantly echoes the traditional Hawaiian shirt Saturday night auditorium sign-off. The visual language of Johnson and the Malloys further reinforces this theme of connectedness. It addition to the sweet joy the scene communicates, it's significant that to the gloriously seductive rhythms and lyrics of "Witchi Tai To" the credits sequence piles some of the world's most distinctive surfers literally and symbolically into the same boat, a little rubber raft that finally sends them together over the falls. In a similar way, one of the best stretches of *Thicker Than Water* occurs when a half dozen of these exceptional athletes take the same unexceptional green singlefin out for a spin one after another, eventually handing it over to a talented sprout. To voiceovers of recalled first cutbacks and fifth grade, the surfing underlines individual stylistic nuances, plus the fact that Slater and Machado always look great on anything. More, though, we're hit with a back-to-basics sense of what these men share today as the grown-up versions of the green kids their fathers took surfing. Presumably for a Kelly Slater, whose life was a particularly intense flurry of commitments, adulation, and big checkbook promotions, hooking up with these pals and their "shoestring" venture reads as a way to re-connect with that simple truth. "All the attention can just take a hike," he sighs. "It hasn't fulfilled my life."

It was during the eighteen month period of filming that the then-six time world champion dropped out of the tour circus. Clearly seeking a change from the grind of constant solicitation, Slater jumped on a boat trip proposed by *Surfer* and went on to co-produce *The September Sessions* with Emmett Malloy. To hear his mates in the DVD bonus commentaries, he wasn't the only one burned-out by the scene and eager to get away. Quite a six-pack showed up: Kelly, Dorian, Machado, Luke Egan, Ross Williams, and, basically saying you're not going without me, Brad Gerlach. *The September Sessions* finds the group alone on magical reefs, some known, some name-them-yourself, in the Metawais off Sumatra. All but about four of the video's 28 minutes cover the sessions in question, with the odd shot of flat pirogues echoing the surfboard form and the little bit left catching seasicky boredom cut by the wondrous privilege of slipping off the boat to surf secret perfection. Kelly's occasional voice-overs emotionally frame what's happening on screen: "I was traveling, doing all these ... things apart from riding waves and being exactly where I want to be."

There at last, interestingly, the freedom of the surfing veers almost to responsibility: how can you let waves like that go when a week later you'll be back opening a new Quiksilver outlet or signing paper? It's fun to see that even these guys get surfed out and need to break up tiring days with bodyboards and sublime, surprisingly photogenic bodysurfing. Malloy's cuts lie tight with a musical menu sensitively adapted to the flow and surprise of the wave action. The primary interest is the "Sessions," of course: just surfing, no "rules and jerseys and numbers," with a relaxed air to things and particular nods again to Slater for, among much else, the endless barrel past the camera that opens the movie, and Machado, who turns what might seem like a handicap, that lankiness, to rubbery advantage in his sinuous carving and slackly cool pullouts. The second word of the title is equally important, though. Johnson's previous movie begins with and lingers on a kid's first times out, seeking encouragement from elders and discovering what it all means. *The September Sessions* implicitly looks backward from its position very emphatically on the other side of summer. Starved for encouragement of a different kind, these boys, now men, find it by plunging again into that pure meaning.

"It's still there if you're willing to look for it," says Chris Malloy in *One California Day*. Referring to the intact enchantment of the state, he could also be evoking that magic even a Slater can misplace but that any surfer can find again just by taking the time. In their 2007 video Jason Baffa and Mark Jeremias scour what many might consider the least likely of places to look, a Golden State that's become a kind of tepid nowhere on the world surfing map and which is everywhere synonymous with crowds, traffic, and McMansions. Yet as they cruise a thousand miles of coast they find at least eight figures who do get it and suggest that they are emblematic of more. Richly different individuals from 20 to 70, they share surfing's old-time religion, with its tolerant simplicities and generous connections. Conscious of being part of an historical continuum and not the summit of creation, they share the conviction that experiencing the instant matters more than to be seen experiencing it. Two years before *One California Day* the Baffa-shot and -directed *Singlefin: Yellow* spoke to the same sentiments. Shaping the eponymous vintage 9'6" from a template created by his father, El Segundo's Tyler Hatzikian sends it down south to shortboard wizard Beau Young (and not co-incidentally, surf family scion), who will take it around the block and in turn move it along to another surfer, and so on, for a total of six-plus sets of hands and feet from Australia through Japan and Hawaii. Before the next leg the surfers talk about their surfing lives in their most narrow and broadest senses, and gradually find their way with Yellow. In the case of Bonga Perkins that means the two of them eating some heavy stuff at Backdoor Pipeline before finally coming to an understanding. Yellow is the descendant of the communal green board in *Thicker Than Water*; it's interesting that, neighbors on the spectrum, the two colors share much despite flagrantly different outward appearances. As in the earlier film, the board represents a kind of connective spiritual tissue for surfers of distinctly varied technique, temperament, and personal background. A link to a common past, it is a shared platform for a certain solidarity of soul and purpose across undeniable lines of difference, and reminder of what unifies rather than divides those who paddle out each morning.

As the first word of its title hints, *One California Day* is about surfing as a whole and not a series of confining compartments set off by style or board length, filthy localism or the arrogant parochialism of age that says the era you surf(ed) in is the only one that counts. In *Yellow* Hatzikian said "sometimes you get pinned into … a certain type of surfing; it's good to mix it up." "It's just surfing," add the pair of innovative ride-anything young Orange Countians Alex Knost and Tyler Warren, freed by their open negotiations with the past and impatient with prescriptive labels like retro, soul, and high-performance. To acoustic guitar that reminds you the Sandals were a California band, the film's opening includes the now classic figure of accelerated traffic in the perpetual SoCal Carmageddon. But over this and gorgeous 16mm contrasting shots of the state's still glorious natural setting comes the reassuring voice of a young Skip Frye closing in on 70. The two generations he represents with the great, and iconoclastic, Joel Tudor set the tone with their reminder that "any time you paddle out you become part of a much larger picture." Jeremias and Baffa will present that composite picture as they travel the state, visiting the O.C.'s Knost and Warren, and with Jimmy Gamboa for a surprisingly upbeat look at a Malibu of friendly lineups and convivial ghosts. The Central Coast brings the inspiring country boy Malloys and Joe Curren of the free surfing Rincon royalty line. Shaper Tyler Hatzikian road trips us north to check in with the Noll dynasty, tending the guttering flame of redwood board tradition in damp Crescent City. Yellow's proud father Tyler follows further lines of continuity south to Dale Velzy and, when the moustachioed legend passes, a commemorative ceremony addressed by Bruce Brown and an impressively attended paddle-out funeral.

While the surfing globe once turned on a California-Hawaii axis, it was a daunting and original challenge to set a surf movie there in 2007. Looking back on that often forgotten history is certainly part of the method. "The five star boat trip to Indo" would be the easier choice, Chris Malloy admits, but it can be more fun—because more hard won—to find real adventure in your own backyard. Recounting a ten-mile DIY "staycation" in *Stoked and Broke*, young contemporary Cyrus Sutton would certainly agree. It's a question of attitude. "The further off, the nearer the surface," wrote Thoreau. "The nearer home, the deeper." Or as he wrote elsewhere in his journal, "it takes a man of genius to travel in his own country."[75] In the cold, kelpy green Baffa and Jeremias offer a series of subtle West Coast pleasures that get under your skin, like young Warren inverting things to project punkish cool tap-dancing across the longboard in the small right at Blackies; he correctly evokes earlier California homeboys Dewey Weber and Steve Bigler, even if an even more precise analogy might be the faraway footwook of late '60s Aussie imp Kevin Brennan. Starting out with Malloy at the family farm near Ojai, you forget there can be fifth generation Californians; from a clan around that long, they're the right guys to underline the full historical and geographical identity of their home state with a rugged surfari to Baja. The outrigger strapped to the van allows access to a perfect unnamed point break; more poetically, it recalls the historical DNA of every surf trip in the great migrations of the Pacific islands.

By luck main shooting was under way when a sizeable swell rolled in, offering rare size and volume to spots like Rincon and Santa Barbara's Sandspit. It's moving to watch the younger Curren in action and hear him, unassuming, go on about his exceptional family and the tension they know as well as any between surfing and being famous for surfing. Its title suggesting each day's little part in time's long sweep, *One California Day* opens to the scene from Brown's *Slippery When Wet* when the mailbox at the Velzy & Jacobs shop symbolically delivers an invitation to a way of life; it draws to a conclusion after Dale's funeral, the whole surfing family in attendance. Afterwards, while next generation shaper Hatzikian makes his way north along the coast at sunset, it starts to rain. Slippery when wet, the visual language is eloquent as each individual drop plops heavily into growing rivulets that slip off to join the sea. Prefacing the credits, surfer Devon Howard's discreet narration delicately underlines the theme of cyclic renewal. In the rhythmic rise and fall, a lone surfer scans the horizon, then paddles for a wave born long before it rolled into this coast at that moment.

Perhaps because their very agenda involves a certain graceful, grateful patience, videos originating in surfing's so-called "retro movement" have been among those offering the most subtle and lasting pleasures. Contrast with the noisy energy of the alternative may have something to do with it as well. In the larger picture, they have little more than niche appeal compared with the frenetic grab of louder films made for a vastly larger youth-driven audience and featuring the hyperactively spectacular, skate-inspired surfing of each new generation since the early '90s. Each new generation, that is, plus Kelly Slater. Since the Duke no one has more iconically dominated surfing for so long a period. Slater won eleven world titles from 1992 to 2111 while essentially creating the profession of video pro with appearances in different productions well north of 100, and all this time still managing to communicate enough of the gentle soul surfer ethos to lodge comfortably within Jack Johnson's laid-back cinematic vision. No one has more right to see no distinction between the two than Kelly, as he indicates on screen in *Waveriders*. Once, though, surfing's major billboard and only true household name was just the cute kid who brought a welcome end to some suburban lawn goof-around boxing gone a little rough with the slightly plaintive bleat, "Let's go video some surfing!" That scene comes from Taylor Steele's landmark 1992 independent production *Momentum*. It's a very rare change of tone in a film devoting only three of its supercharged 37 minutes to something other than a soundtrack of rampaging punk and the point-and-shoot videotaping of high performance surfing. High performance as in very high, since the subject of Steele's movie is the hyper-intense wave work of what would soon be called the New School. Brought into this circle through childhood pal Rob Machado, the 20-year-old Steele assembled young guns like Machado, Slater, Chris Malloy, Ross Williams, and Shane Dorian. *Momentum* is their graduation party: only the best parts of their best rides shot straight-on from the sand with zero in-water work and, beyond the grainy opening credits closeout wave and one brief creaky wipeout, no slow motion. But for a generation of grommets, Sprung Monkey and Bad Religion jack-hammering over a festival of wild snapbacks, airs, and floaters, who cared? How radical was it to be these guys?

If in fact New School surfing was, like all innovation, less an abrupt turning point than part of a continuum —in this case running through surfers like Martin Potter and Cheyne Horan—*Momentum* helped make it feel Totally New. With his full-speed-ahead montage of intense, unfinished snippets of longer rides, Steele was certainly responding to reduced attention spans. He furthermore kept things simple: California-Mexico-Hawaii, a sequence of mini-chapters announced by no frills titles ("Shane Dorian," "Baja," "Secret Break"), a roaring bad attitude earscape, glue-footed surfers relentlessly shredding and busting airs. As Keith Beattie notes, "Steele made a virtue of ... his unsophisticated home video equipment"; one result is a presentation marked by the "wilful technical crudity" that Susan Sontag recognized in experimental filmmaking and which here suggests a defiant renewal of surfing's rough-edged marginality.[76] The skateboard-influenced moves and blunt presentation are as brutally in-your-face as the music and the title's unarguable physics. The kids dug it and imitators predictably followed. Brash, noisy, and popular, *Filthy Habits* had softened up viewers for what would be Steele's knock-out punch. After *Momentum* and its sequels full-blast visual and aural assault was more norm than exception. Asked in 2008 whether he might consider "pure surfing films a lost art" in the video era, John Severson referred to today's "wall-to-wall surfing with rap tracks." Perhaps regretting the dismissive air, he immediately conceded that "some might say these are finally 'pure' surf films."[77]

Severson's ambivalence is understandable. While most have the nuance of an adrenaline shot, certain videos broadly within the *Momentum* vein do simultaneously communicate the rebellious kick of early surfing movies and an alert, contemporary aesthetic temper. Going solo after a precocious career in the Taylor Steele stable, Australian Kai Neville put his finger to the zeitgeist's pulse and made three such films in 2009–2012. Much anticipated ("It's Finally Here," breathlessly announced the *Surfer* review by Stuart Cornuelle) and then rewarded (*Surfer* Poll Video of the Year), *Mödern Collective* introduced the New New School to the surfing world just as Steele had done with their predecessors two decades earlier. Here in what Nick Braithwaite calls "the surf video for a new generation," in *Lost Atlas* and *Dear Suburbia* (sic), he took the best of today's Air Patrol on the road for a series of short, intense sessions showcasing the most radical contemporary maneuvers, "rodeo flips," 360°s and more. We're talking guys just then blasting into their surfing maturity like Dane Reynolds, Dusty Payne, and Jordy Smith, as well as hot rookies like John John Florence, Kolohe Andino, and Margaret River super grom Jack Robinson. From arty black and white portraits of the principals, their impassive sculptural forms sheathed in cloudy undulations, the trance-like opening of *Modern Collective* announces the edgy newness of Neville's project by, ironically, sampling Timothy Leary's half-century old "turn on, tune in, drop out" monologue: "If you're over the age of 40 I'm not sure you should listen to this record." Playful, feisty, sincere, this epigraph and Leary's eerily calm follow-ups about the Philosopher's Stone and other airy matters aid in the creation of the film's vaguely mystical atmosphere, its slightly "off" existential tingle. Occasional sound and image distortions add to the mix, along with unsettling editing shifts and a constantly surprising synth punk/electronic pop soundtrack cut deliciously at one moment by the Castaways' "Liar, Liar."

That selection accompanies the first of the video's twelve unnarrated sections/sessions, "In the Woods." The French forest in question fronts a shorebreak far from the tubular ideal. The point's not wave perfection, though, since sloppy onshore conditions are in fact the ticket when the whole idea is to ramp up repeatedly for the next two seconds of sublime aerial adventure; it's fun asking if, evoking the "squared circle" of the Philosopher's Stone, the film's triangular logo and on-screen crystal pyramid are there to evoke with a wink the difficult, ultimately rewarding alchemical transformation of such four foot leaden wedges into gold? In any case, Neville usually bides his time through a number of unsuccessful attempts to stick a move before the money shots start rolling in. Due to their historical context, the earlier quantum leaps of Slater and company were more eye-catchingly new than what this crew offers. But even after two decades of ultra-progressive surfing it's hard not to be impressed by the gyroscopic torsion and gravity-defiance of these maniacs seemingly able, on top of everything else, to right themselves on their toy boards in the most impossible conditions. Even if its plucky verbal enactment of torch passing strays towards pomposity, there's enough new here to justify the wrap-up graphic "This is not THE END … This is THE BEGINNING."

Alternating full-speed and slow motion, Neville's 16mm image is usually razor-edged and handsomely color rich even if the video recalls Steele's first film in its lack of water shots. While Dane Reynolds gets a section to himself—in a hazy black and white echoing the sepia vapor aesthetic of certain transitional shots—the organization is generally by session as we bounce about to favorites like Morocco, Australia, and Indonesia. The title shifts attention away from individual performances, but standout moments do come from a Jordy Smith directing flight operations in Western Australia, Dion Agius on some lefts during a sunset session, and Reynolds, low-key but consistently charismatic whether wet or not. The brief non-surfing sequences tend to address interactions within the "collective" more than the locations themselves, which are often reduced to a couple of rice paddy shots or an emblematic kangaroo. The overly serious feel of the whole seems calculated; filming a bare minimum of downtime goofing-off, Neville steers wide of the comic set piece to concentrate not only on the best new surfing but on the off-center vibe of the generation it speaks most directly to. From "Beautiful Decay" through "Here Is Nowhere" and "Terra Firma / Sea (Antonym)," the section titles catch a certain post-modern ease with the instabilities of irony and contradiction. The Millennial "Parallel Universe" is also a place where shared generational identity can paradoxically be defined at least in part by an extreme individualism. In Neville's film a "collective" functions together but to perform the most showy "watch me" surfing moves, where the point is repeatedly to detach oneself literally from the wave and visually from the performance of others as an autonomous locus of pure action, attitude, and image.

Bradley Corbett could be writing about any of Neville's videos and not just the beautiful *Lost Atlas* and its sometimes bratty cast when he said that "it busies itself defining the aesthetic of now. From graphic design, to apparel, to surfboard design, to music, to the candid conversations between the surfers, to the way these young millionaires flit about the globe, the viewer gets a distinct sense of where this all is and where it is going." To get there, though, it seems at times that Neville is straining too hard for effects. *Dear Suburbia* (2012) has won the same big prizes as *Mödern Collective* but is a lesser film largely for this reason, though a certain intellectual and moral disconnect doesn't help either. Begin with the good stuff, though, and there is a lot. The videographer certainly made some strong choices, notably widening the collective to include guys like cool daddy Craig Anderson, John John, and grom phenom Jack Robinson, and bringing on Rick Rifici for some spectacularly rich and expressive water photography. There's more on the surfing below, but the sessions are all outstanding, and one breathtaking.. Leaving behind the already interesting techno and mutant disco of *Mödern Collective*, Neville's soundtrack is a real bijou, with familiar surprises from the last three decades, including "Just Like Honey" and Joy Division's "Atmosphere" bringing on the, well, atmosphere. On the sinister side Nick Cave's "Red Right Hand" and John Maus's eerie Tears for Fears-flavored reprise of Body Count's "Cop Killer" chip in a note of creepy menace that's inexplicably just right to accompany luxuriantly shot state-of-the-art surfing. Though maybe its appropriateness can be partially explained by Maus himself, who argues that "any worthwhile political or artistic agenda should be about seeking an undoing of the situation as it stands."[78] That seems to be what Neville is after in his insistent positioning of surfing as everything that the eponymous "suburbia" isn't.

Fine—in fact, name a surf film in which that idea is not at least implicit. The problem with *Dear Suburbia,* isn't its message but the hipster art school aesthetic Neville stretches to breaking point in trying to communicate it. Getting things started, a weird dirge ushers in, variously, a wooden Dane Reynolds wrapped in Old Glory, a stuffed animal, a broken Barbie, a dog on a chair, and a dry pool. Constructed on the principle that the banal becomes hauntingly strange the second it's framed, these and similarly blunt shots of blank house faces and hollow rooms are easy shorthand for arid souls and lives, especially next to the companionship and colorful high emotion of the surfline. The culprit, though, is less this tic than those recurring art installations, the ironic "shrines" Neville uses to mark the border between certain sessions. An undraped young lady, household objects like Mickey Mouse ears and donuts, such phallic knickknacks as garden hoses, baguettes, and bananas, they assemble themselves periodically into Dada-esque sculptures speaking presumably about twisted, frustrated dear queer suburbia. While it's hard to tell whether this is *Dali for Idiots* or just a hoot, it certainly communicates a high degree of self-satisfaction and contributes loads of needless irritation to 43 minutes of film. The umlaut in *Mödern Collective* was harmless visual affectation; the title of the later film finishes with a provocative comma that's useless unless to suggest a letter's salutation, but that can't be for there's no real communication here, given the film's cultivated attitude of easy, self-regarding superiority. Plus there's the old brick problem for those who live in glass houses. It's an old school reflection, but where does a film bracketed by a half-dozen prominently displayed corporate logos get off critiquing our shallow conventional lives? "Finally, Capitalism and Art have been blended in a seamless coherent whole," flows the vitriol of a wildcat blog review. "The distinction between content, meaning and commerce has become invisible: personality becomes brand, the perfect trojan horse to mind fuck youth under the guise of anti-suburbia."[79]

Happily, there is the glorious surfing, which in each new Neville film seems kicked up another implausible notch. Coded by sheep and fog, an interesting session finds Craig Anderson tearing in New Zealand, and Kolohe Andino in a motley wetsuit and the minuscule Robinson conduct a recital at what looks like Yallingup. Starring Florence and Reynolds, the Japan sequence is something else, though. Heavy, extremely fast typhoon-generated tubing right-handers set the stage. This is not the stuff for an aerial show, though we do get two or three. The interest here is deep play within the barrel punctuated by moves that seem to echo changelessly across the decades the powerful "involvement surfing" of Peterson and Young. Rising high, slipping low, accelerating and slowing at will, Dane and John carve the wave face then occasionally drop off, notching neatly again back into the pocket. The small handful of airs feels pro-forma; these guys communicate more joy, it seems, in playing out the implications of a powerful, beautifully formed tube. Neville knew what he had, placing these the best five minutes of the movie at the end. So doing, he seems to be courting the old dichotomy between the dynamic continuous precision of the blue water sculpted line and the spasmodic moments of abrupt display and explosive grace that are ultra-progressive surfing. We've heard it before, riding with the wave or against it, an endless restatement of a tension that's not ever going to go away in the surf movie or in the surfing it serves. The same can be said, of course, of the recurrent dust-up, inherent in the choices driving *Dear Suburbia*, between disinterested surfing cool and the commerce/convention nexus.

Among other things, Neville worked with Taylor Steele on the funny, deconstructive *Stranger Than Fiction*, and the director of *Momentum* produced *Mödern Collective*. The parallel with Steele's early work has been frequently made, and after its splashy start one can only wish Neville as rich and varied a subsequent career. *Momentum* pushed generational buttons in part because of its napalm soundtrack and uncompromising, monolithic energy. Thanks to Slater's first pro tour crown, the filmmaker's audience was understandably curious about the exciting young posse already called the *Momentum* Generation, and

Steele unsurprisingly revisited this territory in two sequels. Yet over time the director would mature with his audience and their stars. Re-thinking his reflexive dissing of "wall-to-wall surfing with rap tracks," Severson's follow-up could speak to Steele's career: "Evolving is the key word here. Look for change." Since the mid-'90s that career has continually evolved towards greater depth and complexity in narrative strategy and character development. While the technical advancement of his work has brilliantly kept pace, Steele recently claimed that "flashier edits and cooler angles" are secondary, articulating what over time had become evident in his work, that his focus had increasingly turned to "making movies with more of a story behind them."[80]

For Steele the parallel attempt "to humanize these athletes and make their lives more relatable"[81] would begin very timidly with his third video *Focus* (1994). At a point where, terrific as it is, the sheer charge of the surfing alone may have started to ring limitingly hollow, Slater, Machado, Shane Dorian, the Malloy brothers, Taylor Knox, and the other larger-than-life wave heroes begin, interestingly, to double up in the films as hapless shoreside civilians. In *Focus*, instead of just the spare identifying label on the screen, Benji Weatherley and Greg Browning clown around, respectively, on a skateboard and in a laundromat dryer before the mini-chapters devoted to their surfing. By the end of the 1990s the dudes are still filmed the same way surfing like the same gods on the same mid-size shorebreaks, but their exploits are now framed by playful narrative structures and quick brushstrokes of personality. *The Show* (1997) features the crew in dumb thumbnail movie or TV parodies (*The Godfather*, *Rocky*, *Twilight Zone*). The next, *Loose Change*, begins with a thunderthroat

Missing, director Taylor Steele (2013). Australia-based cinematographer Tim Wreyford films Mick Fanning as Taylor Steele ponders the next shot. Tobias Bolaños International Airport, Costa Rica, en route for someplace (Ted Grambeau/Adventures in Light).

announcer declaiming, "They are the most talented surfers in the world, but can you imagine for one second what their lives would be like if they never surfed?" Somewhere between horsing around and a school play, the corny "skits" that develop these thin conceits (as well as the outtakes under the closing credits) do start to humanize the best surfers in the world: game but much better on a board than the boards, they're a bunch of frisky young guys having fun and struggling just like you and me in front of a camera. Viewing Steele's films in order is like time-lapse photography—you're watching a dozen surfers do more amazing things each year and a dozen youngbloods grow up. It's funny, though, that the filmmaker who did more than anyone to introduce elite surfing's Gen × to the world would do so in ways that finally recall the feeling of the classic surf movie. We want to see our best surfers both as superhuman denizens of the deep and as simple human beings, and sometimes specifically as awkward, goofy youngsters who crack up when they're together. Since the days of Bud Browne surf cinéastes have been happy to oblige. Maybe the top performer/just a guy combination works because that's what most real surfers, even the best, remain. You believe Mick Fanning in *Missing* when he say that "once I step away from that, I'm just your everyday person."

More active professionally than ever in the new century, Steele is taking his camera on the road to destinations so fresh—i.e., Iceland, Peru, and Vietnam for *Castles in the Sky*—that the place seems at times as much the point as the sumptuous waves. To a soundtrack that has you taking notes during the credits, the cinematography of Alex Berger and Todd Heater yields rich, densely colored hyper-slow motion in the service of a surfing become over time expressive of far more than just raging hormones. Increasingly complex characterization comes into play, encouraged by more sophisticated, thoughtful narrative framing. Based on just such an intriguing narrative proposition, Steele's 2013 *Missing* asks what happens when we take a regimented-to-the minute competitive pro like Fanning out of his over-scheduled existence and away to a handful of exotic surprise destinations. What happens is an impressionistic jumble of experiences that include some shyly under-exploited Pamplona bull-running (recalling *Waves of Change* cultural filler), a very careful chill-out with an immense silverback in Rwanda, and a visit to the ruins of the star's ancestral home in Ireland. Punctuating the land scenes are high-powered surfing, alone or trading barrels with such as John John Florence at a chopper-accessed secret dream break, Joel Parkinson at Cloudbreak, and Tom Curren, whose cameo shows he can still bring it. Shooting for a compressed three weeks in seven different countries, Steele offers moments of stunningly nuanced visual beauty, particularly when playing with hue and texture where sky meets water; it's not going too far to reference the delicate visual rush of a Turner or Jane Wilson canvas. His now more neo-folk and world-flavored soundtrack ear is again faultless, and craft of all sort shines quietly throughout. The opening images shift abruptly from a ghostly extraterrestrial form glimpsed through a milky cloud to the teeming human warmth of a dark Rwandan hut with an exuberant crowd of villagers surrounding the slightly overwhelmed Fanning. In a similar way, the film's rich aural and visual palette deliberately cuts at times to spectral black and white and distorted sound effects that communicate something of the weird nowhereness of airports and customs—and perhaps as well the too-extensive stretches of our lives lost in translation and not given to the here and now.

The film's flaw is its casting. As a surfer, what's not to like about the three-time world champ? No featherweight, Fanning conveys a solid physical presence that makes his gravity-defying vaults and spins all the more impressive, while allowing him to bully his way through a closing barrel. Unfortunately, when not in the water he can make the 36 minutes of movie time drag. Mick Fanning comes off as the nicest guy in the world, but this is a film about a kidnappee blindsided by the unexpected. It demands a more charismatic central personality capable of surprising the viewer, and himself. What's really gone missing is that necessary spark. Wrapping things up, Fanning trots out a series of banalities: "the experience as a whole was just incredible ... the trip of a lifetime ... an experience I'll tell my grandkids about." The auteur who cast Rob Machado in *The Drifter* certainly knows charisma when he sees it. Despite a different premise, the 2009 movie's equally about the need "to break out of that comfort zone, to truly leave home behind," but the soulful burn of Machado's eyes rises from depths lacking in *Missing*. The protagonist of the latter lets down what is otherwise top-level film conception and realization.

Steele's ceaseless tinkering with storytelling has continued with the refinement of an approach to film production pioneered by Scott Dittrich and, as of *Tales of the Seven Seas*, his assemblage of the work of multiple cameramen in multiple locations. On May 2, 2012, Steele and director Nathan Myers mustered 25 filmmakers to shoot a film called *Here & Now* in which all of the action takes place across the globe in one single day and the title signals where the best of those places is. The same year it was on to a radically different narrative approach for the release of the entrancing *This Time Tomorrow*. Though Steele didn't have to convince anyone but himself, it's almost too bad with a pitch like this: a monster swell has risen in the South Pacific—let's race two surfers northeast through Tahiti, Mexico, California, and finally on to Alaska, surfing essentially the same wave as it and they make their way halfway around the world. Again, the idea wasn't new—bodyboard wizard Mike Stewart tracked a swell north in 1996, *In God's Hands* fictionalized a similar pursuit, and *Chasing the Swell* used an Oahu-Mavericks-Todos Santos series to structure a look at paddle-in big wave surfing—but Steele would bring it to more enthralling cinematic life. The storm swell he needed rose in late August, 2011. Overnight, even with plans in place, it was red alert for Dave Rastovich and Craig Anderson trying to stay awake for eight days and 20,349 miles. Two of the world's best-loved free surfers—one-time competitive pros now happily out of that circuit—they stumble off with full quivers to Tahiti, where the Billabong Pro is milking every drop from the swell. Don't ask how Rasta manages (most of) a ride unbelievable even to his partner—one of the most beautifully filmed ultra-slow motion barrels ever at the endlessly shot Teahupoo—though the more typical vibe of the film comes when the two have to "scrounge up a boat" during the media circus and find a quiet right for themselves.

With some eventual help from friends like Kelly Slater and Chris Del Moro, the surfing in Tahiti, on a mud road Mexican point break, at Malibu, or off a bear-happy Alaska coast (where the starch has definitely gone out of the swell) includes the required aerials and 180° snaps off the top even if in general it tends more towards energy-conserving efficient lines. Plus Rastovich looks like he invented bodysurfing. With a few effective color-rich brushstrokes Steele culturally contextualizes the hopscotching of our weary pair. A whirring computer graphic of the advancing swell (eerily recalling newscast treatments of tsunamis) and intermittent "technical" on-screen indicators ("Day 4 Mexico 9:15 a.m. 15,663 miles") contrast neatly with the rumpled humanity of Ando and Rasta, whose raggedy good-natures more than communicate the "next level strangeness" of the whole thing. Rastovich's dazzling smile keeps lighting up the place. The fatigue's zeroing in, though, and, Biblically, it's only on the seventh day that these surf gods can rest. Craig curled up for a snooze *literally on PCH at 3 a.m.* is one of those moments you remember from surf films.

This Time Tomorrow offers a new cinematic take on surfing while inscribing itself wholeheartedly within a long tradition. Alliteration furthers the title's suggestions of echoing continuity. Perhaps the more so because uncommented, shots on the Pacific Coast Highway and the rush hour crowding of Malibu's acutely familiar combers push nostalgia buttons back through Ted Jepsen, *Gidget*, and so many others. Most importantly, the video taps into the mythic resonance that made *The Endless Summer* unforgettable. Who after all is this pair of surfers, a regular and a goofyfoot, if not Hynson and August with dreads and a very today jet-lag buzz? Peering through a glass, darkly, a half-century earlier, Brown's film dimly sensed the world of globalized economic, cultural, and environmental interdependence fully enacted here. Where *The Endless Summer* enlisted—by resisting—the seasonal myth, the later film seeks meanings in its daily counterpart, the solar cycle in which "this time" and "tomorrow" cancel themselves in a kindred urge to stop time, to make the present "endless." At some level this is the dream of anyone who's ever paddled through the soup. Surfing "each new expression of the same storm," the protagonists of *This Time Tomorrow* incarnate a philosophical fantasy inherent as well in the quest of August and Hynson: to make possible the Heraclitan impossibility of stepping twice into the same river, and twice onto the same wave.[82]

This Time Tomorrow, director Taylor Steele (2012). After a muddy slog through waist-deep water along the Mexican coast, Steele filming a peerless point break. The waves to themselves, Craig Anderson, Dave Rastovich, and Alex Gray traded tubes for five hours (Todd Glaser/A-Frame).

After the independently produced *Momentum*, Steele gradually developed a series of sponsorship arrangements that don't seem to have compromised his maturation into the leading creative force in the field. He is a highly contemporary individual talent who has honored a long surf film tradition by pushing its classic recurring elements (exciting breaks, wave pyrotechnics, striking individuals, travel, cultural context, music) into new, unexpected areas. It's clear he knows "we're not curing cancer … we're making surf movies,"[83] but it's also apparent in his exceptional body of work that he never takes the genre any less than seriously. Yet where Steele is simultaneously most alive to today's wired world and most faithful to the age-old truth of surfing as profoundly personal experience may finally be in the generous way he has encouraged a generation of surfers to make their own films. Co-produced with Nathan Myers, clearly parallel to the experience of *Here and Now, Innersection* is at once an evolving online contest and a film declined in now yearly versions. The pair's alertly modern idea was to solicit three minute action profiles from surfer/filmmaker duos (or larger teams), put them online at *innersection.tv*, ask viewers to rate them, and then bring the best together in a feature video. For the final step the film's buyers vote for the best section and a prize of a $100,000. The producers received 150 mini-videos for the first film in 2011, gradually winnowing to a tight 25 that includes sections by big names like Joel Parkinson, Craig Anderson, Clay Marzo, John John Florence, and Kelly Slater, but also some very hot (relative) unknowns. Among the latter, the first edition turned a spotlight on winning team Matt Meola and director/editor Elliot Leboe (who would in turn direct the winning 2012 clip with Albee Layer). Though underwritten by O'Neill, the puckish Meola was still "just some surfer from Maui"[84] until the film set off a flow of offers. The buzz online and in surf publications has been abundant and not only because *Surfer* and *Surfing Life* are part of the long sponsor list. In the very young tradition of social media and online democratization, *Innersection* is an excitingly visionary experiment in the crowd sourcing of surf film content and quality.

It was of course only a matter of time until the urge to film surfing and the potential of the Internet would intersect. Such are the changes ahead that, despite the inundation of responses to "surfing" on YouTube, for the most part that potential is still largely unimagined today. Steele and others, though, have taken important early steps in exploiting the confluence of the web and the local mall availability of high quality digital film, sound, and editing technology. In the summer of 2015, for example, RED Digital Cinema and *Surfer* launched a promising by-invitation surf film competition to be judged in part by online viewers. Among many other things, the web portals of the specialist magazines regularly post individual and commercial efforts, encouraging surf community dialogue and reaction, while such outlets as the Surf Channel and Surfer.TV warehouse vast amounts of accessible video footage. Billabong's participatory XXL awards evolve in near-real time as swells and surfers hook up, and the ASP—now WSL—regularly streams contests and offers wide access to past performances; over six million viewers (a third on mobile devices) tuned into the WSL YouTube broadcast platform for the Billabong Pipe Masters in December, 2014.[85] Hotshot iconoclast/walking brand Dane Reynolds turns out little videos with tart design, personality, and the dynamite surfing of himself and crew, uploading them to his personal site alongside art, musing, photos, and things generally Dane. Kai Neville has gone elaborately in something like that direction with What Youth, a hybrid lifestyle/video hub and experimental locus for the restless, prolific energy of Neville and others. The many quality surfing-oriented blogs and sites include Korduroy.tv and Liquid Salt; while the latter does not feature surfing videos, it does foster a thoughtful, non-sectarian environment conducive to the best filmmaking.

Corporate light years away, it's no accident that GoPro is one of the most prominent sponsors for *Innersection*. Obviously, such a project means opportunities for high visibility use of its popular camera technology and new smartphone apps. With the 2014 IPO, however, it's become apparent that GoPro is moving beyond its wildly successful camera sales to position itself as a major media outlet. According to a pertinent piece by James Trew, the company moved over seven million units in 2011–2013, and some 6000 uploads from the company's equipment pour in daily. Already "sitting on a content golden goose," CEO Nicholas Woodman recently signed up a team of 100 performers from across the extreme sports spectrum, including Kelly Slater. In the hands of the right athletes," observes Ryan Mac in *Forbes*, "the footage shot on a point-of-view action camera is viral crack." With its own in-flight entertainment channels and video-gaming content links, GoPro's the leading brand channel on Facebook, Instagram, and YouTube. Yet as active as GoPro is today, the IPO re-boot's being read as a sharp turn into new directions perhaps not yet even fully clear to the company itself. What seems obvious is that surfing will play an important role. The outfit conceived on an Indo surfari sponsors the World Surf League, smaller competitions, and its own surf team. While its efforts necessarily target a huge audience across a wide span of sports and outdoor activities, the question is less whether GoPro will move beyond raw footage and the "super selfie" to the more elaborate surf movie form, but when and how.

For the moment, though, the most exciting interface between the surfing world and the new technologies remains *Innersection*. Its wonderful title works on many levels, from the wave section to the discrete cinematic parcels that combine to form the video, and perhaps most saliently to the punning notion of intersection. For in the web site and finished film, that is exactly what Steele and Myers are facilitating, a digital crossroads where the acutely private moment and the desire to share and publically celebrate that moment meet. One of the most remarkable qualities of *Innersection 2011* is how, composed of 25 different sections, surfers, directors, and musical selections, it nevertheless functions as a coherent whole. Signing the final product, Steele worked closely with each team to re-edit, vary wave choice, shuffle musical selections.

The toughest logistics ever, he's said, but the work paid off, as just one small example of countless effective montage and musical choices may show. Color values tilted to near black and while, the final left-breaking barrel out of which Joel Parkinson charges segues into the similar tones of a shadowy corridor along which a skateboarding John John Florence completes the left to right visual glide. There's diversity *and* flow as one generation hands off to the next, tour vet to superkid, one hallway to another, soaring alt-rock lift to dirty street punk, surfboard to skateboard. Working with dozens of different artists of surf and film, trusting proportion to emerge from difference, Steele and Myers tease this kind of harmonic echoing and variation repeatedly out of their dealings with a vast range of divergent notes. Refusing the status quo in their frequent changes to *Innersection*, furthering "the next revolution in surf filmmaking,"[86] they also send lines of intersection back to its earliest days. The surf movie has always been a collaborative experience, mobilizing the intensely personal experience and expression of surfers, the filmmaker's interpretative intermediary presence, and the viewer's infusion of life and meaning into what is still only projected light through the catalytic act of viewing. Today clicks and blog discussions may have largely replaced whoops and whistling bottle caps, but the surf community viewers inhabit remains as real as the multi-purpose room at John Adams Junior High School that fall evening in 1953.

~ 3 ~

In Hollywood's Hands
The Feature Film Surfing Narrative

> By that long scan of waves, myself call'd back, resumed upon myself,
> In every crest some undulating light or shade....
> —Walt Whitman, "By that Long Scan of Waves"

On August 22, 2012, the Big Kahuna died. In the mid–Fifties Terry Tracy left a stable position in banking to throw together a scrap-lumber hut on the beach in Malibu with a band of surfing originals including Da Cat Himself, Miki Dora. Brentwood's own Kathy Kohner, five-foot and 15, somehow infiltrated the Pit Crew, and, famously, her tales of shooting the curl as the group's adopted mascot would find their way into her father's 1957 novel and eventually onto the big screen in the 1959 Hollywood hit *Gidget*. In fact, a summer or two before the film came out county authorities demolished Tubesteak's digs, after which he took a job driving a delivery truck and finally retired in Orange County. Kathy went off to college in Oregon, married Marvin Zuckerman, and raised a family; over seventy today, she greeted diners for years at Duke's Malibu, where her job was to tell stories from back in the day. The real life narrative arc of Terry and Kathy roughly parallels that of the film, with Kahuna finally going back to work, Gidget together at last with Moondoggie, and in the closing shot a beach that once brimmed with muscles and bikinis now back-to-school empty. Both stories speak of carefree youth and a necessary reckoning with the adult world, of enchanted parentheses and inexorable Septembers.

The tensions of these real and screen lives— between the perceived flatness of a conventional model of existence and the vivid personal freedoms and challenges of surfing— have in large part remained those of the film genre *Gidget* engendered. In the half-century since, from the *Beach Party* franchise and its Sixties spin-offs, through *Big Wednesday*, *North Shore*, *Blue Crush*, *Drift*, and many others, and on to *Chasing Mavericks* and *Perfect Wave* in 2012 and 2014, filmmakers have gone to the sand more than three dozen times to produce narratives either focused expressly on surfing as sport or obsessive life choice, or at least as significant background informing and directing the film's meaning. At very best, the critical and commercial results have been mixed. *Gidget* is a fondly remembered marker of American cultural history, *Point Break* remains a cult favorite a quarter century later, and, within the norms of theatrical release, several other films have created some convincing characters and attempted to address the surfing life with a modicum of respect, intelligence, and authenticity. It would be fair to say, though, that the genre has generated an imposing share of stinkers and that, unlike *The Endless Summer*, not a single Hollywood surfing narrative has attained truly lasting critical acclaim or monument status. The norm has been rather lackluster financial results even if, while not blockbusters, *Point Break* and *Gidget* were box office hits, and a number of others have done well commercially. Faced with the Hollywood version of their stoutly defended identity, surfers themselves have generally not approved of what they see as simplification, stereotyping, and outsider exploitation. While such readings can change over time—both *Gidget* and *Big Wednesday* having, for example, advanced from initial rejection to affection to, in memory's haze, near cult status—this attitude is not surprising. Just look at the chemistry of the relationship: on one hand we have the thin skin of a surfing subculture proud of its exclusiveness and quick on the insult for those perceived as pretenders, and on the other the tendency of Hollywood productions to dumb down to the lowest common denominator and stick to reliable one-size-fits-all formulas.

Yet while it's easy to come down on mass-entertainment surfing narratives, it's more interesting to keep an eye open to the meanings behind their attractive surfaces. This demands an open-minded critical viewing of the movies in question within their social and historical context and that of the changing surfing scene they at times accurately—and often inaccurately—reflect. Complex real world products at the juncture of art, entertainment, and commerce, they try with varying degrees of effort and success to come to terms with public images of surfing—from the scuzzy to the mythically romantic—and with some rough understanding of its elusive, shifting reality as chosen life, glamorous escape, empty style locus, art, sport, business. This is a busy intersection. The remarks to follow will address these and other parameters of the complicated and sometimes prickly relationship between Hollywood and surfing. Beyond the dazzling settings, wicked barrels, great tans, and dudespeak, beyond the wooden characterizations and predictable narrative patterns, films born of that union can speak at times with surprising—if not always intentional—pertinence to the larger society and to such themes as growing up, family and home, the seductive lure of commerce and appearance, and a world of dizzying social change, including serious questions of race, class, and gender. Hollywood's invitations to the multiplex are by their very nature inoffensive and consensual; when they venture into the tricky marginal space of the shore and the surfers who inhabit it, their meanings depend largely upon how they deal with the sense of subversive possibility suddenly freed there. While, admittedly, the films often only flirt with rebellion before looping back to obedience, the thematic upshot can occasionally be edgy and troubling. By virtue perhaps of an initial positioning further from the mainstream, certain of the several non-studio surf movie productions, either foreign in origin or low budget independents, have tended towards riskier thematic questionings and less tidy resolutions.

On April 10, 1959, *Gidget* simultaneously displayed the attractiveness of the beach and surf line setting, the intriguing nature of the sandy beatniks who ruled that space, and the compelling potential of the culture clash between their surfing world and that of the heroine's square parents. Before that time, wave riding appeared with extreme infrequency in general audience fictional cinema. On one hand, that's unsurprising for, beyond Hawaii and to a lesser degree Southern California, the general population was unfamiliar with the sport; for that matter, only when it abruptly picked up cultural speed in the 1950s was the surf community itself able to generate its own tiny self-referencing film industry. Yet when we look at some of the rare early cinematic appearances of surfing, what stands out is the obvious visual and narrative possibilities it made available to filmmakers. Only very occasionally do they seem to have recognized that potential. In 1923, for example, *The White Flower* starred Betty Compson as a young Hawaiian of mixed birth who falls in love, and into a love triangle, with a visiting American. In the vivid action drawing of Compson surfing that dominates the movie poster, the starlet's unrestrained tresses flying up at an angle evocatively parallel that of the white water splashing from her moving board to suggest a form of fusion with natural energies. As she aims forthrightly at the viewer, upright with arms spread and seemingly ready to embrace what comes, the breathless text invites us to "see Betty riding the surf" and "shocking us all with her hula!" In two other extant posters, Compson is pictured again surfing, though from a different angle, and dancing the hula. The film was shot in Honolulu, as a publicity photo of Compson makes clear, clad as she is in the same skimpy one-piece as in the poster and, the opposite of demure, gaily waving from a similar standing position just in front of Duke Kahanamoku and three of his brothers posed before their boards.

While the silent Paramount release is now considered officially lost,[1] the plot is well-known, and Compson's character certainly surfed in the film (as, pertinently, women in traditional Hawaiian society did). Such action no doubt helped embody cinematically both the

Poster, *The White Flower*, writer/director Julia Crawford Ivers (1923). Betty Compson portrays a Hawaiian woman who falls for a visiting American. Watch "Betty riding the surf" and "shocking us all with her hula!"

islands exoticism and impulsive willfulness of a character who is at one point tempted to kill her rival before, torn by guilt, deciding to end it all in the mouth of a volcano. True love wins out as the American's fiancée selflessly gives him up to the determined, deserving woman she recognizes as his real soul mate. Looking past the story conventions and the florid period melodrama, there is a kind of proto-feminist decisiveness and energy to this heroine in what is, significantly, one of the rare early films both written and directed by a woman (Julia Crawford Ivers). Surfing seems to play a role in that characterization. (Even practiced by a haole actress, the hula may as well, especially when seen as the Hawaiian cultural "resistance" identified by Momiala Kamahele.) While such a reading remains necessarily partial and circumstantial, it is tempting to view *The White Flower* as a distant precursor to films like *Gidget* and *Blue Crush* in its use of surfing both as a natural element of the young character's environment and as an act of symbolic significance in the creation of female identity.

In a different way, *The White Flower* is a precursor as well of a South Seas romantic adventure released nine years later, King Vidor's *Bird of Paradise*. The RKO production echoes the Pocahontas plot, with a yacht pulling into a remote Polynesian island, a similar love triangle, and the same smoking volcano. One way they differ, though, is in the lack of any surfing imagery in the second. After a dust-up with a shark, the film's American lead (Joel McCrea) and the local Polynesian princess (Dolores Del Rio) fall madly in love; in this case, she's the one who's otherwise promised, so the two slip away illicitly to a distant island, a place cumbersomely labeled "Paradise." Inevitably, the couple is run down and the hero injured, at which point the volcano goes off and the heroine is forced to save her people by satisfying that angry god. Lead Joel McCrea was an accomplished surfer, one of the first in the industry, and it's even said that he secured his part in this movie by teaching the movie's producer to surf.[2] Accordingly, one might imagine the enlistment of wave riding at least as local color (the case in the 1951 remake) and possibly, say, as signifier of a certain feminine strength and rebelliousness or of the Western hero's adoption of local ways. Instead, *Bird of Paradise* turns quickly from a few scene-setting outriggers to a conventional "forbidden love" story arc emphasizing eroticism (including a controversial nude swimming scene), fusional connection, and the white male's imposed linguistic and cultural dominance ("You're mine now"). Instructively, the numerous versions of the movie poster invariably place the couple together in a romantic embrace, whereas in those of *The White Flower* the heroine, drawn into a similarly intense relationship, nonetheless appears at all times alone and fully engaged in an autonomous activity with overtones of assertive cultural expression, whether it be dancing the hula or surfing.

During the emergence and institutionalization of Waikiki as a tourist destination and the later Tiki pop culture boom with its collective American dream of paradisiacal world of leisure and sensuality, several dozen films were set in Hawaii, where surfing was a colorful, visually entrancing, and readily available aspect of the cultural environment. Yet as the example of *Bird of Paradise* indicates, it was clearly difficult for industry professionals to think outside of standard visual and narrative conventions and place this intriguing activity meaningfully within their standard story constraints. While the Australian film *Tall Timbers* (1937) supported its lifesaving romance plot efficiently with location surfing footage, the best most films could manage was Waikiki to Diamond Head establishing shots or background stock of gliding surfers. *Waikiki Wedding* (1937) and *Hawaiian Nights* (1939), for example, used such footage for palmy atmosphere before turning to musical comedy doings that could occur anywhere. For the most part, if it existed at all on screen, surfing was part of a thin cultural veneer providing an initial sheen of exoticism before the film, again, got back to the business of its classical narrative patterns and characterizations. It's not coincidental that surfing became an appropriate subject in itself only when it had at last sufficiently entered white, mainstream American society. Before that, while it was a pleasure for tourists to watch and a fun enough amusement on vacation, surfing remained a colorful activity associated with the dark-skinned *otherness* of distant climes.

Curiously, the acting career of the indisputable face of surfing for decades, Duke Kahanamoku, finds little place for the remarkable skills that made his reputation or for anything close to the realities of the traditional culture he so perfectly embodied. Flush with Olympic gold, famous for highly publicized exhibitions on both mainland coasts and a daring rescue of eight people in heavy Newport Beach seas, the legendary surfer and swimmer was recruited into small supporting parts in a dozen Hollywood productions alongside actors like Robert Young and Henry Fonda. Despite the fact that a good two-thirds of these movies were set in the South Seas, only one in any way pretends to exploit his surfing ability. In a few uncredited seconds from the first minute or two of *The Black Camel*, a Charlie Chan mystery from 1931 set in Honolulu, Kahanamoku plays a beachboy giving surfing lessons. In others he's an Arab heavy, a trapper, a pirate. The opening voiceover of *Wake of the Red Witch* (1948) simulates sympathy for the white man's theft of the "idyllic peace and beauty of the South Pacific," but it's really about the rivalry between two white men, not to mention shirtless John Wayne killing a giant octopus. He's the Duke who counts. As the role was written, the local chieftain Kahanamoku portrays is interchangeable with an Apache. In any case, he never gets wet.

The studio execs may have stayed at the Royal Hawaiian and lived in the Malibu Colony, but using surfing in their films was another question. In the annexes and back workrooms of their studios, though, at least one band of the oddballs who drew the cartoons didn't hesitate. More than the specialist photographs of Doc Ball, more than the occasional newsreel or furtive background shot of waves in a feature film, if there is one sure sign that the word on surfing was getting out to the un-sandy masses, it's *Hawaiian Holiday*, a 1937 "Silly Symphony" from Walt Disney. Over eight minutes in length, it brings together the whole gang on the beach under a few scene-setting palm trees. Mickey strums Hawaiian tunes on ukulele, an undulating Minnie dances the hula, and Pluto wrangles with feisty crabs. Clearly the star, as the opening image makes clear, Goofy recklessly challenges surf which puts him through the spin cycle and pile drives him into dry land. With the typical extraordinary range of Disney's animation teams, the waves manage at once to be dumb funny, anthropomorphically nasty, and possessed of a frothy, sculpted loveliness drawn straight from Hokusai. Like endless other mini animated epics, this cartoon illustrates a variation on the timeless theme of the arrogant individual chastised by a recalcitrant natural world. While it is (speciously) considered the source of the term goofy-footed for surfers who, like its hero, lead with their right foot,[3] in fact *Hawaiian Holiday* says little more about the islands and surfing than that they were beginning to lodge in the public consciousness. Three years after the opening of Don the Beachcomber and two before the Golden Gate International Exposition Fair celebrating Polynesian peoples, that is a relevant cultural observation.

In fact, two full decades before the Disney cartoon, 1917 brought *Bobby Bumps, Surf Rider* from animation pioneer J.R. Bray, one of about 60 silent black and white cartoon featurettes from 1915–25 starring the same little boy and his dog. While rudimentary, its nearly four minutes are surprising in their forward-looking embrace of the then very unfamiliar sport and its novel attractions. Bobby and his pup spy striped bathing costumed surfers gliding by in the straight-on fashion of the day and would love to join the action. So they swipe an ironing board from a maid in the elaborately stereotyped cartoon blackface then common. She tries to scold Bobby, who mistakenly runs her over, at which point she is pursued by a shark—which she eventually whups and turns into her own surfboard. When the feisty maid jumps across to join tandem Bobby and dog on their board, it's time for a spanking and the punishment of laundry duty. Apparently enough Americans were sufficiently familiar with surfing for this all to make sense, but if they weren't such a cartoon was certainly part of their education. It's not surprising that animators awoke to surfing before "more serious" filmmakers. With its potentially violent man-nature interface, curious physical gestures, and the easily evoked exoticism of colorful locales (not to mention the suggestion of skimpy attire), surfing offered ample visual and thematic possibilities. Just as important, it seems, is the obligatory creativity and alert reactivity to cultural change necessary to the profession of cartoonist. "Cartooning is idea creativity on overdrive": written about their print counterparts, Robert Mankoff's reflection applies equally to film animators who, forced to churn out countless stories on demand, were required at all times to remain alert to the next new thing. Created by small teams of imaginative eccentrics obliged to improvise and unconstrained by the serious financial risk of full-length features, the short cartoon is a nimble media speedboat next to the ocean liner of the feature film.

To get the big ship finally out of port in 1959 would take a finally ensconced local surfing culture and a reassuringly bowdlerized script safely borrowed from a novel whose best-selling status demonstrated statistically to the execs that surfing was there to stay. Along with its intentional and unintentional treatments of changing gender standards and the first stirrings of the next decade's rebellious kids, the film *Gidget* confirmed that surfing was indeed a viable subject. Soon Frankie and Annette also wanted to go to the beach. The only surfing they did, though, was on the wave of the new sport's faddish popularity in a seemingly endless string of *Beach Party* extravaganzas. Bruce Brown's famous response to that crass exploitation of an emerging youth culture was *The Endless Summer*, which iconically revitalized the image and self-image of surfing and

***Bobby Bumps, Surf Rider*, director Earl Hurd (1917). In this Bray Studios production, Bobby and his pooch learn to surf on a pilfered ironing board; the maid is not amused (Tommy Stathes and the Bray Animation Project).**

surfers. Taking Mike and Robert around the world, Bruce pulled off a rarity by fusing the confidential surf movie and the big theatrical release to communicate the essence of surfing movingly to both the broadest general audience and the sunburned faithful in the islands and on the coast. Even if *Step Into Liquid* and *Riding Giants* later managed to speak meaningfully to both audiences, a miracle like *The Endless Summer* was an elusive achievement; the surf movie and the Hollywood production have since largely gone their separate ways in their treatment of a surfing world that has changed as dramatically as the larger world it alternately reflects and rejects.

Directed primarily to a hardcore audience, surf community movies and videos tend to speak a long-familiar visual and narrative language in their individual variations on a tried-and-true formula that goes back as far as Bud Browne. The Hollywood release, by contrast, is necessarily hybrid, addressing to the widest possible general audience its attempt to transform the surfing life and stoke—or at least public perceptions of that life and stoke—into a circumscribed number of characters and fictional circumstances that ring familiar bells for the greatest number. For Tinseltown, this too often means melodramatic focusing and foreshortening in the form of suspenseful contests or the buildup to thrilling big wave challenges. Whereas, of course, the very nature of surfing for the 99 percent is an undramatic, ingrained dailiness of small tests and pleasures. The task is further complicated by the fact that the surfing subculture to which such films must remain at least minimally faithful has gone through decades of constant mutation. Since the 1970s surfing has played an ever-growing role within mainstream Western culture and its globalized interpretations across an increasingly interconnected world economy and media network. It has generated, among other things, a sophisticated competition and star system, a profitable range of clothing and accessory industries, and an alliance of attitude and style with a booming alternate sports sector. Yet at the same time surfing has never stopped being a shoreline refuge for rebels and outcasts, a life choice obstinately cultivating a nonchalant critique of the dominant culture from its margin. The challenge of the feature film is to package these and a few more of the thousand other things surfing and surfers are into 90 believable minutes of comprehensible narrative conflict and resolution, structuring the whole to speak pertinently to contemporary social and moral issues while, ideally, revealing a universal truth or two.

Given such a check list, the surprising thing is not that such films fail but instead how many do meet a certain number of these criteria. The core of the discussion to follow will be the close critical examination of the most significant Hollywood contributions to the genre, a few of which have been successful, perhaps even memorably so, and too many others unfortunately forgettable. The organization will combine the chronological and thematic. The opening section ("Where the Boards Are") will cover the genre's creation in the release of *Gidget* and its almost entirely commercial elaboration in the *Beach Party*-ing '60s through the first steps towards a more serious representation of surfing in the hybrid *Ride the Wild Surf*. Their delicious absurdities aside, these movies intriguingly address the tension between freedom and restraint that would animate the emerging youth culture of the 1960s; part of that meaning lies in their treatment of the image and identity of the surfer at a critical juncture when the social jury was still very much out: healthy athlete, beatnik, vigorous outdoorsman, hood, or just nice kid who'll go back to school when playtime is over. In the second section, "Catch a Wave," the analysis turns from a chronological presentation to focus on what one might call the "classic" mode of the surfing narrative, with its elaboration upon a coming-of-age formula already sketched out by *Gidget* and *Ride the Wild Surf*. Drawing on a few representative examples from *Big Wednesday* and *North Shore* to *Blue Juice* to *Chasing Mavericks*, this discussion will address the recurring narrative and character patterns to which a remarkable percentage of surfing narratives faithfully cleave: drawn to surfing and its bracing values and, sometimes, temptations, an immature protagonist faces a series of trials, at which point a wise mentor intervenes, re-centering the hero and preparing him or her for a concluding challenge or competition revelatory of personal growth. It's comically easy, of course, to dismiss this schema as a clichéd, implausible variant lifted loosely from the formula of the classic sports film. That said, the density of its recurrence speaks pertinently to a widespread image on the part of the general movie-going public—and many real surfers themselves—of the surfing life as a theater of identity creation and a space where the negative rebellion against a normative existence and the positive embrace of alternative values intersect. The final chapter, "Heroes and Villains," then turns to the way certain surfing feature films have widened their purview to examine broader social and political issues. Chief among these are women's roles and changing gender standards, questions of race and ethnicity, the treatment of the environment, and the insistent temptation of profit and image in a consumption society. Interestingly, the cinematic conventions in place are so powerful that many of the films in question continue as well to remain faithful to the standard coming-of-age narrative and character patterns traced in the second section.

The announced progress of this three-part organization—the genre's frothy early days, the classic narrative arc, the social relevance of certain surfing films—might suggest that these are entirely separate subjects. This is far from the case. In fact, one has to look no further than *Gidget* for proof that such distinctions are extremely permeable. The 1959 hit was the first true full-length surfing fiction, and its discussion could already fit into any of the above categories. First of all, its 95 minutes constituted the prototype of the beachsploitation film that would dominate the 1960s. At the same time the adaptation of Frederick Kohner's novel created a simplified version of the coming-of-age story and character template that would go on to pattern the vast majority of surfing features for the next half century. Finally, in its giddy embodiment of personal liberty and female empowerment, *Gidget* was nothing less than a political statement. Even if, in predictable Hollywood fashion, the movie retreats considerably from the more daring positions taken by the novel on which it is based, *Gidget* is an indisputably feminist work. Both of its times' normative sense of womanhood and looking ahead to a different future, *Gidget* does send its heroine off with Moondoggie at the end, but much more importantly it has sent her outside. No matter what she says about the male lead at the end of the movie, when she finds her own wave, one she can stand up alone on, that is really the ultimate.

~ ~ ~ ~ ~

Where the Boards Are

When Gidget and Moondoggie walk out of frame in the closing shot of *Gidget*, they are leaving their own Little Eden. While the couple's Miltonian wandering steps and slow betray a micro-hint of regret, their return to solid suburban lives as Francie and Jeffrey has a safe Fifties inevitability, one Hollywood-crafted to will into gray-flannelled order the real, more subversive truth of the film, that just over the cultural horizon lay new notions of social organization, sexual behavior, and feminist possibility. For Gidget's beach is a place of experimentation with those options, a theater for the competing demands of duty and desire at precisely that Ike-to-JFK turning point in American cultural history. Casual alertness to the cultural breeze helps explain the movie's popularity and strangely lasting appeal, but just as important is its (naïve by recent standards, fresh by the time's) affectionate openness to the charms of the surfing life. With its neatly prepared surprise ending, the film also has a structure and narrative pacing tight enough to keep you watching even today, and this despite the wooden acting and gratingly "declaimed" dialogue delivery style.

The plotting is clever. A teenage tomboy, Francie[4] gets dragged from her Donna Reed home to the beach by boycrazy friends. There she meets a band of surf bums who, amazingly to this girl from the hardworking suburbs, just hang out and ride the wild surf. When circumstances lead to an accidental glide down a wave's face, it's no looking back for the cute innocent who soon wheedles the dough necessary for a board. Preferring that Francie date the reliable son of a business associate, her parents nevertheless pay up, almost more worried she'll never grow up than that she will. It would seem that she will if we're to judge by the company she keeps, notably the seasoned Kahuna—the gang's leader, a Rochester-in-trunks—and his younger lieutenant Moondoggie. James Darren dreamy, the latter rescues Francie from some stubborn kelp to, unsurprisingly, set the romantic comedy plot into motion: her crush grows but he's apparently not having it, for Moondoggie claims he's rejected his rich father's world and has eyes only for the open road he'll soon be hitting with the Kahuna. Along the way Gidget gains surfing cred, the band surprised that a girl would do anything on the sand but wiggle or "lose" her ball near the guys' towels. Cheerful lunks with just a touch of leering menace, they dub their mascot girl + midget = Gidget and, mugging madly, tease her in the stagy verbal rhythms of the Sharks and Jets.

Moral and dramatic complications ensue in the last reel when the much anticipated "luau" finally comes round. Gidget prepares for the big night with an elaborate stratagem: she pays one of the fellows to pretend he's with her in order, says she, to make the Kahuna jealous—when in fact it's Moondoggie in her sights. Today almost comical in its innocence, the luau's amalgam of flaring tiki torches, throbbing bongos, and horizontal couples certainly pushed erotic buttons for a '59 teenage audience. Now imagine the blossoming Gidget's surprise when she tiptoes into this orgiastic scene to find that the guy she hired to "court" her passed the gig on to Moondoggie! The attraction's steamingly mutual, but the ruse is so firmly in place that some inevitable misunderstandings send an indignant Gidget off—and straight into the experienced arms of Kahuna. Back at a borrowed bachelor pad, though, honor outs as Moondoggie shows up to declare himself with a right to Kahuna's chin, while Gidget runs off in the confusion. The film's coda tries to make clear that the summer was just that, an interlude, pleasurable and perhaps even necessary, but meant to end so that adult business could begin. Francie's sweet surprise is that when, resigned, she agrees at last to meet the son of Daddy's colleague, it turns out that young man is none other than Moondoggie. Fed up with the Kahuna's phoniness, Jeffrey's heading back to college. The new couple visit their old haunts in the closing frames. The crew has all gone back to school, and the Kahuna's breaking down his shack and returning to work. A chance look at an ID badge indicates that he's an airline pilot. Even the Big Kahuna, it seems, can't shake responsibility.

With its different conclusion and other tweaks, Gabrielle Upton's efficient and very Hollywood adaptation of Frederick Kohner's novel tried hard to put the genie back in the bottle, but it was too late for that. It was probably too late in 1957 when the book shot up to number seven on the *New York Times* bestseller list, just above another sign of the times, Jack Kerouac's *On the Road*. The Czech émigré who found success as a Hollywood screenwriter, Broadway playwright, and, following through on *Gidget*, author of a dozen books including several *Gidget* sequels, was intrigued by his daughter Kathy's fascination with the emergent Malibu surf scene. The 15-year-old whose mother gave Buzzy Trent and Matt Kivlin rides to the beach would slip out of her upscale Brentwood home to hang with a virtual surfing hall of fame, legends like Miki Dora, Mickey Munoz, and the guy who sold her her first board, Mike Doyle. Picking up on Kathy's sense that something special was happening and her desire to memorialize it, Kohner listened hard to her teen slang and tales, knocking together a fictionalized first-person version of her experiences in six weeks. It's a remarkable feat of empathy. A non-surfer and non-native speaker, the foreign-born psychology Ph.D. manages to talk the talk of a late '50s L.A. teenager, with only the occasional verbal miscalculation (a pompous teacher, for example, "dishing out a lot of bilge water"[5]). He convincingly communicates how irritating and manipulative adults can be and the churning emotions of first adolescent love. Perhaps most exceptionally, his lean sentences render the inexpressible sense impressions and rush of surfing better than any purple excess: "The only sound in the vast moving green was the hissing of the board over the water. A couple of times it almost dropped away under my feet, but I found it again and stood my ground" (149).

Gidget is not *Adventures of Huckleberry Finn*, *The Catcher in the Rye*, or *To Kill a Mockingbird*, but it is a far from negligible contribution to that notably American line of salty first-person juvenile narrations. Huck's all in a sweat about true stories and fiction and his tetchy relationship with that author Mark Twain; Gidget too fusses about her "true story on my word of honor" and the barfy-looking Mr. Glicksberg, the English comp teacher—and figure of the author father—who's coaching her through the writing. For both, the initiatory journey to follow will be framed throughout by the extremes of true and false, the authentic and the phony. With a nod to Huck, Francie imagines starting hers "on the bank of a river," but we learn soon enough the ocean shore will be where, beginning significantly on Independence Day, she too will explore "the perennial American theme—whether to drop out of society's mainstream or live the expected life."[6] Kohner recognized the thematic potential of the surfspace and the new subculture in representing this tension. Living in a hut on speared lobster and canned beans, scoring waves at will, the "surf bum" Kahuna is the antithesis of the Cold War suburban husband battling crab grass. "The only way to get economic independence," his assured chiasmus settles matters, "is to be independent of economics" (42). Kahuna's present-moment Malibu world of instinct and freedom is just a pause on the road with Kerouac or, presiding tropically on his flimsy provisional walls, Gauguin. The breeze of freedom here extends to the novel's relatively uncensored presentation of physical desire and changing sexual mores. As the guys check out the "boobs" and "jugs" in *Playboy*, Gidget "lapped up every word of that sexy talk, every single syllable of it" (50). A "nice girl," she's instructed, "goes on a date, goes to bed, goes home." Not coincidentally, it's just after this steamy build-up that she and Moondoggie take to the waves for some tandem surfing. While over the long term both he and the Kahuna will preserve Francie's 15-year-old honor, you wouldn't know it with the couple's sexualized delight in picking up "the same rhythm" and going "on a bareback ride" and waiting "for another good hump." Under a blazing sun he gets up and stays up, "meaning he didn't spill, and I had my hands around his head and felt just great."

In the Eisenhower '50s one doubts a white bread American father could have pulled off a novel like this. Kohner's cosmopolitan European background certainly figures in the apparent ease he displays when so empathetically representing Francie's emerging physical desire and the hot sensuality of the beach. With "the surf pounding against the dunes ... supplying the proper background music," Francie muses, "maybe this was the right moment—maybe I would wake up in the morning and I would have become a woman overnight" (140). No wonder the cover-cited *Pittsburgh Press* reviewer found it all "shocking" before adding that it was "wonderfully entertaining." The daughter Kohner represents in the novel has apparently assimilated much of the same European bohemianism, speaking French, travelling widely and living abroad, referring confidently to Freud and Adler. With her "novels from Sexville" (3), Francie is also quite a reader, referencing Bernardin de St. Pierre's *Paul and Virginie* and a straight off the shelf 1956 scorcher by Françoise Sagan (not to mention the obscure Ovidian myth of Baucis and Philemon). A story of paradise lost, the eighteenth century novel suggests how an idyllic tropical environment of pure natural love between two young people can be ruined by social customs while Sagan's *A Certain Smile*, published a year after *Lolita* first titillated Paris, treats a passionate love affair between a student and an older man. Far from innocent choices, they suggest a programmatic effort to distinguish the novel's moral and social atmosphere from a slowly changing but still far less progressive American norm. They also deliver up a protagonist who is kilometers away from the average California high school sophomore in 1957. Most obviously, Francie is well-travelled, multi-lingual, and raised around the latest ideas because her model Kathy Kohner was. In retrospect, it's tempting to see the odd European-ness of this novel about surfing the far western edge of America as pointing the way as well towards another vector of change for young people that was lying just over the cultural horizon. Kahuna vaunts the merits of a non-materialistic life on the move open to the next day and the new experience. While his tramping pursuit of the swell draws on an old hobo tradition, it also looks ahead to the next decade, that moment when the Grand Tour suddenly went democratic and American kids en masse started lugging their backpacks to *Europe on Five Dollars a Day*. By 1970 Joni Mitchell was in Europe writing a song called "California." Old hat to impatient adolescent Francie, what she and her generation learned there about the body and different forms of social organization and Simone de Beauvoir would play a sizeable role in the social upheavals of the period.

Kohner was certainly familiar with *Le deuxième sexe*, if *Gidget* is any indication. While the basics of his story differ relatively little from the earlier plot summary of the film, that little bit is crucial. Unlike the movie's clever Moondoggie twist, Francie knows his backstory all along and must deal directly with her burgeoning affection, Jeff's absent girlfriend, and the maladroit swerves between his distant, horny, and tender selves. Their relationship in the novel is textured and imperfect; not just teen dreaming about the inaccessible, it forces the girl becoming a young woman to call repeatedly on her own developing intelligence

3. In Hollywood's Hands 155

and emotional resources. Stepping up to complicate this Hollywood-appropriate attraction is, of course, Gidget's parallel but less-standard affection for the surfing life. While the at first condescending crew overcomes initial resistance to mentor the novice surfer—a generosity actually described as typical by many early women surfers[7]—normative images of

Gidget, director Paul Wendkos: The Little Girl with Big Ideas bargaining for a board. Left to right: Cliff Robertson as Kahuna, Burt Metcalfe as Lord Byron, Sandra Dee as Gidget, Doug McClure as Waikiki, Joby Baker as Stinky (kneeling), Tom Laughlin as Lover Boy, and Robert Ellis as Hot Shot (Columbia Pictures/Photofest).

'50s femininity return regularly to throw into relief Francie's outdoorsy athleticism and her chosen tomboy place in the male gang. Sure, part of her ticket into the crew means sneaking food from home and thus replicating the nurturing feminine role, but her ponytail, no nonsense manner, and lack of "falsies" set her apart from such as the Kahuna's languorous ex- and the "coozies" who slink into the luau. Like the former tripping across the sand with heels and parasol, the leopard-skinned clad latter show up on the beach dyed and bejewelled. Francie's instinctive reaction to their arrival and its modeling of willing female objectification is "a quick dunking in the surf" (124).

That same instinctive movement from dry land to the sea is what marks the novel's conclusion and most distinguishes it from that of the movie version. As Jeff and Kahuna duke it out over Gidget, she sprints for the surfline, her board suddenly as light as feathers. The surf's big and the men warn her off, but "No, I wouldn't go back. Not for the life of me" (148–9). The dramatic insistence here underlines the stakes: nothing less than "the life of me." Not so much fleeing as pursuing an alternative, Francie resists the stereotypical male worries about feminine fragility and their battle for possession; she resists male modification or framing of her atypical action and its affirmation of female persistence, focus, and physical force, instead transforming the men's script of patronizing concern into one of positive reinforcement: "Shoot the curl ... shoot it!" Symbolically resisting a preordained place in the home, she masters waves "high as houses." As the water hisses green around her, at last "I ... stood my ground." Following this defiant statement and triumphant action, a coda does return to the larger forces of conventional femininity in Cold War America, with Francie accepting Jeff's pin before boot camp in Texas. Yet even as Kohner's novel completes its romance plot it also subverts it: as Krista Comer writes, Francie's first-person narration insists on Jeff's fraternity pin as a sign of liberation from "gender norms and peer pressure enforced by *other girls* so that she can enact instead a different kind of femininity"[8] (45). Rejecting a sentimental discourse of romance, Francie insists that she tore up the gushy love letter she earlier wrote and goes so far as to relegate her summer with Jeff to "dream" and momentary Kahuna attraction to "curiosity" (154) "But with the board and the sun and the waves it was for real. All things considered," she concludes, "maybe I was just a woman in love with a surfboard." The original subtitle for Kohner's novel was "The Little Girl with Big Ideas." Far from a sign of ambivalence, the tension between the introduction's "little girl" and conclusion's "woman" confirms the novel's feminist coming-of-age ambition.

Columbia bought the rights to *Gidget* only a month after the novel's publication. Moving quickly, the execs implicitly indicated what they wanted done with this potentially controversial material by tapping the lead writer for the popular soap opera *The Secret Storm* to do up the movie script. Upton's re-work is considerably tamer due in large part to the trick ending and the happy couple's more clearly indicated suburban future. Drawing on Kohner's original while working occasional expressive changes, she does, however, have a good sense of the symbolic detail and mythic undercurrents of little Francie's tale. For, as slight and hokey as it can seem, *Gidget* does in fact flirt with myth, its heroine an Ugly Duckling, its hero a prince in hiding, its disguise ruse and surprise twist straight from Elizabethan comedy. Though only at film's end is it off to work they go, Gidget's seven-strong beach crew could be tall dwarves, with their muscular mutual support for the heroine and their customized nicknames. On the sand, as Kohner already indicated, such sobriquets are the norm. There the guys are only Stinky or Loverboy, and the token of Francie's acceptance into the beach clan is the gift of the title Gidget. Then there's the mysterious Kahuna. Plosive monosyllabic prose at last overwriting assonantal poetry, his real handle in the film, we finally discover, is Burt Vails. The family name hints at the ultimately superficial nature of the aliases adopted by all these supposed marginals along the shore—thinly shrouding but in no way deeply altering fundamentally conventional selves. As Kahuna admits, that Hawaiian mask on the hut wall in fact comes from Acapulco, a location already famous notably for transforming shoreline exploits into mere spectacle. At the death of his pet bird—a wild pirate's squawking partner, an evident image of freedom—the illusions begin to fade, until the only wings left to Burt the Korean War vet lead back to a branch of what President Eisenhower would denounce less than a year later as the military industrial complex. Jeffrey's pseudonym is most significant of all. When this character who most ostentatiously breaks with his past life circles back to his businessman father's world, we realize that Moondoggie was never the lone wolf his nickname promised, but only a domesticated pup pretending to howl. And as the film closes, the protagonists are clearly once again Jeffrey and Francie. The fraternity pin he gives her gestures ironically at the band of beach brothers that is now just a memory. Unlike the novel's ending, where Jeff's absence enables Gidget's return to the waves, here his pin fastens the couple into a stable, socially acceptable relationship and securely fixed identities.

Yet, despite such seeming confidence in its representation of suburban middle-class certitudes, the film's deeper truth may actually be just how fragile they are. For, no matter what, to dash onto the beach in *Gidget* is to enter a space of experimentation with new cultural possibilities. The original trailer already picks up on this idea, referring to "the Story of the Beach Generation." Bogus as he may later turn out, by the surf Kahuna lives up to his title, a shaman presiding over disturbing initiatory rites and opportunities. He may plan to check out in an impossibly corny way (no less than "jumping a freight train"), but the surfing life he and the crew have fashioned on the shore actually questions the assumed value of work while implicitly endorsing a subversively collective model of social organization. The gang's leader, we're told in Upton's script, is "into existentialism," and it's clear those Surfrider Beach bongos are echoing others up the coast at North Beach. Unsurprisingly, given its parentage in Kohner's novel, *Gidget* signals the changes to come perhaps most noticeably in its treatment of gender and sexuality. Just over the horizon of the new decade, of course, lay the sexual revolution, and the film has a hormonal physicality which recalls the novel's treatment of the same questions and which surprises even today. The innocent Francie's girlfriends fret that she's "studied up on everything but sex," while even her June Cleaver mother recognizes the "biological fact: the female matures earlier than the male." When the girls go off to the beach it's on a—the term is repeated insistently—"man hunt," while the perspective is later reversed by the beach crew to corresponding fear of "jail bait." Standing, remarkably, under a sign offering "Hot Dogs," one of Gidget's voracious girlfriends savors the "six hunks of male, enough for seconds!" awaiting her. And isn't the pad Kahuna leads our heroine back to already a '70s Hefner-approved den of stylish iniquity.

While, Hollywood *oblige*, the protected young thing growing up in *Gidget* finally resists premarital relations, she does offer a refreshing vision of new feminist possibility. A century earlier in *Jane Eyre* another girl stared across open reaches and asserted that women have the same need for action and opportunity as their brothers. Gazing across the sea's suggestive, dangerous expanse, then taking on its barrier of breakers, no-nonsense Gidget finds that field, at once challenging the resistant model of the prim Valley housewife and that of the coiffed bimbo with her useless beach ball. Four years later Brian Wilson's "Surfer Girl" proposes that the couple hit the waves together. While the guy in the song may still hold the key to the "woody" (!), the world is very clearly changing. And soon, as other pop culture monuments would have it, manic Mondays will become the norm and, on Fridays, girls just wanna' have fun. It's that very fact which perhaps best explains the desperate rearguard quality of the screenplay's comfortable suburban ending. The film ropes the heroine back into a respectable status quo and the romantic plot twist masks the quiet anxiety of its denouement precisely because the world *Gidget* unwittingly foreshadows is just too much fun.

Throughout the 1960s this tension between the adult world and a youth culture in disturbing emergence and way ready for fun will again play out in the sand, though generally in an even safer and more saleable manner. Responding to the success of *Gidget* and a surf boom that would fill the transistors and turn Mr. Magoo into a surfing *Hula Magoo*, about thirty "beach movies" appeared between 1960 and 1968. For the most part quickly shot cheapos, they took crowds of cute teenage party animals to attractive locations for intertwined romantic intrigues, lots of skin, and comic misunderstandings. The location of choice was the summertime beach, with occasional surrogates like the ski slopes or Lake Arrowhead. While a number of independents and other studios rushed in to launch their own bald appeals to the new baby boom youth market, the big player was American International Pictures. With *Beach Party* and its six successors, AIP went profitably mainstream after the company's low-budget horror and J.D. shockers in the '50s, essentially shifting from a thrill- and fear-driven take on youth culture to its playfully mindless celebration. The fantasy space these and other movies created corresponded to the dreamed freedoms of that initial post–World War II American generation raised in prosperous, monotonous suburbia. At least at first, if that collective space of the mind could be said to have a geographical location, it was the sunny coastline of Southern California. While their playground would soon be imagined similarly in places like Honolulu, Daytona Beach, and Fort Lauderdale, the entitled white kids from mass-transport allergic L.A. and Orange County were certainly among the first 16-year-olds in history to expect not only a driver's licence but a pink slip. When the Beach Boys reference that proof of car ownership in "Little Deuce Coupe," they are glorifying a teen dream of personal autonomy and mobility, and the best way to get to the beach.

Even if the revelation and affectionate examination of surfing culture are at the heart of the film that got all this going, for the most part the beach movies are more about what happens on the sand than in the waves. Some form of surfing does figure in most of them, but only one—the hybrid *Ride the Wild Surf*—can be said to treat in any kind of depth the meanings of surfing and its relation to central elements of plot or character development. To speculate why, it's not difficult to imagine the reasoning of studio executives. *Gidget* was about the choices of growing up, with the tangible surfing world semi-realistically portrayed in the film embodying for the protected suburbanite a refreshingly different range of life values. But why continue any kind of serious exploration of a subculture most producers didn't understand anyway when they could simply piggyback on its image? In other words, even if its surfing served only as background and atmosphere, *Gidget* still had a lot to offer in simple entertainment value to the average American teen: a largely adult-free setting, scanty garments, romantic entanglements, a wild nighttime bacchanal, songs by James Darren and the Four Preps. As such, *Gidget* really is a rough draft of the beach movies to follow and their "successful simple formula" as identified by Thomas Lisanti, the Gibbon of the genre's rise and fall: "Start with attractive swimsuit-clad teenagers twisting on the sand, add a dash of surfing footage, mix in romantic misunderstandings, stir in popular musical performers, add aging comedians for comic relief, and whisk in villainous bikers or predatory adults."[9] The movie pros recognized that the small real surfing community would always be happier with its own parallel cinematic universe of Bud Browne and John Severson. As for the rest of the kids, why not just "a dash" of surfing for its fad value, fun tribal language, visual attractiveness, and as a handy signifier of youthful freedom?

Considering simply the bottom line, they're weren't wrong. Compare, for example, the $1.5 million dollar gross of *Gidget* to the $3.5 million, $4.2 million, and $2.2 million takes of, respectively, *Where the Boys Are* (1960), *Blue Hawaii* (1961), and *Gidget Goes Hawaiian* (1961). One's a sequel and the others are clearly riding the same pop cultural wave as *Gidget*. Set over spring break in Florida, *Where the Boys Are* dispenses with surfing altogether to concentrate on Connie Francis's singing and conventional romance plots entwined around the "good girl"–"bad girl" debate. Pulling Elvis out of a slump (while occasioning one of his most memorable love songs), *Blue Hawaii* does call on a few slim action shots and the waveriding King in studio tank rear projection to insist upon the free, rebellious nature of a character who, 90 minutes later, will get hitched and start a business. Of the three, where you'd rightly expect the most surfing is the *Gidget* sequel. Bringing in a new female lead opposite one of only two survivors from the original cast, James Darren as Moondoggie, *Gidget Goes Hawaiian* can't not put its heroine on the waves. More mature and slightly more physically imposing than Sandra Dee, Debra Walley actually seems to pop up at Waikiki and ride tandem in a boat-based travelling shot; in others, Linda Benson stands in for the lead more successfully than did, say, Diane Kibborn and a be-wigged Mickey Munoz or Johnny Fain in *Gidget*. Walley's Gidget entrances the guys with her surfing prowess and gutsy if inept water ski-jumping, her eager athleticism heightening the contrast with her manipulative, water-allergic rival Abby. Yet, while the surfing does reinforce Gidget's difference, she's finally on a trip safely orchestrated by her parents and far more into complicated love triangles and formulaic Hollywood romantic misunderstandings than in the original movie, with its genuine, if at times sweetly naive, attempts to slip Mom and Dad and get at what surfing might mean to a life. If the waves have a pro-forma nature here, just wait for the second sequel, where Francie heads off to the Eternal City, and then the TV series and TV movies. Tossing the role from actress to actress like the overinflated beach balls Francie once scorned, the franchise confirmed that Gidget was no longer a woman in love with a surfboard but a brand.

The beach movies are clearly branded entertainment products set in a teen- and bikini-friendly environment to which corporate America was happy to lay claim. If surfing and publishing legend Steve Pezman's cheerfully wild exaggerations in *Step Into Liquid* are to be believed, America's 2000 pre-*Gidget* surfers were four million by 1964. His simile for the craze—"like a Hula Hoop that never went away"—highlights how the business world saw the lasting potential of the new craze. The beach party movies are all about commodification, starting with the transformation of an authentic surfing subculture into a saleable style reference and cinematic shorthand. The world they delivered was a sandy Disneyland, where kids could let off steam and dabble in titillation while threatening no one and never leaving a risk-free environment. Emblematically led by ultra-safe Frankie Avalon and Annette Funicello, equally clean-cut white kids surf, sip Cokes, fall in love, break into song, and have madcap adventures in that last summer before adulthood. Gary Morris has written incisively about the films and their portrayal of the beach as America's happy, healthy sandbox-refuge from a very unsettling reality of racial conflict, war, a dead president, nuclear threat, and beatniks not only morphing into hippies but multiplying. In this filmic universe, surfing is presented less as marginal behavior than as a wholesome, outdoorsy alternative to boredom and deviance. Though that might sound positive, surfers were unamused by the Hollywood version; Stacy Peralta speaks for many when rolling his eyes at "the goofy essence of what they think surfing is: guys sitting on the beach all day long playing guitar."[10] Planing off the dangerous edge half-sharpened by the Kahuna, AIP thus confirmed such other forms of entertainment co-optation as the made-for-Top 40 surf music craze and TV's *Surfside 6*. Gary Morris aptly identifies the "schizoid air" of the films, one "typical of the period of social flux in which they were made." For all the unbridled agitation they seem meant to portray, they in fact are about reassuring white middle-class America that the world was perfectly comprehensible and that its children were just having some good clean fun before getting on with the important stuff.

The movies are schizoid in another way as well. With their chaste lovers, systematic beatnik jokes, and retread adult actors direct from a well-worn parental past, they indeed send a comforting message to suburbia. Yet despite pious intention the form of the films says something else entirely. A weird non-linearity rules: "they are a patchwork quilt of motifs and formal strategies, alternately distanced and in-your-face, heavy with subplots and random songs, cartoon characterizations, slow-motion and speeded-up visual effects, and even blatant audience acknowledgements ... structurally the films are practically anarchic." Morris adds that the form of such 1965 wonders as *Beach Blanket Bingo* and *How to Stuff a Wild Bikini* was "influenced by America's social decline." This is, if anything, an understatement. While one might easily recognize the *zeitgeist* in the films' portrayals of the teen tribe's resistance to rapacious adult developers or ad men, the zany harmlessness of the villains effectively erases any vaguely political implications. Not so for the off-the-wall structural and stylistic choices of the *Beach Party* franchise and its spin-offs, where a saucy, random surrealism, despite vast differences of tone and intention, is not without recalling "Desolation Row." It is difficult to view the films today and not register somewhere in their genial mess the confused, rudderless society just offshore ready to storm that desperately happy strand. The Beach Boys were still singing "All Summer Long," but the Summer of Love was coming. Only a year and a half after sour social ferment and a new youth culture brought an end to these films *Rowan & Martin's Laugh-in* would hit the air. Counterculture seeping into culture, there was the same metaphor of the non-stop party and the strangely similar—but now fully knowing—comedy of wacky deconstruction.

A good place to see that unthreatening weirdness in action would be the brace of films with which AIP launched its series, *Beach Party* (1963) and *Muscle Beach Party* (1964). The similarity in titles is no accident for both begin with the same emblem of teen freedom, hot rods racing to the shore, and star virtually the same large, attractive cast frolicking at the same stretch of Malibu sand. Even if frail and very American Bandstand East Coast,

Frankie Avalon's portrayed as the natural leader of a band of surfers; no navel visible due to contract restraints, ex–Mouseketeer Annette is his virginal, marriage-fixated flame. Frankie wants more, songs are sung, no one works, complications ensue. Innuendo and absurdities run amok, and twisting Candy violates the laws of physics in the closing credits of both movies. Swap the biker heavies, intrusive adult scientist, and hot foreign chick who falls for Frankie in the first with the bodybuilder heavies, intrusive adult businessman, and hot foreign chick who falls for Frankie in the second, and the films are virtually identical. So too is the presentation of surfing, alongside which *Gidget* comes off as *cinéma verité*. Punctuating the italicized beach jargon, occasional calls of "surf's up!" send the guys, Annette, and another girl or two whooping off into the gnarly ankle slappers of Paradise Cove. The latter then abruptly morph into stock footage and rear projection of waves three to five times their size in an incoherent collection of Californian and Hawaiian breaks, lefts, rights, solo surfers, massed groups, hot-doggers, "comic" wipeout artists. This goes on in three or four little bursts, perhaps six minutes total in each film, just enough to remind viewers that this beach is the land of the free and the home of the cool.

Real surfers were associated with the projects, top performers like Johnny Fain, Linda Benson, and Miki Dora, as well as Dick Dale for the music and Windansea regular and cult surf artist Mike Dormer, who collaborated with Lee Teacher on the lively trash "Hot Curl" opening graphics for *Muscle Beach Party*. The vision of surfing, though, is generally that of some distracted parent from the Valley, reduced to a few shards of overheard lingo and the general sense of a fun and athletic, if not completely comprehensible, way to fill in the summer months when you really should be working. Viewed with a mega-dose of indulgence, though, and despite all their absurdities, *Beach Party* and *Muscle Beach Party* might actually hint at a pertinent notion or two about surfing. The framing device of the earlier movie, for example, is an anthropologist's observation of the curious rites and rituals of the exotic cult that is American youth. Cornily mouthed behind the cartoonish "professor" beard of actor Bob Cummings, such a characterization nevertheless had a certain relevance vis-à-vis an increasingly tribal youth culture in the 1960s, especially one further divided into an even more hermetic surfing subculture. Following real examples like Da' Cat or The Bull, and the lead of the elaborately monikered *Gidget* crew, Deadhead, Big Boy, and other surfer nicknames flourish around the *Party* firepits. On one hand the sign of an imagined or perceived identity shift accompanying entry into the surfer life, the alternate clan distinction of such nicknames also speaks to what was becoming more widely recognized in American youth culture as the stifling conformity of the prosaic suburbs. More precise issues of contemporary surf culture and identity wander similarly into the narrative confusion. In *Muscle Beach Party*, for instance, the bad-guy bodybuilders led by Don Rickles are a regimented goon squad of superficial beefcake; their arrival and subsequent conflict with the laidback surfing crew about who controls the beach raise the question both of poser Valley kooks invading the scene ("they're not for real") and, as this is Malibu, of precious space on overly crowded breaks. In the same movie Frankie repeatedly delivers lines worthy of the Kahuna (or Da' Cat) about wanting only what's free and avoiding the prison of "Time Payment City, ice-boxes, and TV's." When he's tempted by Luciana Paluzzi's luscious contessa to give up the surfing life for her yacht and fabulous wealth, the crew abruptly wises him up to the sell-out. Pop-culture schematic and sentimental as it is, the weight given to the conflict does vaguely gesture towards suspicions about the seduction of capital and commerce then awakening in the younger population and in a surfing subculture alert to the early stirrings of professionalism and sponsorship.

Okay, but let's not exaggerate. For the most part, of course, the unthreatening world of innocent sex, cartoon conflict, absurd adults, and waves for the taking created by *Muscle*

Beach Party, director William Asher (1963): Annette Funicello as Dee Dee, Frankie Avalon as Frankie. Boards waxed and breaking into song on the way to the beach. Notice how Frankie's board is trying to take advantage of Dee Dee's (American International Pictures/Photofest).

Beach Party and consort was hermetic and, very soon, self-parodying. It's hard not to think of these movies embodying the last little bit of sun before the dirty political storms of the late '60s. When *How to Stuff a Wild Bikini* came out on July 14, 1965, surfer Frankie was in the naval reserve. That was 28 days before Southern California summer heat abruptly meant the flames of the Watts Riots and two weeks before Lyndon Johnson doubled monthly draft quotas, sending Vietnam troop levels to 200,000. In the decades since the last of the genre, *The Sweet Ride*, made its way off the sand, the *Beach Party* movies have maintained an affectionate little place in the public imagination for their silly innocence of theme and general good humor, and probably as well for the comically transparent nature of their blatantly commercial motivations. Unsurprisingly, in the decades since, similarly commercial motivations have tried to harness that affection, revisiting the genre every few years with a blend of wistful nostalgia and aware parody. The year 1987, for example, would bring a long-awaited trip *Back to the Beach*, an aptly named sequel starring a now married Frankie and Annette as stressed-out Ohio car salesman and housewife. Together with their rebellious son, they decide on a much-needed Hawaiian vacation, stopping in California en route to visit their daughter, now mixed up with a surfer. They're soon detoured back to their old beach for a host of typically incoherent Beach Party adventures, a raft of songs, some funny B-level cameos, and, eventually, Frankie's return to surfing excellence after his traumatizing accident two decades earlier.

By rights, *Back to the Beach* should just be a pale attempt to rip off young babyboomers nostalgic about their teen years, but in fact it's a blast. Annette is prettier now at 45 than as a pinched Disney prude. Her real-life friendship with Avalon is apparent in the patent chemistry and neat comic timing missing the first time around. Played by Demian Slade, their fractious son debuts irritatingly but soon starts swiping scenes with a humorously elaborate youthful identity crisis; in one sight gag, the funnier because not followed up on, the perfectly coiffed mother is on one side of a kitchen counter spray-painted on the other by the kid with a menacing skull and crossbones. On the cusp between over-the-top parody and affectionate attention to the melodies and lyrics of some great songs, the musical performances are sensational, including Dick Dale on "California Sun" and Pee Wee Herman (!) with "Surfin' Bird." All this, of course, does not make *Back to the Beach* a "real movie," but that's the point. Filmed from the same beach now invaded by punks, it would almost be disappointing if the surfing shots distinguished between Hawaiian and Californian footage, though they do playfully take on the joys of studio rear projection. Cameos from pop icons like Jerry Mathers and Bob Denver weave in and out of an appropriately wrinkled narrative fabric where you can break into song at will or flirt with Connie Stevens, and where Annette's Mouseketeer past and Avalon's "Venus" are just as much a part of the story as their fictional doings. Refusing to adopt an attitude of superiority towards its subject matter, the movie and its 17 (!) screenwriters stir together memories from the earlier films and random trimmings from popular culture into a jokey soup. Far from serious cooking, this simple comfort food is served up with generosity and affection. Part of the pleasure here is the clearly communicated sense that *Back to the Beach* was fun to make and that the moviemakers want its audience to share fully in the fun.

This is the big difference with another movie heading back to that same stretch of sand, *Psycho Beach Party*. The 2000 theatrical release adapted by Charles Busch from his own 1987 play is all attitude and no heart. The story of multi-personalitied Florence, who's dubbed Chicklet by the surf gang she wants to join and who may or may not have committed the slasher murders terrorizing Malibu Beach, is a vexingly knowing parody of *Gidget* and lurid low-budget 50s teenage noir. Garish, extravagantly mannered, smirking more than playful, it resembles Andy Warhol's earlier *San Diego Surf* in its irritating in-grown posing and arch gay-camp waspishness. Writing in *The Village Voice*, Dennis Lim rightly laments how "the viewer is left to ponder the number of levels on which this counts as a pointless exercise." Bad as it is, though, *Psycho Beach Party* couldn't kill the sub-genre. One wonders if that was the motivation behind *National Lampoon Presents Endless Bummer*, a 2009 embarrassment that puts paid forever to the venerable *Lampoon* reputation for very funny, if raunchy, films. *Psycho Beach Party* at least had an point of view, as annoyingly self-satisfied as it was. Unwittingly perfect of title, *Endless Bummer* is such an uninvolving mess that it's not clear whether it is some kind of updated-beach-party-meets-classic-teen-movie hybrid or a parody of those things, or just a parody of the act of filmmaking. Set in Ventura, the "plot" turns around a blond surfer type whose custom board, made by the obligatory shaper guru, gets stolen, at which point an expedition across the border into the dreaded Valley leads to its recovery, accidental destruction, and the concluding "Surf Party" (that gave the movie its European DVD title). That some form of these events occurred to John Drury, who wrote the screenplay, does not make them interesting, even if a lively '80s soundtrack covering artists like Joan Jett and The Specials helps a bit. Studded with studiedly "funny" lines and cardboard teen stereotypes, the bland whole has drawn a impressive series of bad news customer reviews on sites like Amazon and IMDB whose virulence is, if anything, understatement.

Happily, four years later Disney would show that going mindlessly back to the beach didn't have to mean mindless screenwriting. A Disney Channel production, *Teen Beach Movie* (2013) is dedicated to the studio's own recently deceased Annette Funicello. Shot in Puerto Rico with the high production values one associates with Disney, it is aimed at a teen audience but works as light, playfully nostalgic entertainment for adults as well. Brady and McKenzie are young surfers in love, but the latter, forced by a pretentious aunt and family tradition, will have to leave her island paradise tomorrow for a snobby prep school. When she paddles out one last time to ride a big swell and Brady tries to rescue her, a mammoth wave sends them back to 1962 and into *Wet Side Story*, the favorite beach party film of Mack's board-shaping father. There the couple tumbles into the romantic intrigues of a full scale musical that, as its title indicates, involves tension between rival groups, in this case the surfers and the greasers. To this add a mad scientist trying to manipulate the weather and transform the surfers' beach into a luxury tourist complex, and a dozen cleverly written, skillfully produced original vocal numbers, with titles like "Cruisin' for a Bruisin'" and "Surf's Up." Even if *Teen Beach Movie* strays from the strict beach party formula and is a transparent attempt to capitalize on the success of the studio's 2006 *High School Musical*, it takes a clever, respectful angle on the old films that has certainly piqued the curiosity of more than one kid today about the corny originals and their innocent tics. Plus the surfing is lavishly filmed and stunt-doubled. As in so many movies, it plays the customary role of counterpoint to stilted conventionality, here as represented by Mack's two-dimensional air-kissing aunt. At the same time, the figure of the wise elder transmitting the family's sacred board to the new generation suggests the way a surfer is always part of a continuum with a meaningful past. In the end, in fact, it seems fair to say the same about this eminently lighthearted cinematic journey back to some very familiar sands.

The Beach Party era was, of course, a brief historical moment. By 1964 Bruce Brown was already touring along the West Coast and in Hawaii with *The Endless Summer*, which in its 1966 theatrical form would forever change the public's view of surfing and conspire with social change to stop the Beach Party. Already, though, within the genre itself there were indications of changes under way. Six months after the inexplicable mid-winter release of *Muscle Beach Party*, Columbia's *Ride the Wild Surf* hit American screens with its luaus and flirting, yet also with its real surfing and a somewhat more than cursory glance at the sport's emerging monetization. It's a strange, if far from disagreeable, amalgam of a movie. One of the film's odd-coupled parents is certainly the giddy beach romance and its familiar attempt to cash in on the teen market with the same old partying, swimsuits, and bitchen settings. The other is the hardcore surf movie tradition of Bud Browne and Bob Evans. Or as Eugene Archer put it in the *New York Times*, "the beach-bound antics of the adolescents … are innocuous enough—but man, those waves!" When Butch Van Artsdalen and Mike Diffenderfer on big Makaha are cut briefly into the conclusion of *Muscle Beach Party*, the result is beyond ridiculous. *Ride the Wild Surf*, by contrast, offers convincing miles of such footage. The film Don Taylor took over from Art Napoleon may be similarly marred by the recurrent problem of obvious studio tank close-ups and embarrassingly obvious rear projection, but the long stretches of exceptional surfing at Haleiwa, Sunset, Makaha, Pipeline, and Waimea Bay are dazzling and, furthermore, germane to the dry land characterizations and plot. Executive fingerprints are certainly all over the latter, though, and its offer of … not one, not two, but three love stories! A trio of handsome mainlanders—played by the just still bankable Tab Hunter, teen heartthrob Fabian, and TV's *Lawman* Peter Brown—head to Oahu to test themselves against the North Shore's winter swell and the other surfers lured by its challenge and danger. Conveniently, each has an opposites-attract (and hair color-coordinated) love complication, with resulting pressures from Susan Hart, Shelley Fabares, and Barbara Eden, respectively, to man-up to responsibility, go back to college, or, in the case of Brown's trustfunder Chase, liberate the inner wildman. As the trailer pitch put it, the movie's about "the guys who go for the action and the gals who go for the action guys."

It's significant that the action came first. Cinematographer Joseph Biroc and the film's screenwriting producers Jo and Art Napoleon actually went to Hawaii in the heavy winter of '63 to shoot surfers Miki Dora, Butch Van Artsdalen, Greg Noll, and Phil Edwards on the great North Shore breaks. Only with that expensive 35 mm footage in the can—and the story possibilities it suggested—did the couple cobble together the screenplay. Certainly, the waves are what you remember about *Ride the Wild Surf*, long swathes of which not only resemble the more modest surf community movies but are composed of exactly the same rides, for Biroc's tripod was far from alone when those breaks went off. The film explicitly recognizes the growing attention to surfing of photographers, filmmakers, and even television, with background cameras moving in and out of frame, a TV commentator for the tense final competition, and the repeated appearances of an experienced boardmaker and surf photographer. Inspired by (though not resembling) Phil Sauer, the entrepreneurial shaper who furnished boards for the film and directed its stunt work, the cigar-chomping vet arbitrates conflicts between the surfers, orients a viewing public short on insider knowledge, and, most importantly, raises the issue of surfing for money. "There's getting to be some loot in it," we're told. The film's heavy, for example, generates a regular income with his own signature board. Unconcerned with narrative subtlety, the plot abruptly manufactures tension between our three polite Californians and the thuggish gang of Eskimo, played by an earnestly glowering Jim Mitchum in the same jailhouse shorts as his double Greg Noll. High melodrama frequently ensues ("I'll get you for this, buddy boy!") before the formulaic sport film Big Competition conclusion that would essentially establish the model for the genre. Fabian's Jody Wallis will show himself the best of the three and end up in the thick of the contest at Waimea Bay. For him the stakes are not just pride but a similar sponsoring contract.

Jody needs the cash because, five years after the Kahuna, he's a self-identified "surf bum" who wants to live off the sport and chuck the rest; but after meeting Shelley Fabares's (pallid) Brie, who informs him "there are wonderful and useful things to do in the world," maybe he'll wake up and use the sponsorship jackpot to go back to school and give the career of oceanographer another shot. Roughneck Steamer Lane and well-bred Chase Colton have their own romantic quandaries, but tucked into all of them is the tussle already quietly staged in *Gidget* between their love for the "the waves and lying in the sand and doing nothing" and presumably worthwhile employment. Two of the female love interests are very clearly the super-ego to the childish male id; urging Chase to follow his instinct, the unconventional judoka played by spunky Barbara Eden comes off as the opposite, but the couple's relation is informed by exactly the same pretty nagging and cajoling. At the end the women seem to prevail, though a touch of interesting ambiguity may surround the case of Jody. *Ride the Wild Surf* concludes with a competition that brings all the principals to Waimea. Finally, and unsurprisingly, fourteen of the sixteen competitors throw in the beach towel, with only Eskimo and Jody left to duke it out. Time after time the two wipe out as we're told (though the visuals don't fully support this) that the swell is shifting, the wave is closing down, and it's suicide out there. When Eskimo at last gives up, grudgingly granting that "you're all right," the Dora-doubled Jody tries again, fails, and then finally makes the wave, riding triumphantly all the way through the shorebreak. The closing credits start rolling when, again before the TV cameras and still photographers, the cheering crowd surrounds the hero as he takes his girl in his arms. Mercifully, there's no moralistic follow-up. In fact, given the memory of Jody's very pale affirmation of a new direction ("Why don't I?") and the emotional lift of the great Jan & Dean anthem, the final impression is less one of a young man going back to school that of one finding his authentic life choice confirmed. It was his own girlfriend who said "you can be anything you want!"

The real highlight of *Ride the Wild Surf*, though, is not the plot but "those waves!" and this despite the lack of in-water shooting, the rear projection and close-up implausibilities, and the miraculous speed with which competitors recover their boards to catch an absurd number of Waimea monsters. Even the usually difficult Miki Dora recognized the achievement. The Malibu ace who'd never ridden surf of that size noted (in rare first person plural) that "we did something that had never been done before. Big-wave riding was filmed in 35mm. They were good people and really wanted to understand surfing."[11] The latter is made clear, among other things, by the film's respectful attention to geography, not just namechecking the famous North Shore breaks but carefully indicating their specificities, communicating their spatial relation to each other, and presenting their largely rural context. This was necessary information for 1964 audiences, and, their time well spent in Hawaii, the Napoleons communicate it better than certain surf community moviemakers.

At times the film even has the same moves, such as when Chase jumps at Waimea Falls, a beyond-familiar figure in the early surf movie. Another bit of essential pedagogy concerns the mechanics of wave formation. As we first meet our trio, they've made a pilgrimage to the Bay only to discover the supposed behemoth in its normal calm and flat incarnation. Several times during the film's 101 minutes, though, fraught radio commentary about an incoming storm front builds up suspense while making clear what's needed for Waimea to perform. These are landmark first lessons for the landlubber audience in what would become a long series of such sessions in subsequent surf films.

Writing in *The Daily Beast*, Laird Hamilton's not the least ironic when he names *Ride the Wild Surf* one of the twelve most memorable surfing movies. Yet while the achievement of "real surfing in it" was true in spades, time might have obscured his memory of its bogus elements. With the striped shorts and legs spread like he's doing squats, Eskimo's stand-in remembers. "Who can believe that shit," growls Noll in *Riding Giants* (though sour grapes from the earlier era's premier big wave rider for not scoring the Mitchum role he coveted may have something to do with the attitude). Finally, the split verdict's just right, for *Ride the Wild Surf* is a Hollywood commodity with feet planted in two separate worlds. While the beach movies forming part of its own ancestry would continue to spill blithely out for a bit longer, it was a significant step towards more authentic and respectful treatment of surfing action and the surfing life, one whose relative box office success indicated a substantial mainstream curiosity about the real thing. In 1966, of course, Brown would be the right man with the right film at the right time, at once enchanting the general public with an authentic surf movie and condemning the most blatantly ersatz commercial treatments of surfing to the scrap heap. *The Endless Summer* merits the legendary status it has universally been accorded; when the familiar graphics of the film poster appear four decades later in the bedroom of the protagonist in *Soul Surfer*, it reads not as set design thematics but just as what surfers still have on their walls. After Hollywood's early commercial forays into the beach scene, Brown offered a different kind of product, one that felt so noncommercial that he couldn't find a distributor and had to release the film independently to prove it could fill seats. After weeks of word-of-mouth sell-outs in the surf capitals of Wichita and New York, Columbia finally picked it up for wide-scale distribution. Until *Roger & Me* in 1989, *The Endless Summer* was the highest grossing documentary ever and, if we are to judge from Amazon DVD sales rankings fifty years after its release, it's only outperformed by *Gidget* and *Point Break*, with user comments breaking regularly towards "Classic!"

In the beach towns, of course, a movie for surfers by surfers was nothing new, but for inland general audiences it was. A fresh, salty breeze, *The Endless Summer* is no Hollywood scriptmeister working up his daughter's adventures or writer/producer pair toiling for Desilu who, their finger profitably to the cultural pulse, could just as easily turn out a hippy film five years after *Ride the Wild Surf*. For the first time, at least for a mass audience, Brown got on film something close to the essential of the sport that had left its fad days behind and was beginning to take up other kinds of cultural, economic, and institutional space. What most teases that essence into being is Brown's affectionate, knowledgeable filming of the surfing action which, contextualized by occasional land scenes and the thin narration-directed "plot," constitutes 80 percent of the film. Seasoned by a lifetime of surfing and a decade of movies for other surfers, his technique was furthermore marked by a certain confidence born in those glory days of *Tokyo Olympiad*, the Sabols' early NFL Films, and the Wide World of Sports. Back in that first era of broadcast color before the image glut of later TV and Internet, just getting close to the action with quality footage of the finely trained body in competitive movement was considered by most viewers exuberantly fresh enough in itself to communicate simple human truths about nerve and discipline, the thrill of victory or the agony of defeat.

While Brown was an early practitioner of in-water shooting and on-board camerawork with his Bell and Howell Autoload, it's his standard mid-distance shots that carry the film. Often set early morning or late afternoon (good surfing windows but most important, most atmospherically lit and shadowed), they tell a simple, irresistible story of human energy and natural force, of figure and field in an always shifting, ever re-correcting dynamic. His camera can pan tightly in to focus on footwork or back to place a crowd of surfers and a pod of dolphins in suggestive parallel, but most shots are content to be long mid-distance takes with the surfer in constant adjustment to the break, there where the smooth water wall and its collapsed past meet. At that equally mobile and still point of the breaking world, Brown's surfers for the first time showed a mass audience that surfing is simultaneously about full release and careful discipline, about complete freedom and a form of enslavement to those moments of freedom. The Kahuna had to *talk* about the surfing life (a finally arid message in the mouth of the stiff, landlocked Cliff Robertson). Through the loving attention of a cameraman calmly assured that the action can communicate everything it means by itself, Brown takes us visually to that cusp of order and flow, obsession and insouciance, discipline and the stoke that is surfing to the committed for whom the sport spills over into the life. His imagery establishing the terms, Brown enabled the waves of narrative surf films to follow—even if it meant waiting a while.

Most obviously, no longer was it possible to fake the surfing scenes like before, with those bogus flat water close-ups and rear projection. In the decades to follow, as Hollywood returned to the shore, submersed and embarked subjective camerawork would increasingly complement the can't fail straight-on shot. Pro stand-ins would always get work, but the new norm would become actors comfortable enough in the small stuff to suspend viewer disbelief for the transition to bigger waves unsurprisingly out of their range: a reasonable paddle out and a wait in actual swell—or perhaps a really caught wave, in the case of certain actor-surfers—and the audience was on board. In more recent years, the impression has become nearly perfect, not only with well chosen stand-ins but also with recent CGI face replacement technology. Creating the cinematic illusion of real surfing with its inherent tension and drama was vital for the waves could no longer simply be a colorful backdrop to conventional romance. If such films were to reward any kind of serious narrative and thematic ambition, the surfline would have to become a credible space where the story can take meaningful hold, where its characters live intensely and ask what matters about identity, personal values, making a buck, dropping out, growing up, getting old, the compromises life extorts. For over a decade, though, no one in Hollywood seriously took up the challenge. Perhaps it was simply the daunting simplicity and legitimacy of Brown's vision; perhaps it was the distracting spasms of social upheaval or those concurrent upheavals in a surfing world shaken by the new board technology that radically changed the experience or a new competition scene that changed how we look at it. Yet while the studios shied away, the "surfing movie" plunged forward with redoubled vigor and creativity. Responding first to

Brown's example, then seemingly energized by the revolutions in the street and in the curl, filmmakers north and south released some of the genre's signal efforts in films such as *Pacific Vibrations*, *Morning of the Earth*, *The Innermost Limits of Pure Fun*, and *Five Summer Stories*.

~ ~ ~ ~ ~

Catch a Wave

In this sense then, it's appropriate that it took surfers themselves to lead the larger cinema entertainment industry back into the telling of surfing stories. In 1977, for example, a script written by surfer-model-actor Phillip Avalon came to Australian screens as *Summer City*. A shoestring feature that found a certain success following its estival December release, the tale of four mates on an early '60s blowout road trip north of Sidney before losing one of their number to marriage includes a certain Mel Gibson in his first role, that of a hardcore surfie. Before things get bloody following the seduction of a gun-happy local farmer's daughter, the movie flits tonally between lighthearted drinking, flirting, and mucking about, and more sober background tensions about looming maturity. Watching surfers, the responsible member of the group carefully grills Gibson's Scollop, then just drying off: "Where's the future in it? ... There's nowhere to go." "That's right," he mumbles, "There's nowhere to go. It's all there already." While, five years after *Deliverance*, *Summer City* is finally more about the male bonding adventure gone sickeningly wrong, surfing nevertheless contributes to its secondary concern with maturity welcomed and resisted. Set in a an efficiently evoked Australian surfing milieu, the film's small, under-the-radar drama has more in common than one might think with the big deal surfing feature that would arrive with a major Hollywood splash just six months later and, at $11 million, run 180 times more in production costs. Dennis Aaberg and John Milius, who co-wrote the script of *Big Wednesday*, also grew up surfing, but this time at Malibu's First Point. Like the Australian picture, the Warner Bros. production Milius would direct follows a group of surfing friends and, at least in its opening chapter, places them back in the early 1960s. This narrative decision, of course, recalls another end-of-summer movie, *American Graffiti* (1973), the smash hit teen film by Milius's friend George Lucas that served as an evident influence on *Big Wednesday*. In retrospect, the narrative and thematic attraction of the prior decade seems clear. In a Western world shattered by years of political, social, and stylistic change, generational division, assassination, and the American (and Australian) trauma of Vietnam, the early 1960s represented an easily sentimentalized earlier haven of relative simplicity and peace before history veered into bumpier terrain. It's no surprise that the coming-of-age film—which each of these is—would want to visit this place. Yet as all three show in their very different ways, the seed of corruption germinates just under the surface of even the most idyllically remembered scene.

When he made *Big Wednesday*, Milius was starting to ride high in Hollywood with *Dillinger* and *The Wind and the Lion*, and was thus able to write his own ticket for this treasured private project. Everyone agrees that its genesis was Aaberg's observations of the early Malibu scene, and particularly a kick of a party, in a 1974 *Surfer*-published (very) short story called "No Pants Mance." The name Mance, by the way, does more than rhyme with Lance Carson, a wildman nose walker from back in the day and, if this is possible, something of a rival to Dora as a "character." The brother of Kemp Aaberg, a legendary '60s regularfooter who made more than the odd appearance in Bruce Brown's films, Denny brought humor and an offhand precision of observation to the script. Milius brought supercharged ambition, an overheated sense of the mythic, and a gift for the zinger, qualities that a year later would cough Captain Kilgore up on that shore in Nam. Riffing from "the smell of napalm in the morning" to "Charlie don't surf," Milius was on to his kind of subject in *Apocalypse Now*, there where the dank sump hole meets the sweepingly gestural. Despite his autobiographical links to the subject, whether three surfing buds growing up in L.A. County was is another question, but Milius certainly started well by buying the rights to the 1961 John Severson title. *Big Wednesday* is such a good handle that it alone may have tipped the balance in the famous three-way point swap with Lucas and Spielberg. Between them, *Star Wars* and *Close Encounters* would haul in over a billion dollars worldwide, whereas *Big Wednesday* was a critical and popular flop, only making its initial investment back (and pulling off a partial reputation recovery) years later on video. Meanwhile, the title stuck in the cultural imagination, becoming over time everything from another surf movie (*Biggest Wednesday*) to a pale ale to a New Zealand lottery event, and when a massive swell hit California particularly hard in the middle of the last week of August 2014, what else could you call that day? The title functions so well because it yokes a banal weekly moment—no *Saturday Night Fever* or *Friday Night Lights*—with a generic adjective whose very modesty of suggestion is what, paradoxically, ignites the imagination.

The suggestive reach of the title says something about Milius's ambition in *Big Wednesday*, ambition that is both its strength and weakness. His autobiographically flavored tale of surfing pals from carefree adolescence through the inevitable readjustments of age cleaves believably to the details and the feeling of a '60s and early '70s Southern California youth culture, even if the three are predictably (cf. *Ride the Wild Surf*) schematic and representative in their differences—the preternaturally gifted but troubled one, the maniac, the responsible guy. Running them up through adulthood, as Twain once said about his characters, Milius goes occasionally off course, most notably in his repeated attempts to universalize and mythify the whole enterprise. It's important to remember the movie industry context at this time. The 1970s were the heroic era of the New Hollywood, when a fearless reach for scope in the genre film overnight became a challenging new norm. *Big Wednesday* clearly aims to be surfing's *American Graffiti* but unlike Lucas—or Coppola in *The Godfather*, Towne-Polanski in *Chinatown*, etc.—Milius seems unwilling to back off from the overdramatic heightening of meaning. He seems afraid to trust his core material to speak for itself. Trying to hoist it into the great, he finally limits the power of a solid central narrative, some excellent acting by William Katt, Jan-Michael Vincent, Gary Busey, and Sam Melville, and surfing sequences that nearly four decades later are still marvelously credible and moving. There, certainly, Milius was right to shoot high, bringing Greg MacGillivray on board to coordinate the surfing scenes, dropping legends like Bud Browne, George Greenough, and Dan Merkel into the water, and shooting for a total of *20 weeks* on El Salvadoran point breaks, at the Ranch, and, for the epic conclusion, at Sunset Beach.

Milius follows his trio from 1962 through 1974 as they haltingly come of age in a jumble of surfing, pranks, draft dodging, chicks, and keggers. While his film was criticized by Janet

Maslin as "too often incoherent," the frequent sacrifice of narrative focus and coherence to the piquant moment in fact jibes well enough with the confusions of adolescence and the mixed-up, tie-died intensities of the period. There's the local surf god Matt, his problems with alcohol, and the mostly refused duties great talent and minor fame impose; crazy Leroy "the Masochist," played by Gary Busey and so almost as such derisively funny and self-destructive; and Jack who becomes the lifeguard shooing a burned-out Matt off the beach, then, again uniformed, heading reliably off to Vietnam. Character is left to emerge from the action and the gab, which is fine for the most part, though at times a short shot of appropriate backstory wouldn't hurt. How do these guys know each other? Why "the Masochist" (and why a nickname of four syllables)? More seriously, why and when did surfing become so important to each of their lives? Embedding some of this information discreetly into the jumble would probably add more than it would subtract, for at the end we care relatively little about these characters simply because we don't know them as well as we might, given their two hours of constant interaction with each other and their radically changing society. In between the high quality surfing scenes—seamlessly managed by remarkable look-alikes Peter Townend, Billy Hamilton, and other perfectly chosen doubles—the guys party, hit Tijuana, split up, marry, father children, try to make sense of the changes, and all, again, periodically punctuated by their coming together to surf. The parallel between the personal and social metamorphoses can be moving, but once again it's more effective when Milius doesn't try to say too much. The night before Jack's ship-out the guys watch the Watts Riots on TV in silence, a far more resonant moment than the baroque draft dodging histrionics that precede it. When Jack comes back from the War but not their friend Waxer, the buddies meet for the first time in three years for a session at sunset, the end of more than one kind of innocence is writ large.

Too large, perhaps. Actually, that particular scene does work with a certain delicacy for it's credible that these reunited friends would meet up on their boards, and where else to find secure footing in treacherous personal and social currents? Yet unfortunately even the film's most eloquent moments are often deformed by an invasive, distracting portentousness. In an interview with Andrew Stille, Milius proudly speaks about his "coming-of-age story with Arthurian overtones" and how its protagonists' troubled lives would be "made larger than life by their experience with the sea." Yet in the same remarks he said that those "who truly understand myth don't use it consciously." The filmmaker who imports from Aaberg's short story the metaphor of kings to describe his three surfers uses myth very consciously. The main problem is the relentlessly highlighted quadripartite structure of the film, announced by simple print on black screen: "The South Swell, summer 1962," "The West Swell, fall 1965," "The North Swell, winter 1968," and, yes, "The Great Swell, spring 1974." It's such an intrusively present ordering device that when "Sherry" pops up in the excellent period soundtrack, calling on the Four Seasons seems intentionally heavy of intent. The seasonal myth does bring order to a rambling twelve years of messy lives and social history and to a thematic arc of innocence-loss-redemption, but where it most goes wrong is in the voiceover introducing each chapter. It's never clear precisely who is speaking: perhaps the filmmaker himself, who includes a snap of his young self in the series of nostalgic black and whites that movingly underlie the credits? Framed by the epic sweep of Basil Poledouris's musical score and in prose that says way too much undergraduate Hemingway, the script strains unashamedly for the tingle. Like this from 1968: "The north swell

Big Wednesday, director John Milius (1978): Gary Busey as Leroy "the Masochist" Smith, Jan-Michael Vincent as Matt Johnson, William Katt as Jack Barlow (Warner Bros./Photofest).

was cold and lonely and dangerous. I remember … but now it all seemed to be behind us. Change wasn't in the beach or the rocks—it was in the people." Or 1974: "Who knows where the wind comes from? Is it the breath of God? Where do the great swells come from, and for what? It was a time we'd waited for for so long."

In a Hollywood landscape littered by flimsy entertainment products, it's hard to knock generous ambition, and the *auteur* passion and sincerity of the film are palpable. It seems, though, that Milius loved his highly personal material not wisely but too well. The first time we see the trio as such they are descending to the beach through the visual frame of a columned neo-antique portico that appropriately underlines their identities—voiced over, typically, before demonstrated on screen—as, again, the local "kings." Fine, yet when as grown-ups they return to the same scene for the Great Swell and the climactic surfing sequence, the framing calls annoying attention to itself, the steps are weedy, and the architecture sprawls in extravagant ruin. Classic cinematic bookending as in *Shane* or *The Searchers*, in Milius's hands it's more of the same "overly bombastic storytelling," more "trying to accomplish too much."[12] And it's not only the cinematic language that is italicized. When a waitress newly arrived in L.A. reflects that "back home being young was just something you did until you grew up; here it's everything," the lapidary formula evokes screenwriter self-satisfaction far more than real speech. In another register, so too for the prophetic verbal freight of the friends' admired counselor, the board shaper Bear: "You hear talk of a big day every now and then—it'll be a swell so big and so strong it'll wash clean everything that went before it. That's when the board will be ready. That's when Matt, Jack, and Leroy can distinguish themselves. That's the day they can draw the line." Please.

Here much less would be more, especially since the core narrative by itself does the job, giving density to the sweet frivolity of the *Gidget* growing-up model while also widening its scope to treat more consciously and in more clearly realized detail those times that were a-changing. When Milius is not overdoing things, the young protagonists return believably to the beach to center their friendship, look together for meaning and direction in their changing selves and world, and, finally, take a step over that line into adulthood. In his influential *Playing and Reality*, Donald Winnicott offers terms that can perhaps cast light on the function of this psycho-physical space in *Big Wednesday* and, more largely, the film genre it teamed with *Gidget* to create. While Winnicott's subject was early infancy, his conceptualization of "transitional space" and "transitional objects" resonates analogically when one considers these young individuals obsessively returning to the same place with toys that seem to prolong childhood but in fact help lead to its end. To master the board is progressively to achieve a certain self-mastery when faced with the sets, some calmly manageable, others ominously rising, that life rolls in from its inexhaustible depths. Riding waves is furthermore a formalized, structured encounter with raw pulses of physical energy, an energy clearly parallel to the raging hormonal forces throbbing within the adolescent self. Teenaged girls riding horses come to mind here as a similarly symbolic harnessing of brute natural force during this stretch of profound personal transition.

For our three surfers, the formal moment of transition occurs when they head out on the Big Wednesday in question, its title a sly wink at hump-day, when the week's beginning tips into its end. Jack's back from Nam, Leroy from Pipeline, Matt from his boozy decline. Some convincingly filmed big wave rides, music heavy on the brass, Matt's wipeout and climactic rescue by his buddies, and then the three find themselves on the shore shyly approached by a wide-eyed blond kid with the lost board. "Keep it," advises the ace, more movingly than cornily fusing the moment of personal transition with the act of transmission, an intersection immediately confirmed when, just before leaving the beach for good, the trio looks seaward to admire a young Gerry Lopez. He's as talented as they say and, adds Leroy, "so were we." Importantly, the board Matt re-gifts is the work of the cool, mysterious shaper Bear. Older, bearded, troubled himself, formulaically cranky but generous, he turns the character first sketched out by the Kahuna and glancingly evoked in the photographer Phil from *Ride the Wild Surf* into a fully drawn prototype for the mentor figure who will return in some form in nearly every subsequent surf film. Bringing shape to the transitional object, advising and often scolding his younger acolytes, Bear and his successors are rare adults able to stand outside adult society, a position from which they dispense wisdom to facilitate the young person's transition to a later life phase. *Big Wednesday* figures that moment as the dreaded move "inland."

In an emerging post–War American tradition marked by Nicolas Ray's *Rebel Without a Cause* and Salinger's *The Catcher in the Rye*, adolescence registers as "a social litmus test, a time of life during which subjects more easily detect phoniness."[13] Since a full-bore version of "the teenager's attitude of disdain" is incompatible with most conceptions of successful adult life, the challenge is to make the passage while keeping a certain edge of resistance that protects some portion of the authentic self. Master of the surf transitional space, the older guru prepares his charges for an extreme final ocean challenge that forces them to reconnect with the best of that childhood self and enables a next phase that, while different, will always at some level be animated by what was learned there. "Though inland far we be," Wordsworth wrote about coming of age in the "Intimations Ode," "Our Souls have sight of that immortal sea" where "Children sport upon the shore, / And hear the mighty waters rolling evermore." Preparing the new generation for this transition, the elder mentor furthermore illustrates a paradox central to surfing, that a sport which emblematizes modern youth culture so perfectly in fact is animated by a deep respect for ancestral wisdom and the past. Significantly, in *Big Wednesday* as in numerous other surf films, biological parents play little or no role. Their part belongs instead to the mentoring elder who offers to those who show themselves worthy a place in an ancient line of descendance and the responsibilities which accompany it.

For good or for ill, *Big Wednesday* set firmly into place the character type of the wise elder and the narrative arc enlisting his counsel to prepare the young protagonist(s) for a heavily symbolic challenge. While the movie pattern does address in coming-of-age an eminently legitimate theme and while it gestures towards the significant role of tradition within the surfing world, its repeated use speaks more clearly to a certain anxiety about surfing in the wider culture and to Hollywood's dependence on manufactured conflict and neat resolution. Time and again surfing is presented in largely positive terms, but not as a lifetime avocation so much as a beautifully photogenic space of initiation and testing. It's something you do with stoked intensity until it's time to take up the reassuringly settled concerns of normative life. In the constraints of the ninety minute format, the theatrical release draws on the sport film formula to figure the process of growth as a series of conflicts to be resolved in a single—and, again, wildly photogenic—final surfing competition or confrontation with waves of exceptional size or danger. With inevitable variations, this basic pattern spins out of *Gidget, Ride the Wild Surf* and *Big Wednesday* to structure movies such as *North Shore, Blue Juice, Newcastle, Soul Surfer, Drift, Blue Crush, Point Break*, and *Chasing Mavericks*. Within the surfing community part of the abundant appeal of the animated feature *Surf's Up* (and to a lesser degree the *SpongeBob SquarePants* franchise[14]) is the knowing way it plays with these very conventions. Nor is cinema the only medium to rely on them. Perhaps the best surfing novel, Tim Winton's *Breath* is a densely imagined and richly textured reading experience. It goes far beyond the formula, but it nevertheless gives us a rudderless kid with nearly invisible parents, a memorably troubled surf-elder, a great wave that punctuates a life, and a protagonist-narrator now on its other side who still surfs but does so differently today as husband and father.

In the 1987 *North Shore* that pattern couldn't be more clear: a naïve protagonist from the mainland leaves his struggling single mother for Hawaii, where luck and talent lead to the tutelage of the tenebrous Chandler, a (yep) bearded board maker whose rigorous idealism helps the young man learn what he wants from the waves and from himself, and face the final challenge in the Pipeline Open. Somewhat less corny than this pitch might indicate, William Phelps's film is farfetched but unpretentiously efficient in its dealings with the appealing narrative tension between innocence and experience. Launched as if by Jet Ski, it opens the instant Rick Kane takes the Arizona State Surf Championship (!?), and before minute five the cute tow-head has left pool-generated waves to test himself against the most rugged waves in the world on Oahu's eponymous North Shore. Some of the abundant implausibility washes off when, a few missteps and chance encounters later, lead Matt Adler shows that even extravagantly wide-eyed he can hold his own on reasonable Hawaiian breakers without a stunt double. His character as written and portrayed has a tabula rasa earnestness that hovers between sweet and irksome, for this supposedly top surfer has apparently never read *Surfer* and doesn't know what a rhino chaser, duck dive, or haole is. Such off-the-plane innocence sets Rick up for more than a few falls—most notably when he inadvertently crosses Gerry Lopez's Vince, honcho in the local surf posse—but it also leads to the crucial relationship with the mysterious board shaper. Rick's an artist pressured by Mom to take a big scholarship back East, Chandler an artist forced to make a living selling to big name show-offs. Rick works to remake Chandler's surfboard logo and in exchange learns from the master how to read waves and write the next chapter of his life.

Outstanding performances on the waves and an attentively observed local surfing culture bring some ballast to this charmingly innocent hot air balloon. As a Tinseltown surfer, Adler was not alone, for the actors portraying his two allies, Gregory Harrison (Chandler), all cool sobriety, and John Philbin (Turtle), also hold their own plausibly, only handling off to doubles at Pipe and other hairy breaks. The casting of the film's heavies runs more or less the other direction, with top surfers like Lopez and Laird Hamilton having to make a similar stretch, but this time from the board to the boards. Pros Mark Occhilupo and Robbie Page also show up in pleasantly amateur little cameos that help introduce our innocent abroad to the North Shore scene and the generalist audience to a few necessary surfing

North Shore, director William Phelps (1987): Stand-off between Laird Hamilton as the arrogant Lance Burkhart and Gregory Harrison as the soul surfing Chandler. Photographer: John Paragon as the Professor; background: Matt Adler as Rick Kane (partially obscured) and John Philbin as Turtle (Universal Pictures/Photofest).

basics. It's absurd that Rick would, of all people, get a lift from two of the best surfers on the planet, but together they do help paint a believable background of sugar cane burnoffs, wave-centrism, and localist tensions. A lifelong surfer who spent a couple of months absorbing local vocabulary and speech patterns, Philbin makes the most of his thankless supporting role as Turtle, the third-wheel local who befriends Rick then watches the new arrival strike up a friendship with Turtle's boss Chandler. Shruggingly cool of body language with a lazy tonal lag to his surf pidgin, Turtle is right up there with Captain Kilgore and that surfer dude stoned since the third grade, Jeff Spicoli, in the extremely small category of movie characters with real surfer DNA. Like Sean Penn in his breakthrough role in *Fast Times at Ridgemont High*, Philbin so thoroughly inhabits the caricature that it becomes character.

The film's most absorbing stretch is the central chapters when the successive improvements in Rick's design parallel his surfing apprenticeship. Chandler offers him a rigorous education in literal and symbolic depth, beginning significantly with a dive to the reef—for "most surfers never look under the water"—then sequencing gravely through an imposing array of lined-up boards that visually represent the full tradition, from the skegless ancient koa wood 130 pounder to the most alert of the new short sticks. As Rick learns both to look at the world around him and to respect the past, his design efforts improve, from the first, all flash but "soulless," through the image Chandler at last approves, a surfer emerging as if born from the curl. More than a necessary concession to commerce, the logo's creation here enacts the trying quest to bring into meaningful accord surface and depth, signifier and signified, in a world that generally rewards their dissociation. There the stars are the Lance Burkharts—icily chiseled and self-regarding in his portrayal by Laird Hamilton—who "think a wave's just for carving up, hot-dogging, imposing their own style" for the spoils of fame. Whereas the shaper insists, "a pure surfer goes with the wave." Chandler is attractively true to his name, the traditional artisan nurturing a guttering flame. In this decade of an exploding ASP, exponentially growing surfwear industry, and Gordon Gekko, he transmits his discomfort with competition and sponsorship, his sense of a moral dichotomy between old-school soul surfers and the facile shredders who score big on the circuit. The inevitable crisis of conscience follows when Rick's developing wave skills win him a place in the Pipeline Open—"you want your picture in the surf magazines?" growls Chandler—where, just as inevitably, he'll make it through to the finals opposite Burkhart.

The film works in the predictable complication of Rick's romance with an Hawaiian beauty, then links it interestingly to ugly haole-local racial tensions. Where the latter could have remained generic, instead the movie identifies Rick's antagonists as Da Hui, the Black Shorts who surfaced in the '70s with a nationalist/localist agenda briefly explained by the shaper as historically justified; more precisely, a punk in the group's the bad guy, whereas its leader, played with stoic menace by Gerry Lopez, represents both the local standard of surfing excellence and a slowly revealed fair-mindedness. As the protagonist navigates these hazards, Phelps remains focused on his moral dilemma until the big competition and its have-it-all ending. Rick loses the final due only to Burkhart's literally underhanded cheating, wins it in the eyes of friends, former foes, and himself, gets the shaka from Vince and his picture on the cover of *Surfer*, then finally chooses art school after all. While not without recalling *Gidget*, this merging of incompatibly parallel lines seems more satisfying if only because *North Shore* so fervently communicates the belief that hard-won self-knowledge is what matters, not its medium of waves or paint.

In so doing, it explicitly develops an emphasis, one hinted at in earlier films but apparent only in the voiceovers from *Big Wednesday*, upon the intensely introspective, even mystical aspect of the wet physicality that is surfing. Rick's apprenticeship is all very Luke Wavewalker, its roots in a similar mulch of vaguely Eastern thought and rough matter from the West's Romantic tradition. When Chandler obliges Rick to observe for long stretches the churning of the waves, he is discreetly requiring his young charge to look inward with at least as much focus. Presupposing a world and self inextricably mingled in life's currents, this fusion of attention comes naturally to a sport that perhaps more than any other demands an immersive reactiveness and empathetic alertness to the fluid environment on the part of the actor within that environment. External and internal reality, the rhythm of the waves and the beating of the heart: "Sea of stretch'd ground-swells, / Sea breathing broad and convulsive breaths / … I am integral with you." Overblown in that way of his, Whitman recalls in "Song of Myself" those thrilling, embarrassing winds of Milius that might be the breath of God. Phelps is truer to the laconic cool of surfing discourse; his is in fact a similarly full-throated lyricism, but one stronger for the way he holds it in check.

These Zen romantic winds power the surf in what we might identify as the "classic" films of the genre. Over and over again some form of the watery rite of passage concludes a personal quest running down two paths so densely intertwined that they become one, the hesitantly growing ease of the waterman paralleling—becoming—the growing self's hesitant progress towards confident maturity. The access to deeper truths enabled by the surf guru invariably includes the recovery of lost or threatened values in a world menaced by materialism and preoccupied with image. Not surprisingly, this form of narrative has appeared with insistence in the last three decades as, since the Reagan-Thatcher '80s, the triumph of the commercial has become nearly complete. In the surfing world, that unthinking obsession with free markets is frequently, if not always fairly, equated with the sport's monetized ASP institutionalization, the rampant growth of surfwear subsidiaries and sponsorship, the new aerial slashing that seems to favor style over substance, and an attitude alliance with the posing, in-your-face extreme sports sector. Not surprisingly, the Hollywood-born mentor figure's frequent recurrence came just as surfing itself, led by a baby boom demographic but not only, was re-discovering the quiet pleasures of the longboard and celebrating surfing's continuity with its past and a go-with-the-flow tolerance in a gently retro series of surf videos like *Sprout*, *Thicker Than Water*, and *One California Day*.

While nostalgia shades that recurring figure's worldview in the theatrical releases of recent decades, it positively rules a little-known 2005 production called *The Ride*. You've got to give it to *The Ride* for bringing together a self-involved, arrogant world champ from 2002 with, as mentor, none other than … Duke Kahanamoku! Nathan Kurosawa (no relation) wrote, produced, and directed this pleasantly amateur little fable of time-travel, shot in less than a month entirely in Hawaii with local talent. When snarling, entitled Californian David Monroe wipes out at Sunset, he's rescued 91 years earlier at Waikiki by the Duke, who ignores the hotshot's very bad manners, coaching him along in the pidgin of a century ago with lessons like, "Bruddah', ride the water, not the board" and "the spirit is what transports you." They hang out with the two other beachboys and about five assorted beachgoing passersby (this is a very low budget operation). Eventually Scot Davis's David gets beyond his comically one-dimensional anger, gratefully joins their ranks, falls in love with a proto-feminist Hawaiian beauty, and realizes, yes, the meaning of life. It is easy to make fun of the low production values, lame transitions, and characterizations even Kurosawa recognizes as "a little over the top,"[15] but the sheer good will of the whole thing can be hard to resist, especially as incarnated by Sean Kaawa. The exceptionally charismatic first-time actor (and reggae band leader) pulls off the intimidating feat of non-hagiographically portraying a Duke believably jibing with the accounts of the man's simplicity and generous dignity. He completes Monroe's apprenticeship with a compulsory big wave paddle-out on the North Shore, at which point the nicknamed "Ghost" wipes out and returns to the 21st century, but, of course, not to a mercenary view of surfing. Newly gracious in victory, still dazed, he heads to Honolulu and meets the now-aged son of one of his 1911 pals, then goes to Duke's for dinner and the mobius strip narrative conclusion time travel movies can be counted on to provide. Beginning in the overheated Huntington Beach surfing–BMX–skateboard circus, the film takes viewers, as its subtitle goes, "Back to the Soul of Surfing." It's a predictable, sentimental journey that occasionally swings through some mildly interesting territory thanks to Kaawa's performance and the sincerity of its good intentions.

If the soul of surfing's the concern of *The Ride*, in the overtly Christian *The Perfect Wave* it's the soul of a surfer. Starring Scott Eastwood, the 2014 release that surfs off recent returns to fundamentalism worldwide but which made it to only a few screens is based on the St. Paul-like account of an '80s surfer living the hedonistic moment who survived a near-death experience diving in Mauritius and today preaches the Word. The Duke might have seemed like a stretch, but none other than God Himself plays the spiritual guide in this loose (if often visually lush) play on the familiar coming-of-age narrative formula. The autobiographical details are updated to today. A California-born Kiwi (never really explained), Ian disregards the reservations of his devout, conventional parents and heads off with a bud on what he rightly identifies as a "dream surf trip": somehow never at a lack for funds or happy coincidences, they make it to Australia's Gold Coast and then to Bali and Jeffrey's Bay, with their ultimate goal Cape St. Francis and "Bruce's beauties" from *The Endless Summer*. Except that, after the movie's subtitle "A Surfer's Glimpse into Eternity" and the born-again matriarch's insistence that her non-believing son need only ask and God will respond, it's clear immediately what the perfect wave really is. Launched with a particularly talky introduction, Eastwood's character loves to rhapsodize in voiceover about his spiritual sense of surfing as a kind of eternity in the moment (while copping unacknowledged quotations from surfers like Phil Edwards and Buzzy Trent). It's hard to say if Eastwood does a good job portraying this figure for, beyond a bland, watery spirituality apparent from minute one, he goes through zero character development. Ian's romance with the most interesting character in the movie heads nowhere, nor does the potentially enriching friendship he strikes up with the soul surfing Lachlan; ditto for the young man's artistic talents (cf. *North Shore*), revealed at a crucial instant and then forgotten. Until his character abruptly has a sit-down with God, Clint's son is left with little to exhibit beyond a likeably soulful gaze and his chiseled chin and abs.

The plot as such is a very pretty progression of beautifully filmed surfing scenes (including fine underwater shooting), punctuated by plausible local color and cursory glances at the road's nightlife temptations and casual meet-ups. To the credit of the writers and director, the story checks in at the right places and communicates something of the mechanics and aesthetics of a very contemporary surf trip. But if you're actually going to

J-Bay and Bali and seem to want to present the scene realistically, why illustrate the best wave one of the characters nails with a shot from Pipeline or take the endless barrel in the credits from Skeleton Bay on Africa's Atlantic coast? Supposedly enhancing the plot and preparing its payoff, a large number of portentously faith-based details call attention to themselves, like a trip to an island that is "literally paradise," our pair getting symbolically lost in the desert, a pal rebuked for being of "little faith," the hero put off by Bali's "idol worship," the dive buddy's warning that "if you get confused, head towards the light," and even the Endless Summer that in this context clearly awaits the just. If these constant road signs are not clear, the inspirational lyrics of the soppy soundtrack do the trick. That final dive leads to a nearly fatal jellyfish sting and panicked flatlining at the hospital. You really have to be with the religious program not to squirm when He announces in his James Mason accent, "Ian, I am the true light and in me there is no darkness." After a bit of posthumous chatting, the surfer miraculously bounces back to announce that "I've ridden my wave." This in turn inspires a friend to do some surfing of his own and download "the e-version Bible ... and I started to read it." Why not, since that's where this *Perfect Wave* was breaking all along? But unless one is deeply of the converted, the sledgehammer subtlety of this 94 minute sermon is very tough on the ears.

Extremely "uneasy" in its "mix of the hang-loose mindset ... and reborn Christian fundamentalism,"[16] *The Perfect Wave* cleaves imperfectly to the familiar surf movie plot structure. The essential is present, though: dispersing the required instruction into the visionary pleading of Ian's mother and the final counseling session with the Heavenly Father, and delivering in its heavy-handed way on the metaphorical promise of that long sought perfect wave, the movie treats surfing yet again as an act of introspection and emblematic phase in a process of personal transformation. Here as often elsewhere that process implies leaving behind the very surfing that led symbolically towards enlightenment. That's certainly the case in *Blue Juice*, a loose-limbed 1995 comedy drama. Even if this forgettably lightweight effort can seem like a study in character complexity next to the pious simplifications of *The Perfect Wave*, it's still apparent all along that boy-man JC (no relation) will surf the Boneyard at the end and learn what he has to learn. In the script co-written and directed by Carl Prechezer, the thirtyish hero is planning a global surfari with Chloe, who has another agenda, settling down with her man and making a go of a Cornwall café. Then JC's mates blow in, and the intentional jumble of a plot is off and stumbling with lots of boozy, matey stuff and a publicity scheme to get JC back out at the dreaded break where he was severely injured, even as the couple, played by likably handsome Sean Pertwee and a particularly fetching young Catherine Zeta-Jones, keeps on very attractively squabbling. This is a surfing crowd so, true to the realities of the British scene, they spend a lot of time waiting. The requisite guru figure, a laconic mystic called Shaper, intones repeatedly, "It's coming." Which is apparent from the opening shots when, in a motif to be picked up later in *Blue Crush* (and, in slightly different terms, *The Perfect Wave*), the hero wakes from a brutal reef wipeout nightmare. Between then and the same break's fearsome reappearance at the conclusion, the story veers from frenetic, noisy male fun to instants of quiet chemistry and charm when it's just Chloe and JC. The tonal shift feeds the theme of choice between lighting out or settling down. Along the way, drawing on the *American Graffiti* device of the recurring radio announcer, Prechezer goes very heavy on cute "English eccentricity"; here as with the excessively wacky crew he assembles to tempt JC, the film's off-beat tone often feels overly calculated.

A year before *Trainspotting* Ewan McGregor plays the wackiest, a London chum named Dean, a drug-addled journalist who's pulled a fast one to get the famous JC back out, and again into the tabloids. Only it's Dean who's tossed up now on the Boneyard rocks, which means that, to position himself for the rescue, JC of course rides the monster slab. It was coming, as the Shaper prophesied, and with it the introspective plunge to values deep within the self that will lead to the hero's no-regrets decision to scrap not only the surf trip but the whole hero trip, and join Chloe in realizing her dream. When the film concludes, a baby's already in the crib. A hollered "It's going off!" sends his mates scrambling for their boards, but the couple remains in each other's arms. For JC there will be no "going off." With the waves below the cliff reduced to cute graphics traced on the window, the conclusion suggests the domesticating impulse of normative femininity; the woman who never gets near the water and insists on adding that very window to the house in the opening scenes will later deflate a plastic globe symbolic of the link the film establishes between surfing and open-ended freedom of movement. Finally, though, the terms assertively established by the narrative coerce an alternate reading: the warm, fuzzy tenderness of the central relationship so clearly outweighs the often distasteful machinations and zaniness of the friends that it's comforting to view JC's decision as an affirmation of personal growth. Together the couple runs the Aqua Shack, a name carefully chosen to suggest the healthy compromises of newly entered adult life in its fusion of one partner's love for the water and the other's desire for a home.

The portrayal of surfing within various versions of this mentor-assisted coming-of-age formula was so fully familiar by 2007 that by it could confidently take the form of a PG general audience parody, and one featuring animated penguins at that. After, in short order, *Happy Feet*, *Madagascar*, and *The March of the Penguins*, opting for the adorable Antarcticans as subject was either brainless or a no brainer. Sony and directors Ash Brannon and Chris Buck rightly believed the latter, for in *Surf's Up*, their entertaining mockumentary tracing the career of a young hotshot off to challenge the best at the Big Z Memorial, they created one of the rare films equally loved in the multiplex and the surf shop. The imposing $100 million budget is visible and audible in the rich depth and detail of scenic and sonic design, the sharply drawn characters, and the spot-on dialogue captured by the self-reflexively present documentary team and given comic life by actors like Jon Heder and Shia Labeouf. The fun of *Surf's Up* is that it has a hoot at the genre's insistent conventions while at the same time milking them for all they're worth. Already Cody Maverick's name is so cool and referenced it's funny; as the best surfer in Shiverpool hopping a whale north to tropical Pen Gu for the contest, he picks up a buddy named Chicken Joe—though Turtle would do just as well for the parody has lovingly chosen *North Shore* as its primary target. There's the arrogant antagonist, the girlfriend Lani (cf. Kiani), the grizzled veteran advisor, the victory in defeat.

For Cody the contest is a pilgrimage to the very break where Big Z, the idol he met as a grommet, disappeared in a monster wave. Conflict with the rude heavy sends the kid to nurse his wounds in the jungle, where he meets a mysterious boardmaker called the Geek—who turns out, of course, to be the now-reclusive former champ. Hilariously voiced by Jeff Bridges, the Geek Totally Abides. After some preliminary wrangling, he will coach his charge through the shaping of a traditional koa board. The analogy's clear between Cody's first impatient hacks at the surface and contemporary wave shredding. The Geek

Surf's Up, directors Ash Brannon and Chris Buck (2007): The Geek (voice Jeff Bridges) and Cody Maverick (voice Shia LaBeouf) shaping a traditional koa board. The Geek says to avoid choppy cuts and slashes and just go with the grain (Sony Pictures/Photofest).

says to use long, smooth strokes, to go with the grain as you go with the wave, and, apparently like Quattrocento sculpture from Carrara marble, the board waiting in the islands hardwood will reveal itself. Despite his competition-resistant instinct, he will also coach Cody into the finals, in the process planing off the kid's showy contemporary insistence that every ride be filmed. There the kid affronts the cheating Tank and finally loses while really winning, his true victory being the joy of surfing and bringing the soul surfing sage out of the woods and back into the waves he loves. Unlike *The Incredibles*, which drops the conceit almost immediately, the documentary framing of *Surf's Up* runs throughout the film, mixing interviews with off-camera exchanges, black and white "archival" film, background pieces, outtakes, and exquisitely animated underwater footage that reads visually like the work of Jack McCoy or Dan Merkel. The filmmakers are not just true to surfing but to the way it is represented; they quote from *Step Into Liquid* when the Geek bows to the wave he's riding or Chicken Joe reveals his home spot as Sheboygan, and from innumerable surfing movies for the brief historical sequence or goof-off time at the blowhole or mud-sliding the slope. There's a paddle-out memorial and the guest appearance of two of the coolest surfing penguins in the world, Rod Machado and Kelly Slater, plus a whole web of pop cultural references from Pee Wee Herman to Don King, With its self-regarding fractures and interstices and its grateful homages, *Surf's Up* treats the surfing tradition with respect while being very much of the post-modern moment. Part of its appeal to the surfing community is that the film's producers clearly made the effort to get to know the scene; once they've done that, giving it the *Office* treatment comes off as a sign of respect and a fun, self-effacing reminder how close the representation of surfing reality (and, at times, surfing reality itself) can be to caricature.

Just how close would again be evident five years later when the (deliciously labeled in the credits) "true story" of *Surf's Up* was followed by the pretty close to true story of *Chasing Mavericks*. In its playful vein, the former recognizes the nearly obligatory nature of certain features the surfing movie tends to take very much to heart, like the crusty veteran and the crucial competition or once-in-a-lifetime wave as an arena of deeply personal testing. There, as film after film would have it, successful resolution can mean the return of threatened integrity or triumph over physical disability, recovery from emotional loss or the mastery of the self's private demons. This moment of passage in the transitional space of surf and sand is presented nearly always as the result of arduous physical and psychological training. As serious about these things as *Surf's Up* is lighthearted, *Chasing Mavericks* is in fact almost literally one long preparation sequence. Yet the very seriousness that might burden a purely fictional story and crush its drama into melodrama functions as an appropriate counterweight in Curtis Hanson's respectful 2012 treatment of the very heavy, if very brief, surfing life of Jay Moriarity. Corky Carroll is right to call *Chasing Mavericks* "right on the money" and add that "it was as accurate as possible." Exactly: the film works so well not because it follows age-old movie formulas but because it follows the narrative contours of a real life which showed that occasionally the old formulas apply perfectly.

Chasing Mavericks traces the trajectory of Jay Moriarity's short life, from his Santa Cruz childhood as a surfing phenom through his obsession, finally achieved at 16, with riding the mythical Mavericks break just north near Half Moon Bay. Moriarity learned at the feet of Frosty Hesson, one of the rare pioneers to surf the huge waves that break only rarely under the spell of severe Pacific storms. Though as early as 1930 Carmel's Robinson Jeffers may have sighted them in "November Surf" as great summits surging out of the west, up through the '80s and early '90s they were still considered more legend than fact. Sensitively directed by Hanson (until health issues forced his replacement for the last fortnight of principal photography), *Chasing Mavericks* resembles in some ways *8 Mile*, with its empathy for the marginal teenager and, once more, "professional" and personal challenges so merged as to become one. As frequently elsewhere in the genre, the acolyte's relationship with the guru—again bearded, gruff, finally lovable—powers the narrative. Abandoned by Jay's military father, his single mom can't hold a job let alone look after her son; in the sweet, seemingly functional family next door, Frosty in fact has problems playing his own role as dad, such is his love for the ocean and dedication to his Mavericks secret. By turns shredder and longboarder, Jay is tops on the local curls, but after sneaking a view of Frosty on a day when Mavericks is firing, he won't rest until he has gone out too. You've got to train me, he begs, and despite Frosty's early hesitation and stern warnings the spectator knows the rest.

Hanson and the film's screenwriters are unabashed in their treatment of this relationship, actually giving the older surfer's longsuffering wife these words: "There are all kinds of sons, Frosty. Some are born to you and some just occur to you." As if that didn't also occur to the viewing audience. Still, while it would be better if less emphatically underlined, the narrative is indeed structured efficiently around a father-son relationship. Symbolically orphaned, Jay wants to be like the admired adult, and five-sixths of the film will consist of his methodical preparation by what the film's heavy, again underlining, calls his "rent-a-dad." With the push-ups and black-outs, lessons in nutrition and wave tactics, endless pummeling in the impact zone and paddleboarding across Monterey Bay, it's hard at times not

Chasing Mavericks, directors Curtis Hanson, Michael Apted (2012): Anthony Tashnick stunt-doubling for Jonny Weston as Jay Moriarity (Twentieth Century–Fox Film Corporation/Photofest).

to see Rocky's sides of beef and hear that soaring score. Preparation sequences have their satisfactions to be sure, heightening tension and voluptuously postponing the film's climax, while satisfying a certain curiosity by seeming to break the whole of a complex action or profession into its constituent parts. *Chasing Mavericks* makes clear that, once again in the surfing movie, more than just waveriding is at stake: it's about, says the exacting guide, "building a solid human foundation—physical, mental, emotional, spiritual." This follows an earlier, and more resonant, warning, that the secret of big wave surfing is "how you perform when everything goes wrong," when mountains of water are "pushing you down into a place that's so deep and so dark you don't want to be there." That dark place will show, of course, in the parallel personal histories of the essentially abandoned Jay and his older mentor who, we discover, was left similarly alone and who then, in the film's major surprise, loses his lovely, supportive wife to a stroke. How to survive such a world? Teaching Jay how to get out through impossibly pounding surf, Frosty says if you look hard enough there's always a way.

A la North Shore, the two dive to explore Mavericks on a calm day, where a not-yet-ready Jay panics in its spooky, shark-laden depths. Echoing the warning above while preparing the three minute post-wipeout pushdown in the closing sequence, Hanson sets in place an important image pattern of enclosure and imprisonment. Every letter Jay receives from his estranged father he locks unopened in a kind of strongbox. The first two-thirds of the film place the boy in closed or tight spaces that visually echo the clenched emotional restriction and fear represented by the box. He keeps returning to a sketch of a diver straightjacketed by a squid's tentacles, and his room, frequently in half-light, squats in a narrow, somber trailer-like structure haunted by the absent father and the mother's absent expression. Jay's escape is surfing, but even then his go-to spot is an inlet accessed only by climbing down or jumping off high wallish cliffs. His kicks with friends lead him twice to suburban pools. Behind the fences of a vacant house, the empty first pool is a commandeered skateboard park, where bristling antagonism and the kids' clacking circuits suggest lives of sterile confinement and repetition; the filled pool they later leap into, a scene of whooping fun and promising mutual attraction with Jay's love interest, hints at progress, but the action remains within a severely immured space. Only when the boy first spies Frosty and his crew at Mavericks do vistas open wide, his envious, disbelieving reaction shot intercut with spacious sweeps of the immense horizon, the endless Pacific, and that wave.

That wave is the thing. The film opens to a voice over haunting shots of a form swimming underwater: "We all come from the sea but we are not all *of* the sea. We who are, we children of the tides, must return to it again and again." Uncontextualized, wincewothy to put Milius to shame, these words are nevertheless eventually redeemed by the film's quiet coda—commemorating Jay Moriarity's tragic death in a diving accident seven years after the events of the film—but most of all their straining towards myth is validated by that wave. For against the brutal fact of the thing as framed by Hanson no verbal lyricism, including the lines to follow, can weigh in as anything but understatement. The director clearly knew it was all about the break—thus the film's title and the way he tactically limits our views of the great swell in action to the barest of minimums until the enormous closing scenes. It's past 20 minutes in that Jay's breath catches with his first sight of Mavericks, and until he actually suits up to surf it they will have only one other brief moment together, when he gapes helplessly from the cliff at a wiped-out surfer swept alone into the rocky Boneyard, a near-drowning that effectively sets up the terminal sequence. The rest of the time it is an absence, a toxic vacuum filling gradually with dread and anticipation. For one thing Mavericks simply doesn't exist until the right—or wrong—storm conditions align. Throughout the film Jay obsesses about getting a specialist weather radio; when he does and it at last pronounces the magic wave intervals in his room's teeming dark, it is the fetishistic tribal object signifying that the moment of passage has come. The surf movie has always tapped into images of the hunt, of surfing safaris and bristling quivers. Earlier Frosty had said of a quiet Mavericks that "the lion sleeps." The big wave board the young Masai receives from his chief is called, significantly, a "spear," and the last words he hears before taking off is "kill it!" The chasing done, it is time to slay the beast.

To get a sense of the beast, first know that it's a 45 minute paddle just to make it out at Mavericks. Hanson communicates something of the size, alternating widely framed, sweeping helicopter shots with in-water camera work shooting up the wave's vertiginous face and then towards the vast vista shoreward after the unfathomable mass of its ugly lead-green shoulder has passed. Most scores would lay it on at this point, but the sound people go instead for a hint of anticipatory martial percussion to prepare the ear for the real payoff, the series of textured vapor detonations as the curls contract and finally explode. Like Rimbaud's "The Drunken Boat," where among "the breakers and currents / I have seen ... what men believed they saw," huge motorcraft ferrying surfers into position reel and barely heave over the almost literally inconceivable incoming ridges. Jay's pro forma antagonist—a low-rent surfer with a foul mouth and little narrative reason to exist—opts for the easier route out on one of those boats, but happily, after a minute of tension in the lineup, Hanson drops the Hollywoody duel one fears is coming. The moon-faced 16-year-old and his wave are more than enough duel.

When Moriarity at last paddles out through the ice-cold chop, it is to the break that would kill Mark Foo the first day the Hawaiian big wave elite turned up to surf the spot, and 96 hours after Jay's real-life first drop. As Steve Pezman later ranted in *Riding Giants*, Mavericks is "so gnarly and rocky and ... violent, it's just hateful, it's hateful." The kid somehow takes off on a wave that looks a dozen times his height and, in live footage from the day integrated seamlessly into the film, his over-the-falls wipeout merits terrifyingly its rep as one of the worst ever witnessed. Of course—after minutes under, board tombstoning then finally snapped off the leash—Jay will conquer the wave. Because expected, and clearly a montage of several separate rides, the soaring representation of his triumph oddly lessens the effect. The older and younger man embrace, a hagiographic series of surf magazine covers follows, then the news of Jay's death, echoing with fresh meaning the film's haunted undersea opening. But it's all decline from the emotional oomph the masterful camerawork and discreetly stirring score elicit from the wave itself when its pure, foul, rearing hatefulness is still the protagonist's future. In his Romantic masterpiece *Howards End*, Forster wrote about another remarkable life and death in terms of a "great wave." What marks such a wave is that it strews at our feet "fragments torn from the unknown."

~ ~ ~ ~ ~

Heroes and Villains

One of the ironies of *Chasing Mavericks* is that, while it was inspired by the form and details of a recently lived life, it has a strange intemporality. Except for the moment Frosty spies the cameras at Mavericks and pronounces "the end of the innocence," the film speaks only incidentally to its times, preferring to develop instead the merged inward-outward focus of a troubled personal adolescence meeting a monumental natural force. In this Hanson's film is actually something of a rarity, for surf movies have from the beginning tended to reflect implicitly, and at times directly comment upon, that larger world out there that is not the beach. Surfing may be a niche activity set in a physically marginal space, but as Southern California's Jackson Browne reminds us, "Looking East" with your back to the sea can be a point of fertile perspective. All about puberty and sweet summer romance, *Gidget* and her *Beach Party*-ing chums in fact signaled fierce culture wars to follow. While *The Endless Summer* inadvertently underlined American global dominance, *Big Wednesday* very advertently widened its scope to treat among other things a painful symptom of that dominance, the Vietnam War, and its seething cultural inflammation. With *Apocalypse Now* and the truism that "Charlie don't surf," six foot peaks and great rights and lefts could never again be quite the theater of utter insouciance they might have once seemed. From *North Shore* through *The Ride*, the sweet coming-of-age fable applies as much to a surfing ethos faced with the enticements and trade-offs of economic adulthood. Even Bear, the revered and archetypal spiritual guide from Milius's film, morphs temporarily into a cigar smoking, sweatshop-running surf brand magnate.

In the decades since, several surf films have even more explicitly addressed what is for lack of a better term called the real world, with its changing gender norms, social fractures, environmental degradation, and commercial pressures upon the self. Most have remained true to the genre's dominant coming-of-age-on-the-beach model, some almost to the letter, others much more roughly so. Perhaps unsurprisingly, with the women's movement in the '70s and the hyper-ascendance of already entrenched corporate power during and since the Reagan Revolution, it is the temptations of commerce and the question of changing female roles that have most frequently emerged, sometimes unintentionally and in very contradictory manners, from such diverse narratives as *Drift*, *In God's Hands*, *Point Break*, *Surfer, Dude*, *Newcastle*, *Brice de Nice*, *Soul Surfer*, and *Blue Crush*. In the latter pair, both from the first decade of the new century, the two issues entwine in intriguing ways. Equally clever of title, *Blue Crush* and *Soul Surfer* follow stories of young surfers trying to make it on the women's tour who, once again confronted with obstacles and aided by demanding mentors, battle predictably through to forms of personally measured victory. A significant sign of a changing world is that, while gender questions still enter the protagonists' stories when they find themselves classically torn between a culturally imposed urge to seek value in male approval and their own growing sense of confident self-esteem, they do not figure as the blanket girls-can't-surf prejudice that so frequently marked the genre in earlier decades. It is heartening that in neither film do guys ever give the girls a hard time for practicing "their" sport. No insults, not even any good-natured ribbing: Anne Marie and Bethany are just surfers, and good ones at that. Kathy Kohner must be proud.

Her Gidget, of course, forced open that door, even if screenwriter Upton as quickly tried to close it. Yet while Annette pops up on the board in rear projection and a talented woman surfer passes unacknowledged in a shot in *Big Wednesday*, the place for women in early surf films is still generally the sand. The Beach Boys' "Girls on the Beach" and the 1965 film of the same name make this perfectly clear. Kiani, the love interest in *North Shore* shows up there picturesquely as an earthy, natural force on horseback, like the Susan Hart character in *Ride the Wild Surf*, and her role is roughly the same, standing by her man and bringing out the best in him. Traditionally alluring and feminine with, literally, flowers in her hair, Kiani anticipates the film's all-boxes-checked ending by simultaneously awakening Rick to the deep meaning of her Hawaiian culture—of which he later displays more understanding than the local hoods in a crucial fight scene—and encouraging him to knuckle down and accept his New York art school scholarship. His guru's wife is a similarly nurturing figure who'll slip in an occasional coaxing word when her idealistic husband misses the point but who leaves the waves to the men. In *Blue Juice* that traditional woman nags the thirtyish hero to leave his childish surfing ways and draws a clear gender line between men as active, irresponsible primates and women as staid homebodies. As such Chloe might be seen as a rearguard throwback, especially given the female lead in *Point Break* four years earlier. Edgy, dangerous Tyler not only shreds with the best but teaches the ropes to the Keanu Reeves character. Remember, this was the decade of *Baywatch* when, while shoehorned into that red tanksuit, Pamela Anderson nonetheless played a lifeguard. In any case, somewhere in those years, according to Dana Brown's awkward backhand compliment from *Step Into Liquid*, it apparently became "no longer an insult to 'surf like a girl.'"

To get an honest sense, though, of the clear social progress represented by such indications and by the admittedly exceptional young protagonists of *Blue Crush* and *Soul Surfer*, it's important not to sugarcoat things: one has only to look at the surf videos of the last few years to see that for every *One Winter Story* or *Litmus* dozens still depict a men-only surfing universe. That is certainly the world portrayed in what we might consider two dark companion piece predecessors to the triumphant Hollywood productions above, *Puberty Blues* and *Blackrock*. Released, respectively, in 1981 and 1997, both are Australian films set in realistically portrayed teen worlds of intense peer pressure where, among other things, "chicks don't surf." True to the highly particular realities of Australian youth culture and the local beach scene south of Sydney and in the Newcastle area, they nonetheless speak forcefully to a wider audience elsewhere and to the still too frequent adolescent reproduction of sexist norms in the gender-segregated beachspace. *Puberty Blues* is the relatively faithful, if slightly sanitized, adaptation of the 1979 novel by Kathy Lette and Gabrielle Carey; a classic today, it was scandalous at the time for its spot-on Oz-slang profanity and casual ease with issues like teen sex, abortion, and drugs. With its Holden panel vans and molls, its spunks and towners, *Puberty Blues* couldn't be more Australian, but anyone who can remember the frantic need to fit in at that age and the cross-hairs of other kids' withering judgement will get this film. In any case, it would be hard to name a movie that better understands and more sharply delineates the place of surfing in a community. *Puberty Blues* knows what it means as a intensely felt marker of certain freedoms and pleasures unavailable to girls, or at least to those who want to fit in.

Which is all 16-year-old Deb and Sue care about. Bumped up for legal purposes from the 13 of the novel, these very ordinary little girls labor across the jammed beach in the opening scene, detailing on the way the prestige rankings of its different sectors, from "dickhead land" to their ultimate destination, Greenhills where the top surfers hang. They know the drill as, zeroing in on the latter, they enumerate and later enact with desperate, comical precision the ritual humiliations necessary to get there. This means sucking up and passing along test answers and refusing to rat, but at the end the in-chicks let you smoke with them in the loo, and you can tell the others to rack off. Yet while the gatekeepers to this kingdom of cool are the girls, its royalty are the boys. Utterly faithful to the spirit of the book, Bruce Beresford's soberly efficient direction perfectly captures the insecure yearnings of the former and, once they make the grade, the latter's confident sense of owning their little world: "The better they surfed, the higher their rank. The passport into a surfie gang for boys was a surfboard, a pair of boardshorts, a pair of straight-legged Levis, a packet of Marlboro cigarettes and long, blonde hair. To graduate into the surfie gang you had to have your name called out at assembly, regular canings, and have 'broken in' a couple of young surfie chicks. The surfie boys had a special walk. They bounded along in their rubber thongs, keeping their torsos stiff, sturdy as a lighthouse."[17] *Puberty Blues* is full of such *had to*'s, a few for boys, of course, but mostly for girls, little tyrannies like never eating in public or holding your bladder all afternoon, and bigger ones like jumping on demand into the back of the van with the Vaseline and the guy you've essentially been assigned.

The terms are clear. The boys surf and the girls watch, as the first guy Deb "goes around" with angrily recalls when she dares to close her eyes while decoratively tanning on the beach. Referenced in several stretches of nicely shot action on a clean right, surfing is their only real passion, a sole grace note in grungy little existences. The "plainness" Janet Maslin recognizes in *Puberty Blues* is one of the film's strengths, an unflinchingly rendered daily middle-class drabness that at first might explain the attractions of the exotic surfie group to these equally plain girls until it becomes clear to the viewer and eventually the girls themselves that the supposedly exciting new life they struggled to enter is every bit as dismal. As booze hands off to weed (and eventually to heroin, though this is less stressed than in the novel), the tribal rituals become increasingly rudimentary and mechanical, perhaps some emotionless sex but mainly just joint after joint. In her early enthusiasms and later creeping disaffection, Debbie gradually emerges as the central character in part because of a tense, unaccompanied wait for a late period but equally because of the complexity of personality Nell Schofield brings to the role. Behind the dumpy yearning and striving mimicry she communicates the stirrings of courage in a gutsy self at last insisting on sorting through the bad choices and slim offerings of her twisted teen world. In town with the other girls, Deb pauses before a jeweler's window to admire the "friendship rings" that seal relationships—that is, until you're "dropped," sometime not even by the guy himself but via a third party. Later this scene is echoed in a similar stare, this time through the surf shop window at an array of the forbidden boards, racked like weapons for the taking. Gidget had that moment too, when she saw Stinky's handicraft and started to get ideas. At last, sick of fetching snacks for stoned, paranoid boyfriends and all the rest, Debbie and Sue bug off, pooling their resources to take on the beach and its institutionalized sexual discriminations with a taboo board of their own.

The conclusion finds the two gamely trooping with their used equipment until they arrive at Greenhills and its astonished catcalls: "Girls don't surf! Jesus, who do they think they are?" It may be pearl city for their first attempts, but as the pair says about being dropped, "Who cares?" At last goofyfoot Deb gets up—Schofield snagged the role largely because she could surf—and a few female faces turn with provisional interest, though Beresford has the light hand and wisely avoids the sentimentality of a mass Hollywood-style female rebellion. In any case, this is very much a personal matter. The bookend final shot features the girls and the same stretch of sand as at the start. This time, though, they look down from a dominant position on the bluff, and the crowd which had earlier swallowed them up has now disappeared, the two images collaborating as quiet visual confirmation of that declaration of independence signed along the shoreline. The board Sue and Deb learn on is decorated with the flamboyant image of a tiger. In their teenage jungle girls are fully expected to be catty, but the big predators remain the boys. The tiger embodies forbidden energy and ferocity, while suggesting a Blakean turnaround of innocence into experience, once-docile lambs trailing the flock to the slaughter transformed by an understanding of their own power and possibilities. Since the novel and film, of course, it would be foolish to deny that women and girls have achieved more access to that power and those possibilities both in a larger Western society and in the lineup. Before we pat ourselves too much on the back, though, consider that when Australia's Network Ten brought out a two-season series version of *Puberty Blues* in 2012, it was acclaimed less as the accurate '70s time-capsule it was than as a reflection of today's realities. The culture of adolescence it "disturbingly illuminates," wrote Graeme Blundell, "seems not so much dated as distressingly contemporary."

Unfortunately, the same might be said of *Blackrock*, the 1997 portrait of a surf-driven Australian youth scene with its guys' too familiar solidarity and dismissive objectification of girls and women. Here beautifully filmed by no less than George Greenough, surfing is again the one domain of elegant mastery and meaning for largely directionless teenage partiers. They come together for a wild, boozy rave organized by young Jared to welcome back Ricko, his charismatic friend and rough edged older brother-figure returning from a long surf trip. Clearing his head after a scuffle, Jared squats a rock above the beach, where he spies one of the girls, Tracy, having sex with a friend of his. Things go south fast when other guys arrive and violently gang-rape the girl. Frozen, Jared watches her stumble off, only to discover the hungover next morning that she was found dead and probably murdered. The central conflict turns on Jared's refusal to dob on his mates as the inquest gets rolling and suspects, including his sweet, upscale girlfriend's brother, are brought in. With an occasional pause to sully the victim, the surfies carry on as before, while one of Tracy's friends goes unhinged with grief and anger. Intertwined with these tensions is the story of Jared's single mom, who has just discovered her breast cancer but can't manage to sit her mute, increasingly alienated son down long enough to tell him. *Blackrock* is the adaptation of the 1996 play of the same name by Nick Enright, itself an extension of Enright's earlier *A Property of the Clan* (1992). With its title drawn from the police report, the original was clearly inspired by the sensational rape and murder of 14-year-old Leigh Leigh near Newcastle in November, 1989. Donna Lee Brien has skillfully examined the way Australian audiences unsurprisingly read the film as similarly inspired. It fact, as she argues, the movie makes no reference to the murder, preferring in its significantly fictionalized narrative to de-emphasize the circumstances and motivations of the crime and examine through the invented characters of Jared and others larger issues of mateship, ambient sexism, and personal responsibility.

Blackrock was not generally well reviewed, which is surprising given its strong central performance by Laurence Breuls, between explosions just letting the edges of emotion escape from a tightly wound character. Director Steven Vidler has a sure sense of closely observed place and social class in the film's Newcastle area setting, as well as an alert contemporary awareness of the media as voracious feeder on human remains. When Ricko confesses to Jared and the net tightens, Vidler tarts up the conclusion needlessly, but overall offers a convincing portrayal of a real world of troubled kids with wildly misplaced priorities. Like *Puberty Blues*, this film is less about surfing than about a nasty, claustrophobic social ecosystem where surfing means at least two contradictory things. On one hand, especially as shot by Greenough, it's a momentary escape into beauty and harmony with an environment very different from the endemic bleakness of industrial and flat suburban settings; on the other, it's a just another mark of rank enlisted into an vile system of sexual apartheid. Deb and Sue get out by paddling out. Vidler takes aim at pervasive sexism differently, though that's not at first apparent in a movie tending to direct attention from a girl's personal horror to a boy's decision about what to do with it. Critic David Rooney called the secondary mother-son conflict in *Blackrock* "the drama's unconvincing and distracting element." This is to miss the point, for to make of the divorced mother's breast cancer a substantial subplot is in fact to raise in a another way the issue of gender and thus subtly establish a parallel with its dominant role in the film's central fact of sexual violence. Enright's screenplay develops the woman's lonely fears, her feverish attempts to cope, and her absolute inability to persuade an oblivious young male to listen, let alone care about a woman's life-and-death drama. With actress Linda Cropper's convincingly understated vulnerability and instants of abrupt courage, her character's personal struggle embodies what is just another metastatic stage of the same social disease, an ugly disregard for feminine dignity that can go so far as to make a young girl sexual recreation and then write "slut" on her tombstone.

With their often dark realism, *Puberty Blues* and *Blackrock* are radically different in tone and plot from the brace of big budget Hollywood productions treating, among others, questions of gender in surfing that appeared in the early years of the new century. From 2002 and 2011, respectively, *Blue Crush* and *Soul Surfer* both place aspiring young blond pro surfers on the same perfect Hawaiian beaches, where, aided by sage counselors, each will overcome hardship to qualify in extremis for a big competition, which she will technically lose but in personal terms win. Formulaically familiar as it is, shamelessly echoing *North Shore* and *Big Wednesday*, *Blue Crush* nevertheless has an honest, scuffed contemporary zip which is lacking in the pious certitudes of *Soul Surfer* and which in certain ways links the film with the more uncompromising social vision of the two Australian films. To be sure, Anne Marie from *Blue Crush* confronts nothing like the gender barriers faced by girls in the earlier works, but, contradicting common impressions of her idyllic islands, she does come from distinctly straitened social circumstances "on the other side of the island," there where you struggle to pay your rent. Anne Marie's a good surfer, though, and she needs the sponsorship cash that a top performance in the Pipeline Masters might bring in. (Interestingly, real-life competition for women surfers at Pipeline did not occur until after *Blue Crush*, and perhaps, life-following-art, in response to it.) The film was loosely inspired by Susan Orlean's 1998 *Women Outside* profile on Maui girl surfers, most from poor single-parent families, together trying to get through the impact zone. What remains from the original piece is its blend of near-trailer trash social realism with surfing's perfect dream, and the sense of a hard-won, daily threatened female community. *Blue Crush* is a teen entertainment product transferring its protagonist to Oahu's sexy breaks and tracing the classic sports comeback trajectory, but it stands apart among most Hollywood contributions to the genre for the semi-ambitious way it entwines the heroine's troubled surf quest with questions of social class, race, and gender.

Like *Big Wednesday*, *Blue Crush* drew its title from a previous surfing movie, in this case Bill Ballard's incisive, celebratory 1998 look at the women of surfing past and present. Drawing on archival footage and sterling sequences from surfers like Megan Abubo, Layne Beachley, and Rochelle Ballard, the video's beautifully scored 66 minutes essentially made the all-woman surf movie commercially possible and enabled later films like *Dear and Yonder* and *The Women and the Waves*. In a nice touch, many of the women featured in the earlier movie appeared in the later, either as themselves or through seamless digital face replacement as doubles for the actors. The wordplay in the title of the Universal release works perfectly; furthermore, it could not have come from a film more central to then-consolidating sense of a female surfing community. In *Blue Crush* that community is small but well-knit, a necessity given the sweat and hassles of getting along. Anne Marie (Kate Bosworth) shares run-down digs with two girlfriends and a kid sister on the edge of delinquency. Abandoned by her mother who's run off to the mainland with some guy, the surfing older sister cares for her difficult sibling like the similarly alone surfing protagonist of the animated *Lilo & Stich* from the same year. The three friends hit the surf when they're not working in neat little uniforms as housekeepers at a nearby luxury hotel or getting chewed out for driving Penny late to school. Anne Marie's the star, a local wild card invite to Pipe, with one week left to prepare—but also with, as the pre-credit sequence displays, nightmares due to a wipeout near-drowning. To this narrative complication then add the NFL team staying at the hotel and its absurdly handsome/nice quarterback; Matt crosses glances with Anne Marie, asks for surfing lessons, and suddenly she's choosing silk sheets and room service over training. As the protagonist yields to the attractions of fame, wealth, and afternoon massages, her little sister falls even more apart and her friends try to get her back on the board. Finally, following an unpleasant encounter with the team's hot, nasty "wives and girlfriends," Anne Marie sorts out what's important. Among other things, the film's $30+ million budget shows in the quality in-water work by Sonny Miller and the convincing technical doubling by Rochelle Ballard. The heroine surfs impressively after an early stumble, in the end scoring a Billabong sponsorship and a closing hug with Mr. Right.

Fairy tale narrative arc and, yes, brand name placement, but overall the film communicates a largely credible sense of the serious financial need and social class barriers present even in paradise. For the tight household of girls in the film, surfing exists simultaneously as a state of pure being and pleasure into which they apparently fell at birth and as a way out of a pretty tough life landside. They are always struggling to make the rent; when let go by the hotel, they jump on the comparatively big dough in surf lessons for Matt and his rambunctious teammates. Interestingly, the film is quietly framed throughout by the ethnicity that often runs parallel with class in Hawaii. Even if a little blondie, Anne Marie is insistently presented as a local,[18] and her elaborately tattooed, similarly low-rent male friends are all ethnically Hawaiian. From the opening scenes, they act as enabling support for her ambitions, urging her out to Pipeline and "blocking" so she can select the best practice waves. But certain submerged resentments surface when they find their friend with her new beau at a secret break, picking a fight with him because, as they say, "we grew here, you flew here." Back in *North Shore* Chandler had similarly addressed the mainlander's problems of island integration, reminding the hero that we took their land, so naturally they want at least to hold on to their waves. Anne Marie's other close ethnically Hawaiian friend is Eden, her too-symbolically named roommate and, in a nice twist on the motif, the film's by now inevitable mentor figure. Yes, she's also a surfboard shaper.

Guilting her friend back to work, renting an expensive Jet Ski for training, Eden is the protagonist's conscience, one all the more necessary in that familiar pattern of the central figure without parental guidance. The woman as counselor is particularly appropriate in *Blue Crush* because the idea of feminine solidarity runs central to the film. The male figure threatening to fracture the female community is, significantly, the high school testosterone stereotype, not only a football star but the cutest of quarterbacks. The animal attraction in the first glance is there, but the Anne Marie of the initial scenes is a centered, ambitious bustler who bristles at the obvious come-on that follows. She's too busy for such nonsense. When her resolve cracks, her surfing goes to pot, her roommates struggle with resentments, and her sister loses what little order her life had before. The crunch comes one evening during a gala team dinner with Anne Marie in the knockout dress her new boyfriend bought her: "Let's go show you off!," he bubbles. This moment of stereotypical female objectification is punctuated by an overheard restroom conversation among the mini-skirted wags, who can't see what Matt's doing slumming like that. Against female solidarity we have the age-old stereotype of women whose fundamental identity is that of catty Caroline Bingley rivals for male attention. Our heroine storms out, only to dive in the water fully

Blue Crush, director John Stockwell (2002): Matthew Davis as Matt Tollman and Kate Bosworth as Anne Marie Chadwick. Reversing the Moondoggie/Gidget apprenticeship, Anne Marie teaches quarterback Matt to surf (Universal Studios/Photofest; photographer: John P. Johnson).

clothed. A moment underwater, and then she's floating next to him in his tie. "What should I do?" she begs. Matt winningly replies, "The girl I first met would never ask a man what to do."

That Anne Marie would head underwater at this moment of crisis is consistent with the film's imagery, which, again, begins with an oft-repeated nightmare sequence of submerged, churning terror. As in *Chasing Mavericks*, the claustrophobic underwater fears link surfing trauma with that of a life struggling to get to the surface. Another near-drowning will follow, and when she finally gets back to work and makes it through to round two at Pipe, Anne Marie repeatedly refuses waves; and then at last taking off, it's a hairy wipeout and another long beating. By the time she makes it back out, it's too late to get the requisite number of waves to beat the real Keala Kennelly against whom she's opposed. But Kennelly's surprisingly willing to help, working on the psych-out and coaching Anne Marie into position. Result: a perfect ten that turns loss into triumph and sponsorship. This, the film's second feminine mentor figure, might cynically be seen as good PR for the real-life surfer in question, and in any case the competition was already essentially over when she started helping. Yet she may also be viewed as embodying an alternative model of behavior to that traditionally offered by men: when last sighted in *North Shore*, the Laird Hamilton bad guy was pulling the hero's board leash so he couldn't catch a winning wave. The network of support women offer women is central as well in another film from the new century, the often sharply observed (if a few drops too sweet) 2011 coming-of-age fable *Beautiful Wave*. It figures with particularly acute meaning in *Blue Crush*, for this is a movie largely about women getting by in a tough world and needing desperately to hang (ten) together.

For these women as, it seems, for the real Maui girls whose story informs the film, surfing is surfing first, natural and necessary as breathing, and only accessorily a business opportunity that circumstance won't let you refuse. In the 2011 *Soul Surfer* the opposite seems like the case. Gender counts in the film in that protagonist Bethany will fuss about her handicap and attractiveness to boys, but it's much less thematically important than the obsessive way the film reminds us of the burgeoning, increasingly invasive commercialization of surfing, or for that matter of our ad-infested daily lives. Its treatment is largely unintentional and the effect is, to be honest, far from flattering to its protagonist and those who tell her story. *Soul Surfer* recounts with what seems to be relative fidelity the much publicized tale of Bethany Hamilton, the young pro surfer who lost her arm in a shark attack but who fought back to make it again on the circuit. An audience already familiar with this narrative arc thus arrives more than primed for the heartwarming—and universally applicable—comeback story to follow. And unsurprisingly, if annoyingly, they will hear from first frame to last that "life is a lot like surfing. When you get caught in the impact zone you have to get right back up because you never know what's over the next wave. And if you have faith anything's possible." The extraordinary biographical facts do lessen the corniness of such a message, of course, but there's a lot to lessen: a family unironically perfect in a way one hasn't seen in cinema for decades, a villainess whose name Malina could be from a Disney fairy tale and who happens to be the sole non-blonde in the lineup, not one but two intense preparation scenes. And the religion: much more than a dollop, a primary ingredient. "I think I got my strength from Jesus Christ," the real-life Bethany witnesses in the closing credits. Apparently, if you have faith anything's possible.

And thus the film's title, instead of the more usual sense of soul surfer, that centered individual seeking neither attention nor first place but harmony with the wave and the self. Revealingly, after the cute opening Super 8 footage of the little girl with surfing parents and salt water in her veins, Bethany avows that "from my first wave I wanted to be a pro surfer." Given surfing's carefully cultivated mythology of counter-cultural spiritual purity, the tendency of other films in the genre—*Surf's Up*, *Big Wednesday*, *North Shore*, *Drift*, *The Ride*, *Surfer, Dude*, etc.—has been at least to question the meaning and personal costs in the professional sport and the accompanying sell-out to commercial motives and interests. Not so *Soul Surfer*, which not only smilingly accepts as given Bethany's career choice but which is in itself a virtual orgy of product placement. One feels the film, like the surfer herself, was in large part sponsored by Rip Curl. But the namechecking goes far beyond this brand to others and finally to the jaw-dropping moment when preparation for a mission to aid Thai tsunami victims rewards us with a lingering full-screen shot of a pallet of Spam. Agreed, even one can of Spam is an inherently comic object, but the embarrassing ripple of theater laughter was at least as much in response to the inescapable fact of the film's insistent merchandising.

Despite such a moment, the central facts of the narrative are gripping, a girl who gets her arm bitten off, goes back in the ocean (amazing in itself), and then surfs again at an elite level. To make phases two and three of this narrative sequence—the subject matter of the film—work, the precipitating first event demands delicate treatment. As throughout the movie, the opening surfing sequences are sumptuously shot and convincingly doubled. About 25 minutes in, as Bethany and family friends wait tranquilly for the next wave, the literally out-of-the-blue shark attack occurs. This happens quickly, cleanly, almost abstractly, with no creepy pre-predation music and the minimum of graphic effects. Even Bruce at Universal Studios is scarier than this fakey maw which surges upward and disappears, and which, except for Dad's later comparison of the scarred board to the now reassuringly deceased shark's teeth, is essentially forgotten almost immediately after it occurs. To de-emphasize the attack by hurrying through then erasing it afterward seems part of director Sean McNamara's plans: focusing viewer attention intently upon the protagonist's recovery and necessary return to surfing, he does not want his audience to hear those notes from John Williams and get all *Jaws*-y any time anybody goes near the water. The issue is in fact only addressed once, and this in order to be summarily dismissed. "Aren't you afraid?" asks a friend. "I'm more afraid of not surfing," replies Bethany. Issue closed.

Anyway, who would be afraid with Dennis Quaid and Helen Hunt as their loving, encouraging, longboarding, attractive, scripture-quoting, non-working, endlessly available parents? *Soul Surfer* breaks the genre's unwritten rule of the protagonist's weak biological family links and subsequent adoption by the crusty but generous spiritual guide. Quaid's empathetic counselor is, not surprisingly, also a boardmaker. When Bethany fails in her first comeback because she's not able to get out one-handed through heavy surf, he devises an innovation for her board; and all along he's there to train her and offer that kind of advice that applies equally to surfing and to life. In this film, however, the real mentor is the Great Boardmaker in the Sky. The religious apotheosis of *Soul Surfer* occurs before Bethany's second competitive comeback when she accompanies her church group to Thailand to help those suffering, rather neatly, from devastating waves. Seeking a larger purpose, she predictably encourages some understandably hesitant local children to enter the water and try surfing. In context, though, the scene comes suddenly, and creepily, to resemble a missionary-conducted immersion baptism.

The effect is more than a slight malaise, as it is elsewhere when we hear quotations from *Jeremiah* or earnest spiritual counsel from Bethany's youth minister. Certainly sincere and often moving due to the exceptional biographical events upon which it is based, *Soul Surfer* is a marvel of well-shot surfing sequences coordinated by Brian Keaulana and formidable special effects, including remarkable continuity between a CGI-enhanced Bosworth and the surfing Hamilton. The film nevertheless suffers from a goody-goody self-righteousness and a smug failure to question certain assumptions upon which its heroine stands. Like Rick in *North Shore* or Anne-Marie in *Blue Crush*, Bethany wins, while technically losing, the final competition; "I didn't come to win," she reassures us, "I came to surf." Okay, but this seemingly blithe disregard for fame and honors is in fact underlain by a fully developed mentality of sponsorship and merchandising. *Soul Surfer* is not unpleasant to watch despite the occasional wince, but the impossible-not-to-root-for comeback mechanics of its remarkable core story still come off as disagreeable when so sanctimoniously framed by whitebread Family Values and by a certain Christian Right's unthinking fusion of free market capitalism and old-time religion.

The title of the 1998 film *In God's Hands* seems to identify a kindred spiritual bent, but what the much-awaited TriStar release most shares with *Soul Surfer* is the finally disappointing use it makes of a very high potential subject. Zalman King's ambitious project certainly wants to be about the Important Issues facing surfing at century's end, specifically the lures and compromises of professionalism and the anti-traditional temptation to rely on machines in the surfing of big waves. Unfortunately, the tool chosen for this purpose by screenwriters King and Matt George is a fictional narrative that at its best distracts from some of the most fabulous surfing footage ever assembled and at its worst is, without exaggeration, cringe-inducing. *In God's Hands* is a great surfing movie trapped in the body of a schlocky Hollywood B-movie. Perhaps the first warning sign is the need to echo *Ride the Wild Surf* and *Big Wednesday* and cover all narrative bets with a trio of very different protagonists. Mickey, Shane, and Keoni represent three generations, from the voluble 35-year-old burn-out who once almost hit it big on the pro circuit and who has a hard time with change, to the infinitely taciturn, infinitely talented 22-year-old, to the bushy-tailed apprentice. Travelling together through the Indian Ocean, they train for mammoth waves, then take them on in Hawaii where old-school Mickey will lose his life. These very different guys obviously care for each other, but, beyond the fact that they all love to surf, *why*? The film never addresses the question, dogmatically asserting their friendship without ever displaying any real personal history or chemistry so that, in what should be the moving ending, it's hard to buy into the grin-allergic Shane's ardent memory of "one of those friends when you just think about 'em you smile." The problem with this film is that you're often smiling but at the wrong moments.

Coming out of a movie and TV career in soft-core erotica, director King has the facile Hollywood knack for keeping things very pretty and very superficial. With on-site shooting in stunning locations and highly professional camerawork and lighting, the production values are consistently high but unfortunately at the service of thin, undeveloped characters and a story that, while visually sumptuous, is riddled with implausibility, clichés, and manufactured crises. The tale begins and ends with the framing device of Shane's Mexican train trip for what we eventually find is his second meet-up with a lethal wave and tribute to the friend it killed. In between, our intrepid trio will surf like gods, but as often, it seems, they'll get tossed in jail in Madagascar, busted out, pursued in skeleton costumes to an improbably waiting seaplane by a canoe full of worked-up locals, and travel to Bali in a "tramp steamer," upon the deck of which they will construct a skateboard ramp. When not partaking in the frenetic party and concert scene, they meet up with the real-life big wave elite and train like commandos to ride monster slabs with the then-new tow-in technology. Before they head off to Maui to do battle with Jaws in the spectacular last chapter, Shane will take up with and sadly leave the captain's daughter, Keoni will get malaria, Mickey will gripe about jet-skis. Watching over their progress is the mysterious Wyatt, the photographer-magus-fixer who believes in Shane as the once-in-a-generation talent, shows up miraculously to distribute pearls to corrupt officials, and, in the guise of writing a book, philosophizes in voice-over about surfing. Poor Shaun Tomson, he of the melodious upper-crust South African accent, is obliged by a burdensome script to illustrate his pronouncement that "every sport has its mythologies" by citing the example of ... Mickey Mantle?

To the film's credit (and risk), real surfers were cast in the other important roles as well. While this helps immeasurably in the water, on land the results are uneven. Matty Liu's prior TV and movie experience shows in his relative ease with the one-dimensional emotions he's asked to portray, whether it's bright-eyed rookie curiosity or the painful fatigue of malaria (that has him, oddly, sprinting madly about at one point and from which he bounces back instantly once the fever drops). More central to the story are Matt George as Mickey and Patrick Shane Dorian as Shane Daniel. George's character is a muscled, verbose bundle of misused charisma. Lex Luthor bald before today's Kelly and the whole cool cueball thing, he's an attractive character who'd be much more so if he weren't written to be such a "character." Mickey's a recognizable movie type, the kind of guy who lives big, smokes cigars, boxes, slaps down royal flushes, chases dames, and can develop an elaborate marlin metaphor about them while locked up in a foreign prison. We are probably supposed to think of all that as a facade for the wounded heart of the surfer who missed his chance and is resisting change now as a kind of personal affront. In the end, the whiny way he keeps repeating "you can do it" about paddling into huge waves poorly serves the romantic soul surfer side of the movie's staged debate. When the action turns to Hawaii and Mickey goes fatally down in the mountainous wave he in fact does paddle into, details reveal a death wish that seems more motivated by movie conventions than the guy's earlier tour disappointments and first mild dose of mid-life crisis.

Where George is all over the place in his portrayal, Dorian's Shane is almost pathologically mute. One generously presumes this is because of his intensity of purpose, though vacancy remains another possibility when interminably long soulful stares only yield monosyllabic replies or, in response to Wyatt's evident, falsely profound observation that surfing is tribal in nature, a baffling "I never thought of it that way." While, notably in the Western, the silent man expressing himself with his actions is a classic, it seems the filmmakers exaggerated in their parsimonious allotment of lines to the surfer; Dorian is certainly a novice actor with a very limited range, but he's not the "fence post" critic Jane Ganahl recognizes, and his voice does have an almost feminine timbre that can be oddly affecting. In any case, he is model handsome, which was apparently a good fit for King who can't stop posing him silently with his exquisite cipher of a girlfriend in front of endless reaches of sea and cloud. Nestled in the warm shadows of a soft-core-porn-meets-perfume-ad aesthetic, they gaze moodily at each other and into the picturesque distance. The wince factor of the deal gets a good tow-in by the love interest's sensitive roughneck of a father: "She recognizes herself in ya', same eyes, same heart, without lies, taking only what you need, giving only what you can." Much less dreadful as dialogue is the single longest expanse of speech Dorian is granted, when his character poetically explains wave mechanics to her and, with a movingly unadorned sincerity, speaks about the curl where "whatever I'm doing, why I'm doing it, in that moment it all makes sense." Illustrated by pebbles dropped in a pond, his remarks address the way a big wave folds around an island and keeps going. "All you would need to do to ride it again," he purrs, "is find out where it's heading next and beat it there, however you can." Recalling the 1996 trans–Pacific wave-chasing of Dorian's buddy Mike Stewart (also in the film) and anticipating that of *Chasing the Swell* and Taylor Steele's recent *This Time Tomorrow*, the image prepares the conclusion when Shane will memorialize Mickey's passing by catching up to the same swell at Todos Santos.

In its long Hawaiian act, with the exception of Mickey's continued petulance and, of course, his death, the film replaces its earlier melodrama with the much truer drama of some of the biggest waves on earth. These were the pre-*Riding Giants* days when towing-in needed more explanation. During and after a extended, nicely shot small wave Bali sequence of training sessions (running, lugging boulders underwater, etc.), *In God's Hands* calls on surfers playing themselves like Stewart, Rush Randle, Pete Cabrinha, Laird Hamilton's rugged consigliere Darrick Doerner, and water safety boss Brian Keaulana. Together they provide ample illustration of and lessons in the physical preparation required, why you need to wait for the tow rope to whip, and how to survive 80 yards on the wipeout

Mach 10 Express. Necessary for non-surfers, the shop talk is agreeable for a specialist public because, even with the stiff acting, it's coming from guys with serious cred. The staged corniness of a "What's your greatest fear?" round-robin washes right off in winter Jaws at its thick, monstrous worst. Before multiple perspective cameras and a perfectly rendered slow motion norm cut occasionally to suddenly thrilling full speed, the film's star not surprisingly leads the charge. Dorian's velocity is exceptional, a tiny figure clattering down the face and fighting back in the camera's direction over the grisly bulge of the passing shoulder. When swallowed up from behind one time, the wipeout leads to effective subjective shooting and a dramatically enacted white water rescue, where the wordy previous warnings trotted out by Keaulana suddenly crystallize into a choreography of military precision. Already sensational in artistically filmed Bali training sessions, Randle adds tight corkscrews to his pull-outs, and Cabrinha somehow shrugs off the legendary right backside. The two most exceptional takeaways are Stewart as he belly slams down the mountain while impossibly holding on (and, yeah right, spinning a 360°), plus a pumped Brian Keaulana in the best ride of all tight out of an explosively spitting barrel. In the end credits, the film's dedication to Todd Chesser movingly closes the frame on this exceptionally surfed and filmed sequence. Chesser doubled for George in certain scenes; on February 13, 1997, he was inked in for the Mickey death scene during the huge swell but chose instead to surf Oahu, where he drowned at Outside Alligators.

When he first accepted the work, Chesser blogged that "maybe this time Hollywood will get it right." Despite the other-dimensional surfing, the lost opportunities of *In God's Hands* proved him wrong, unfortunately transforming what on one level looks like far more than a $10 M budget into a schmaltzy travelogue for human cardboard cut-outs. Dorian's Sphinx-like performance on land is less the problem, though, than an ambient overseriousness and a heavy priorities tilt towards lush visuals and trite, short attention span-friendly conflicts. A film needs a foundation of plausible action and characters we believe in if it's seriously to take on the key surfing questions ostensibly posed in *In God's Hands* about the relationship between professionalism and the surfer's soul, and how much is gained or lost when machines start taking on the work. Perhaps the closest King's film comes is when, murmuring about his obsessive life choice, Shane observes that "most everybody wants something else from it. I'm afraid if I ask for more it'll all disappear." Even if it's dicey to mix fiction and real life, this nonetheless comes from a well-known surfer five years into an ASP competitive career that would last six more. Also, if the movie had given at least some vague sense of the money network that allows these guys and their expensive Jet Skis to leapfrog all over the world, it might more reasonably have been able to deal with the economic realities of top level surfing; in other words, to rely on a few clandestine black pearls doled out by the mysterious Shaun Tomson character is to beg the question. While the jet-ski assistance issue comes up repeatedly in Mickey's nagging and histrionic face-offs with Doerner, the results on Maui are so spectacular that there's really little debate.[19] Having it both ways, though, the screenplay directs Keoni to reflect that "Mickey was right, you know. I hate the sound of those damn Jet Skis." Impassive stare, long pause: "Me too," Shane elaborates. Refusing to deal seriously with the issues it pretends to raise, *In God's Hands* finally displays a lack of consideration for the surfing world around which its story is structured. The movie's messages are so jumbled that it's not finally clear what it's about. A sign of that confusion is perhaps *Les Dieux du Surf*, the French language title of the film: "The Surf Gods," in other words precisely the opposite meaning of the English title.

Mixed messages are not always a problem, though, especially when they are intelligent and intentional. This is the case for the 2013 Australian production *Drift*, one of the most consistently enjoyable of the genre and a film which, even as it takes great liberties with the letter of surfing's historical record, truly understands its spirit and communicates the often contradictory essentials of its recent evolutions with honesty and affection. The subject, the creation myth of the surf gear and surfwear industry, is certainly less than gripping on paper. Lodged within the tale of two brothers in early '70s Western Australia, though, *Drift* generates such dramatic heat from their different personalities and choices that it could easily have done without the generic bad guy complications written too conventionally into the script. Drawn from a fussy banker's dismissal of a loan request to jumpstart a serious boardmaking operation, the ironic title of the new company is that of the film. The *I* assonance and "curl" graphics of the logo make it clear that the genesis of Rip Curl and Quiksilver broadly provided the inspiration. Rough outlines of the Torquay doings of Brian Singer, Doug Warbrick, and Alan Green have been transferred out west and heavily fictionalized in the story of the brothers and a mate discovering among other things that peddling boards and home-sewn wetsuits along the coast beat a life sentence turning out jarrah planks at the mill. Alongside its close attention to the details of this little human drama and the piecemeal daily assembly of a new business model, *Drift* also portrays the exciting tumult of the newly Aussie-centric surf world just after the short board paradigm shift and just before an onrushing competitive circuit.

The 1960 preamble finds Mrs. Kelly and the two young sons stealing away from her abusive alcoholic of a husband and motoring from Sydney across the sub-continent; encouraged by engine trouble and tasty waves, they settle in dodgy Margaret River, cow-town rustic and far from hospitable in those days before it became the Napa Valley. In a haunted black and white, the windscreen-framed landscape shot like it dreamed itself, these several quietly spectacular minutes of film evoke at once the loneliness, risk, and romance of the family's adventure, and of their longshot commercial venture to follow. In an evocative transition to the 1972 present recalling the opening of Jack Johnson's *Thicker Than Water*, the sepia barrel Jimmy enters as a talented grom splashes to startling full color the instant the now-strapping man charges out. Long-haired Jimmy (Xavier Samuel) is the hotshot surfer, a wildman charmer living by the few rules of his gift; Myles Pollard's older Andy is the responsible one pulling hard time for his brother and mother at the mill. When he gets out, it's to a future that, he says, has been staring them in the face all along, the handcrafting of boards and wetsuits jury-rigged by Mom's sewing machine for sale out there on the underprovisioned surfing frontier. The wider story includes Sam Worthington as hippy surf photographer J.B. in his Griffin-style magical mystery van and as guardian of Andy's eventual love interest, winsome Makaha carver Lani; there's also the movie's weak point, some unmotivated biker types, leather jackets and all, who deal drugs and have it out for the Kelly boys, though only God or Syd Field knows why. Alternating business boom and bust with refused loans and glorious surfing, the narrative includes a partner's tragic Kev Brennan junky end and the temptation to chuck it all and franchise the smarmy big competitor's products. Since this is a surfing movie, it will apparently all come down to a final competition. Jimmy doesn't win the five grand but he does boost an anachronistic air caught on film by J.B. After a bookend rescue scene, it looks like the jig is up, but when the boys show at the store (neatly opposite the bank), business is suddenly booming thanks to the newspaper-published photo. "Welcome to the Future of Surfing," goes the caption.

Oh-so-conventional story elements are amply present, not only in the dramatic lost/won contest but also the remote parental authority and the colorful Sam Worthington role as weathered surfing conscience. Not to mention the schematically different brothers, at one screenplay moment unfortunately referred to as yin and yang. Here, though, such attempts at easy narrative poetry are less corny than they could be because directors Ben Nott and Morgan O'Neill have so fully anchored them in the believable human prose of getting a business up and running. It's daring to believe that it can be involving to hear surfers talk about economies of scale and negotiate a passel of blanks on credit, but that's the case as we come to identify particularly with Andy's dogged attempts to wrest a decent living from a surfing life. Rendered with respectful detail, the central business drama of *Drift* is furthermore contextualized within the recent history of surfing by a screenwriter and directors who clearly know what's important about that history. Critics have rightly pointed out the multiple anachronisms in verbal expression, in the floaters or decades-early aerial maneuver and Zodiac tow-in surfing. Yet while the effect could be the absurd liberties of a *Return to the* (Surfing) *Future*, it's actually Picasso's lies that tell the truth. With Indo hash in hollowed-out boards and, wonderful detail, a Greenough-style kneeboard in the lineup, *Drift* gives us the heart of surfing in the early '70s, that time of extreme cultural ferment and modernization, when the short board revolution had just happened and the competitive revolution shortly would, and where the seeds of so many other subsequent changes were planted as well. Worthington's Merry Prankster photographer projects grainy surf movies, submerses his yellow-housed camera abundantly, and most importantly serves as a lightning rod for the highly charged debates of the period. The purpose of his grumpy-affectionate articulation seems primarily to highlight the multiple contradictions around which the modern surfing scene has constructed itself in the last several decades. He can spot a lone surfer off a point "not provin' himself against anyone." "We're pounding up and down the coast selling shit and he's out there," J.B. adds, "You can't buy what he's got, especially if he's not selling." Then the same photographer will organize a promotional shoot (and stunning session) at an intimidating reef slab dubbed "the Morgue." When the motor floods and the camera's lost, the disgust of the pro who lives by the sold image reflects the uniquely contemporary sense that something really hasn't happened unless it's on film. Positioned throughout the movie at the edge between soul surfer purity and commercial accommodation, J.B. says about the Drift storefront that it's "either the start of something big or the beginning of the end." "Mass production, here we come!," he'll freely taunt, then advise that you have to "exploit the system or it exploits you."

This tension is not accidental in a film about the delicate meeting between entrepreneurial struggles and sheer surfing stoke. The latter certainly gets first class treatment in *Drift*. Samuel, Pollard, and Worthington handle the water like the good Aussie amphibians they are, and the transitions to stunt doubling come off without a hitch. Among other great performers, goofyfoot Craig Anderson, his lanky, slumping brio clearly reverse-imaged in post-production, shared the coverage of Samuel with top Margaret River local Shaun Green. Shot largely by Rick Jakovich and Rick Rifici, the surfing scenes are a neatly edited and masterfully paced blend of in-water, subjective, aerial, and standard shore-based shots, of slow-motion and abrupt full speed. While never stooping to cheap melodrama even at the most crucial junctures of the contest, the shooting consistently captures the immersive beauty and urgency of surfing as well as the desolate blue-white magnificence of Western Australia. Filmed at some hideous bombora, the big wave sequence begins (like Noll at Waimea or Edwards at Pipeline) with Jimmy's spat-out "Fuck it!" From there the condensed dramatic pressure of the sequence builds steadily through the moment the team's Zodiac is overrun by an onrushing wall and tossed like flotsam. *Drift* finally works so well as a film because it recognizes and accepts the way the cool nerve and wild abandonment that are surfing can, and perhaps must, find some kind of accommodation with the prosaic demands of economic reality. *North Shore* serves heavy doses of soul surfing sermonizing, then shoehorns its hero and story into forced have-it-all resolution. *Drift* makes it clear all along that surfing's magic kingdom only really exists in honest relation to the unenchanted dry world of loans and bills. Reflecting the treasured ideals of surfers and their bad conscience, the surfing movie has tended to imagine the two in constant conflict. Even if it's the story of the founding of a multi-billion dollar industry, *Drift* suggests instead that in the complicated mixed motives of their daily lives what real surfers really do is work out their own private armistice.

Under what conditions one does is a big question in numerous surfing films. It is essentially the only one in the featherweight Matthew McConaughey vehicle *Surfer, Dude*, which appeared five years before *Drift* but, more importantly, three complicated decades after its subject, those halting early steps towards today's elaborate web of commodification and sponsoring. McConaughey's character is identified in the film's opening sequence by a thunder throat announcer: "Guess who's coming back! That's right, legendary soul surfer Steve Addington!" The narrative complication to this Malibu homecoming from the world's other great breaks is in that TV voice, since the Add Man's cool, low pressure gear sponsor has sold out to a bigger corporate group—and now they'll only keep him on if he agrees to participate in *Free Surfer*, their upcoming reality show and "first person immersion video game." Tan, shirtless, and barefoot when arriving at LAX, as throughout the film's 85 minutes, Add answers the customs official's question if surfing counts as a job with a pause and crinkled grin: "Not really." Therein lies the pinch—his manager buddy, for all the laid back vibe lent him by Woody Harrelson, knows that the checks have run out and it might be time to go to work for producer Eddie Zarno, former surfer and full-time shark.

At first glance, the film seems like a way to make some change by placing real life buds McConaughey and Harrelson together on their own home turf of Malibu to brah'-talk each other, which they indeed do charmingly. *Surfer, Dude* is a little more than that, however, in the comic, easygoing social satire that quickly falls into place. Zarno needs Addington's effortless cool to pull off what, over lush images of azure swells and bikinied chicks, the same media voice identifies as "the coolest reality show of the summer: the best surfers from around the world will be living in *this* house and partying with *these* girls!" Addington and Jack slip in and out of *this* house, negotiating, refusing to sign, and we soon get the picture: cameras everywhere, the cleavage and synthetic crises of reality TV, the "surfing" room where the technicians want Steve's cooperation in fabricating his game avatar. "Wave porn," mutters one of his Jeff Spicoli slacker buddies. The production design underlines the contrast central to the movie, between reality and reality show, the dusty, shaggy edges of life and the smooth sheen of deceptive appearance. From the brushy Latigo Canyon hillsides through the leathered mugs of rumpled gurus Scott Glenn and Willie Nelson, warm earth tones predominate outside the house. Inside, it's not beer sloshing in a plastic cup but vodka eased into crystal, ivory walls, silvers, greys, frigid cathode blues.

Looming over Point Dume, the spectacular white pad is an "early Klaus Woo." Addington can only stare when he hears that its style is "Post Post-Modern Revival." For jargon, this nonsense and surfer talk, is part of the meaning and the fun of *Surfer, Dude*. In Add's world we hear about keeping the stoke and how "that harshed my morning mellow"; in Zarno's, "we own his image, and image is reality, so we own him." A real surfer and one gone bad, they remain as far apart spiritually as they are alphabetically. "Now I cut deals," replies Zarno to Addington's memory of a great cutback. Whereas all the latter wants to do is surf "out there." The secondary narrative tension, though, is that the waves have shut down for weeks, which drives the protagonist to go so far as to swear off women and weed until they return. The word's never mentioned but it's clearly a karma question for, love interest nonetheless developed and plot complications seen to, it's only when Zarno is at last sent packing that the onshores pick up and the swells rise. Down in Baja on an earlier road trip Steve had performed a requisite figure in the genre, rising briefly out of his normal cheerful surfgrunt to offer lyrical tribute to the mystical something "special" in the sport: "What's special about the wind? Surfing is to be with that mystery, to ride that mystery as long as you can. And when it's over that's cool 'cause you know you were there."

Heartfelt stuff and brief so as not to overstay its welcome, such sentiments pleasantly underlie the broad satire aimed at a contemporary commercial and entertainment infrastructure of facile image and manipulation. In the film, however, surfers themselves can also come in for a touch of good-natured, if not always fully intentional, satire. First, the title hints, as sweetheart stoner boneheads, yet perhaps more importantly as, if not quite hypocrites, at least stealth commercial players. The Addington-style surfer as Emersonian rustic has no truck with commerce, but isn't it exactly that quality that makes him an attractive potential billboard? Zarno reminds McConaughey's character that he was being paid not for surfing but for wearing certain shorts on a certain board; plus he's called, isn't he, the Add Man. Though we're supposed to sigh knowingly when the evil producer evokes the "surfing industry," is there a better term for the interlocking financial interests of competition organizers, clothes and gear manufacturers, the surfing elite, and the producers of subsidiary entertainment products, including this very film? How then to position the surfer protagonist appropriately in relation to this economic system—not fully enmeshed, of course, but close enough to be credible for an audience that wants to celebrate its stars and wasn't born yesterday. According to certain patterns in, now, decades of films, this generally means, it seems, accepting need but not greed as motivation, and ambition but only insofar as it is framed by a wider could-give-a-shit soul surfer ethos. That line is thin and permeable, however. "They all come round eventually," Zarno says, with a distressing perceptiveness. When Add does, only serious second thoughts and his new girlfriend's company president of a father can resolve the problem. The bare feet of the latter in the closing sequence apparently mean he's a cool dude, but is there not embarrassing irony in East Coast corporate cavalry saving the day for a legendary soul surfer?

At the Saturday matinee, to be sure, most viewers will simply see the McConaughey figure as catching the kind of break he deserves. For in the surf film, accommodation with the business world or fame machine generally splashes away like it never happened once the hero's back on the board and immersed again in that surfing dream whose only requirements, we're led to believe, are self- or wave-imposed. But the accommodation did happen, and it does happen in some way in virtually every surfing movie (even the largely innocent *Chasing Mavericks*, whose epilogue accords considerable space to Jay Moriarity's later celebrity). One curious exception to this rule is the work that will conclude these remarks, *Point Break* (1991). Even 25 years later and despite not-unjustified descriptions as melodramatic, Kathryn Bigelow's second film remains a cult classic. At least in part, this is because of its uncompromising portrayal of surfing as entry into an inviolable, resolutely pure spiritual and psychic state. Given the economic realities that a film like *Drift* addresses directly and almost every surf narrative find ways to admit, this is a lush fantasy but one not without its own special, and multiple, ironies. While there actually is a truly Manichean split between surfing purity and "society" in the film, the intriguing overall effect is more to dissolve lines of division than reinforce them. Beyond rebels, the surfers are outlaws, whereas social force is represented by nothing less than the FBI. Much of the interest of the movie lies in what it goes on to do with such apparently irreconcilable opposites. *Point Break* pretends to be an adrenaline action movie with the requisite good guys and bad guys, but in fact it's all about moral nuance, the deceptiveness of appearance, and the inadequacy of simple categories. It's not hard to see how all of these speak to the complex reality of the surfing life.

As the film gets rolling, the categories would certainly seem to be clear. The Keanu Reeves character is a young Bureau hotshot sent to LA to beef up a robbery division tormented by an unsolved series of bank jobs starring the "Ex-Presidents," a highly professional gang trademarked by their LBJ, Nixon, Reagan, and Carter masks. A few American male insult greetings into the narrative, Johnny Utah gains the respect of his cynical veteran partner, played by *Big Wednesday*'s own Gary Busey, and together they pursue the latter's hunch, based on tan lines and a precise heist calendar, that the robbers are surfers. To infiltrate the scene, Johnny learns to surf, which leads to romance with his tough-love coach Tyler and, more troublingly, to a mutual attraction with Bodhi, surfing high priest and, incidentally, bank robbing gang leader. Though she will almost immediately entwine their worlds, Bigelow takes pains at first to distinguish the star student-athlete whose family name Utah evokes a landlocked homegrown fundamentalism from the mystical waterman named for an Eastern wisdom beyond understanding. The memorable opening credits present the two figures in evocative opposition, with multiple abrupt cuts between the FBI agent on the training course, all staccato movement and jerkily repeated shots at bad guy cardboard targets, and the supplely immersed camera view of a surfer, presumably Bodhi, whose every movement is fluidly one with the wave's energy. Here aggression is methodically channeled, numerically evaluated, and tightly focused on decisive later action; there the surfer glides in graceful adaptation to the liquid moment. Yet the complicated moral vision of *Point Break* is such that even as these terms set themselves apart, they also seem to merge—like the titles' two words and the lead actors' names which first appear on opposing sides of the screen, then slide slowly across each other to take their final transposed positions on the other side. The training day sequence with its targets gliding left and right visually echoes this movement as well as the horizontal sweeps of the surfer's continuing relationship with the wave. The rain soaking Reeves as he shoots furthermore suggests a link between the two sequences and their central figures. Significantly, the visual last word goes to Bodhi,

Poster, *Point Break*, director Kathryn Bigelow (1991): The bilateral symmetry of the poster design highlights the film's ambiguities.

whose waves finally swamp the camera, in a sense submerging the screen and, by juxtaposition, the young agent who will soon be swept away by what they represent.

Surfers are "some kind of tribe," we're once again told. Here their world is instinct and Dionysian bonfires on the open sand, while the Bureau offices are a tight warren of cages where the discourse locksteps through statistics and "data-based analysis." When Johnny moves to the beach, he leaves the indoor swimming pool and its sour agents fumbling blindfolded to pick up sunken bricks for the blind ecstasy of night surfing. "You don't need to see the wave; just accept its energy," Bodhi advises. Signaled by little giveaways like surf talk in the office or familiarity with a certain break, Johnny gradually goes native. For much of the film, he's unaware that this band and its attractive guru are the criminals he's seeking, so when that at last becomes apparent his sense of duty is already tightly wound into a confusing web of affection and heady self-discovery. Such complication is the point in a narrative crafted to call into question conventional assumptions. These guys are bank robbers, but their Presidential disguises suggest a parallel, politically subversive agenda: "I am not a crook," mimics the V-fingered Nixon figure before leaving with the cash. Or as Bodhi later says, no longer suggesting but underlining with a thick marker, "This was never about the money. It was us vs. the system, that system that kills the human spirit…. Those dead souls inching along in their car coffins—we show them that the human spirit is still alive." Perhaps sincere, perhaps wildly self-justifying, such rage against the machine is in any case disconcertingly explicit, for Patrick Swayze's Bodhi is far more convincing when he communicates in the quieter language of seduction and infectious enthusiasm—in other words, when talking and living surfing. Again, one of the reasons the film has stuck with viewers is its uncompromising faith in the ideal of surfing—the utter here- and now-ness, the otherworldly float—an ideal that by its very nature is more subversive than any political slogan. Bodhi speaks of "a state of mind, that place where you lose yourself and you find yourself."

When you go to that place and you're an FBI operative, things get complicated. Following the familiar surf movie pattern, Johnny invents an undercover backstory of orphanhood that prepares him symbolically for initiation into the new tribe first by his exacting coach and then, more meaningfully, by what his partner calls the "Zen surf master." Before the last reel, admittedly under duress, Johnny is nevertheless taking part in a bank job and helping form a perfect circle while sky-diving with his surrogate family of a gang. On one level he does his sworn duty, ceaselessly pursuing his target until, as Bodhi himself says, he (sort of) "gets his guy." On another, courting his own demons, he easily crosses lines of allegiance between institutional order and impulse, showing up late to his own bust, tossing procedure to the ocean winds, and, most notably, refusing an unrefusable kill shot. In the world of *Point Break* such lines are made to be crossed. When Johnny first sights Bodhi making small work of a five-foot wall, Tyler identifies him as "a searcher." Besides the obvious philosophical sense, the term suggests thematic links with the John Ford film. And indeed there is similar room for hero and anti-hero, thwarted binary oppositions, and unsettling excursions into alternate cultures and realities. In its referencing of the American cultural tradition of the criminal or gangster as hero, *Point Break* furthermore anticipates later forms of troubling complicity between lawman and outlaw in such films as *Heat* and *The Silence of the Lambs*.

Another complicity just under the surface is, of course, the erotic tension between the Reeves and Swayze characters. The primary contribution of the beautifully filmed but otherwise murky coming-of-age story in the 2008 Australian film *Newcastle* is the introduction of gay male characters and the narrative mechanics of their sexual attraction. In *Point Break* that attraction is palpable if never avowed, its point a weighty contribution to the film's already mercurial atmosphere. The two men share the same girlfriend—"what's mine is yours"—a Lori Petty coiffed for maximum androgyny and bearing the gender indeterminate name of Tyler. There's mooning and wrestling and languorous looks. The great action pursuit through the backyards and kitchens of Venice ends with the two protagonists locked in each other's gaze; finally refusing the shot, Johnny falls back, aims his revolver vertically, firing off a dozen stiff rounds to a monstrous groan of release. This list can go on and should, for a certain gay sexual tension is one more way *Point Break* explores the question of transgression and border crossing. Like this remarkable juxtaposition: the now wised-up Bodhi who says mysteriously, "I know exactly what to do with him," then cut to a beefcake shot of a doe-eyed, shirtless Johnny gazing longingly up at the camera directly above his bed. When both figures, finally aware of the other's true identity, play forward in their edgy game, the skydiving sequence offers a veritable festival of loaded language and action. "We gonna' jump or jerk off?" it begins, then "you want me so much, it's like acid in your mouth." Free falling, they hug in the air, urging each other to "pull it, pull it," and when the pair finally hits the ground they are tangled in a chute that for all the world resembles a particularly energetic night's bedclothes. In the epic final scene, when Johnny runs down his prey in Australia during the Fifty Year Storm, the love interest whose kidnapping was his ostensible motivation in much of the last part of film has completely vanished. What counts is that he "gets his guy." He could slap the cuffs on normally but chooses instead to handcuff himself to Bodhi. It's not surprising that you can go on YouTube and among the other parodies find a mash-up of such scenes entitled "Point Brokeback."

Point Break is indeed parody heaven. Partly it's the actors, Keanu Reeves, never cuter than here or more wooden as an actor, plus the cult film excess of Patrick Swayze, that '80s *Ghost*, *Dirty Dancing*, and *Road House* hard guy heartthrob. Not to mention the abs and scalloped peroxide fringe. Throughout, the film throws two genres, the cop and surfing film, into collision, testing their limits, only to go baroquely over the top in the infamous second skydiving scene. The first was Johnny's initiation, where we could, with indulgent popcorn-fed generosity, just perhaps accept the sophisticated skydiving manoeuvres. Later when, apparently for the girl whose motivational weight we never really buy, Johnny flings himself out of the plane, confident he can streak down, pick up the seven second lead of Bodhi, and share his parachute, we are entering bafflingly stupid—but joyfully parodic—cinematic air space. The two cops in *Hot Fuzz* who ruminate on Johnny and Bodhi get a surefire laugh but are also tapping into a warm surge of affectionate memory for a handful of scenes and verbal exchanges that are as unforgettable as they are easy targets for irony. The same goes for Jean Dujardin in his 2005 French comedy *Brice de Nice*. Though empty-headed Brice can't actually surf, he sits stylishly off the Côte d'Azur in endless wait for non-existent waves, starting each day with a devotional pause before a *Point Break* poster and quoting the wisdom of Bodhi at every available juncture. Well before *The Artist*, *Brice de Nice* and Michel Hazanavicius's *OSS 117* films had showcased Dujardin's subtly physical comic gift and gentle knack for tipping charm into smarm. Siphoning the comic potential from Bodhi philoso-babble while in no way dissing it, Dujardin deftly punctures his character's empty pretence to reveal a moving emotional neediness and thirst for something grander. Brice is ridiculous but in touching pursuit of an ideal. Which is pretty much how we feel about Bodhi.

Point Break is a genre and gender bender, and a total kick, but people don't just remember it for the howlers. In its way parody is as sincere a form of flattery as imitation, imitation that, among other things, has already given us the apparently unending *Fast and Furious* franchise and will soon produce a *Point Break* re-make—to be directed by the cinematographer of *The Fast and the Furious*. There is clearly something in Bigelow's film that arrests and fascinates, most likely its unsteady demarcation between good and evil, desire and duty, one kind of theft and another. Not surprisingly, the beach where Bodhi and Johnny tangle in affectionate aggression serves at least partially as disputed borderland in this fluid, continuing transaction between civilization and its discontents. Yet the surf line also means something entirely other, for behind the abundant half certitudes and contradictions that compose *Point Break* stands at least one uncompromising absolute, the redemptive heart truth of surfing: to glide as one with water, to walk on it, leads to a place so intensely of this world it lifts you beyond it. Every surf film seeks words and images to evoke this spot, but it has to be believed to be seen, and few seem to believe as intensely as *Point Break*. In waves where Johnny is born into a new self, Bodhi goes to complete a cycle as natural as the swell, wanting "the ultimate ... and ready to pay the ultimate price." Repeated at least twice elsewhere in the film, the adjective seems consciously to echo across the decades the squealed "It's the ultimate!" and sheer animal delight of a certain Francie after her first life-changing ride on Moondoggie's board. As Kahuna would find in August 2012, we all finally pay the ultimate price. What matters is that instant in that summer, that wave, that lift, that drop.

Conclusion: Zero Summer

> Where is the summer, the unimaginable
> Zero summer?
> —T.S. Eliot, *Little Gidding*

In the fall of 1953 Bud Browne turned some modest Hawaiian vacation movies into a genre, heading a thousand-strong parade of specialist surf community films and, later, videos that has continued non-stop for more than six decades. In the spring of 1959 the Hollywood pros joined the lineup with *Gidget*, the first of what have since become several dozen narrative theatrical releases centered on surfing and the surfing life. Despite their ostensibly shared subject, as film types they're coconuts and pineapples. The surfing movie and video have a small, reliably surfer-based audience. While filmmakers from John Severson to Taylor Steele have remained alert to powerful social rumblings off the beach and to stylistic and economic changes within surfing itself—the shortboard, the temptations of money and fame, the near obsession with the road—their real subject matter has always remained, very simply, the stoke. The mainstream theatrical narrative, by contrast, serves a much more diverse and diffuse audience whose vague sense of surfing derives very minimally from experience and very largely from its different perceptions within the popular culture. As varied and sometimes contradictory as those perceptions might be, viewer expectations have conspired with the marketplace requirements of date night-friendly film narrative to yield the wearily consistent result of stories often gravitating towards the same classic roster of character types and foreseeable narrative conventions. Yes, the surf community movies have tended towards adherence to their own formulaic blends, but the genre has in general painted its admittedly smaller canvas much more successfully and has certainly been far truer to the real feel and rhythms of the surfing life than most of its imposing Hollywood counterparts. From Bud Browne and Bruce Brown through Jack McCoy and Jack Johnson, none has had anything close to the seed budget and initial support of the big studios, but all have had utter assurance about their subject matter and perfect knowledge of their audience.

Films demand an audience, and not coincidentally the surfing movie started beaming from its clackety projectors more or less the minute the California-based surf culture boom had generated one. Its immense popularity within the very young surfing community—drawn by a few flyers and word of mouth, *500 maniacs stormed Browne's first showing*[1]—clearly expressed at least two strongly felt desires: surfers (and the curious) wanted to have the otherwise completely unavailable experience of watching surf riding footage; just as importantly, in Ike's elephant gray America they wanted an event around which to affirm a cool alternate identity, bond communally, and further the exciting creation of a vivid new subculture. As Dylan would soon announce about larger cultural currents, something was happening, and though exactly what wasn't clear at the time specialists have certainly given it thought since. In recent years theorists have repeatedly recognized ways this leisure activity with such a profound respect for a deeply rooted tradition paradoxically constitutes a radical break with the guiding continuums that mark so much of modern life. Critics like Michel Maffesoli, Gilles Deleuze, David Harvey, and Mark Stranger have characterized surfing as emblematically post-modern in nature: its subculture rejects the rational, utilitarian layerings, distancings, and structurings of modernity, what it means to live, as Saul Bellow deplored, "In a city…. In a mass. Transformed by science. Under organized power. Subject to tremendous controls. In a condition caused by mechanization."[2] Turning from this state of affairs to the morning horizon, surfing instead offers unmediated sensual experience and "an aestheticized lifestyle that resolves around a communion with nature and (grounded) neo-tribal forms of sociation."[3] Unlike other sports—invariably goal-directed, physically circumscribed, chronologically delimited—surfing "swims, even wallows, in the fragmentary and the chaotic currents of change,"[4] and this even in the case of mathematically scored competitions and decades of ultra-commodification. As Gilles Deleuze and others have argued, prolonging and intensifying the earlier Romantic rupture, surfers break with the rational structures of industrial and post-industrial life by radically entering and exiting an existing natural dynamic, their only objective as such being fleeting instants of what has been variously identified as "flow" or "peak experience."[5] This is, of course, what surfers themselves have long labeled the stoke, in its most heightened form the plenitude when time stands still and intense physical presentness means out of body otherness. While the surfing film can be many things and glide with its audience in multiple directions, including the essentially documentary, it remains bound by the foundational obligation to make creative use of the visual and aural resources available to cinema and convey on screen something as close as possible to those moments of intensely ephemeral, intensely personal, intensely heightened experience.

The most telling difference between the surfing movie and the fictional studio surfing feature is the former's nearly exclusive focus upon the stoke. Yet while the ecstatic experience the term connotes is perhaps the only thing all surfers have in common, it's also the most utterly evanescent and uniquely individual of occurrences, and thus by its very nature to a large degree incommunicable. As John Grissim argues in his aptly titled and still-fresh *Pure Stoke*, "the experience itself is the only true descriptive, something that seems to happen when the knower, the act of knowing, and the knowledge become one."[6] The dream of every surf movie is to find an unspoken cinematic language able to evoke that Yeatsian instant, to whisper something as close as possible to surfing's evanescent moments of meditative fusion and scream its fleeting raptures. When that happens here comes the magic word again, starting with Night One of Surf Movie History: "When I showed my surf films in California," Bud Browne recalled with typically clipped understatement, "the audience was stoked, and of course that made me stoked too."[7] For lack of a better term, movies like those by the Bud who would title a vignette in one "The Stoked Life" are frequently referred to as "documentaries." While as we have seen that's a perfectly appropriate term for certain films that have contributed a great deal to the surfing scene, for the most part what distinguishes them from others of the genre is that, while the surf movie spectacle may accessorily inform, it "is viewed not for knowledge, but for sensation."[8] As Keith Beattie correctly argues, surfing movies intentionally eschew the overarching claims of objective truth and a purposive sobriety for "a discourse of delirium."[9] Drawing here on terms from cinema theorist Bill Nichols, Beattie stresses the way the surfing movie brings its invariably "heightened and frequently excessive visual and aural intensity ... to bear on the isolated act of surfing in order to reveal its secrets and meanings."

Mediating the unmediated ecstasy, sharing those secrets and meanings, this has remained the mission, from the first surf movie nights though the film uploaded this afternoon from The Surf Network. That route has certainly been strewn with numerous unimaginative efforts of no more than very ordinary quality. It's tough to make a surfing movie that's unpleasant to watch if only because, as Grissim again affectionately notes, few things film better than a surfer at one with a breaking wave. But for the surf moviemaking planets really to align takes more than even very fine performances on exceptional waves. It takes more than careful allegiance to or clever enhancement of the expressive patterns that have come to orient the genre, either the Bud Browne-initiated formula of intense rides plus comic bits plus local color, or the Bruce Brown-confirmed model of the surfing journey of initiation and discovery. The handful of truly memorable movies and videos combine true intelligence and instinct, great luck and a great eye. Grinning but with the far horizon in sight, they speak with pertinence and easy intimacy to the good times in the surfline, but also, compellingly, to their times. To paraphrase Springsteen on rock and roll, the best surf movies never forget it's only surfing but treat their subject like it's all that matters in the world.

Every list is as individual as every surfer's experience, but this highlights reel will hardly surprise, starting as it does with a brace by Browne, say, *Gun Ho!* and *Going Surfin'*, Bruce Brown's soulful *Surfing Hollow Days*, and the genre's inevitable centerpiece, *The Endless Summer*. The latter's title was a nostalgic dream but, insistently pointing the way abroad, Brown also pointed the way ahead. *The Endless Summer* reinforces the complementary, already emerging models of picaresque wandering and the urgently motivated quest that would drive most later surf movies, while genially embodying the romantic receptiveness and fraternal yearnings of a new generation. Stirred by a world at cultural war and profound revolutions within the surfing nation, that generation then brought us films like John Severson's trippy, militant *Pacific Vibrations*, Freeman/MacGillivray's *Five Summer Stories* and its generous wiseacre sincerity, the primitivist idealism of Alby Falzon's *Morning of the Earth*, and George Greenough's unforgettable voyages within and beyond *The Innermost Limits of Pure Fun*. Finishing out a decade in which the shift of new short board surfing power to the South became abundantly clear and an agitated Hawaiian winter began to clarify the nagging professionalism debate, two of the finest films, Bill Delaney's *Free Ride* and Jack McCoy et al's *Storm Riders*, inevitably feature the new Australian and South African elite.

Ten films from three decades which would average nearly that many per year: a provocatively small haul, for dozens of other movies by these filmmakers and their dedicated rivals and friends have rightfully set more than one room on fire. When lighting strikes and the surfing movie's at its best, the exaltation is loud and contagious, you can't wait to go out tomorrow, and when you do you're, consciously or not, driven by different energies and ambushed by new perspectives. It is pompous to say life-changing, but the Hollister

Bay Theatre, Seal Beach, California (1974). A long line of spectators for the latest incarnation of MacGillivray/Freeman's *Five Summer Stories* snakes out of frame. Summertime and the promise of "new stories" … (MacGillivray Freeman Films).

Ranch sunset right in *Pacific Vibrations* resonates into an existence long after its viewing, like the plaintive guitar licks of "Wooden Ships," Crosby and Stills trading lyrics as disabused soldiers making their own peace. In between conquering summits of moving water never before seen on film, Browne's hero-clowns Buzzy Trent and company do more than have a total blast and make us wish we'd been there; framed as they are by Browne, they also limn a post–War American masculinity casting back to the hard man frontier archetype and ahead to counter-cultural rejections of the suburban nightmare. For the dream instead, see the still point of a turning world in Shaun Tomson's suspended magic at Off the Wall, chill Gerry Lopez petting the monster at Pipeline, Mike Hynson slipped into the perfectly tailored pocket at Cape St. Francis, Greenough stopping time with a 17 pound rig on his back at Lennox Head. Accommodation with the money men will apparently always be a puzzler: is there a better statement of the surfing world's deep ambivalence than the peripatetic restlessness of McCoy's *Storm Riders* and its luminous non-resolution in the cool witnessing of a pod of dolphins recognizing Wayne Lynch as one of their own?

Since the mid–1980s, of course, video has had the best of the traditional surf movie and such communally shared moments. Film festivals and special showings still occasionally bring the juice, and crossover efforts like *Riding Giants* and *Step Into Liquid* have stepped up with style and heart, but viewing has largely become an individual or small group experience. There's sure a lot of it, if you count video-supplemented blogs, WSL contest streaming, online awards for big waves and wipeouts, various surf channels, innovative forms of crowd-sourced filmmaking, and regular check-ins at, say, the Volcom site. With the Betamax, VHS, and DVD shakedown, relatively inexpensive high quality digital technology and Internet now rule a video field at once intensely Web-connected and splintered into an array of personal and tribal framings of surfing as everything from punk shredding to log riding. In some cases responding to à la carte demand, in others still aiming at a broad surfing audience, the movie economic model has changed radically. Most notably the heavyweight surf products and lifestyle clothing industry that has boomed in the last three decades has very actively moved into film production and sponsorship. While the sharp drop in production costs due to new, widely available technology has led to a proliferation of fresh, homecrafted movies shared online and helped serious fully independent films stay above water, the norms are either hybrid semi-independent efforts with several brand names discreetly cropping up on opening and closing credits or full-scale promotional videos that today are so sophisticated and entertaining they hardly register as such. Mini-tours and festival appearances often support DVD, Internet download, streaming, and specialist cable sales, while corporate films, as well as certain individual efforts, usually find their ways to dedicated web sites and directly online. Next to the celluloid hell Greg Noll remembers of shooting, rushing through editing, renting halls, selling tickets, pleading with the projector, and then doing it again the next evening and next year, pro quality laptop editing, Go-Pro's, and a fully developed infrastructure of potential partners have certainly made things easier. But then you've got to find your audience in all that dispersion and break through the image overload and static to be seen and heard. The subject being surfing, you still have to live with the stand you take on the money question, and you have to have something to say.

That's the key. While Doc Ball got it pithily right about surfers—"next to surf riding they like images of same"[10]—it's not enough just to put some good wave footage out there. Today, with so much quality surfing available on YouTube alone, the best films have to have a strong point of view and clear thematic focus to stand out. This has, of course, always been the case, but with the image glut the importance of a confident, striking personal vision is capital. Camcorder pointing and shooting, Taylor Steele got away with unimaginative presentation and crummy technical values in *Momentum* essentially because he was pointing and shooting at Kelly Slater and other extraterrestrials just entering the surfing atmosphere; in *Evolution* Paul Witzig had pulled off the same trick with Wayne Lynch. The shock value of that kind of talent goes only so far, though; while the *Momentum* model of shredfest-plus-roaring soundtrack still has its awesomeness for the video game-suckled successors of that first MTV generation, it's worn thin for many others.

As irony would have it, of the multiple hundreds of videos in a production line that seems only to be accelerating, the same Taylor Steele has created some of the most singular and compelling. Riding the momentum of that first movie and its popular sequels, Steele has matured into a surf storyteller of the first order. His films scratch surfing's exotic travel itch in unusual ways, drawing together individuals of character and style within intriguing narrative and situational framing. In *This Time Tomorrow* he affectionately references the deep history of surfing and its cinematic representations, offering a fresh contemporary take on the human urge to resist time's passage and the way every wave ever surfed is just a "new expression of the same storm." Steele is both an exciting creative force and a generous hub of encouragement and inspiration for others. The same could be said of now-legend Jack McCoy, whose career has spanned the film-to-video transition and who has shown that artistry and heart can out even in overt accommodation with the economic realities of surfing sponsorship. Mixing state of the art action, edgily homemade animation, and off-wave antics from Occy and others, *The Green Iguana* playfully enlists the oldest formulas in the surf movie quiver, McCoy's signature attention to the visual image, and a memorable soundtrack in the service of an urgent contemporary environmental message. In his long career and his attempts early this century to revive the tradition of live communal viewings, McCoy signals a temperament at one with that of a loose so-called "retro" movement that has generated a number of the most involving and soulfully felt videos of recent years.

Aussie Andrew Kidman, for example, communicates a raggedy off-beat affection for the past that lives in every surfer. Pure poetry sends Stephanie Gilmore down the line at Greenmount, her weathered, warmly back-lit longboard session a mystical *pentimento* to the ghostly forms of Michael Peterson in *Morning of the Earth*. Working in the same vein, Thomas Campbell takes us far afield in *Sprout*, but his visits to Noosa Head, Indonesia, and Central America are less the disjointed wanderings of the surfer as global nomad than statements of tolerant relationship and rooted connection. With his film's ride-anything generosity and happy mess of a structure gratefully recalling the earliest movies, Campbell cheerfully erases borders between the silly sectarian divisions of wave-riding, the arts, and the generations. Surfing's intense presentness as a gift and continuum from before animates as well Jack Johnson's work with the Molloy clan. The warmly felt pulse of *Thicker Than Water* is a series of lovingly shot, soulful sequences with the same loose band travelling the surfing world. From the striking opening montage and its truth that the child is father to the man to the equal truth that we're all in the same boat in the last, Johnson's film speaks of the generations and transmissions of a surfing life, of any life. True to that theme in their many film appearances, the Molloys grace *One California Day* with their dusty simplicity. So much the past today, their Golden State was once surfing's bright future. The lovely trust animating Mark Jeremias and Jason Baffa's film lies in each present instant and in Chris Molloy's observation that the magic "is still there if you're willing to look for it." Travelling the coast like Doc Ball, the filmmakers visit with quietly charismatic *California Surfriders*, among them spiritual father Skip Frye, kid Alex Knost, and brother and son Joe Curren, whose words and lives testify to the age-old verities that it's all about now and that being seen surfing is not the same as surfing. Starting things off, a quotation from Bruce Brown's first movie evokes Dale Velzy, all piss and vinegar in those days as he shaped the early boards and the history of surfing. It concludes with his descendant in spirit and deed Tyler Hatzikian driving the rainy coast after Dale's funeral, each individual windshield-splattered drop making its way to a swelling river, back to the sea, and into tomorrow's wave.

Today, of course, the sheer volume of videoed surfing is intimidating. The quality is unsurprisingly uneven, but in the work of artists like these and, again, Dana Brown and Stacy Peralta within the more purely documentary mode, the achievement can be of muscular thematic reach and lingering nuance. These films and certain others have taken their place in a long line marked by imaginative energy, thoughtfulness, loving patience, the quiet modesty of honest ambition, and a confident personal sense that surfing's intimate secrets and meanings will always be worth sharing. A surf video today means a handful of hot surfers in a handful of exotic locations. While visually exciting, the films of Johnson, Steele, Kidman, and the others are showing to viewers today and to the next generation that heart and mind can make a surfing movie much more than just visually exciting. With the exploding democratization of surf filmmaking due to technological advancements, the Internet, and online collaborative forms, the future of the surfing video seems particularly promising. Unfortunately, it's less easy to be sanguine about Hollywood and its treatments of the surfing life. Despite early resentments, *Gidget* is now indulgently remembered for its pioneering status, corny sweetness, and the scraps of bracing honesty torn from the timely novel which inspired it. Since then, however, the studios have too consistently missed the mark in their attempts to delineate believable characters and shape credible narratives around an activity almost universally perceived in popular culture as synonymous with easygoing youthful resistance to authority, but also variously read as an obsessive life choice, a competitive sport, part of an industry, a style choice, the route to fame and riches, an environmentalist commitment, a watery path towards mystic understanding, and what stoners do with the rest of their time. To cook up 90 minutes of requisite conflict and twists into a Hollywood-standard resolution often means incoherently stirring together the first of these ingredients with one or more of the others. Featuring attractive, undraped young people and hyperphotogenic settings and action, the resulting movies are at least going to be easy on the eyes. The trouble is, those same eyes often end up rolling when confronted with the clichéd character types and transparently predictable narrative patterns that have come to compose many of these films.

Reverse engineering from surfing narratives like *North Shore* or *Blue Juice* or *The Ride* back to the scriptmeisters who assembled them, it's not tough to imagine the professional logic. A youthful style-setter with a tangy tribal language, surfing is a cool, visually attractive amalgam of competing values, both vigorous outdoor activity and slacker escape route, expression of soulful purity and high stakes competitive arena. Pushed by the need to appeal to general audiences, the movie pros have for five-plus decades tended to return mechanically to the lowest common denominator identification of surfing with troubled youthful transitions, in turn grafting to the stories that result various combinations of these and other meanings in order to dramatize the temptations and choices of growing up. The crowd of beachsploitation flicks in the 1960s shimmied repeatedly in this thematic and narrative vicinity, but Frankie and Annette's adventures were, finally, more products with surfing in them than surfing movies. As of *Big Wednesday*, though, on average every two years or so producers have gone to the sand with more serious intent. While the resulting films for the most part differ significantly from the Beach Party trifles, they too often fall into the same pattern of cookie-cutter resemblance and adherence to formula. A half century later most narrative surfing releases are still treating surfing much the same way as they did in *Gidget* or *Ride the Wild Surf*. They're still replacing adult authority with the tender concern of the love interest and the tough love of the wise surfing mentor; they're still resolving predictable coming-of-age conflict with the equally foreseeable sports movie contrivance of the dramatic final competition or personal trial.

Perhaps because the coming-of-age theme actually does speak to a real facet of surfing experience—grommets will be always be earning their place in the lineup—the films have rarely been total bombs. Most certainly have their moments, a stretch of dialogue igniting the imagination, some well-cut glass or a bomb or two to catch the delirium, the nostalgic note struck deep inside by a sunset go-out. But in too many we always more or less know what's coming as the surfing that in fact is wound mysteriously into the messy complexities of so many normal existences is reduced to a representative handful of thinly developed characters, a few familiar storytelling arrangements, and some flashy action backed by dramatic percussion. Too often "the sport is presented only in terms of thrills, challenge, and conflict," Matt Warshaw summarizes," and almost never is it viewed as simply integrated into a person's life."[11] Amongst those employing the recurrent coming-of-age formula, certain of the more fully achieved, it seems, have been films inspired by real events or the life stories of actual surfers or groups. Perhaps this is simply because, to use the term again, surfing is in fact naturally "integrated" into such lives and resulting narratives, and not shoehorned in for its colorful visual and dramatic potential.

Biographical fidelity or inspiration is no guarantee of quality, as *Soul Surfer* and *The Perfect Wave* demonstrate, both marred by creepy preachiness, or the autobiographically flavored *Big Wednesday* with its distracting mythical bombast. But when the right tone is held, as it is in the patient dramatic build that is *Chasing Mavericks*, the story recruits the viewer into empathetic identification with an intriguing life. *Drift* generously fictionalizes the surfwear industry creation saga but movingly brings to life the sport's divided heart. Its plot formulas and liberties with history aside, the story of two brothers lends credible human density to Mark Stranger's argument that surfing's commodification has somehow managed to occur "to a significant degree without losing touch with the foundational surfing aesthetic."[12] While the climax of *Blue Crush* ties a pretty Hollywood bow, overall the gritty low-rent energy of its surfing plot draws affectingly from the real-life Maui girls who inspired it. Delving much earlier into the meanings of that surfing-gender interface, autobiography took us memorably towards the sunny emotional innocence of *Gidget*; it led as well into the considerably darker surfing-ordered teen codes of *Puberty Blues*, a film as tonally opposed to the 1959 hit in its caustic, comic remembering as it is its clear thematic successor.

These movies have been honorable achievements, but Warshaw's correct again to observe that neither the studios nor the independents have yet come up with that truly first-rate narrative release, the film that holds up fully as such and as a meaningful cinematic engagement with surfing and the surfing life choice. When it comes, the form it may take is extremely hard to predict if we are to judge by four films that in their distinctly varied ways might have come the closest: the showy major studio hit *Point Break*, discussed earlier in this analysis; two hyper-discreet, under-the-radar Japanese features, *A Scene at the Sea* and *Still the Water*; and the equally confidential, low-budget West Coast effort *Ocean Tribe*. These films are radically diverse in style, tone, and plot, yet at some profound level they rejoin each other in an uncontrived, integrated understanding of the transformative feelings and deeper meanings of surfing. Breaking with or at least refreshing the expected formulas, they frame its urgent ordinariness with quietly fostered, never labored intimations of mythic reach. The four films brim abundantly with life and the vivid sense that surfing is, in Daniel Duane's terms, an irreplaceable, stirringly intense "way of being in the world"[13]; perhaps it's coincidence, perhaps not, but at the same time they stake part of their meaning on narrative conclusions that in each case confront the unignorable fact of death through that of a pivotal character. To view surfing this way, at the moving crest of nothing less than the great, entwined forces of life and death, is to frame it as a deeply Romantic urge, the mobile crux of the two great opposites and a multitude of other mingled contradictions, a tension seeking synthesis in that rich "liminal zone" of "binary oppositions"[14] that is the surfspace.

Getting back to basics can perhaps mean something more than just words there at "that narrow strip of land over which the ocean waves and moon-powered tides are masters—that margin of territory that remains wild despite the proximity of cities."[15]

Point Break is by far the best known of these films. Evoked at length elsewhere and certainly still contested by many viewers, *Point Break* turns elaborate twists on the cop genre in its garish account of bank robbers, FBI agents, and Johnny Utah's transgressive border crossings. Introduced intriguingly in the credits, then developed with unexpected sobriety as a narrative lever, surfing serves as a credible locus for the protagonist's identity transformation and exploration of troubled common ground with the seductive guru Bodhi. Its frequent melodramatic excesses have made *Point Break* an easy target, but the film has a cult status due to far more than just adorable Keanu. In large part what lingers from its viewing is the surprisingly sincere and realized vision of surfing as a portal opening on another order of existence. Monk-outlaw Bodhi is a '90s Miki Dora, articulating intuitive meanings in communion with the wave and nihilistically deconstructing others with his gang's ex–President masks and trigger fingers. In the film's terms, the surfing space into which he initiates Johnny seems at first to emblematize the opposite of conventional dry land doings—for our cop, the world of robbers—but over time it comes to represent something more interesting, the teeming borderland between those oppositions and many more.

Beneath its heavy overlay of Hollywood sound, fury, and baroque narrative derring-do, *Point Break* deploys a surprisingly quiet and contemplative surfing plot. *A Scene at the Sea* is at once its total stylistic opposite and, in Kitano's sweet portrayal of initiation into a new way of being, its intriguing, mute Japanese cousin. Its title assertively anodyne, the tranquil 1991 break with the director's prior violent gangster films shelters the quietest and most minimal of stories: hearing- and speech-impaired, young trash collector Shigeru salvages an abandoned surfboard, repairs it, and becomes obsessed with learning to surf; accompanied by his equally deaf girlfriend, he improves to competition level, and the two briefly quarrel and make up before Shigeru's mysterious death and a ritualistic wave funeral rite. As different as the two films are, they present physically similar young men who stumble upon the surfing life while on the job and obsessively pursue its new sensations to the point of suspicious rebukes on the part of their colleagues. The Bodhi of *Point Break* cryptically enunciates the mystical and spiritual attractions of surfing; Kitano does so as well but through long stretches of silence, drawing the viewer delicately into identification with the deaf protagonist and the urgency, flagrant if utterly unspoken, that animates him. A professional surfer who at least as late as 2009 was still on the longboard circuit, Claude Maki shares with Keanu Reeves a fetching Bambi impassivity and innocence; in both actors the result is the sense of a vulnerable, unfinished self, one tugged at by inchoate inner yearnings which, finally, only surfing seems to express and respond to. Johnny is drawn from manichaean clarity and its strict FBI cubicles to the fertile fringes of instinct and ambiguity emblematized by the surfing life. For Shigeru surfing represents a roughly parallel awakening from the limits and enclosures of a sensorially shuttered existence to one revelling in fusion with the fluid world, a new profusion of sense impressions, and previously unthought possibilities of expression. Leading Shigeru and Johnny's double Bodhi to death in their conclusions, both films furthermore view surfing not only as integrated indispensably into an individual's life but into the great lift and drop of life itself. Romantic in the

Poster, *A Scene at the Sea*, director Takeshi Kitano (1991): Hiroko Ôshima as Takato, Claude Maki as Shigeru (Second Sight Films/Photofest).

largest sense, they twin the vital new sense of being it proffers with its natural completion in the act of symbolic reabsorption back into the sea.

Crackling with that life throughout, *Ocean Tribe* concludes with exactly that symbolic reabsorption made literal. Less geographically and tonally exotic than Kitano's extremely atypical exercise in style, it nevertheless indicates similarly fresh directions for the surfing movie, notably through its subversive play with cinematic expectations. Will Geiger's low-budget 1997 independent effort certainly seems to cover some standard cinematic territory, with its California beaches, anxious boy-men, and raucous road trip dynamics. If anything, though, the narrative pattern that eventually emerges intentionally deconstructs the eminently familiar conventions of mentor-assisted personal growth and the climactic final test. Geiger's interesting personal twist is to graft a poignant, biographically inspired story of four friends springing their terminally ill buddy from the hospital for one last surfari to other filmic conventions, notably those of the traditional surfing movie. When Noah, Lance, Jeb, and Schwartz, each very different and differently troubled, literally kidnap the initially morose, unwilling Bob, they head boozily south from the Santa Cruz area in a psychedelically painted vintage ambulance to catch a big swell in Baja. On one hand, this is *Sideways* meets *The Big Chill*, with youth in the rearview mirror and thoughts of the Big D dodging the headlights. But it also appealingly communicates the rough made-up appearance and feel of old surf movie safaris like, say, *Surf Crazy*. Even if it looks like Rick Griffin decorated their vehicle, when the friends get their fuzz buzzed empathetically to resemble chemo-bald Bob they recall and physically resemble '50s Brown and his zany band of four striking out for "Old Mexico" in 1959. Noah's voiceover calls to mind the genre's traditional narrator as warm, drily humorous, often lyrical guide. Along the way the guys chilling with dolphins recall other *Storm Riders*, and then there's classic tropes like getting skunked, la turista, punctuating the surfing with stunts like roof riding, the inaccessible killer break, a campfire board sacrifice, local informants and scoring a secret spot. From the finicky young doctor to crazy Jeb packing an ounce around Baja like a real life Mike Hynson, the full range of character types hearkens back to *Ride the Wild Surf* or *Big Wednesday*, but just as much to the blend of styles all the best surf moviemakers since Bud Browne have instinctively sought in their performers.

As the gang careens south, the fine 35mm surfing sequences, some shot by Jeff Neu, feature a top surfer-actor—Mark Matheisen as Lance—and others comfortable enough for the smooth hand-off to well-coached doubles who generally dial back the riding to the credible level of experienced, committed amateurs. With their communicated ease in the water and, again, the loosey-goosey surf film vibe of the trip, Geiger convincingly portrays surfing as a casually integrated, unselfconsciously indispensable aspect of thirtyish lives skittish about the problems back home that come with that new territory. The one facing the toughest transition is obviously Bob. The trap of sentimentality gapes, but Geiger skips past by immediately hustling Bob off center stage and according his story little more weight than those of his buddies, with their own interlocking resentments and apprehensions. The effect is a palpable lightening of the mood. We get saltily realistic dialogue from believably written characters full of credibly flawed affection for each other. Instead of phony enlightenment or the kind of carefully paced revelation the situation threatens to deliver, we get a (mostly) happy mutual splashing about in the now. Unlike that transmitted by the familiar narrative surf film mentors guiding their charges along a dramatic trajectory through life's transitions, the wisdom here is that there's no wisdom to transmit, only affection and company to share. The de-dramatizing continues in the conclusion with its nod at the Hollywood pro forma monumental personal challenge. Geiger's script leads the posse to a dynamite secret break (doubled, it seems, by an impressive Todos Santos). Frail Bob insists his way through his friends' natural hesitation and the impact zone. A good session follows at some point during which, with zero dramatic buildup, he very abruptly and inelegantly disappears into a wave; by the time the body's pulled out of the water, it's all over.

The anticlimactic story mechanics and tone seem intentional. Exceptional throughout, the acting here communicates the acute human emotion of such a moment but no more. As he does with the film's musical score or when creating an earlier opportunity for histrionic sentiment—Bob's romantic interlude in Tijuana—Geiger's tendency is to back discreetly off, clearly preferring heart to heartstrings. Finally, it is this emotional understatement that makes *Ocean Tribe* so moving, for the loss and sadness it recounts are lodged within a narrative context closer to that of life than to conventional cinematic strategies that push the tears and the lessons. When the closing credits lead off with a dedication to the real Bob Cook, this comes less as surprise than confirmation. Geiger's reticent discretion helps absolve the film of weaknesses like narrator Noah's thinly developed love quandary, some mismatched paddle-outs to rough surf, and the overdone local met in Baja. It's also what gives him the right to bookend the film with the repeated voiceover and (Dan Merkel-shot) visual parallel between this band of friends and the pod of dolphins who refuse to abandon a weakened member. When Milius goes mythic in *Big Wednesday* the Jungian hammering wears. Here the parallel seems forced the first time around but soon glides naturally into the developing narrative of watery comradeship because the friendship it represents is so instinctive and the ocean such a casual truth in its characters' lives. When their friend dies, his only family them, the four return his body to the sea, a scene juxtaposed with the last shot of Noah and his wife cradling their newborn on the shore. Like Kitano and Bigelow, Geiger again identifies surfing with the most primal of rhythms.

What *A Scene and the Sea*, *Point Break*, and *Ocean Tribe* show most about the surf movie as genre is that external form matters far less than heart. If the great narrative surfing film one day comes, it may be another over-the-top take on a wholly different genre or a mysterious exercise in reticence or perhaps a fresh twist on a seemingly by-the-numbers return to the coming-of-age script. It can be these things or almost anything else it wishes but it will have to create plausible characters and remain defiantly true to at least two motivations: depicting the ways surfing really *matters* to real people, and suggesting what it *means* within larger currents of human understanding and significance. Unfortunately, the record so far has been too many movies blindly adhering to approved character types and story patterns, and too few seriously willing or able to speak to the real secrets and meanings of surfing. Without that central thematic commitment, plot and character can't amount to much. With it, anything is possible, even making a surfing film with, literally, no surfing in it. Naomi Kawase's haunting 2014 fable *Still the Water* remains as urgently attached to surfing's age-old truths as it entrancingly demonstrates the ample imaginative potential of a genre too often content with the tired tried-and-true. In an interview with Didier Péron, the filmmaker reveals that she was doubly inspired by the loss of her adoptive mother and by the revelation of family roots leading back to the tropical archipelago of Amami far to the south of the Japanese mainland. Written by Kawase in three inspired days and shot for the most part in a series of single takes, the magical result is two gracefully intertwined stories of a dying woman and of her daughter's tentative romance with a young man terrified of the sea after his discovery of a corpse in the surfline.

Amami's jungly overgrowth trembles with mystic suggestion. Its green abundance seemingly sprouted from a cerulean sea at times savage at others still, the island and its

Still the Water, director Naomi Kawase (2014). Jun Yoshinaga as Kyoko and Nijirô Murakami as Kaito crossing the wave to the still water (Soda Pictures/Photofest).

small local population retain the ancient animisms with their liquid infusions of spirit and matter. Suffering as her shaman mother withers, lovely young Kyoko finds comfort and budding love with a still traumatized and hesitant Kaito. The calm, sinuous narrative flows back and forth between a coming death and an emerging love against a richly suggestive backdrop in which such elements as the unsimulated bleeding out of a goat, the revelation of the drowned man's identity, Kaito's mother's new romance, and Kyoko's achingly beautiful underwater swims in her prim school uniform all play their part. The latter recall the *anime* of Miyazaki, and indeed we are in a similar world of spiritual wonder, blurry transfers of sea and land, and borders dissolving before your eyes, where the densely entangled trunks and branches of a monumental banyan within sight of the deathbed suggest nature's one uniting force and the futility of our rational categories and divisions. Midway in these two-hours of graciously meditative disclosures, Kawase introduces surfing through the figure of Kyoko's father. A sunripened waterman with a small beach cafe and a centered economy of movement, he calmly accompanies the two journeying women in his life, his wife through the tragic gaiety of her last days and his daughter towards love and blossoming womanhood. Accordingly, he takes an interest in her Kaito and the real and symbolic fear of the sea that has chilled him, recurringly advising via his daughter that surfing is a way to master those fears and find the true self within them.

Significantly, *Still the Water* begins with the diametrical opposite of its title, a robust, beautifully filmed breaker surging noisily left to right across the frame. The reference to Hokusai is evident. Frothing with vitality and power, bearing down symbolically on snowy, half-divine Mount Fuji, "The Great Wave" is the perfect emblem for a film about the fluid blendings of death in life, stillness in energy, transcendence in being. It returns in the older surfer's generous enthusiasms about the sheer vitality the expiring wave transmits, a physical presentness so complete it resembles nothingness. "When you surf," he attests, "you take hold of the last stage of the wave…. When you feel that force with your body, the energy becomes nothing and there is a sense that all, including yourself, is still." There's a mythical tremor in these words, but not only—surfers will also hear an accurate description of a very real state of being. Ideally titled, rare in the hushed symbolic beauty of its images and storytelling, *Still the Water* has not a single barrel or cutback, but it has a truer feeling for the intimate personal whisperings and larger philosophical framings of surfing than many films full of them. Even as it remotely evokes the stale mentor-acolyte pattern, it is a luminous reminder that cinema can represent surfing utterly otherwise while never losing sight of its complex home truths.

The generous opportunity and exacting challenge of surfing as cinematic subject lie in that complexity. In often sharply different ways, each of the films above addresses its vast symbolic potential, an expansive spectrum perhaps best captured by Kawase's paradoxical image of the intense new life born the instant a wave dies. The wave's liberating crash back into itself, poet Galway Kinnell wrote in "Spindrift," beats rhythm to a chant both of time's limits and of its eternal continuity. From the moment Western power first spied Tahitian pleasure gliding by, the truths of surfing have been similarly contradictory, complementary, multiple. Surfing is freedom and servitude, wild youth and rooted tradition, independence and tribal bonds, escape and a job, discovery and expression, innocence and experience, a going from and a going to. A chosen life within a life, it is also life, with the same injustices, temptations, ego trips, and distractions in the surfline as on the street. The filmmakers responsible for the most convincing treatments of surfing in cinema know that stories and characters vital enough to give some breath to larger questions and desires are only possible if they can also communicate the satisfactions that can get a person out of a warm bed and into icy water at six a.m. For over sixty years those satisfactions have remained the nearly sole preoccupation of the surf community film and video; with the new technical means, talents like Taylor Steele and Thomas Campbell, and the apparent willingness of a rising generation both to remember and to re-imagine, it's safe to say that the each year will continue to contribute a new film or two of particularly memorable service to the stoke. As for the narrative film, that's less sure. The tension between morning glass and morning class, between youthful insouciance and adult responsibility is a reality of surfing, but not *the only* surfing reality, as Hollywood persists in believing. It is likely that the trial-by-tube growing up drama will continue to grace our screens, and always possible that it will go somewhere interesting in the process. The genre's real future, though, is elsewhere. Garish, mute, raucous, mystical, the films above each find ways to remain true to the lift and drop of surfing's complex reality while daringly opening on new possibilities in its cinematic representation. Exploring new forms, renewing the old, their most fully achieved successors will be similarly resonant with its entangled heart-truths and salty with the felt pleasures of dawn patrol and the last ride at sunset.

Chapter Notes

Chapter 1

1. Warshaw (*History*, *Encyclopedia*, etc.) refers to the title of Browne's first film in the plural as *Hawaiian Surfing Movies*. Drawing on the usage of the Bud Browne Film Archives, this analysis will employ the singular.
2. Warshaw, *Encyclopedia*, 582.
3. Warshaw, *History*, 11. The historical account to follow draws significantly from Warshaw and Westwick.
4. Westwick, 314.
5. *Fifty Years of Surfing on Film*. The quotations to follow are from the same DVD.
6. The leading professional organization is called the Surf Industry Manufacturers Association.
7. As recently as August 2013 a special issue of *Surfer* devoted to "The Greatest Rides of All Time" still refers to the 1777 sighting as "the initial written record of surfing—a moment when Western colonial culture met ancient Polynesian wave riding for the very first time" ("Unknown Surfer").
8. The May 1769 account by Joseph Banks follows. There may be an earlier written record as well. In *Jardin de récif* (17) Nolwenn Roussel quotes Louis Antoine de Bougainville, commander of *La Boudeuse*, who reports in his "notes" concerning the ship's nine day stay in Tahiti in April 1768 that the Tahitians "were capable of attaining the crest of waves and standing up on planks" (translation JE). That account does not appear in de Bougainville's published record of the voyage. Roussel's book includes no bibliographical reference. I have tried unsuccessfully to contact her and have not been able to locate the notes to which she refers.
9. Joseph Banks, Entry 29 May 1769. (Punctuation and spelling modernized). I became aware of this earlier sighting thanks to Richard Holmes's *The Age of Wonder*.
10. Warshaw, *Zero Break*, 3–4.
11. For example, the first chapter of Holmes's *The Age of Wonder* is entitled "Joseph Banks in Paradise."
12. Benjamin, 256.
13. Nathaniel B. Emerson, quoted in Westwick, 19.
14. "Beach Breezes."
15. Westwick, 104.
16. Kohner, 38.
17. Carlin, 35.
18. Higgins.
19. "Cruisy Way to Surf."
20. Thoreau, *Cape Cod*, 224.
21. Joyce, 169–73.
22. Hemingway, 198.
23. Deleuze, 121.
24. Trompenaars; Wang, 97.
25. Casey, 72.
26. Woolf, 130.
27. Duane, 239.
28. Concert remarks, Bruce Springsteen and the E Street Band, Hunter Valley, Australia, February 23, 2014: ""This is a song I wrote for a night like this. So let me get this right: it's the end of summer, right?".

Chapter 2

1. Beattie, 134.
2. Image reproduced in Manificat.
3. Métraux, 91–2 (translation JE).
4. Nichols, 94.
5. The heroine of Kohner's novel is named Franzie, whereas in the movie version she is referred to as Francie; a similar disparity exists between Kohner's Kahoona and the name Kahuna from the film and popular usage. For harmony's sake, these remarks will use Francie and Kahuna in reference both to the novel and the film.
6. Warshaw, *Surf Movie*, 11.
7. Beattie, 135.
8. In *History* (422) Warshaw estimates 10 percent–20 percent, whereas Higgins quotes a 2005 market-research company figure of 33 percent.
9. "Noa Deane."
10. Aufderheide, 40.
11. Low point would, of course, be a more appropriate term for the period marked by the Boer War, a campaign so shameful that it would effectively begin the process of de-colonization.
12. Low, 52.
13. Ball, *California Surfriders*, 52, 34.
14. McClelland and Gault-Williams. I draw frequently upon these valuable sources of information about the life and career of Browne and other early figures.

15. Anna Trent Moore of the Bud Browne Film Archives stresses Browne's love of Tahiti and pride in the Tahitian travelogue he made but, unfortunately, only showed twice; during the trips to Tahiti Browne also did extensive photography, including many soulful portraits.
16. Tschorn.
17. Mark (235) cites a former lifeguard named Cal Porter, who contends that Venice H.S. student surfer Tuley Clark showed films at noon at the school and charged a nickel for admission. That said, Porter, who attended Browne's inaugural showing, clearly grants that it was Browne who "started the whole surf movie idea."
18. Chidester, 55.
19. Thompson.
20. *Fifty Years of Surfing on Film.*
21. Gault-Williams.
22. Gault-Williams.
23. Bradley.
24. Nick Carroll, 208.
25. Grissim, 102.
26. Wollen, 556. The remarks to follow draw heavily upon Wollen's analysis (553–562).
27. Ehrenreich, 29.
28. *Slippery When Wet* (DVD), commentary. The quotations in the following paragraph come from the same source.
29. As things have turned out, it could be argued that in his casting Brown instinctively illustrated two opposing faces of surfing. Robert is Blackie August's son and as such minor surfing nobility. Polite and well-bred, he's to all appearances the perfect son-in-law or, attests Robert "Wingnut" Weaver of Brown's later *The Endless Summer II*, "the example of how to live your life" (*Endless Summer Revisited*). More self-centered and difficult, Hynson by contrast quarreled easily and squandered much of his magnificent talent in drugs.
30. Duane, 180.
31. Comer, for example, highlights the film's "classic colonial stereotypes" and "sophomoric racisms" (62).
32. Taylor recounts in detail Hynson's chance glimpse of a "small 'Malibu,'" his eventual discovery of the break, and the 40 minute session.
33. For example, see brucebrownfilms.com, Holden, Taylor, and Lisanti (270).
34. In fact, the ride in question was a splice of two later rides (Taylor).
35. *The Endless Summer Revisited.*
36. *The Paul Witzig Trilogy* (2010).
37. Warshaw, *Encyclopedia*, 190.
38. *Crystal Voyager.*
39. Quoted in Warshaw, *Encyclopedia*, 720.
40. David Adams, 74.
41. Bannerman.
42. Raymond. The pages to follow include several quotations from the Library of Congress interview.
43. "SURFER Poll Lifetime Achievement: John Severson."
44. Severson, *Surf*. The remarks to follow draw extensively upon the early chapter "Surf Films." Later remarks on *Pacific Vibrations* draw upon subsequent chapters. The book's pages are unnumbered.
45. Kampion, 108.
46. Quotation from *Entertainment Today*, cited on *Pacific Vibrations* advertising poster.
47. *Beowulf*, lines 506–8.
48. Warshaw *Encyclopedia*, 353.
49. "Surf Filmmaker Hal Jepsen Passes On."
50. Rodgers.
51. "*1971 quand Jeff Hakman*."
52. Using the same melody, "Sidewalk Surfin'" is essentially "Catch A Wave" with different lyrics.
53. Nick Carroll, 209.
54. McKinnon.
55. Ledonne.
56. For example, see Baumgarten, Levy, and Mapes.
57. *Box Office Mojo* reports $3.6 M domestic gross for *Step* vs. $2.1M for *ESII*; RottenTomatoes.com reports 82 percent positive reviews for *Step* vs. 50 percent for *ESII*, and average ratings of, respectively, 6.9/10 vs. 5.8/10. The quotation is the so-called "Critics Consensus" of *RottenTomatoes*.
58. Raymond.
59. Bellah, 144.
60. Quoted in Baker, 113.
61. Butler, 400. For the quotation that follows, see p. 398.
62. Isaiah Walker (87) takes particular issue with this claim.
63. Thoms, 188.
64. Nelson.
65. "Manufacturing Stoke."
66. "Director Jarrod Tallman."
67. Hawk.
68. Housman's article on the streaming of McCoy's *A Deeper Shade of Blue* again highlights McCoy's ambivalence about surfing's corporatization and changes in the surfing movie. Among other things, McCoy neatly balances disappointment and pride that today's "surf industry ... going off the rails" failed to step forward to finance the film. Similarly, McCoy laments how "über-availability ... on the internet" will be "the nail in the coffin of big screen surf movie releases," while taking evident pleasure in the fact that the new movie on-line will reach more viewers than any of his 24 other films.
69. See Baker (113 and elsewhere) re. this tendency in recent surf films.
70. Warshaw, *Encyclopedia*, 552.
71. Baker, 112.
72. Sakamoto.
73. Roth.
74. Sakamoto.
75. Thoreau, *Journal*, 7 Sept. 1851; 6 August 1851.
76. Beattie, 143; Sontag, 207.
77. Raymond.
78. Richards.
79. Shearer.
80. "Taylor Steele Interview"; Myers.
81. Beer.

82. In the title of his 1992 video *Can't Step Twice on the Same Piece of Water,* Alby Falzon evokes Heraclitus directly.
83. "Inside Taylor Steele's *Innersection.*"
84. Ito.
85. Minsberg.
86. "Inside Taylor Steele's *Innersection.*"

Chapter 3

1. "The White Flower / Betty Compson [motion picture]."
2. Thoms, 45.
3. In "Extreme Goofy," Corky Carroll makes this argument. So does "'Hawaiian Holiday,'" while further asserting (wrongly) that the Disney cartoon was the first animated surfing feature.
4. The heroine of Kohner's novel is named Franzie, whereas in the movie version she is referred to as Francie; a similar disparity exists between Kohner's Kahoona and the name Kahuna from the film and popular usage. For harmony's sake, these remarks will use Francie and Kahuna in reference both to the novel and the film.
5. Kohner, 3. In the paragraphs that follow, page numbers for quotations from the novel appear parenthetically.
6. Stillman, xiv.
7. Comer, 48.
8. Comer, 45.
9. Lisanti, 7.
10. Saint Louis.
11. Lisanti, 142.
12. "Big Wednesday Redux."
13. Konstantinou.
14. SpongeBob surfs in the 2015 animated/live action feature *The SpongeBob Movie: Sponge Out of Water,* but it's in a 2009 Nickelodeon episode, "SpongeBob SquarePants vs. The Big One," that the mentor/final challenge pattern more clearly appears. Voiced by Johnny Depp, top surfer Jack Kahuna Laguna coaches the hero and his friends to ride The Big One, the gnarly wave that is their only way home from a remote tropical island. Bruce Brown provided the cameo narration.
15. Tsai.
16. Houlihan.
17. Lette, 7.
18. Brislin (108) critiques the way the script "distances" Anne Marie from the Hawaiian community through its concentration on a conventional haole love story, arguing that *Lilo & Stich* presents Hawaiian life and values more authentically.
19. One irony of the film's tow-in debate is that Dorian would go on to pioneer the return to paddle-in big wave surfing.

Chapter 4

1. "Surf Movie Pioneer." While Anna Trent Moore of the Bud Browne Film Archives cannot confirm the precise figure of 500, she recalls Browne's impression of a very large, enthusiastic crowd.
2. Bellow, 344.
3. Stranger 13; Maffesoli.
4. Harvey, 44.
5. Deleuze, 121; Csikszentmihalyi; Maslow.
6. Grissim, 154.
7. *Fifty Years of Surfing on Film.*
8. Cowie, 9.
9. Beattie, 132, 134.
10. Ball 1946, 84.
11. Warshaw *Encyclopedia,* 211.
12. Stranger, 14.
13. Duane, xiv.
14. Ford 8; Shields.
15. Dakin; quoted in Winton, *Land's Edge,* frontispiece.

Bibliography

There are three parts: Books, Articles and Websites; Film, Video, Animation and Television; Music

Books, Articles and Websites

Aaberg, Denny. "No Pants Mance." *Surfer* (May 1974).

———. "Surfing the Innermost Limits of Pure Fun; Denny Aaberg & FARM's Soundtrack Tribute to George Greenough." Switch-foot.com (Santa Barbara, June 2005). http://www.switch-foot.com/the-inner-most-limits-of-pure-fun.

Abrams, M.H., et al. *The Norton Anthology of English Literature*, vol. 2, 4th ed. New York: W.W. Norton, 1979.

Adams, David. *Colonial Odysseys: Empire and Epic in the Modernist Novel*. Ithaca: Cornell University Press, 2003.

"Andrew Kidman." andrewkidman.com.

Anolik, Lili. "One Summer, Forever." *Vanity Fair* (March 2014).

Archer, Eugene. "Ride the Wild Surf." *New York Times*, December 24, 1964.

Arnold, Matthew. "Dover Beach" (1867). Abrams, M.H., et al. *The Norton Anthology of English Literature*, vol. 2, 4th ed. New York: W.W. Norton, 1979.

Aufderheide, Patricia. *Documentary Film: A Very Short Introduction*. New York: Oxford University Press, 2007.

Baker, Tim. "The Emancipation of the Surfs: Surf Culture Comes of Age," in Bruce Boal, ed., *The Surfing Yearbook*. Layton, UT: Gibbs Smith, 2009.

Ball, Doc. *California Surfriders* (1946). Republished as *Early California Surfriders*. Ventura, CA: Pacific, 1995.

———. "Surf Boarders Capture California." *National Geographic*, vol. 86 (September 1944).

Banks, Joseph. *The Endeavour Journal of Sir Joseph Banks, 1768–1771*. Digital text, State Library of New South Wales, University of Sydney Library, Sydney 1997. Entry 29 May 1769. http://setis.library.usyd.edu.au/ozlit/pdf/p00021.pdf.

Bannerman, Mark. "Spirit of Akasha: Why Filmmaker Andrew Kidman Is Paying Homage to Cult Classic Morning of the Earth." *ABC News*, January 24, 2014. http://www.abc.net.au/news/2014-01-24/spirit-of-akasha-homage-classic-surfing-film-morning-of-earth/5214588.

Bart, Peter. "Fellini of the Foam." *New York Times*, June 12, 1966.

Bartholomew, Wayne. "Bustin' Down the Door." *Surfer* (January 1977).

Baumgarten, Marjorie. Review, *The Endless Summer II*. *Austin Chronicle*, June 10, 1994.

"Beach Breezes." *The Daily Surf*, July 20, 1885.

Beattie, Keith. "Radical Delirium: Surf Film, Video and the Documentary Mode," in James Skinner, Keith Gilbert, Allan Edwards, eds. *Some Like It Hot: The Beach as a Cultural Dimension*. Oxford: Meyer and Meyer Sport, 2003.

Beer, Jeff. "Taylor Steele's 'Here & Now' Surfs the World in a Single Day." Co-CREATE: Creativity/Culture/Commerce, June 13, 2012. http://www.fastcocreate.com/1680926/taylor-steeles-here-now-surfs-the-world-in-a-single-day.

Bellah, Robert N., Richard Madsen, William M. Sullivan, Ann Swidler, and Steven M. Tipton. *Habits of the Heart: Individualism and Commitment in American Life*. Berkeley: University of California Press, 1985.

Bellow, Saul. *Herzog*. New York: Penguin, 1992.

Benjamin, Walter. *Illuminations*. Translated by Harry Zohn. New York: Schocken, 1969.

Beowulf: A Verse Translation. Translated by Seamus Heaney. Edited by Daniel Donoghue. New York: W.W. Norton, 2002.

"Big Wednesday Redux." The Surfer's Journal. http://www.surfersjournal.com/pdf_article/big-wednesday-redux.

"Bill Viola." Exhibition notes, Grand Palais, Paris, Spring 2014.

Bishop, Elizabeth. "Pleasure Seas." *The Complete Poems: 1927–1979*. New York: Farrar, Straus and Giroux, 1983.

Blake, Thomas Edward. "Waves and Thrills at Waikiki." *National Geographic*, vol. 67 (May 1935).

Blake, Tom. *Hawaiian Surfboard*. Honolulu: Paradise of the Pacific, 1935.

Blundell, Graeme. "Puberty Blues Takes Us Back to the 70s." *The Australian*, August 11, 2012. http://www.theaustralian.com.au/arts/review/puberty-

blues-takes-us-back-to-the-70s/story-fn9n8gph-1226446162736.
Booth, Douglas. "Surfing Films and Videos: Adolescent Fun, Alternative Lifestyle, Adventure Industry." *Journal of Sport History* (Fall 1996).
Borte, Jason. "New School." Surfing A to Z. Surfline. http://www.surfline.com/surfing-a-to-z/new-school-history_870/ .
Bowles, Paul. "The Art of Fiction," interview with Jeffrey Bailey. *The Paris Review* 81 (Fall 1981).
Bradley, Ryan. "Q+A: Greg Noll on Surfing as Art, Life." NationalGeographic.com, May 17, 2007.
Braithwaite, Nick. "Modern Collective—Surf Movie Review." Surfing Stoke, June 29, 2010. http://www.surfingstoke.com/reviews/surf-movies/modern-collective/.
Brien, Donna Lee. "'Based on a True Story': The Problem of the Perception of Biographical Truth in Narratives Based on Real Lives." *TEXT* 13, no. 4 (October 2, 2009). http://www.textjournal.com.au/oct09/brien.htm.
Brislin, Tom. "Exotics, Erotics, and Coconuts: Stereotypes of Pacific Islanders," in Lester, Paul Martin, and Susan Dente Ross, eds., *Images That Injure: Pictorial Stereotypes in the Media*, 2d ed. Westport, CT: Praeger, 2003.
Brontë, Charlotte. *Jane Eyre: A Norton Critical Edition*. New York: W.W. Norton, 1971.
Brown, Joe. Review, *The Endless Summer II*. *Washington Post*, June 3, 1994.
Butler, Kelly Jean. "'Their Culture Has Survived: Witnessing to (Dis-) Possession in Bra Boys (2007)." *Journal of Australian Studies* 33:4 (December 2009).
Byron, Lord. Canto II, Canto CVI, *Don Juan* (1819). Edited by Jerome J. McCann. *Lord Byron: The Major Works*. New York: Oxford University Press, 2008.
Cairns, Ian. "We're Number One." *Surfer* (May 1976).
Camper, Fred. "Naming, and Defining, Avant-Garde or Experimental Film." http://www.fredcamper.com/Film/AvantGardeDefinition.html.
Carlin, Peter Ames. *Catch a Wave: The Rise, Fall and Redemption of the Beach Boys' Brian Wilson*. New York: Rodale, 2006.
Carroll, Corky. "Extreme Goofy 10/29/08." http://corkycarroll.com/blog/?p=62.
_____. "For When the Waves Aren't There, These Surf Movies Are." *Orange County Register*, July 30, 2014.
Carroll, Nick. "Subculture," in Nick Carroll, ed. *The Next Wave: A Survey of World Surfing*. Sydney: Angus and Robertson, 1991.
Casey, Susan. *The Wave*. New York: Anchor, 2010.
Chamberlain, Melissa. "Classic Surf Film 'Pacific Vibrations' to Make World HD Premiere at U.S. Open of Surfing." Surfer blog post, July 29, 2010. http://www.surfermag.com/blogs/industry-news/classic-surf-film-%E2%80%9Cpacific-vibrations%E2%80%9D-to-make-world-hd-premiere-at-us-open-of-surfing-august-1-2/.
Chesser, Todd. Blog post, Surfer, December 16, 1996. http://forum.surfermag.com/forum/ubbthreads.php?ubb=showflat&Number=1100774&site_id=1#import.
Chidester, Brian, and Domenic Priore. *Pop Surf Culture: Music, Design, Film, and Fashion from the Bohemian Surf Boom*. Santa Monica, CA: Santa Monica, 2008.
Colburn, Bolton, Ben Finney, et al. *Surf Culture: The Art History of Surfing*. Laguna Beach, CA: Laguna Art Museum/Ginko, 2002.
Comer, Krista. *Surfer Girls in the New World Order*. Durham, NC: Duke University Press, 2010.
Corbett, Bradley. "Slater's Dream and the 'Lost Atlas': A Meandering Review of the New Kai Neville Film." The Surfer's Journal, August 2011. http://www.surfersjournal.com/journal_entry/slaters-dream-and-lost-atlas-meandering-review-new-kai-neville-film
Cornuelle, Stuart. "It's Finally Here: *Modern Collective*: A Review." Surfer, October 20, 2009. http://www.surfingmagazine.com/video/it%E2%80%99s-finally-here/
Cowie, Elizabeth. *Recording Reality, Desiring the Real*. Minneapolis: University of Minnesota Press, 2011.
"Cruisy Way to Surf." Ansett Australia Airlines Magazine, 1996, quoted in bennettsurfboards.com/cruisy_way_to_surf.html.
Csikszentmihalyi, Mihaly, and Isabella Selega Csikszentmihalyi, eds. *Optimal Experience: Psychological Studies of Flow in Consciousness*. Cambridge: Cambridge University Press, 1992.
Dakin, William J. *Australian Seashores: A Guide to the Temperate Seashores for the Beach Lover, the Naturalist, the Shore-Fisherman and the Student*. North Ryde, NSW: Angus and Robertson, 1987.
de Bougainville, Louis-Antoine. *Voyage autour du monde par la frégate du Roi La Boudeuse et la flute L'Etoile; en 1766, 1767, 1768 & 1769*. Paris: Saillant Nyon, 1771.
Deleuze, Gilles. *Negotiations, 1972–1990*. Translated by Martin Joughin. New York: Columbia University Press, 1995.
"Devoted Surfers." Undated letter to Alfred Hitchcock concerning "Low Clouds and Coastal Fog," January 18, 1963, episode of the *Alfred Hitchcock Hour*. Letter displayed at Universal Studios, Hollywood.
DiMartino, Jay. "Surfing History: The Best Surfing Documentary Movies Ever Made." About.com Surfing/Bodyboarding. http://surfing.about.com/od/dvdvideo/a/Surfing-History-The-Best-Surfing-Documentary-Movies-Ever-Made.htm.
"Director Jarrod Tallman on the Making of the

Filthy Habits Sequel." Surfer, July 22, 2010. http://www.surfermag.com/features/jarrod_tallman_on_still_filthy/.

"Documentary Movies at the Box Office." Box officemojo.com. http://www.boxofficemojo.com/genres/chart/?id=documentary.htm.

Duane, Daniel. *Caught Inside: A Surfer's Year on the California Coast*. New York: North Point, 1996.

Ehrenreich, Barbara. The *Hearts of Men: American Dreams and the Flight from Commitment*. New York: Anchor, 1983.

Eisner, Lisa, and Roman Alonso. "The Swell Life." *New York Times*, August 20, 2006.

Eliot, T.S. "Little Gidding" (1942). M.H. Abrams, et al. *The Norton Anthology of English Literature*, vol. 2, 4th ed. New York: W.W. Norton, 1979.

Engle, John. "August and Everything After: A Half Century of Surfing in Cinema." Bright Lights Film Journal, April 30, 2013.

Enright, Nick. *Blackrock*. Strawberry Hills, Sydney: Currency, 1996.

Evans, Bob. "Locked In." *Surfing World* (September 1964).

Falzon, Albert. "*Morning of the Earth*: 25th Anniversary." http://www.youtube.com/watch?v=FONstndO9OQ.

Feldman, Jonathan. "Thomas Campbell Captures the Surf World's Creative Spirit." Paper, February 25, 2013. http://www.papermag.com/2013/02/thomas_campbell_captures_the_s.php.

"Film Fest Billabong Jack McCoy." jackmccoy.com. http://www.jackmccoy.com/filmfest-reports.htm.

Finney, Ben, and James D. Houston. *Surfing: A History of the Ancient Hawaiian Sport*. Rohnert Park, CA: Pomegranate Artbooks, 1996.

Ford, Alexander Hume. "A Boy's Paradise in the Pacific." *St. Nicholas Illustrated Magazine for Boys and Girls*. Vacation Number (August 1908).

_____. "Riding the Surf in Hawaii." *Collier's* (August 14, 1909).

Ford, Nick, and David Browne. *Surfing and Social Theory: Experience, Embodiment and Narrative of the Dream Glide*. London: Routledge, 2006.

Forster, E.M. *Howards End*. London: Penguin, 1989.

Ganahl, Jane. "Big Waves, Little Drama." SFGATE, May 8, 1998. http://www.sfgate.com/news/article/Big-waves-little-drama-3090777.php.

Gault-Williams, Malcolm. *Legendary Surfers: A Definitive History of Surfing's Culture and Heroes*. http://www.legendarysurfers.com/.

"The George Greenough Interview, Part 1." FlexSpoon: Living the Greenough Legacy, June 1, 2009. http://flexspoon.com/george-greenough/the-george-greenough-interview-part-1.

"The Greatest Rides of All Time." *Surfer* Special Edition (August 2013).

Grissim, John. *Pure Stoke*. New York: Harper Colophon, 1982.

Hamilton, Laird. "A Surf Star's Favorite Surfing Movies." The Daily Beast, September 23, 2010. http://www.thedailybeast.com/articles/2010/09/23/surf-star-laird-hamiltons-favorite-surfing-movies.html.

Harvey, David. *The Condition of Postmodernity: An Inquiry into the Origins of Social Change*. Cambridge: Blackwell, 1990.

"'Hawaiian Holiday' Is the First Animated Surf Movie Ever." SurferToday.com. http://www.surfertoday.com/surfing/8072-hawaiian-holiday-is-the-first-animated-surf-movie-ever.

Hawk, Steve. "Search and Destroy." *Outside* (April 2004).

Hemingway, Ernest. *The Sun Also Rises*. London: Panther, 1985.

Higgins, Matt. "Women of the Waves Seek Equal Pay," *New York Times*, March 7, 2007.

Holden, Stephen. "*Endless Summer 2*: In Search of the Perfect Wave, or Something." *New York Times*, June 3, 1994.

_____. "No More Hunt for the Perfect Wave; the Thrill is Finding the Scariest." *New York Times*, July 9, 2004.

Hollywood Don't Surf! "Production Notes." Press release, 2010. http://www.festival-cannes.fr/assets/Image/Direct/034959.pdf.

Holmes, Paul. "In Trim: Bruce Brown's Endless Epic: The Story of the Filmmaker and the Film that Changed the Surfing World." The Bluegrass Special.com, June 2010.

Holmes, Richard. *The Age of Wonder: How the Romantic Generation Discovered the Beauty and Terror of Science*. London: HarperPress, 2009.

Houlihan, Mary. "'The Perfect Wave': Surf the Swells or Serve the Lord?" ChicagoSun-Times.com, July 10, 2014. http://www.suntimes.com/entertainment/movies/28554368–421/the-perfect-wave-surf-the-swells-or-serve-the-lord.html#.VDLFMhZKSua.

Housman, Justin. "Jack McCoy on Surf Films." Surfer blog, June 6, 2013. http://www.surfermag.com/blogs/culture/jack-mccoy-and-the-future-of-surf-movies/.

"Hui Nalu O Hawaii." Website of Hui Nalu Canoe Club. www.huinalucanoeclub.com/.

Ito, Daniel Ikaika. "Meeting Meola at the 'Innersection': Talking with Matt Meola about his 'Innersection' Win." ESPN/Action Sports, March 4, 2011. http://espn.go.com/action/surfing/news/story?page=matt-meola-interview.

"Inside Taylor Steele's *Innersection*." Carve, January 4, 2011. http://www.carvemag.com/2011/01/inside-taylor-steeles-innersection/#.U5mKFCjl9kd.

JackMcCoy.com.

Jeffers, Robinson. "November Surf." *The Collected Poetry of Robinson Jeffers: 1928–1938*. Stanford, CA: Stanford University Press, 1988.

Jeremias, Mark. "The Surfer's Studio Interview: Mark Jeremias." Smash, October 2012. Posted by Tyler Warren: http://smashsurf.com/the-surfers-studio-the-mark-jeremias-interview/.

Jobs, Richard Ivan. "AHR Forums: Youth Movements, Travel, Protest, and Europe in 1968." *The American Historical Review* 114.2 (2009).

Joyce, James. *A Portrait of the Artist as a Young Man*. New York: Penguin, 1978.

Kalinak, Kathryn. *Settling the Score: Music and the Classical Hollywood Film*. Madison: University of Wisconsin Press, 1992.

Kamahele, Momiala. "Hula as Resistance." *Forward Motion* 2.3 (1992).

Kampion, Drew. *Stoked! A History of Surf Culture*. Layton, UT: Gibbs Smith, 2003.

Kinnell, Galway. "Spindrift." *The Avenue Bearing the Initial of Christ into the New World: Poems 1946–1964*. Boston: Houghton Mifflin, 1974.

Kodak/Atlab. National Film and Sound Archive: Kodak/Atlab Cinema Collection. http://nfsa.gov.au/collection/film/film-partnerships/kodakatlab/.

Kohner, Frederick. *Gidget*. New York: Berkley, 2001.

Konstantinou, Lee. "Learning to Be Yourself." (Review article, Abigail Cheever, *Real Phonies: Cultures of Authenticity in Post-World War II America*.) *Twentieth-Century Literature* 56.2 (Summer 2010).

Leary, Timothy. "Timothy Leary—Turn On, Tune In, Drop Out (1966)." https://www.youtube.com/watch?v=qEnYFE70N5M.

Ledonne, Rob. "Remembering *The Endless Summer*: A Look Back at Bruce Brown's Masterpiece." Surfer, November 30, 2013. http://www.surfermag.com/features/the-greatest-surf-film-ever-made/.

Lette, Kathy, and Gabrielle Carey. *Puberty Blues*. London: Picador, 2002.

Levy, Emmanuel. Review, *The Endless Summer II*. Variety (June 6, 1994).

"Lifetime Achievement: John Severson." 2011 Surfer Poll award. Surfer, December 26, 2011. http://www.surfermag.com/surfer-poll/lifetime-achievement-john-severson/.

Lim, Dennis. "The Day the Laughter Died." *The Village Voice* (August 1, 2000). http://www.villagevoice.com/2000-08-01/film/the-day-the-laughter-died/.

Lisanti, Thomas. *Hollywood Surf and Beach Movies: The First Wave, 1959–1969*. Jefferson, NC: McFarland, 2005.

London, Jack. "Riding the South Seas Surf." *Woman's Home Companion* 34.10 (October 1907).

Low, Rachel, and Roger Manvell. *The History of the British Film: 1896–1906*. London: Allen and Unwin, 1948.

Lynch, Gary. "Doc Ball, Legendary Lensman," April 10, 1990. Quoted in Gault-Williams.

Mac, Ryan. "The Mad Billionaire Behind GoPro: The World's Hottest Camera Company." *Forbes* (March 25, 2013).

Maffesoli, Michel. *The Time of the Tribes: The Decline of Individualism in Mass Society*. London: Sage, 1996.

Manificat, Hervé. "Découvertes du Surf dans le Pacifique." *Surfer's Journal* 97 (August-September 2013).

Mankoff, Robert. "The Creative Life of a Cartoonist." New Yorker, May 9, 2012. http://www.newyorker.com/cartoons/bob-mankoff/the-creative-life-cycle-of-a-cartoonist.

"Manufacturing Stoke: An Interview with P.M.K. from Misfit Pictures." TransWorld Surf, April 26, 2011.

Mapes, Marty. Review, *The Endless Summer II*. Movie Habit, January 23, 1998. http://www.moviehabit.com/reviews/end_aw98.shtml.

Marcus, Ben. "From Polynesia, with Love: The History of Surfing from Captain Cook to the Present." www.surfingforlife.com.

Mark, Richard. *Our Lifeguard Family: Honoring Your Service: The First 100 Years*. Los Angeles: Los Angeles County Fire Department, Lifeguard and Marine Operations, 2009.

Maslin, Janet. "'Big Wednesday' Gets Caught in Some Rough Surf: Buddyhood of Surfing." *New York Times*, July 28, 1978.

_____. "'Puberty Blues.'" *New York Times*, July 15, 1983.

Maslow, Abraham. *Religions, Values, and Peak-Experience*. Hammondsworth: Penguin, 1962.

McClelland, Gordon. "Scenes from the Life and Times of Bud Browne." *The Surfer's Journal* (Winter 1995).

McKinnon, Andrew. "A Tribute to Joe Engel 1960–2006." SRO Surf, September 30, 2006. http://www.srosurf.com/gennews/engel.htm.

McLuhan, Marshall, and Quentin Fiore. *The Medium is the Massage: An Inventory of Effects*. New York: Bantam, 1967.

Mekas, Jonas. "The Filmmaker's Cooperative: A Brief History." The New American Cinema Group: The Filmmakers' Coop. http://film-makerscoop.com/about/history.

Métraux, Alfred. *L'Ile de Pâques*. Paris: Gallimard, 1941.

Michaels, Lorne. "Lorne Michaels on the 1970s and the Birth of Saturday Night Live." *Vanity Fair* (October 2013).

Michaels, Samantha. "My Perfect Adventure: Chris Molloy." Outside Online, November 30, 2012. http://www.outsideonline.com/outdoor-adventure/my-perfect-adventure/My-Perfect-Adventure-Chris-Malloy.html.

Minsberg, Talya, and Nick Corasaniti. "World Surf League Takes Web-First Approach to Drawing Viewers." *New York Times*, February 22, 2015.

Mitchell, Elvis. "Film: Catch a Wave and You've Got a Documentary." *New York Times*, August 3, 2003.

Montague, John. "Edge." *The Great Cloak*. Winston-Salem, NC: Wake Forest University Press, 1978.

Morris, Gary. "Beyond the Beach: AIP's *Beach Party* Movies." Bright Lights Film Journal, May 1998.

Myers, Nathan. "You Are Here: Taylor Steele." Surfing Magazine, September 22, 2012. http://www.surfingmagazine.com/blogs/you-are-here-taylor-steele/.

Naughton, Kevin. "Has Video Killed the Surf Movie?" *Surfer* (September 26, 1985).

Nelson, Chris. "DIY Surf Films Against the Code. Huck, March 19, 2012. http://www.huckmagazine.com/ride/surf/diy-surf-films/.

Nemerov, Howard. "Sandpipers." *Mirrors & Windows: Poems*. Chicago: University of Chicago Press, 1958.

Nichols, Bill. *Introduction to Documentary*, 2d ed. Bloomington: Indiana University Press, 2010.

"1971: quand Jeff Hakman découvrait la France." Surf Session.com, December 7, 2013. http://www.surfsession.com/2013/12/07/1971-quand-jeff-hakman-decouvrait-la-france/.

"Noa Deane and Dion Agius Apologise for Surfer Poll Awards." *Stab*, December 9, 2014. http://stabmag.com/noa-deane-and-dion-agius-apologise-for-surfer-poll-awards/.

Orlean, Susan. "Life's Swell." Women Outside, Fall 1998. outsideonline.com, August 23, 2002. http://www.outsideonline.com/adventure-travel/north-america/united-states/hawaii/Life-s-Swell.html.

Péron, Didier. "Naomi Kawase: J'ai des prédispositions à devenir chamane." Libération: Next, September 30, 2014. http://next.liberation.fr/cinema/2014/09/30/j-ai-des-predispositions-a-devenir-chamane_1111794.

Pezman, Steve. "Surfer." Liner notes, *The Cosmic Children*, 1970; DVD Surf Video Network, n.d.

"Quiksilver Earnings Up 10 Percent, Sales Jump 15 Percent in 2nd Quarter." *Daily News Record*, September 26, 1996.

Raymond, Matt. "Surf's Up ... At the Library?" Library of Congress Blog, July 25, 2008. blogs.loc.gov/loc/2008/07/surs-up-at-the-library/.

Reyes, David. "Surfer Tracks Big Swell across Pacific." *Los Angeles Times*, August 2, 1996.

Richards, Sam. "John Maus: 'If My Music Sounds 80s, You're Hearing Its Medieval Backbone.'" *The Guardian*, November 12, 2011.

Rimbaud, Arthur. "Le Bateau ivre." *Le Bateau ivre et autres poèmes*. Paris: Editions 84, 2014. [Translation JE.]

"Rock Hudson Breaks Shoulder." *New York Times*, August 15, 1953.

Rodgers, Terry. "Hal Jepsen, 66; Surf Filmmaker Made the Waves His Stars." *Union-Tribune San Diego*, February 17, 2006. http://www.uniontrib.com/uniontrib/20060217/news_1m17jepsen.html.

Roethke, Theodore. "The Waking." The *Collected Poems of Theodore Roethke*. New York: Anchor, 1975.

Rolland, Romain. *Un beau visage à tous sens: Choix de lettres de Romain Rolland (1866–1944)*. Paris: Albin Michel, 1967.

Rooney, David. "Review: 'Blackrock.'" *Variety* (February 8, 1998).

Roth, Chloe. "Thomas Campbell: Um ... Duh ... Yeah." Huck, April 26, 2012. http://www.huckmagazine.com/art-and-culture/art-2/thomas-campbell/.

Roussel, Nolwenn. *Jardin de récif: Sur la trace des premiers surfeurs tahitiens*. Biarritz: Atlantica, 2005.

"The Rosy Resurrection." Tracks: The Surfers' Bible, February 11, 2011. http://www.tracksmag.com/201102112570/Tracks-Features/General/The-Rosy-Resurrection.html.

Rukeyser, Muriel. "Palos Verdes Cliffs." *The Collected Poems of Muriel Rukeyser*. New York: McGraw-Hill, 1982.

Saint Louis, Catherine. "Style: Surfing Gauguin." *New York Times*, July 4, 2004.

Sakamoto, Glenn. "Devon Howard." Liquid Salt, May 17, 2012. http://www.liquidsaltmag.com/2012/05/devon-howard/.

Salles, Walter. "Notes for a Theory of the Road Movie." *New York Times*, November 11, 2007.

Schiffter, Frédéric. *Petite philosophie du surf*. Toulouse: Editions Milan, 2005.

Severson, John. *John Severson's Surf*. Bologna: Damiani/Puka Puka, 2014.

―――. "Rare Interview with John Severson and Tom Blake." Interview on Australian TV, 1972. http://www.youtube.com/watch?v=vUQkt395-pU.

Shearer, Steve. "dear suburbia reviewed, by steve shearer." Blog post, September 20, 2012.

Shields, Rob. *Places on the Margin: Alternative Geographies of Modernity*. London: Routledge, 1991.

Sketches of the Life of Bishop Patteson in Melanesia. Society for Promoting Christian Knowledge. New York: Pott, Young & Co., 1876.

Sontag, Susan. "Jack Smith's *Flaming Creatures*," in Gregory Battcock, ed., *The New American Cinema: A Critical Anthology*. New York: Dutton, 1967.

Springsteen, Bruce. Remarks, Bruce Springsteen and the E Street Band concert, Hunter Valley, Australia, February 23, 2014.

Stille, Andrew. "John Milius: American Outsider." Diary of a Screenwriter, May 27, 2013. http://diaryofascreenwriter.blogspot.fr/2013/05/john-milius-american-outsider.html

Stillman, Deanne. "Introduction," in Frederick Kohner, *Gidget*. New York: Berkley, 2001.

Stranger, Mark. *Surfing Life: Surface, Substructure and the Commodification of the Sublime*. Surrey: Ashgate, 2011.

"Surf Filmmaker Hal Jepsen Passes On." Surfer blog post, July 22, 2010. http://www.surfermag.com/features/jepsenrip/.

"Surf Movie Pioneer." *Surfing World* (March 1963).

"Surf Movies." SurferToday.com. http://www.surftoday.com/surf-movies.

"Surfer and Filmmaker Jeff Parker Remembers Being in Michael Jackson's 'Thriller.'" examiner.com, July 8, 2009. http://www.examiner.com/article/surfer-and-filmmaker-jeff-parker-remembers-being-michael-jackson-s-thriller.

"Surfing's Angry Young Men." *Surf Guide* (October 1963), quoted in David Rensin. *All for a Few Perfect Waves: The Audacious Life and Legend of Rebel Surfer Miki Dora*. New York: HarperCollins, 2008

Taylor, Kimball. "Mike Hynson: Cape St. Francis, 1963." *Surfer* Special Edition: The Greatest Rides of all Time (August 2013).

"Taylor Steele Interview at Castles in the Sky Premiere." MeSurfTV, Episode 9, August 1, 2010. https://www.youtube.com/watch?v=SyhgNk2whtc.

Tennyson, Alfred, Lord. "Crossing the Bar" (1889). M.H. Abrams, et al., *The Norton Anthology of English Literature*, vol. 2, 4th ed. New York: W.W. Norton, 1979.

"Thomas, G. Wayne." http://www.gwaynethomas.com/albums/david-elfick.html.

Thomas, Gregory. "Private Paradise." *Surfer* (July 2014).

Thompson, Neal. "Ski Movie Mogul Warren Miller Refuses to Go Downhill." SeattleMet.com, November 23, 2011. http://www.seattlemet.com/arts-and-entertainment/articles/warren-miller-ski-film-legend-december-2011/1.

Thoms, Albie. *Surfmovies: The History of the Surf Film in Australia*. Sydney: Shore Thing, 2000.

Thoreau Henry David. *Walden, and Other Writings*. Edited by William Howarth. New York: Modern Library, 1981.

Thoreau, Henry David. *A Year in Thoreau's Journal: 1851*. New York: Penguin, 1993.

Tomson, Shaun. "Foreword," in Sam George, ed., *Surfer Magazine: 50 Years*. San Francisco: Chronicle, 2010.

Townend, Peter. "Topanga Dayz." Easy Reader News, June 10, 2013. http://www.easyreadernews.com/71184/peter-pt-townends-mates-point-of-view-first-trip-to-southern-california/.

Trew, James. "Extreme Exposure: Inside GoPro's Burgeoning Media Empire." Engadget.com, May 29, 2014. http://www.engadget.com/2014/05/29/gopro-media-business/.

Trompenaars, Fons, and Charles Hampden Turner. *Riding the Waves of Culture: Understanding Cultural Diversity in Business*. New York: McGraw-Hill, 1998.

Tsai, Michael. "Island Film 'The Ride' Catches Waves of Praise." Honolulu Advertiser.com, August 5, 2004. http://the.honoluluadvertiser.com/article/2004/Aug/05/il/il01a.html.

Tschorn, Adam. "In 1946 Fame Was in the Future for Several New Santa Monica Lifeguards." *Los Angeles Times*, July 20, 2008.

"2011 SURFER Poll Lifetime Achievement." YouTube, December 7, 2011. https://www.youtube.com/watch?v=l9Pb1t4t9TE.

"Unknown Surfer, Matavai Bay, Tahiti, 1877." *Surfer* Special Edition: The Greatest Rides of All Time (August 2013).

Walker, Isaiah Helekunihi. *Waves of Resistance: Surfing and History in Twentieth-Century Hawai'i*. Honolulu: University of Hawai'i Press, 2011.

Walker, Maxton. "My Favourite Film: Big Wednesday." TheGuardian.com, December 13, 2011. http://www.theguardian.com/film/2011/dec/13/my-favourite-film-big-wednesday.

Wang, Anyi. "Gangshang de shiji" [A Century on a Small Hillock]. In *Gangshang deshijiWang Anyi zhongpian xiaoshuoji* [A Century on a Small Hillock: Novellas of Wang Anyi] (vol. 4). Shanghai: Shanghai Wenyi Chubanshe, 2013.

Warshaw, Matt. *The Encylopedia of Surfing*. Orlando: Harcourt, 2005

_____. *The History of Surfing*. San Francisco: Chronicle, 2010

_____. *Surf Movie Tonite! Surf Movie Poster Art, 1957–2004*. San Francisco: Chronicle, 2005.

_____, ed. *Zero Break: An Illustrated Collection of Surf Writing, 1777–2004*. Orlando: Harcourt, 2004.

Westwick, Peter, and Peter Neushul. *The World in the Curl: An Unconventional History of Surfing*. New York: Crown, 2013.

"The White Flower / Betty Compson [motion picture]." The Library of Congress American Silent Feature Film Survival Database. http://lcweb2.loc.gov/diglib/ihas/loc.mbrs.sfdb.10551/default.html.

White, Thomas. "Gotta' Surf Somebody: With 'Riding Giants,' It's Not About the Wave." Documentary.org, July 2004. http://www.documentary.org/magazine/gotta-surf-somebody-riding-giants-its-not-about-waves.

Whitman, Walt. "By that Long Scan of Waves" (1884); "Song of Myself" (1891). *Walt Whitman: The Complete Poems*. London: Penguin, 2012.

Winnicott, D. W. *Playing and Reality*. New York: Routledge, 2005.

Winton, Tim. *Breath*. New York: Picador, 2009.
———. *Land's Edge: A Coastal Memoir*. London: Picador, 1998.
Witzig, John. "We're Tops Now." *Surfer* (May 1967).
Witzig, Paul. "I Was Trying to Break from the Traditional Surfing Sound (*Sea of Joy*)." Interview, Somusically, August 23, 2013. https://soundcloud.com/rarecollections/paul-witzig-i-was-trying-to.
Wollen, Peter. "The Auteur Theory." From Gerald Mast and Marshall Cohen, eds., *Film Theory and Criticism: Introductory Readings*, 3d ed. New York: Oxford University Press, 1985.
Woolf, Virginia. *To the Lighthouse*. Ed. David Bradshaw. New York: Oxford World's Classics, 2006.
Wordsworth, William. "The World Is Too Much with Us" (1800); "Ode: Intimations of Immortality from Recollections of Early Childhood" (1807); *The Prelude* (1850). *The Collected Poems of William Wordsworth*. Hertfordshire: Wordsworth, 1994.

Film, Video, Animation and Television

American Graffiti. Universal Pictures, Lucasfilms/Coppola. Dir. George Lucas. Perfs. Richard Dreyfus, Harrison Ford, Ron Howard, Cindy Williams. 1973.
The Angry Sea. Dir. John Severson. Narr. John Severson. Perfs. Tommy Lee, Greg Noll, John Peck, Butch Van Artsdalen. 1963.
Apocalypse Now. American Zoetrope. Dir. Francis Ford Coppola. Perfs. Sam Bottoms, Marlin Brando, Robert Duvall, Martin Sheen. 1979.
Back to the Beach. Paramount Pictures. Dir. Lyndall Hobbs. Perfs. Frankie Avalon, Annette Funicello, Lori Loughlin, Demian Slade, Connie Stevens. 1987.
Barefoot Adventure. Dir. Bruce Brown. Narr. Bruce Brown. Perfs. Joey Cabell, Del Cannon, Mike Diffenderfer, Joey Hamasaki. 1961. DVD reissue, *The Bruce Brown Signature Collection*. Go Entertain. 2012.
Beach Blanket Bingo. American International Pictures. Dir. William Asher. Perfs. Frankie Avalon, Linda Evans, Annette Funicello, Harvey Lembeck, Jody McCrea. 1965.
Beach Party. American International Pictures. Dir. William Asher. Perfs. Frankie Avalon, Bob Cummings, Annette Funicello, Harvey Lembeck, Eva Six. 1963.
Beautiful Wave. Portfolio Films America. Dir. David Mueller. Perfs. Lance Hendriksen, David Thomas Jenkins, Ben Milliken, Patricia Richardson, Aimee Teegarden, Alicia Ziegler. 2011.
The Big Surf. Dir. Bud Browne. Narr. Bud Browne. Perfs. Peter Cole, Greg Noll, Mike Stange, Buzzy Trent. 1957.
Big Wednesday. Dir. John Severson. Perfs. Pat Curren, Ricky Grigg, Greg Harris, Greg Noll. 1961.
Big Wednesday. Warner Bros. Dir. John Milius. Perfs. Gary Busey, Patti D'Arbanville, William Katt, Sam Melville, Jan-Michael Vincent. 1978.
Biggest Wednesday: Condition Black. Dir. Tim Bonython. Perfs. Ken Bradshaw, Ross Clarke-Jones, Noah Johnson, Dave Kalama, Dan Moore. 1998.
Billabong Odyssey. Billabong. Dir. Philip Boston. Perfs. Ken Collins, Shane Dorian, Brad Gerlach, Mike Parsons. 2003.
Bird of Paradise. RKO Radio Pictures. Dir. King Vidor. Perfs. Dolores Del Rio, Joel McCrea. 1932.
The Black Camel. Fox Film Corporation. Dir. Hamilton MacFadden. Perfs. Sally Eilers, Bela Lugosi, Warner Oland, Dorothy Revier. 1931.
Blackrock. Palm Beach Pictures. Dir. Steven Vidler. Perfs. Laurence Breuls, Linda Cropper, Simon Lyndon, Jessica Napier. 1997.
Blue Crush. Billygoat Productions. Dir. Bill Ballard. Perfs. Megan Abubo, Lisa Anderson, Rochelle Ballard, Layne Beachley. 1998.
Blue Crush. Universal Pictures. Dir. John Stockwell. Perfs. Mika Boorem, Kate Bosworth, Matthew Davis, Michelle Rodriguez. 2002.
Blue Hawaii. Paramount Pictures. Dir. Norman Taurog. Perfs. John Archer, Joan Blackman, Elvis Presley, Nancy Walters. 1961.
Blue Juice. Skreba Films. Dir. Carl Prechezer. Perfs. Ewan McGregor, Sean Pertwee, Heathcote Williams, Catherine Zeta-Jones. 1995.
Bobby Bumps, Surf Rider. Bray Productions. Dir. Earl Hurd. 1917.
Bra Boys. Berkela Films. Dir. Sunny Abberton, Macario De Souza. Narr. Russell Crowe. Perfs. Jai Abberton, Koby Abberton, Sunny Abberton, Kelly Slater. 2007.
Brice de Nice. Mandarin Cinéma. Dir. James Huth. Perfs. Elodie Bouchez, Clovis Cornillac, Jean Dujardin, Alexandra Lamy, Bruno Salomone. 2005.
Bustin' Down the Door. Fresh and Smoked. Dir. Jeremy Gosch. Narr. Edward Norton. Perfs. Rabbit Bartholomew, Ian Cairns, Mark Richards, Michael Tomson, Shaun Tomson, Peter Townend. 2008.
Can't Step Twice on the Same Piece of Water: A Surfing Odyssey. Island Records. Dir. Alby Falzon. Perf. Jim Banks. 1992.
Castles in the Sky. Sipping Jetstreams Media. Dir. Taylor Steele. Perfs. Craig Anderson, Tim Curran, Rob Machado, Dave Rastovich, Dane Reynolds, Jordy Smith. 2010.
Cat on a Hot Foam Board. Dir. Bud Browne. Narr. Bud Browne. Perfs. Phil Edwards, Hevs McClelland, LJ Richards, Dewey Weber. 1959.

Cavalcade of Surf. Dir. Bud Browne. Narr. Peter Cole. Perfs. Linda Benson, Pat Curren, Mike Doyle, Buzzy Trent, Dewey Weber. 1962.

Chasing Mavericks. Fox 2000 Pictures. Dir. Curtis Hanson; Michael Apted. Perfs. Gerard Butler, Elisabeth Shue, Abigail Spencer, Jonny Weston. 2012.

Chasing the Swell. Los Angeles Times. Dir. Sachi Cunningham. Perfs. Carlos Burle, Shane Dorian, Mark Healey, Greg Long, Evan Slater, James Taylor. 2010.

The Cosmic Children. Dir. Hal Jepsen. Narr. Hal Jepsen. Perfs. Larry Bertlemann, Jeff Hakman, Barry Kanaiaupuni, J Riddle, George Trapton. 1970. DVD, Surf Video Network, date unavailable.

Cruise Cat. Metro-Goldwyn-Mayer. Tom and Jerry cartoon. Dir. William Hanna, Joseph Barbera. 1952.

Crystal Voyager. Dir. David Elfick. Narr. George Greenough. Perfs. George Greenough, Richie West, Nat Young. 1973.

A Day in the Life of Wayne Lynch. Rip Curl. Dir. Jack McCoy, Dick Hoole, David Lourie. Perf. Wayne Lynch. 1978.

Dear & Yonder. Woodshed Films, Roxy. Dir. Tiffany Campbell, Andria Lessler. Perfs. Belinda Baggs, Linda Benson, Stephanie Gilmore, Kassia Meador, Sofia Mulanovich. 2009.

Dear Suburbia,. Dir. Kai Neville. Perfs. Craig Anderson, Kolohe Andino, John John Florence, Dane Reynolds, Jack Robinson. 2012.

A Deeper Shade of Blue. McCoy Media. Dir. Jack McCoy. Narr. Moses Goods. Perfs. Manoa Drollet, Stephanie Gilmore, Derek Hynd, Gerry Lopez, Jamie O'Brien. 2011.

Dogtown and Z-Boys. Dir. Stacy Peralta. Narr. Sean Penn. Perfs. Jay Adams, Tony Alva, Jeff Ho, Stacy Peralta, Craig Stecyk. 2001.

Down the Barrel. Peligro Pictures, ESPN. Dir. Steven Lawrence. Perf. Rob Machado, Joel Parkinson, Doc Paskowitz, Kalani Robb, Kelly Slater. 2007.

Drift. World Wide Mind Films. Dir. Ben Nott, Morgan O'Neill. Perfs. Lesley-Ann Brandt, Robin Malcolm, Myles Pollard, Xavier Samuel, Sam Worthington. 2013.

The Drifter. Sipping Jetstreams Media. Dir. Taylor Steele. Narr. Rob Machado. Perfs. Rob Machado, Kelly Slater. 2009.

Echoes. Dir. George Greenough. Perf. George Greenough. 1972.

The Endless Summer. Bruce Brown Films. Dir. Bruce Brown. Narr. Bruce Brown. Perfs. Robert August, Mike Hynson. 1964, 1966.

The Endless Summer Revisited. Bruce Brown Films. Dir. Dana Brown. Perfs. Hobie Alter, Robert August, Bruce Brown, Greg Noll, Dale Velzy. 1990.

The Endless Summer II. Bruce Brown Films, New Line Cinema. Dir. Bruce Brown. Narr. Bruce Brown. Perfs. Robert August, Tom Curren, Patrick O'Connell, Robert Weaver, Shaun Tomson. 1994.

The Endless Winter. Prod., Dir. Matt Crocker, James Dean. Narr. Nick Boulting. Perfs. Mitch Corbett, Mark Harris, Pete Russell, Linda Sharp, Rodney Sumpter. 2012.

Evolution. Dir. Paul Witzig. Perfs. Reno Abellira, Peter Drouyn, Midget Farrelly, Wayne Lynch, Ted Spencer, Nat Young. 1969.

Expression Session. Dir. Jim Freeman, Greg MacGillivray. Perfs. Jeff Hakman, David Nuuhiwa, Jock Sutherland, Nat Young. 1971.

The Fantastic Plastic Machine. 20th Century Fox. Dir. Eric and Lowell Blum. Narr. Jay North, Nat Young. Perfs. Steve Bigler, George Greenough, Bob McTavish, Mike Purpus, Nat Young. 1969.

Fast Times at Ridgemont High. Dir. Amy Heckerling. Perfs. Brian Backer, Jennifer Jason Leigh, Judge Reinhold, Sean Penn. 1982.

Filthy Habits. Billabong. Perfs. Ronnie Burns, Richie Collins, Sunny Garcia, Mark Occhilupo. 1987.

Fifty Years of Surfing on Film, Vol. 1: Bud Browne, John Severson, Greg Noll. The Surfer's Journal. Dir. Ira Opper. Narr. Robert Weaver. 2008.

Fifty Years of Surfing on Film, Vol. 2: Bruce Brown, Greg MacGillivray, George Greenough. The Surfer's Journal. Dir. Ira Opper. Narr. Robert Weaver. 2008.

Fifty Years of Surfing on Film, Vol. 3: Paul Witzig, Alby Falzon, Hal Jepsen, Bill Delaney. The Surfer's Journal. Dir. Ira Opper. Narr. Robert Weaver. 2008.

Five Summer Stories. Dir. Jim Freeman, Greg MacGillivray. Narr. Jim Freeman, Greg MacGillivray. Perfs. Bill Hamilton, Margo Godfrey Oberg, Barry Kanaiaupuni, Gerry Lopez, David Nuuhiwa. 1972–1979, 1995.

Focus. Poor Specimen. Dir. Taylor Steele. Perfs. Greg Browning, Taylor Knox, Rob Machado, Kelly Slater, Benji Weatherley, Ross Williams. 1994.

Free and Easy. Dir. Jim Freeman, Greg MacGillivray. Narr. Jim Freeman, Greg MacGillivray. Perfs. Billy Hamilton, Ricky Grigg, Joyce Hoffman, David Nuuhiwa, Jock Sutherland. 1967.

Free Ride. Dir. Bill Delaney. Narr. Jan-Michael Vincent. Perfs. Rabbit Bartholomew, Mark Richards, Shaun Tomson, Peter Townend. 1977, 1983.

Gidget. Columbia Pictures. Dir. Paul Wendkos. Perfs. James Darren, Sandra Dee, Arthur O'Connell, Cliff Robertson. 1959

Gidget Goes Hawaiian. Columbia Pictures. Dir. Paul Wendkos. Perfs. Joby Baker, James Darren, Carl Reiner, Vicki Trickett, Deborah Walley. 1961.

The Girls on the Beach. Paramount Pictures. Dir. Harvey Jacobson. Perfs. Noreen Corcoran, Linda Marshall, Steven Rogers, Martin West. 1965.

Glass Love. Dir. Andrew Kidman. Perfs. Tom Curren, Skip Frye, Derek Hynd, Neal Purchase, Ozzie Wright. 2005.

Going My Wave. Dir. John Severson. Narr. John Severson. Perfs. Mike Hynson, Mickey Munoz, Butch Van Artsdalen, Dave Willingham. 1962.

Going Surfin'. Dir. Bud Browne. Narr. Hevs McClelland. Perfs. Reno Abellira, Larry Bertlemann, Jeff Hakman, Barry Kanaiaupuni, David Nuuhiwa. 1973–1977.

The Golden Breed. Dir. Dale Davis. Narr. Dale Davis. Perfs. Eddie Aikau, Joey Cabell, Ricky Grigg, Felipe Pomar, Nat Young. 1968.

Gone with the Wave. Dir. Phil Wilson. Narr. Johnny Magnus. Perfs. Johnny Fain, Paul Strauch, Buzzy Trent, Dewey Weber. 1964.

The Green Iguana. Billabong. Dir. Jack McCoy. Perfs. Munga Barry, Luke Egan, Sunny Garcia, Peter King, Mark Occhilupo. 1992.

Gun Ho! Dir. Bud Browne. Narr. Peter Cole. Perfs. Candy Calhoun, Phil Edwards, Greg Noll, John Peck, Butch Van Artsdalen. 1963.

Have Board Will Travel. Dir. Don Brown. Perf. Midget Farrelly. 1963.

Hawaii Nine-O. Sports Video Productions, Gorilla Grip. Dir. Tim Bonython. 1990.

Hawaiian Holiday. Walt Disney Productions. Dir. Ben Sharpsteen. 1937.

Hawaiian Nights. Universal Studios. Dir. Albert S. Rogell. Perfs. Johnny Downs, Constance Moore. 1939.

Hawaiian Surfing Movie. Dir. Bud Browne. 1953.

Here & Now: A Day in the Life of Surfing. Sipping Jetstreams Media. Dir. Nathan Myers. Perfs. Reubyn Ash, Stephanie Gilmore, Rob Machado, Dave Rastovich, Kelly Slater, Ozzie Wright. 2012.

Hollywood Don't Surf! MacGillivray Freeman Films. Dir. Sam George, Greg MacGillivray. Narr. Robert Englund. Shown as a work-in-progress 2010, unreleased.

The Hot Generation. Dir. Paul Witzig. Narr. John Thompson. Perfs. Kevin Brennan, Bob McTavish, George Greenough, Ted Spencer, Nat Young. 1967.

How to Stuff a Wild Bikini. American International Pictures. Dir. William Asher. Perfs. Beverly Adams, Annette Funicello, Dwayne Hickman, Harvey Lembeck. 1965.

Hula Magoo. UPA/Columbia. Dir. Paul Fennell. 1965.

In God's Hands. TriStar Pictures. Dir. Zalman King. Perfs. Shane Dorian, Matt George, Matty Liu, Maylin Pultar, Shaun Tomson. 1998.

In Search of Tubular Swells. Dir. Dick Hoole, Jack McCoy. Narr. Jack McCoy. Perfs. Rabbit Bartholomew, Ian Cairns, Gerry Lopez, Mark Richards, Rory Russell. 1976.

The Innermost Limits of Pure Fun. Dir. George Greenough. Perfs. Chris Brock, George Greenough, Bob McTavish, David Treloar. 1969.

Innersection. Prod. Nathan Myers, Taylor Steele. Dir. Matthew Bokor, Greg Browning, Kyle Buthman, Nicolas Dazet, et al. Perfs. Craig Anderson, John John Florence, Matt Meola, Joel Parkinson, Kelly Slater, etc. 2011.

Into the Sea. Dir. Marion Poizeau. Perfs. Easkey Britton, Mona Seraji, Shalha Yasini. 2014.

Kelly Slater and the Young Guns. Quiksilver, Pavilion Productions. Dir. Jason Haynes. Perfs. Jeremy Flores, Luke Munro, Dane Reynolds, Kelly Slater. 2004.

Kelly Slater in Black and White. Dir. Richard Woolcott. Perf. Kelly Slater. 1991.

Kong's Island. Quiksilver. Dir. Jack McCoy, David Lourie. Perfs. Rabbit Bartholomew, Gary Elkerton, Chappy Jennings. 1983.

Letting Go. Quiksilver, Pavilion Productions. Dir. George Opadchy, Jamie Tierney. Narr. Bryan Fisher. Perfs. Andy Irons, Bruce Irons, Brock Little, Mark Richards, Kelly Slater. 2006.

Life as a Movie. Little Buddy Productions. Dir. Benji Weatherley. Perfs. Tom Carroll, Tony Hawk, Yadin Nicol, Kelly Slater, Rizal Tanjung, Tosh Townend, JP Walker. 2008.

Lilo & Stich. Walt Disney Feature Animation. Dir. Chris Sanders, Dean DeBlois. Perfs. Tia Carrere, Daveigh Chase, Jason Scott Lee, Ving Rhames, Chris Sanders. 2002.

Litmus. Dir. The Val Dusty Experiment (Andrew Kidman, Jon Frank, Mark Sutherland). Perfs. Tom Curren, Miki Dora, Joel Fitzgerald, Derek Hynd. 1996.

Locked In! Dir. Bud Browne. Narr. Peter Cole, John Weiser. Perfs. Joey Cabell, Phil Edwards, Jeff Hakman, Joyce Hoffman, John Peck. 1964.

Loose Change. Poor Specimen. Dir. Taylor Steele. Perfs. Shane Dorian, Rob Machado, the Malloys, Kelly Slater, Benji Weatherley. 1999.

Lost Atlas. Dir. Kai Neville. Perfs. Dion Agius, Kolohe Andino, Yadin Nicol, Dusty Payne, Jordy Smith, Chippa Wilson. 2011.

"Low Clouds and Coastal Fog." January 18, 1963, episode of the *Alfred Hitchcock Hour.*

Manufacturing Stoke. Misfit Pictures. Dir. Pierce Michael Kavanagh. Perfs. Lucas Dirkse, Mikko Flemming, Tiare Thompson, Adam Traubman. 2011.

A Matter of Style. Dir. Steve Soderberg. Narr. Steve Soderberg. Perfs. Larry Bertlemann, Terry Fitzgerald, Gerry Lopez, Shaun Tomson, Peter Townend. 1975, 1980.

La Mer (Baignade en mer). Dir. Frères Lumière. "*La Première séance publique payante,*" Institut Lumière, institut-lumiere.org/patrimoine.html. 1895.

Minds in the Water. Dir. Justin Krumb. Perfs. Chris Del Moro, Jack Johnson, Hayden Panettiere, Joel Parkinson, Dave Rastovich. 2011.

Missing. Sipping Jetstreams Media. Dir. Taylor Steele. Perfs. Tom Curren, Mick Fanning, John John Florence, Taylor Knox, Joel Parkinson. 2013.

Moana. Dir. Robert Flaherty. Perfs. Ta'avale, Fa'amgase, Pe'a. 1926.

Mödern Collective. Dir. Kai Neville. Perfs. Mitch Colburn, Yadin Nicol, Dusty Payne, Dane Reynolds, Jordy Smith. 2009.

Momentum. Dir. Taylor Steele. Perfs. Shane Dorian, Taylor Knox, Rob Machado, Kelly Slater, Benji Weatherley, Ross Williams. 1992.

Morning of the Earth. Dir. David Elfick, Alby Falzon. Perfs. Steven Cooney, Terry Fitzgerald, Rusty Miller, Michael Peterson, Nat Young. 1972. VHS, Chili Video. 1998.

Muscle Beach Party. American International Pictures. Dir. William Asher. Perfs. Morey Amsterdam, Frankie Avalon, Annette Funicello, Luciana Paluzzi, Don Rickles. 1964.

Nanook of the North. Dir. Robert Flaherty. Perfs. Allakariallak, Nyla, Cunayou. 1922.

National Lampoon Presents Endless Bummer. Lighthouse Entertainment, Vans Warped Tour. Dir. Sam Pillsbury. Perfs. Khan Chittenden, Jim Piddock, Ray Santiago, Allison Scagliotti. 2009.

Newcastle. Dragonfly Pictures, Three Dogs and a Pony. Dir. Dan Castle. Perfs. Rebecca Breeds, Lachlan Buchanan, Kirk Jenkins, Xavier Samuel, Reshad Strik. 2008.

North Shore. Universal Pictures. Dir. William Phelps. Perfs. Matt Adler, Gregory Harrison, Gerry Lopez, Nia Peeples, John Philbin. 1987.

Occy: The Occumentary. Billabong. Dir. Jack McCoy. Perfs. Mark Occhilupo, Occhilupo family; Rabbit Bartholomew, Tom Carroll, Tom Curren, Brendan Margieson. 1998.

Ocean Fever. Dir. Steve Soderberg. Narr. Steve Soderberg. Perfs. Tom Curren, Buttons Kaluhiokalani, Mark Liddell, Jeff Parker, Shaun Tomson, Peter Townend. 1983.

Ocean Tribe. SeaReel. Dir. Will Geiger. Perfs. Robert Caso, Tony Fazio, Mark Matheisen, Gregg Rainwater, Vaughn Roberts. 1997.

Once Upon a Wave. Dir. Walt Phillips. Narr. Walt Phillips. Perfs. Peter Cole, Ricky Grigg, Greg Noll, Fred Van Dyke. 1963.

One California Day. Dir. Jason Baffa, Mark Jeremias. Narr. Devon Howard. Perfs. Joe Curren, Skip Frye, Tyler Hatzikian, Alex Knost, Chris Malloy, Greg Noll. 2007.

110% Surfing Techniques, Volume. Discovery of Surf Media. Dir. Martin Connolly. Perfs. Martin Connolly, Matz Ginman-Trout, Phil MacDonald. 2010.

One Winter Story. Frank Films. Dir. Sally Lundberg, Elizabeth Pepin. Perfs. Ken Bradshaw, Mike Gerhardt, Sarah Gerhardt. 2007.

Pacific Vibrations. Dir. John Severson. Narr. John Severson. Perfs. Rolf Aurness, Corky Carroll, Rick Griffin, Billy Hamilton, Jock Sutherland. 1970.

Panorama of Ocean Beach and Cliff House. Dir. H.J. Miles. 1903.

The Paul Witzig Trilogy. DVD (*The Hot Generation, Evolution, Sea of Joy*). Witzig Films. 2010.

The Perfect Wave. Divine Inspiration Trading 679, Fabulous Boomtown Boys. Dir. Bruce MacDonald. Perfs. Scott Eastwood, Rachel Hendrix, Rosy Hodge, Cheryl Ladd, Scott Mortensen. 2014.

The Performers. Quiksilver. Dir. Jack McCoy, Harry Hodge. Perfs. Rabbit Bartholomew, Gary Elkerton, Marvin Foster, Chappy Jennings, Wes Laine. 1984.

Point Break. JVC Entertainment, Largo Entertainment. Dir. Kathryn Bigelow. Perfs. Gary Busey, John C. McGinley, Lori Petty, John Philbin, Keanu Reeves, Patrick Swayze. 1991.

The Prince and the Surfer. Crystal Sky Worldwide, Paul Family Films. Dir. Arye Gross, Gregory Gieras. Perfs. Timothy Bottoms, Robert Englund, Sean Kellman, Jennifer O'Neill, Vincent Shiavelli. 1999.

Psyche Out. Dir. Walt Phillips. Narr. Walt Phillips. Perfs. Kemp Aaberg, Lance Carson, Barry Kanaiaupuni, Greg Noll, Butch Van Artsdalen. 1962.

Psycho Beach Party. New Oz Productions, Red Horse Films, Strand Releasing. Dir. Robert Lee King. Perfs. Amy Adams, Lauren Ambrose, Charles Busch, Thomas Gibson, Matt Keeslar. 2000.

Puberty Blues. Limelight Productions. Dir. Bruce Beresford. Perfs. Jad Capelja, Tony Hughes, Sandy Paul, Geoff Rhoe, Nell Schofield. 1981.

The Ride. Third Reef Pictures. Dir. Nathan Kurosawa. Perfs. Scot Davis, Sean Kaawa, Weldon Kekauoha, Mary Paalani. 2003.

Ride the Wild Surf. Jana Film Enterprise, Columbia Pictures. Dir. Art Napoleon; Don Taylor. Perfs. Peter Brown, Barbara Eden, Shelley Fabares, Fabian, Susan Hart, Tab Hunter, James Mitchum. 1964.

Riding Giants. Agi Orsi Productions, Forever Films, Quiksilver Entertainment. Dir. Stacy Peralta. Narr. Stacy Peralta. Perf. Jeff Clark, Laird Hamilton, Greg Noll, Darryl Virostko. 2004.

Rough Sea at Dover. Dir. Robert Paul. 1896.

San Diego Surf. Andy Warhol Foundation. Dir. Andy Warhol; Paul Morrissey. Perfs. Joe Dallesandro, Tom Hompertz, Taylor Mead, Ingrid Superstar, Viva. 1968; 2012.

A Scene at the Sea [Ano natsu, ichiban shizukana umi]. Office Kitano, Toho Company, Totsu. Dir. Takeshi Kitano. Perfs. Toshizo Fujiwara, Sabu Kawahara, Claude Maki, Hiroko Ōshima. 1991.

A Sea Cave Near Lisbon. Dir. Robert Paul. 1898.

A Sea for Yourself. Dir. Hal Jepsen. Narr. Hal Jepsen. Perfs. Jeff Hakman, Barry Kanaiaupuni, Gerry Lopez, J Riddle, Peter Townend. 1973.

Sea of Joy. Dir. Paul Witzig. Perfs. Reno Abellira, Tiger Espere, Wayne Lynch, Ted Spencer, Nat Young. 1971.

The Search. Rip Curl. Dir. Sonny Miller. Perfs. Tom Curren, Frankie Oberholzer. 1990.

Search for Surf. Dir. Greg Noll. Perfs. Pat Curren, Miki Dora, Buffalo Keaulana, Chubby Mitchell, Terry Tracy. 1957–1961.

Searching for Tom Curren. Rip Curl. Dir. Sonny Miller. Perf. Tom Curren. 1996.

The Seedling. Woodshed Films. Dir. Thomas Campbell. Perfs. Skip Frye, Jimmy Gamboa, Devon Howard, Kassia Meador, Joel Tudor. 1999.

The September Sessions. The Moonshine Conspiracy (Emmett Malloy, Kelly Slater). Dir. Jack Johnson. Perfs. Shane Dorian, Luke Egan, Brad Gerlach, Rob Machado, Kelly Slater, Ross Williams. 2000.

The Show. Poor Specimen. Dir. Taylor Steele. Perfs. Shane Dorian, Taylor Knox, Rob Machado, Chris Malloy, Dan Malloy. 1997.

Sik Joy. Billabong. Dir. Jack McCoy. Munga Barry, Luke Egan, Sunny Garcia, Mark Occhilupo. 1994.

Singlefin: Yellow. Singlefin Productions. Dir. Jason Baffa. Perfs. Tyler Hatzikian, Devon Howard, David Kinoshita, Daize Shayne, Bonga Perkins, Beau Young. 2003.

Sipping Jetstreams. Dir. Taylor Steele. Perfs. Shane Dorian, Andy Irons, Dane Reynolds, Kelly Slater. 2006.

Slippery When Wet. Bruce Brown Films. Dir. Bruce Brown. Narr. Bruce Brown. Perfs. Kemp Aaberg, Del Cannon, Phil Edwards, Henry Ford, Freddy Pfahler, Dick Thomas. 1958. DVD reissue, *The Bruce Brown Signature Collection*. Go Entertain. 2012.

Snapshots at the Seashore. Dir. Cecil Hepworth. 1903.

Some Like It Wet! Dir. Brad Page. Narr. John Chapin. Perfs. Miki Dora, Chubby Mitchell, Bruce Van Artsdalen, Dewey Weber. 1965.

Sons of the Surf. Dir. Robert C. Bruce. 1926.

La Sortie de l'usine Lumière à Lyon. Dir. Frères Lumière. "La Première séance publique payante," Institut Lumière, institut-lumiere.org/patrimoine.html. 1895.

Soul Surfer. Enticing Entertainment, Island Film Group, et al. Dir. Sean McNamara. Perfs. Helen Hunt, Lorraine Nicholson, Dennis Quaid, AnnaSophia Robb. 2011.

Spinning Boards. Dir. Bud Browne. Narr. Peter Cole. Perfs. Mike Doyle, Buzzy Trent, Butch Van Artsdalen, Dewey Weber. 1961.

Spirit of Akasha. Warner Bros. Dir. Andrew Kidman. Perfs. Tom Curren, Kye Fitzgerald, Mick Fanning, Stephanie Gilmore, Fergal Smith. 2014.

"SpongeBob SquarePants vs. The Big One." Nickelodeon. *SpongeBob SquarePants*, Season 6, Episode 5. Dir. Andrew Overtoom, Alan Smart. Perfs. Bruce Brown, Rodger Bumpass, Johnny Depp, Davy Jones, Tom Kenny. 2009.

Sprout. Woodshed Films. Dir. Thomas Campbell. Belinda Baggs, Alex Knost, Dave Rastovich, Joel Tudor, Tom Wegener, Ozzie Wright. 2004.

Step Into Liquid. Gotham Group, New Visual Entertainment, Top Secret Productions. Dir. Dana Brown. Narr. Dana Brown. Perfs. Layne Beachley, Jesse Billauer, Laird Hamilton, Alex Knost, Gerry Lopez. 2003.

Still the Water [Futatsume no mado]. Kumie. Dir. Naomi Kawase. Perfs. Miyuki Matsuda, Nijirô Murakami, Tetta Sugimoto, Jun Yoshinaga. 2014.

Stoked and Broke. Dir. Cyrus Sutton. Perfs. Ryan Burch, Cyrus Sutton. 2011.

Storm Riders. Dir. Dick Hoole, Jack McCoy. Narr. Jack McCoy. Perfs. Maurice Cole, Joe Engel, Thornton Fallander, Gerry Lopez, Wayne Lynch. 1982.

Stranger Than Fiction. Poor Specimen. Dir. Taylor Steele. Perfs. Josh Kerr, Clay Marzo, Yadin Nicol, Dane Reynolds, Kalani Robb, Julian Wilson. 2008.

Strictly Hot. Dir. Dale Davis. Narr. Dale Davis. Perfs. Miki Dora, Mike Doyle, Johnny Fain, Mike Hynson, Rusty Miller. 1964.

Summer City. Avalon Films, Michael Jordache Enterprises. Dir. Christopher Fraser. Perfs. Phillip Avalon, Steve Bisley, Mel Gibson, John Jarratt. 1977.

Sunset Surf Craze. Dir. Walt Phillips. Narr. Walt Phillips. Perfs. Linda Benson, Del Cannon, Peter Cole, Pat Curren, Ricky Grigg. 1959.

The Sunshine Sea. See *Waves of Change*. 1971.

Super Session. Dir. Hal Jepsen. Narr. Hal Jepsen. Perfs. Larry Bertlemann, Margo Godfrey Oberg, Jeff Hakman, Barry Kanaiaupuni, Gerry Lopez, Rory Russell. 1975.

Surf. Dir. John Severson. Perfs. George Downing, Buzzy Trent. 1958.

Surf at Monterey. The Thomas Edison Company. Dir. James White. 1897.

Surf Board Riders, Waikiki, Honolulu, Hawaiian Islands. The Thomas Edison Company. Dir. Robert Bonine. 1906.

Surf Classics. Dir. John Severson. Narr. John Severson. Kemp Aaberg, Miki Dora, Mike Doyle, Mickey Munoz, Butch Van Artsdalen. 1964.

Surf Crazy. Dir. Bruce Brown. Narr. Bruce Brown.

Perfs. Joey Cabell, Pat Curren, LJ Richards, Donald Takayama. 1959.

Surf Down Under. Dir. Bud Browne. Narr. Bud Browne. Perfs. Bob Evans, Bluey Mayes, Snowy McAlister, Claude West. 1958.

Surf Fever. Dir. John Severson. Narr. John Severson. Perfs. Kemp Aaberg, Lance Carson, Miki Dora, Mike Doyle, Fred Van Dyke. 1960.

Surf Happy. Dir. Bud Browne. Narr. Bud Browne. Perfs. Joey Cabell, Peter Cole, Pat Curren, Mike Doyle, Ricky Grigg, Buzzy Trent. 1960.

Surf Mania. Dir. Walt Phillips. Narr. Walt Phillips. Perfs. Robert August, Joey Cabell, Peter Cole, Mike Doyle. 1960.

Surf Safari. Dir. John Severson. Narr. John Severson. Perfs. Pat Curren, Mike Doyle, Mickey Munoz, Butch Van Artsdalen, Sonny Vardeman. 1959.

Surf Scenes. The Thomas Edison Company. Dir. Robert Bonine. 1906.

Surf Trek to Hawaii. Dir. Bob Evans. Perfs. Midget Farrelly, Dave Jackman, Bob Pike, Nipper Williams. 1962.

Surfer, Dude. Berk/Lane Entertainment, J.K. Livin Productions, Winchester Capital Partners. Dir. S.R. Bindler. Perfs. Alexie Gilmore, Scott Glenn, Woody Harrelson, Matthew McConaughey, Jeffrey Nordling. 2008.

Surfers: The Movie. Dir. Bill Delaney. Perfs. Tom Curren, Miki Dora, Cheyne Horan, Martin Potter, Kelly Slater. 1990.

Surfing for Life. Dir. David L. Brown. Narr. Beau Bridges. Perfs. Doc Ball, Peter Cole, Rabbit Kekai, John Kelly, Anona Napoleon. 1999.

Surfing Hollow Days. Dir. Bruce Brown. Narr. Bruce Brown. Perfs. Kemp Aaberg, Pat Curren, Phil Edwards, Mike Hynson, LJ Richards. 1962.

Surfing, le sport national des Illes Hawaii. Dir. Pathé Frères. 1911.

Surfing the 50's. Dir. Bud Browne. Narr. Peter Cole, John Kelly. Perfs. Linda Benson, George Downing, Greg Noll, Donald Takayama. 1994.

Surf's Up. Sony Pictures Animation. Dir. Ash Brannon, Chris Buck. Perfs. Diedrich Bader, Jeff Bridges, Zooey Deschanel, Jon Heder, Shia Labeouf. 2007.

Surfwise. Dir. Doug Pray. Perfs. Doc Paskowitz, Paskowitz family. 2007.

The Sweet Ride. 20th Century Fox. Dir. Harvey Hart. Perfs. Jacqueline Bisset, Bob Denver, Tony Franciosa, Michael Sarrazin. 1968.

Tales of the Seven Seas. Dir. Scott Dittrich. Perfs. Rabbit Bartholomew, Larry Bertlemann, Tom Curren, J Riddle, Shaun Tomson. 1981.

Tall Timbers. Cinesound Productions. Dir. Ken G. Hall. Perfs. Frank Harvey, Frank Leighton, Shirley Ann Richards. 1937.

Teen Beach Movie. Disney Channel, Rainforest Productions. Dir. Jeffrey Hornaday. Perfs. Barry Bostwick, Garret Clayton, Suzanne Cryer, Ross Lynch, Maia Mitchell. 2013.

Thicker Than Water. The Moonshine Conspiracy. Dir. Chris Malloy, Emmett Malloy, Jack Johnson. Perfs. Brad Gerlach, Rob Machado, Dan Malloy, Kelly Slater, Raimana Van Bastolaer. 1999.

This Time Tomorrow. Sipping Jetstreams Media. Dir. Taylor Steele. Perfs. Craig Anderson, Chris Del Moro, Dan Malloy, Dave Rastovich, Kelly Slater. 2012.

Ticket to Ride. Dir. Steve Soderberg. Narr. Steve Soderberg. Perfs. Ronnie Burns, Tom Curren, Johnny-Boy Gomes, Buttons Kaluhiokalani, Max Medeiros. 1987.

Ultimate Sessions: The Greatest Moments in Surf Movie History. Opper Sports Productions. Dir. Ira Opper. Narr. John Thoms. Perfs. Steve Cooney, Shane Dorian, Jeff Hakman, Mike Hynson, Jeff Hakman, Buttons Kaluhiokalani, Kelly Slater, Shaun Tomson. 2006.

Villégiature: Premiers bains. Dir. Frères Lumière. 1895.

Waikiki Wedding. Paramount Pictures. Dir. Frank Tuttle. Perfs. Bob Burns, Bing Crosby, Martha Raye, Shirley Ross. 1937.

Wake of the Red Witch. Republic Pictures. Dir. Edward Ludwig. Perfs. Luther Adler, Adele Mara, Gail Russell, John Wayne, Gig Young. 1948.

Water Sportites. British Pathé News. 1931.

Waterlogged. Dir. Bruce Brown. Narr. Bruce Brown. Perfs. Joey Cabell, Mike Diffenderfer, Phil Edwards, Mike Hynson, Greg Noll. 1963.

Waveriders. Prod. Margo Harkin. Dir. Joel Conroy. Narr. Cillian Murphy. Perfs. Gabe Davies, Richard Fitzgerald, Chris Malloy, Dan Malloy, Keith Malloy, Kevin Naughton, Craig Peterson, Kelly Slater. 2008.

Waves of Change. Dir. Jim Freeman, Greg MacGillivray. Perfs. Billy Hamilton, Gerry Lopez, David Nuuhiwa, Keith Paull, Nat Young. 1970, released with changes as *The Sunshine Sea*, 1971.

We Got Surf. Dir. Hal Jepsen. Narr. Hal Jepsen Perfs. Reno Abellira, Simon Anderson, Tom Curren, Gerry Lopez, Shaun Tomson. 1981.

Where the Boys Are. Euterpe, MGM. Dir. Henry Levin. Perfs. Connie Francis, George Hamilton, Dolores Hart, Jim Hutton, Paula Prentiss. 1960.

The White Flower. Famous Players-Lasky. Dir. Julia Crawford Ivers. Perfs. Betty Compson, Edmund Lowe. 1923.

The Women and the Waves. Filmworks Entertainment. Dir. Heather Hudson. Perfs. Linda Benson, Zeuf Hesson, Ashley Lloyd, Kim Mearig, Heather Tiddens. 2009.

The Young Wave Hunters. Dir. Bob Evans. Perfs. Bobby Brown, Joey Cabell, Midget Farrelly, Bob McTavish, Nat Young. 1964.

Music

"All Summer Long." The Beach Boys, 1964.
"Another Brick in the Wall," Pink Floyd, 1979.
"Atmosphere." Joy Division, 1980.
"Boléro." Maurice Ravel, 1928.
"California." Joni Mitchell, 1971.
"California Dreamin.'" The Mamas and the Papas, 1965.
"California Sun." Henry Glover and Maurice Levy, 1961; The Rivieras, 1964; Dick Dale, 1987.
"Carry That Weight." The Beatles, 1969.
"Catch a Wave." Jan & Dean, 1963.
"Cool Change." Little River Band, 1979.
"Cool, Cool Water." The Beach Boys, 1970.
"Cop Killer." Body Count, 1992; John Maus, 2012.
"Cowgirl in the Sand." Neil Young, 1969.
"Cruisin' for a Bruisin.'" Mitch Allan, Jason Evigan, et al., 2013.
"Desolation Row." Bob Dylan, 1965.
"Do It Again." The Beach Boys, 1968.
"Echoes." Pink Floyd, 1971.
"4th of July, Asbury Park (Sandy)." Bruce Springsteen, 1973.
"Gimme Shelter." The Rolling Stones, 1969.
"Girls on the Beach." The Beach Boys, 1964.
"Head Above Water." Hunters & Collectors, 1992.
"Johnny Kool (Part 2)." Brian Setzer, 1996.
"Just Like Honey." The Jesus and Mary Chain, 1985.
"Liar, Liar." The Castaways, 1965.
"Little Deuce Coupe." The Beach Boys, 1963.
"Long Time Gone." Crosby, Stills & Nash, 1969.
"Looking East." Jackson Browne, 1996.
The Original Soundtrack from Five Summer Stories. Honk, 1972.
"Pacific Vibrations." Sky Oats, 1970.
"Pipeline Sequence." Honk, 1972.
"Red Right Hand." Nick Cave and the Bad Seeds, 1994.
"Ride My See-Saw." The Moody Blues, 1968.
"Riders on the Storm." The Doors, 1971.
"Riding the Wind." Kevin Baker, 1996.
"Roll Plymouth Rock." Brian Wilson, Van Dyke Parks, 2004.
"Sherry." The Four Seasons, 1962.
"Sidewalk Surfin.'" Jan & Dean, 1964.
"Strawberry Fields Forever." The Beatles, 1967.
"Surf City." Jan & Dean, 1963.
"Surfer Girl." The Beach Boys, 1963.
"Surfin.'" The Beach Boys, 1961.
"Surfin' Bird." The Trashmen, 1963; Pee Wee Herman, 1987.
"Surfin' Safari." The Beach Boys, 1962.
"Surfin' U.S.A." The Beach Boys, 1963.
"Surf's Up." The Beach Boys, 1971.
"Surf's Up." Al Dee Theodore, Alana Da Fonseca, et al., 2013.
"Take Five." Dave Brubeck Quartet, 1959.
"Tales of Brave Ulysses." Cream, 1967.
"Theme from *The Endless Summer.*" The Sandals, 1966.
"V-12 Cadillac." Farm, 1970.
"Venus." Frankie Avalon, 1959.
"We're Only Gonna' Die for Our Arrogance." Sublime, 1992.
"When I Grow Up (To Be a Man)." The Beach Boys, 1964.
"White Bird." It's a Beautiful Day, 1969.
"White Room." Cream, 1968.
"Witchi Tai To." Jim Pepper; Harpers Bizarre. 1969.
"Wooden Ships." Crosby, Stills & Nash, 1969.
"Zero to Sixty in Five." Pablo Cruise, 1976.

Index

*Numbers in **bold italics** indicate pages with photographs*

Aaberg, Dennis 75, 169, 170, 171
Aaberg, Kemp 58, 170
Abberton, Jai 119
Abberton, Koby *118*
Abberton, Sunny *118*, 119
Abellira, Reno 48, 72, 96
Abubo, Megan 190
Acapulco 59
Adams, Jay 97
Adler, Alfred 154
Adler, Matt *175*
Adventures of Huckleberry Finn 153
aerial camerawork 46, 70, 116, 199
aerial surfing maneuvers 99, 133–136, 138, 139, 177, 198, 199
Agius, Dion 135
Aikau, Eddie 70
Aipa, Ben 48
air mattress surfing *see* surf mat
Ala Moana 3, 54, 57, 82
Alaska 106, 139
Alfred Hitchcock Hour 15
Ali, Muhammad 120
Allen, Paul 62, 63
Alter, Hobart "Hobie" 57
alternate sports *see* extreme sports
Alva, Tony 97
Amami Islands 218
American Grafitti 122, 169, 170, 179
American International Pictures (AIP) 85, 158, 160
Andaman Islands 129
Anderson, Craig 135, 136, 139, *140*, 141, 199
Anderson, Pamela 106, 186
Anderson, William 10, 17
Andino, Kolohe 134, 136
Angourie 60
The Angry Sea 34, 82
animation 5, 89, 97, 124, 127, 148, *149*, 161, 212; *see also* Bobby Bumps, Surf Rider; Dormer, Mike; Evans, Jim;

Griffin, Rick; *Hawaiian Holiday*; *Hula Magoo*; Lamb, John; *SpongeBob SquarePants*; *Surf's Up*
Anolik, Lili 105
apartheid 65, 66, 73
Apocalypse Now 170, 185
Apted, Michael *182*
Archer, Eugene 165
Arnold, Matthew 20
Arriflex camera 87
The Artist 205
ASCAP (American Society of Composers, Authors, and Publishers) 27, 81, 104
Asher, William *162*
Association of Surfing Professionals (ASP) *see* World Surf League (WSL)
Astrodeck 121
August, Oral "Blackie" 110, 224n29
August, Robert 28, *29*, 53, 54, 63–*66*, 67, 68, *87*, 107, 110, 150, 224n29
August, Sam 110
Aurness, Rolf 83, 94
Australia 13, 15, 16, 29, 37, 40, 42–46, 49, 50, 60, 65, 69, 70–80, 91, 97, 98, 100, 101, 103, 104, 107, 119, 120, 124, 126, *128*, 129, 131, 134, 147, 169, 178, 187–190, 198, 199, 209, 212
Australian Championships (1969) 73
Australian Film Development Corporation 77
Avalon, Frankie 2, 27, 64, 92, 149, 160, 161, *162*, 163, 213
Avalon, Phillip 169

Back to the Beach 163
Bad Religion 133
Baffa, Jason 125, 131, 132, 212
Baggs, Belinda 127, 128
Bagley, Bob *29*
Baja, California *see* Mexico

Baker, Joby *155*
Baker, Kevin 125
Bali 30, 77, 79, 103, 178, 179, 195, 196, 197; *see also* Indonesia; Uluwatu
Ball, John "Doc" 26, 39, 40, 44, 46, 51, 148, 211, 212
Ballard, Bill 190
Ballard, Rochelle 111, 190, 191
Banks, Joseph 10, 24, 34
Banzai Pipeline *see* Pipeline
Barefoot Adventure 60, 61, 92
Barr, David 99
La Barre 72, 96
Bartholomew, Wayne "Rabbit" 98, 100, 101, *102*, 119, 120, 122
Basque Coast 71, 88, 96, 107
Baywatch 15, 186
Beach Blanket Bingo 160
The Beach Boys 20, 27, 28, 55, 60, 64, 82, 84, 89, 93, 158, 160, 186; *see also* Wilson, Brian
Beach Party 6, 15, 27, 31, 144, 149, 158–*162*, 163; movies 6, 15, 27, 45, 52, 63, 81, 92, 144, 150, 158–168, 185, 213
Beach Shorts Film Fest 121
beachboys 5, 14, 26, 37, 42, 57, 148, 177, 178
Beachley, Layne 16, 111, 190
"beachspace," varied meanings of 3, 7–9, 17–23, 25, 30, 34–36, 67, 68, 126, 144, 145, 149–154, 156, 158, 168, 171, 173, 174, 187–189, 192, 202, 204, 206, 208, 214, 215, 220
The Beatles 92; *see also* Lennon, John
Beattie, Keith 133, 209
Beaulieu camera 84, 95
Beautiful Wave 192
Becker, Phil 17
Bell & Howell camera 44, 51, 168
Bellow, Saul 208
Bells Beach 65, 101, 103
Benson, Becky 97
Benson, Blanche 97

239

Benson, Linda 47, 49, 91, 159, 161
Beowulf 91
Beresford, Bruce 187
Berger, Alex 138
Bernardin de Saint-Pierre, Jacques-Henri 154
Bertlemann, Larry "Rubberman" 48, 94, 96, 97, 120
Bianco, Jean-Louis 96
Bieber, Justin 105
The Big Chill 217
Big Surf 83
The Big Surf 44
Big Wave Tour 16
Big Wednesday (1961) 82, 84, 170
Big Wednesday (1978) 1, 2, 6, 44, 75, 82, 101, 144, 151, 169–171, *172*–174, 177, 186, 190, 193, 195, 202, 213, 214, 217
Bigelow, Kathryn 202, *203*, 206, 218
Biggest Wednesday: Condition Black 112, 170
Bigler, Steve 132
Billabong 7, 17, 32, 103, 121–5, 141, 191
Billabong Challenge 124
Billabong Odyssey 43, 112, 123, 124
Billabong Pipeline Masters *see* Pipeline Masters
Billabong Pro Tahiti 139
Billauer, Jesse 110
biography (genre) 32, 117, 123, 124, 182–185, 193, 194, 214, 217
Bird of Paradise 147
Biroc, Joseph 165
Bishop, Elizabeth 89
Bishop Museum 25
The Black Camel 148
Black Shorts *see* Da Hui
Blackies 132
Blackrock (play, film) 75, 187–190
Blake, Tom 26, 38, 39, 40, 41, 43, 44, 115
Blow, Mark 34
Blue Crush (1998) 190
Blue Crush (2002) 1, 144, 147, 174, 179, 186, 190–*192*, 193, 194, 214
Blue Hawaii 62, 159
Blue Juice 7, 151, 174, 179, 186, 213
Blum, Eric 74
Blum, Lowell 74
Blundell, Graeme 188
Bobby Bumps, Surf Rider 148, *149*
Bodhi 202, 204–206, 215

Body Count 135
bodyboard 83, 127, 130, 139
bodysurfing 45, 50, 83, 96, 104, 127, 130, 139
Bolex camera 44, 52
Bondi Beach 34
Bonine, Robert 36, 37
Bonython, Tim 112
bonzer 127, *128*
Boone, Pat 91
Bosworth, Kate *192*, 194
Botany Bay 118
Boulting, Ned 117
Bowles, Paul 68
Boyer, Lynne 92
Bra Boys 117, *118*, 119
Bradshaw, Ken 124
Braithwaite, Nick 134
Brandt, Rex 14
Brannon, Ash 180, *181*
Bray, John Randolph 148
Bray Productions *149*
Brennan, Kevin 72, 132, 198
Brentwood 153
Breuls, Laurence 189
Brewer, Dick 70, 72
Brice de Nice 186, 205
Bridges, Jeff 180, *181*
Brien, Donna Lee 189
Brock, Chris 75
Brontë, Charlotte 93, 157
Bronzed Aussies 101
Brown, Bruce 2, 7, 15, 27–*29*, 30, 32, 33, 41, 46, 47, 50, 52–54, 56–65, *66*, 67–70, 77, 78, 80–82, 85, 89, 91, 98, 103, 105–109, 113, 115, 121, 125, 132, 149, 150, 165, 167–170, 178, 207, 209, 212, 217
Brown, Dana 28, 58, 61, 67, 105, 106, 109, *110*, 111, 115, 186, 212
Brown, Peter 165
Brown, Woody 49
Browne, Bud 1, 3, 6, 7, 14, 26, 27, 31, 33, 39, 40, *41*, 42–56, 60–62, 81, 85, 89, 97, 100, 104, 113, 116, 125, 138, 150, 159, 165, 170, 207–210, 217
Browne, Jackson 185
Brubeck, Dave 95
Bruce, Robert C. 37, 38
Buck, Chris 180
budget and box office of surf films 7, 27, 28, 30, 33, 34, 57, 77, 80–82, 85, 104, 159, 180, 191, 197, 207, 211
Bunyip Dreaming 124
Burleigh Heads 72, 101, 103
Burns, Ronnie 99
Burrow, Taj 115
Busch, Charles 163

Busey, Gary 170–*172*, 202
"Bustin' Down the Door," *Bustin' Down the Door* (article, film, events) 98, 100, 101, 117, 119; *see also* Southern Hemisphere, shift of surfing power to
Butler, Kelly Jean 119
Byron, Lord 19
Byron Bay 61, 71, 77

Cabell, Joey 47, 60
Cabrinha, Pete 196, 197
Cairns, Ian 98, 101, 120
Calhoun, Candy 47, 92
Calhoun, Marge 47, 93
California 14–16, 26, 29, 39, 40–42, 45, 49–53, 55, 59–62, 64, 65, 70, 71, 80, 82, 83, 86, 91, *95*, 103, 104, 117, *128*, 131–133, 139, 161, 163, 170, 178, 207, 212, 217; *see also* Central Coast; Los Angeles; Orange County; Santa Barbara; Santa Cruz; Southern California; *individual cities*; *individual surf breaks*
California Surfriders 39, 40, 51, 212; *see also* Ball, John "Doc"
Campbell, Thomas 28, 32, 108, 125–*128*, 129, 212, 221
Canada 30
Cannon, Del 53, 58, 60, 61
canoes 36
Cape St. Francis 67, 77, 107, 178, 210
Carey, Gabrielle 187
Carmichael, Stokely 92
Carroll, Corky 2, 83, 182
Carroll, Tom 107
Carson, Lance 170
cartoons *see* animation
The Castaways 134
Castles in the Sky 138
Cat on a Hot Foam Board 44, 61
The Catcher in the Rye 123, 173
Cavalcade of Surf 44–47
Cave, Nick 135
Central America 127, 212; *see also* Costa Rica; El Salvador
Central Coast (California) 132
Ceylon *128*
Cézanne, Paul 35
Chasing Mavericks 6, 43, 144, 151, 174, 182, *183*–185, 192, 202, 214
Chasing the Swell 139, 196
Chesser, Todd 197
Chinatown 170
La Ciotat 17
Clark, Jeff 112–114
Close Encounters of the Third Kind 170

Cloudbreak 99, 107, 123, 138; *see also* Tavarua
Cole, Maurice 104
Cole, Peter 32, 42, 43, 45, 46, 47, 49, 52, 53
Collins, Richie 123
colonialism and post-colonialism 7–*11*, 12, 30, 31, 37, 65, 77, 81, 83, 91, 104, 108
Columbia Pictures 156, 165, 167
comic interludes in surf movies 6, 7, 26, 42, 44, 46, 48–61, 64, 86, 124, 127, 128, 137, 138, 181, 212
coming-of-age theme 7, 8, 22, 144, 151, 152, 158, 166, 169–171, 173–194, 204, 213, 214, 218, 221
commercialization of surfing 7, 8, 9, 15–17, 27, 28, 30, 32, 51, 68, 69, 84, 91, 96, 97, 101, 103, 104, 106, 109, 115, 117, 121–124, 127, 128, 130, 135, 150, 151, 159–162, 165, 166, 176, 177, 186, 193, 194, 197, 199–201, 207, 211, 214, 224*n*68; *see also* product placement; professionalization of surfing; *individual sponsors*
Compson, Betty *146*
Cooder, Ry 84
Cook, Bob 218
Cook, Capt. James 9, 10, 25, 81, 118
Cook Islands 99
Cooney, Steve 77, *78*, 79
Copyright Act (1976) 104
Corbett, Bradley 135
Corbett, Mitch 117, 118
Coppola, Francis Ford 170
Cornuelle, Stuart 134
Cornwall 179
Cortes Bank 109, 110
The Cosmic Children 94, 95, 96
Costa Rica 28, 107, 110, *128*, *137*
counter-cultural aspects of surfing and surf films 4, 6–8, 10, 15, 19, 20, 21, 27, 30–33, 42, 47, 49, 54–58, 60, 63, 64, 67, 68, 71, 73–94, 104, 126–128, 135, 150, 153, 154, 157, 158, 160, 161, 173, 193, 203
Country Joe and the Fish 79
Cream 79, 84, 95
Crescent City 132
The Cribbar 118
Crocker, Matt 117
Cronulla race riots (2005) 119
Cropper, Linda 189
Crosby, Stills & Nash 76, 84, 210
Cross, Dickie 113
crowded surf spots 27, 31, 32, 96, 97, 161

Crowe, Russell 118
Crystal Voyager 75, 76
cultural imperialism and insensitivity *see* colonialism
Cummings, Bob 161
Cunningham, Mark 127
Curren, Joe 132, 212
Curren, Pat 44, 46, 51, 53, 59
Curren, Tom 97, 107, 117, 123, 125, 126, 138

Da Hui 120, 176
The Daily Beast 167
Dale, Dick 14, 84, 163
Dana Point 83, 89
Darren, James 152, 159
Davis, Dale 52, 70
Davis, Matthew 192
Davis, Scot 177
A Day in the Life of Wayne Lynch 123
Daytona Beach 158
Dean, James 117
Deane, Noa 32
Dear and Yonder 190
Dear Suburbia 134–136
de Beauvoir, Simone 154
de Bougainville, Louis Antoine 223*n*8
Dee, Sandra 6, *155*, 159
A Deeper Shade of Blue 105
The Deer Hunter 79
Delacroix, Eugène 35
Delaney, Bill 69, 94, 100, 101, 209
Deleuze, Gilles 21, 208
Deliverance 169
Del Moro, Chris 139
Del Rio, Dolores 147
Denver, Bob 163
Diamond Head 37, 38, 147
Diffenderfer, Mike 165
Dillinger 169
DiMartino, Jay 124
Dirty Dancing 205
Disney, Walt *see* Walt Disney Studios
Dittrich, Scott 139
documentary 6, 24, 26, 32–34, 112, 117–120, 124, 180, 181, 208, 212
Doerner, Derrick 114, 196, 197
Dogtown 47, 112
Dogtown and Z-Boys 97, 112
dolphins 89, *102*, 104, 168, 217, 218
Don the Beachcomber 148
Donegal 110
The Doors 103
Dora, Miki 20, 51, 69, 83, 88, 116, 126, 144, 153, 161, 165, 166, 170, 215

Dorian, Patrick Shane 100, 130, 133, 137, 195–197, 225*n*19
Dormer, Mike 161
Down the Barrel 105, 123
Downing, George 43, 49, 53
Doyle, Mike 45, 64, 69, 88, 153
Dream Syndicate 123
Drift 144, 174, 186, 193, 198–200, 202, 214
The Drifter 139
Drouyn, Peter 70, 72
drugs 72, 75, 180, 187, 188, 198, 199, 224*n*29; *see also* marijuana
Drury, John 164
Duane, Daniel 22, 66, 214
Dujardin, Jean 205
Duke's Honolulu 178
Duke's Malibu 144
Dungeons 16
Dylan, Bob 15, 207

Earhart, Amelia 38
East Coast (U.S.) 13, 15, 45
East Indies *128*
Easter Island *see* Rapa Nui
Eastwood, Scott 178
Echoes 76
Eden, Barbara 165, 166
Edison, Thomas 5, 25, 34, 36
Edwards, Phil 43–48, 59, 61, 64, 91, 109, 113, 165, 178, 200
Egan, Luke 124, 130
Ehrenreich, Barbara 56
8 Mile 182
Eisenhower, Dwight 152, 154, 157, 207
Eisner, Lisa 127
El Salvador 170
El Segundo 127, 131
Elfick, David 76–*78*
Eliot, T.S. 62, 68, 207
Elkerton, Gary 122
Ellis, Robert *155*
The Endless Summer 1, 2, 3, 6, 7, 27–*29*, 33, 43, 57–60, 62–*66*, 67–70, 74, 80, 83, 98, 100, 103–107, 109, 114, 140, 144, 149, 150, 165, 167, 178, 179, 185, 209
The Endless Summer II 28, 59, 105–108, 110, 112, 114, 115, 121
The Endless Winter 33, 117, 118
Engel, Joe 103
Enlightenment 24
Enright, Nick 189
Ensenada 99
environmentalism in surfing and the surf film 30, 47, 68, 75, 76, 80–86, 88–90, 94, 124, 140, 151, 212, 213
Equal Rights Amendment (ERA) 81, 92

ESPN 105
Evans, Bob 44, 47, 50, 52, 60, 77, 165
Evans, Jim **48**
Evolution 70, **71**, 72, 77, 94, 96, 100, 104, 211
Expo 67 128
"Expression Session" 91, 96
extreme sports 17, 21, 30, 53, 61, 69, 84, 89, 90, 94, 98, 106, 150, 177, 178, 205

Fabares, Shelley 165, 166
Fabian 165, 166
Facebook 142
Fain, Johnny 69, 159, 161
Fallander, Thornton 103
Falzon, Albert "Alby" 52, 58, 68, 72, 73, 76-**78**, 79-81, 89, 93, 94, 124, 125, 209
Fanning, Mick 80, **137**-139
The Fantastic Plastic Machine 74
Farm 75
Farrelly, Bernard "Midget" 46, 52, 60
The Fast and the Furious 206
Faulkner, William 125
Feldman, Jonathan 127
Festival du film de surf d'Anglet 121
Field, Syd 198
Fifty Years of Surfing on Film 1, 42, 50, 51, 223n5
Fiji 60, 108, 123
film finale in big wave competition 45, 46, 59, 111, 150, 156, 166, 176, 178, 180, 181, 184, 185, 192, 196, 198, 213, 217
Filthy Habits 122, 123, 125, 133
financing of surf films *see* budgets and box-office
The Fireballs 48
Fitzgerald, Joel 125, 126
Fitzgerald, Terry 77, 89, 96, 125, 126
Five Summer Stories 2, 31, 44, 48, 75, 77, 80, 81, 84, 85, **87**, 88-94, 101, 105, 169, 209, **210**
Flaherty, Robert 25, 124
Fletcher, Herbie **87**
Florence, John John 129, 134-136, 138, 141
Florida 15, 60, 61
Focus 137
Fonda, Henry 148
Foo, Mark 114, 185
Forbes 142
Ford, Alexander Hume 13, 36
Ford, John 204
Forgotten Island of Santosha 73
Forster, E.M. 185

Fort Lauderdale 158
Foster, Marvin 122
The Four Preps 159
The Four Seasons 171
France 2, 15, 72, **95**, 96, 107
Francie *see* Gidget
Francis, Connie 159
Frank, Jon 125
Free and Easy 85, 86, 92
Free as a Dog 125
Free Ride 2, 28, 100, 119, 209
Freeman, Jim *see* MacGillivray/Freeman
Freeth, George 13, 36, 37, 117
French Polynesia 99
Freud, Sigmund 154
Friday Night Lights 170
Frye, Harry Richard "Skip" 125, 126, 132, 212
Funicello, Annette 2, 27, 92, 149, 160, 161, **162**-164, 186, 213

G-Land *see* Grajagan Bay
Galveston 111
Gamboa, Jimmy 132
Ganahl, Jane 196
Garcia, Sunny 122
Gauguin, Paul 153
Geiger, Will 217, 218
gender issues *see* women in surfing and surf films
George, Matt 195, 197
George, Sam 27, 113
Gerlach, Brad 111, 129, 130
Ghana 64
Ghost 205
Gibson, Mel 169
Gidget (novel, film) 1, 2, 6-8, 14, 26, 27, 40, 45, 50, 52, 57, 75, 92, 93, 106, 113, 140, 144, 145, 149-154, **155**-159, 164, 166, 173, 176, 186, 188, **192**, 207, 213, 214
Gidget (TV series, TV movies) 2, 159
Gidget Goes Hawaiian 62, 159
Gidget Goes to Rome 159
Gilmore, Stephanie 80, 125, 212
Ginsberg, Allen 56
Glass Love 126
Glenn, Scott 200
globalization of surfing 8, 9, 13, 15, 28, 29, 30, 43, 44, 45, 63, 65, 67, 114
Go-Pro 30, 44, 75, 116, 142, 211
The Godfather 170
Godfrey Oberg, Margo 92, 97
Going My Wave 45, 82
Going Surfin' 47, 48, 209
Gold Coast 77, 120, 178
The Golden Breed 3, 69

Golden Gate International Exposition 14, 148
Gomes, Johnny-Boy 99
Gone with the Wave 45
Gorilla Grip 123
Gotcha 116, 123
Graflex camera 39
Grajagan Bay 101, 104, 107, 122
Grannis, Leroy 39, 129
The Grateful Dead 79
La Gravière 96
Gray, Alex **140**
Great Britain 117, 118
Great Lakes surfing 110
"The Great Wave of Kanagawa" 35, 220
Green, Alan 198
Green, Shaun 199
The Green Iguana 124, 212
Greenhills Beach 187, 188
Greenmount Beach 212
Greenough, George 28, 68, 70, 72-76, 78, 81, 89, 93, 94, 100, 127, 170, 188, 189, 199, 209, 210
Griffin, Rick 52, 83, 84, 127, 198, 217
Grigg, Ricky 43, 46
Grissim, John 208
Guéthary 72
Gun Ho! 1, 45-47, 56, 92, 209
guru figure in surf films *see* mentor
Guthrie, Woody 125

Hakman, Jeff 47, 48, 94-96
Haleiwa 49, 51, 69, 95, 97, 165
Half Moon Bay 182
Hamasaki, Joey 92
Hamilton, Bethany 193, 194
Hamilton, Bill 44, 70, 83, 87, 88, 90, 114, 171
Hamilton, Laird 16, 21, 44, 93, 107-114, 119, 167, **175**, 176, 192, 196
Hanalei Bay 86, 89
Hang Ten 15, 97
Hanson, Curtis 182, **183**, 184
Happy Feet 180
Harrelson, Woody 200
Harris, Mark 117, 118
Harrison, Gregory **175**
Hart, Susan 165, 186
Harvey, David 208
Hatzikian, Tyler 127, 131, 132, 212
Have Board Will Travel 45
Hawaii Nine-0 45, 123
Hawaiian Holiday (1937) 148
Hawaiian Holiday (1954) 42
Hawaiian Islands 9, 10, 12-15, 21, 25, 26, 29-31, 37, 38, 40, 42, 43, 45, 49, 51, 54, 55, 57-62,

64, 65, 70, 71, 78, 82, 83, 86, 90, 92, 93, **95**, 96, 99, 100, 103, 107, 111, 113, 114, 120, **128**, 129, 131–133, 145, **146**, 147, 161, 163, 165, 166, 185, 190, 191, 195, 196, 207, 209; *see also* Honolulu; Maui; North Shore; Oahu; *individual surf breaks*
Hawaiian Nights 147
Hawaiian Surfboard 38
Hawaiian Surfing Movie 6, 26, 40–42, 116
Hawk, Tony 98
Hawks, Howard 55
Hayes, Conan 129
Hazanavicius, Michel 205
Heat 204
Heater, Todd 138
Heder, Jon 180
Hefner, Hugh 56, 157
Heiser, Dave 41
Hemingway, Ernest 20, 55, 171
Hemmings, Fred 101
Hepworth, Cecil 37
Heraclitus 140, 225n82
Here & Now: A Day in the Life of Surfing 139, 141
Herman, Pee-Wee 163, 181
Hermosa Beach 2, 17, 58, 121
Hesson, Rick "Frosty" 182–185
High School Musical 164
Hilton, Dave 95
Hoffman, Joyce 47, 92
Hokusai, Katsushika **35**, 148, 220
Hollister Ranch 76, 82, 84, **87**, 95, 170, 209, 210
Hollywood Don't Surf 6, 27
Homer, Winslow 19, 35
homosexuality 204, 205
Honk 89
Honolua Bay 72, 83, 95, 99
Honolulu 14, 25, 43, 45, 57, 84, 88, 94, 148, 158, 178
Hoole, Dick 101, **102**
Hoover, Mike 107
Horan, Cheyne 119, 133
Hossegor 88, 96
Hot Fuzz 205
The Hot Generation 70, **71**, 72
How to Stuff a Wild Bikini 160, 163
Howard, Devon 127, 132
Hudson, Rock 40
Hughes, Russell 71, 73
Hui Nalu Canoe Club 13, 38
hula 37, 84, **146**–148
Hula Magoo 158
Hunt, Helen 194
Hunter, Tab 165
Huntington Beach 46, 47, 59, 91, 178

Hurd, Earl **149**
hydrofoil surfboard 111
Hynd, Derek 119, 123, 125, 126
Hynson, Mike 28, **29**, 63–65, **66**–69, 107, 140, 150, 210, 217, 224n29

Iceland 30, 138
illustration *see* animation
In God's Hands 139, 186, 194–198
In Search of Tubular Swells 45, 101
in-water camerawork *see* water camerawork
The Incredibles 181
India 32, 65, 129
Indian Ocean 65, 195
Indonesia 32, 79, 100, 120, 127, 134, 142, 212; *see also* Bali; Uluwatu
The Innermost Limits of Pure Fun 43, 74–76, 169, 209
Innersection 32, 116, 141, 142
Instagram 142
International Professional Surfers (IPS) 101; *see also* World Surf League (WSL)
Internet 3, 16, 28, 30, 32, 33, 84, 105, 114–116, 124, 141–143, 168, 179, 210, 211, 224n68
Into the Sea 117
Ireland 117, 126, 129, 138
Island Records 124
Ivers, Julia Crawford **146**, 147

J-Bay *see* Jeffreys Bay
Jacobs, Hap 7, 58, 132
Jakovich, Rick 199
James, Don 39
Jan & Dean 8, 27, 97, 166
Japan 15, 65, 103, 131, 136, 214
Java 103
Jaws *see* Peahi
jazz 58, 73, 82, 83, 95, 125, 127
Jeffers, Robinson 182
Jeffrey *see* Moondoggie
Jeffreys Bay 103, 125, 178, 179
Jennings, James "Chappy" 122
Jepsen, Hal 69, 94, **95**–98, 113, 140
Jeremias, Mark 85, 125, 131, 132, 212
Jett, Joan 164
John Adams Junior High School 41, 143
The Johnnys 122
Johnson, Jack 28, 125, 126, 129, 130, 198, 207, 212
Johnson, Lyndon 163
Joy Division 135
Joyce, James 20

Kaawa, Sean 178
Kael, Pauline 63
Kahanamoku, David 37, 38
Kahanamoku, Duke 13, 15, 21, 32, 37, 38, 41, 43, 49, 90, 109, 115, 133, 148, 177, 178
Kahanamoku, William 37
Kahuna 30, 32, 57, 144, 152, 153, **155**–157, 160, 161, 166, 168, 173, 206
Kaio, Kealoha 113
Kalama, Dave 114
Kaluhiokalani, Montgomery "Buttons" 99, 120
Kamahele, Momiala 147
Kampion, Drew 82
Kanaiaupuni, Barry 89, 93–96
Kaopuiki, Joseph "Scooter Boy" 7, 42
Katt, William 170, **172**
Kawase, Naomi 218, **219**, 220
Kealakekua Bay 9
Keaulana, Brian 194, 196, 197
Keaulana, Richard "Buffalo" 43, 45
Kekai, Albert "Rabbit" 7, 32, 42, 43, 109
Kelly, John 49
Kelly Slater and the Young Guns 123
Kelly Slater in Black and White 32, 123
Keltner, Jim 84
Kennedy, John F. 60, 152, 160
Kennelly, Keala 109, **110**, 110, 192
Keough, Byron 46
Kerouac, Jack 56, 60, 153
Kibborn, Diane 159
Kidman, Andrew 32, 80, 108, 125, 126, 128, 129, 212
Kilgore 170, 176
King, Don 109
King, Don (boxing) 181
King, Peter 124
King, Zalman 194–197
Kinnell, Galway 220
Kirra Point 124, 125
Kitano, Takeshi 215, **216**, 218
Kivlin, Matt 153
kneeboard 72, 74, 75, 83, 199
Knost, Alex 110, 127, 131, 132, 212
Knost, Jim 110
Knox, Taylor 137
Kohner, Frederick 57, 75, 151, 153, 154
Kohner, Kathy 14, 144, 153, 154, 186
Kong's Island 122
Korduroy.tv 141
Korean War 157
Korin, Ogata 35

Kottke, Leo 84
Kurosawa, Nathan 177

LaBeouf, Shia 180, *181*
Laine, Wes 122
Lake Arrowhead 158
Lamb, John 89
Laniakea 49
Larronde, Jon 37, 46
Laughlin, Tom *155*
Lawman 165
Layer, Albee 141
Leary, Timothy 134
Leboe, Elliot 141
Leigh, Leigh 189
Lennon, John 86
Lennox Head 76, 210
Lette, Kathy 187
Letting Go 123
Liberia 64
Liddell, Mark 99
Life as a Movie 17
lifeguarding 14, 40, 44, 50, 103
Lightning Bolt surfboards 96, 97
Lilo & Stich 190
Lim, Dennis 164
Liquid Salt 141
Lisanti, Thomas 1, 159
Litmus 31, 125, 126, 128, 187
Liu, Matthew "Matty" 195
Lloyd, Ashley 128
localism 67, 90, 118, 119, 120, 131, 176, 191
Locked In *41*, 45, 46, 47
London, Jack 13, 24, 36
longboard 21, 97, 106, 126–128, 132, 182, 194, 211, 212, 215; revival 17, 32, 108, 126, 127, 177
Loose Change 137
Lopez, Gerry 48, 80, 88, 89, 91, 95–98, 100, 101, *102*, 103, 104, 107–109, 127, 173, 175, 176, 210
Los Angeles, Los Angeles County 26, 39, 61, 94, 158, 172
Los Angeles Times 39
Lost Atlas 16, 134, 135
Louisiana Story 124
Lourie, David *102*
Lucas, George 169
Lumière brothers 17, *18*, 19, 34, 35
Lynch, Wayne *71*–73, 76, 100, *102*–104, 123, 210, 211

Mac, Ryan 142
MacGillivray/Freeman (Greg MacGillivray, Jim Freeman) 28, 44, 47, 48, 52, 69, 77, 80, 84–86, *87*–94, 124, 128, 170, 209, *210*

Machado, Rob 127, 129–131, 133, 137, 139, 181
Madagascar 195
Madagascar 180
Maffesoli, Michel 208
Makaha 14, 40, 42–47, 49, 51, 58, 82, 113, 165, 198
Makaha International Surfing Championships 44, 46, 49, 52, 91
Maki, Claude 215, *216*
Malaysia 103
Malibu 13, 14, 27, 30, 31, 43, 46, 49, 51, 69, 82, 95, 97, 132, 139, 140, 144, 148, 153, 160, 161, 164, 166, 169, 200
"Malibu board" 51, 73
Malloy, Chris 127, 129, 131–133, 212
Malloy, Dan 127, 129
Malloy, Emmett 129, 130
Malloy family 110, 129, 130, 127, 212
Manhattan Beach 51, 98
Mankoff, Robert 149
Mantle, Mickey 195
Manufacturing Stoke 117
The March of the Penguins 180
Margaret River 3, 73, 134, 198, 199
marijuana 17, 71, 73, 77, 80, 82, 188, 199, 201, 213
Maroubra Beach 118
Marquand, John P. 56
Martin, Todd 99
Marzo, Clay 141
masculinity, competing conceptions in early surfing movies 54–56, 210
Maslin, Janet 171, 187
Matheisen, Mark 217
Mathers, Jerry 163
A Matter of Style 98, 100, 119
Maui 72, 86, 111, 141, 190, 193, 197, 214
Maui Surfer Girls 31
Mauritius 73, 178
Maus, John 135
Mavericks 111–114, 139, 182–185
McClelland, Brennan "Hevs" 46, 48
McClure, Doug 155
McConaughey, Matthew 200, 201
McCoy, Jack 28, 32, 44, 101, *102*–105, 107, 109, 111, 113, 122–125, 181, 207, 209–212, 224n68
McCrea, Joel 147
McGregor, Ewan 180
McLuhan, Marshall 86
McNamara, Sean 194

McTavish, Bob 60, 68, 70, 72, 74, 75, 94
Meador, Kassia 126, 128
Medeiros, Max 99
Mekas, Jonas 77, *78*
Méliès, Georges 34
Melville, Sam 170
mentor in surf films 151, 155, 157, 164, 165, 172–177, 185, 190, 191, 194, 199, 201, 204, 205, 213, 215, 217, 220, 225n14
Meola, Matt 141
La Mer ("*Baignade en mer*") 18, 19, 35
Merkel, Dan 44, 100, 170, 181, 218
Metawai Islands 130
Metcalfe, Burt *155*
Métraux, Alfred 25
Mexico 2, 29, 41, 53, 59, 70, 95, 99, *128*, 132, 133, 139, *140*, 195, 201, 217
Michaels, Lorne 90
Miles, H.J. 35
Milius, John 44, 82, 169–171, *172*–174, 177, 184, 185
Miller, Mike 96
Miller, Rusty 46, 77, *78*
Miller, Sonny 191
Miller, Warren 26, 42, 51
Minds in the Water 117
Missing *137*–139
Mr. Magoo 158
Mitchell, James "Chubby" 51
Mitchell, Joni 90, 154
Mitchum, James 63, 166, 167
Miyazaki, Hayao 220
Mödern Collective 134–136
Momentum 34, 37, 50, 94, 121, 122, 125, 127, 133, 136, 141, 211
Monterey 25, 182
Moondoggie 144, 151, 152, 154, 156, 157, 159, *192*, 206
Moonshine Conspiracy 129
Moriarity, Jay 182, *183*–185, 202
Morning of the Earth 27, 58, 76, 77, *78*–80, 90, 94, 103, 105, 124, 125, 169, 209, 212
Morocco 72, *128*, 134
Morris, Gary 160
Morrissey, May Ann 39
Mousketeers 161, 163
Ms. magazine 92
MTV 121, 211
Munoz, Mickey 45, 153, 159
Munro, Mimi 92
Murakami, Nijirô *129*
Muscle Beach Party 160–163, 165
music *see* jazz; punk; rap; soundtrack; surf music
Myers, Nathan 139, 141, 142

myth, mythic reach of surf films 19–23, 58, 77, 84, 89, 151, 156, 157, 170–174, 176, 184, 188, 214, 218–220

Namath, Joe 120
Nanook of the North 124
Napoleon, Art and Jo 165
narration, narrator 42, 44–47, 54, 57, 59–61, 64, 65, 68, 72, 74, 78, 79, 82, 83, 85–87, 97, 98, 101, 106–109, 113, 117, 118, 122, 125, 127, 129, 217, 218
narrative formula: classic structure of surf community movie 3, 6, 7, 26, 42, 43, 52, 53, 57, 86, 88, 150, 207, 209; classic structure of surfing feature film 3, 42, 82, 145, 150–152, 166, 170–177, 179, 182, 194, 207, 213, 214, 218
National Film and Sound Archive Cinema Collection (Kodak/Atlab) 80
National Geographic 29, 36, 38, 39
National Lampoon Presents Endless Bummer 164
Natural Progression surfboards 94
Nauert, Randy 84
Naughton, Kevin 116, 117
Nehru, Jawaharial 76, **78**
Nelson, Willie 200
Network Ten 188
Neushul, Peter *see* Westwick, Peter
Neville, Kai 134–136, 141
New Hollywood 81, 170
New Line Cinema 105
New School 72, 99, 100, 121, 133
New York 63, 126, 167
New York Surf Film Festival 121
New York Times 62, 63, 153, 165
New Yorker 63
New Zealand 60, 61, 64–66, **128**, 136, 170, 178
Newcastle 187, 189
Newcastle 174, 186, 205
Newport Beach 60, 148
NFL Films 168
Ngcobo, Walter 108
Nichols, Bill 209
Nixon, Richard 80, 81, 89
"No Pants Mance" 170
Noll, Greg 2, 16, 41–43, 46, 48–**51**, 54, 57, 60, 68, 112, 113, 121, 132, 161, 165–167, 200, 211
Noosa Heads 60, 71, 80, 127, 212
La Nord 96
North, Jay 74

North Beach (S.F.) 15, 157
North Beach Surf Film Festival 121
North Shore (Oahu) 7, **41**, 43, 51, 53–55, 57, 64, 71, 77, 80, 83, 86, 87, 89, 90, 93, 94, 96, 98, 100, 101, 103, 107, 113, 122, 165, 166, 174, 178
North Shore 7, 144, 151, 174, **175**–178, 180, 183, 186, 191–193, 200, 213
noseriding 64, 74, 126, 127, 132, 170
Nott, Ben 199
Nuuhiwa, David 48, 86, 88, 90

Oahu 7, 37, 43, 59, 60, 64, 97, 103, 104, 139, 165, 190, 197
Oberg, Margo *see* Godfrey Oberg, Margo
Occhilupo, Mark 117, 122, 124, 126, 175
Occy: The Occumentary 117, 124
Ocean Beach 46
Ocean Fever 99
Ocean Tribe 214, 216–218
"Ocean Waves" **35**
O'Connell, Patrick 106–108, 115
Off the Wall 99, 120, 210
The Office 181
OM-Bali Pro 103
Once Upon a Wave 53, 54, 56
One California Day 31, 85, 125, 131, 132, 177, 212
110% Surfing Techniques 117
One Winter Story 31, 187
O'Neill (surf gear) 141
O'Neill, Morgan 199
Opper, Ira 95, 99
Orange County 29, 57, 82, 94, 126, 144, 158
Oregon 144
Orlean, Susan 190
Ōshima, Hiroko **216**
Ours 119
Outrigger Canoe Club 13
Outside Alligators 197

Pablo Cruise 100
Pacific Coast Highway (PCH) 81, 96, 140
Pacific Coast Surfriding Championships 14
Pacific Vibrations 27, 58, 80–85, 92–95, 101, 169, 209, 210
The Packards 48
paddle-out funeral or memorial 21, 132, 181
paddleboard 38, 51, 182
Page, Robbie 175
Palos Verdes 14, 39, 40

Palos Verdes Surf Club 39
Paluzzi, Luciana 161
Pamplona 138
Panorama of Ocean Beach and Cliff House 35
Paradise Cove 161
Paragon, John **175**
Parker, Jeff 99
Parkinson, Joel 138, 141, 142
Paskowitz, Dorian "Doc" 39
Pathé brothers 5, 25, 34, 37
Patteson, John Coleridge **11**
Paul, Robert 34
Paull, Keith 88, 93
Payne, Dusty 16, 134
Peahi 16, 107, 111, 112, 114, 124, 195, 197
Peck, John 43, 46
Penn, Sean 113, 176
Peralta, Stacy 28, 97, 105, 106, 112–115, 160, 212
"perfect wave" 67, 69
The Perfect Wave 6, 144, 178, 179, 214
The Performers 121, 122
Perkins, Gregory "Bonga" 131
Péron, Didier 218
Perth 121
Pertwee, Sean 179
Peru 15, 30, **95**, 96, 138
Peterson, Craig 117
Peterson, Dane 128
Peterson, Michael 77, 80, 97, 125, 126, 136, 212
Peterson, Pete 39
Petty, Lori 205
Pezman, Steve 94, 113, 159, 185
Phelps, William 175, 177
Philbin, John **175**, 176
Philippines 28
Phillips, Walt 52–54
Picasso, Pablo 35
Pink Floyd 76, 122
Pipeline 43, 44, 46, **48**, 52, 61, 70, 80, 86, 89, 91, 94–98, 100, 109, 110, 113, 120, 127, 131, 165, 173, 179, 190, 191, 200, 210
Pipeline Masters 99, 141, 174, 176, 190–192
Pit Crew 144
Pittsburgh Press 154
Playboy 153
Point Break (1991) 2, 3, 144, 145, 167, 174, 186, 202, **203**, 204–206, 214, 215, 218
Point Break remake 206
Point Mugu 97
Polanski, Roman 170
Poledouris, Basil 171
Pollard, Myles 198, 199
Pollock, Jackson 76

Poppler, Jericho 92, 93
Porthleven 118
Portugal 28, 88
post-modernity of surfing and surf films 21, 85–87, 90–93, 135, 136, 160, 181, 208, 215
Potter, Martin 133
Prechezer, Carl 179
The Present 126
Presley, Elvis 15, 62, 64, 159
Prewitt, Paul 100
The Prince and the Surfer 7
product placement 51, 96, 121, 123, 191, 193
professionalization of surfing 7, 8, 13, 15–17, 21, 27, 32, 33, 68, 69, 71, 83, 91–94, 96, 98–101, 103–105, 109, 115, 129, 150, 162, 168, 176, 177, 186, 190, 193–195, 197, 198, 199
A Property of the Clan 189; *see also* Blackrock
Psyche Out 53, 54
Psycho Beach Party (play, film) 163, 164
Puberty Blues (novel, film, series) 187–190, 214
Public Baths 42, 58
Puerto Rico 72, 73, 164
punk rock 125, 127, 133, 134, 142
Purpus, Mike 48, 99

Quaid, Dennis 194
Queens 42
Queensland 68, 74, 100, 103
Quiksilver 16, 96, 106, 112, 121–123, 130, 198

The Ranch *see* Hollister Ranch
Randle, Rush 196, 197
rap 84, 125, 133
Rapa Nui 25, 111
Rarick, Randy 34, 101
Rastovich, Dave 129, 139, **140**
Ravel, Maurice 73
Ray, Nicholas 173
Reagan, Ronald 177
rear projection "surfing" 62, 63, 159, 161, 163, 165, 166, 168, 185
rebelliousness *see* countercultural aspects of surfing and surf films
RED Digital Cinema 141
Redondo Beach 15, 51
Reef 122
Reeves, Keanu 186, 202, **203**, 205, 215
Reno, Angie 89, 96
restaurants 99; *see also* Tavarua
"retro movement" 49, 125–133, 177, 212

Reynolds, Dane 134–136, 141
Richards, John ("Little John," "LJ") 45, 59
Richards, Mark 98, 100–**102**, 103, 119, 120
Rickles, Don 161
Riddle, J 94, 95
The Ride 177, 178, 185, 193, 213
"ride anything" movement 108, 126–129, 131, 212
Ride the Wild Surf 63, 150, 151, 158, 165–167, 170, 173, 174, 186, 195, 213, 217
Riding Giants 6, 34, 97, 105, 112–115, 121, 150, 167, 185, 196, 210
Rifici, Rick 135, 199
Rights-and-Lefts 87
Rimbaud, Arthur 184
Rincon 43, 47, 53, 54, 59–62, 132
Rip Curl 103, 121, 123, 193, 198
RKO Pictures 147
Road House 205
Robertson, Cliff 57, **155**, 168
Robinson, Jack 134–136
Rocky Point 78
Roe v. Wade 92
Roger & Me 167
Rohloff, Grant 52, 113
Rolling Stones 95
romanticism 19, 24, 75–78, 80, 84, 85, 88, 89, 127, 176, 208, 209, 214–216
Rooney, David 189
Roosevelt, Theodore 25
Rothman, Eddie 120
rottontomatoes.com 112
Rough Sea at Dover 34
Rowan and Martin's Laugh-In 160
Roxy 16
The Royal Hawaiian 148
Russell, Rory 95–97, 101
Rwanda 138

Sagan, Françoise 154
Salinger, J.D. 123, 173
Salles, Walter 67
Salt Creek Beach **29**, 64, 89
Samoa 99
Samuel, Xavier 198, 199
San Clemente 62, 80
San Onofre 39, 49, 81
San Diego 96
San Diego Surf 164
San Francisco 113
Sand Bar *see* Sandspit
The Sandals 58, 62–64, 70, 84, 131
Sandspit 61, 132
Santa Barbara 61, 68, 74, 81, 132
Santa Cruz 21, 43, 46, 54, 60, 111, 124, 126, 182, 217

Santa Monica Civic Auditorium 59, 88
Saturday Night Fever 170
Sauer, Phil 165
A Scene at the Sea 214–**216**, 218
"scenic" *see* travelogue
Schofield, Nell 188
Scotland 117, 118
A Sea Cave Near Lisbon 34
A Sea for Yourself **95**, 96
Sea of Joy 70, 73
sea snakes 100
Seal Beach **210**
The Search series 123
Search for Surf 30, 43, **51**, 55, 77, 127
The Searchers 172
Searching for Tom Curren 117, 123
The Secret Storm 156
The Seedling 126
Senegal 64, 65
The September Sessions 125, 129–131
Severn Bore 118
Severson, John 27, 28, 41, 47, 52, 53, 58, 69, 71, 73, 80–85, 91–95, 113, 128, 133, 134, 137, 159, 170, 207, 209
sexism *see* women in surfing and surf films
shaka 21, 128, 176
Shane 172
Shank, Clifford "Bud" 58, 127
sharks 71, 79, 100, 149, 183, 193, 194
The Shins 127
shortboard revolution 21, 27, 33, 48, 49, 68–81, 83, 86, 88, 93–98, 100, 105, 113, 120, 126, 168, 198, 199, 207
The Show 137
Sideways 217
Sik Joy 33, 122
The Silence of the Lambs 204
Simmons, Bob 46
Singer, Brian 198
Singlefin: Yellow 31, 131
Sipping Jetstreams 6
Skateboard Madness 97
skateboarding 17, 32, 47, 48, 53, 89, 91, 97, 98, 106, 112, 126, 133, 137, 142, 178, 184, 195; *see also* extreme sports
Skeleton Bay 179
Skewjack Surf Village 118
Slade, Demian 163
Slater, Kelly 15, 22, 32, 37, 50, 72, 99, 100, 105–107, 109, 117, 119, 123, 129, 130, 133, 134, 136, 137, 141, 142, 181, 211

Index

Slippery When Wet 7, 57, 77, 127, 132, 212
slow-motion filming 28, 45, 54, 78, 88, 89, 95, 116, 122, 133, 134, 138, 197
Smirnoff Pro-Am contest (Sunset Beach) 97
Smith, Jordy 134, 135
Snapshots at the Seashore 37
snow skiing, snowboarding 17, 53, 61, 88, 89, 98, 127, 158
Social Distortion 122
Soderberg, Steve 31, 69, 94, 98–100, 104
Sons of the Surf 37
Sontag, Susan 86, 133
Sony Pictures 112, 180
La Sortie de l'usine 18
Soul Surfer 167, 186, 190, 193, 194, 214
"soul surfing" 32, 126, 139, *175*, 176, 180, 181, 193, 196, 199, 200, 201
soundtrack 26, 33, 40, 42, 46, 49, 58, 72–76, 79, 80–82, 84–86, 88, 89, 92, 93, 95, 100, 103, 111, 114, 116, 121-7, 129–131, 133–138, 170, 179, 184, 190, 211, 212, 214, 218; *see also* jazz; punk rap; rock; surf music; *individual artists and bands*
South Africa 15, 45, 62, 64–**66**, 67, 69, 103, 107, 117, 120, *128*, 195, 209
Southern California 14, 26, 39, 40, 51, 57, 74, 80, 85, 94, 106, 131, 145, 158, 163, 170
Southern Hemisphere, shift of surfing power to 27, 69, 70–80, 94, 98, 100, 101, 103, 105, 120, 126, 209
Spain 16
The Specials 164
Spencer, Ted 72
Spicoli, Jeff 44, 176, 200
Spielberg, Steven 170
Spinning Boards 6, 44, 45, 59
Spinning Wheels 97
Spirit of Akasha 80, 125, 126
SpongeBob SquarePants 174, 225n14
Springsteen, Bruce 22, 209, 223n28
Sprout 125–127, *128*, 129, 177, 212
Sprung Monkey 133
Sri Lanka 127
Standard Oil Company 124
Stange, Mike 45, 46
Star Wars 170, 177
Steamer Lane 21, 34, 49
Steele, Taylor 28, 32, 36, 50, 116,

121, 122, 133, 134, 136, **137**–139, **140**–143, 196, 207, 211, 212, 221
Step Into Liquid 28, 33, 34, 105, 109, **110**–112, 114, 115, 121, 150, 159, 181, 186, 210
stereotypes of surfers and surfing 6, 15, 44, 150, 159–161, 164, 176, 164, 200, 213
Steve Miller Band 83
Stevens, Connie 163
Stewart, Mike 127, 139, 196, 197
Still the Water 214, 218, **219**
Stille, Andrew 171
Stockwell, John **192**
Stoked and Broke 122, 132
Storm Riders **102**, 103, 104, 121, 209
Stranger, Mark 208, 214
Stranger Than Fiction 136
Strictly Hot 69
Stubbies Contest (Burleigh Heads) 103
stunt doubles 159, 161, 165–168, 171, 175, 183, 190, 191, 193, 194, 197, 199, 217
Sublime 124
Sumatra 130
Summer City 169
Summer of Love 81, 160
Sumpter, Rodney 70
The Sunrays 48
Sunset Beach 16, 42, 54, 58, 59, 65, 69, 82, 94–96, 113, 165, 170, 177
Sunset Surf Craze 53, 92
The Sunshine Sea see *Waves of Change*
Super Session 95–97
supertanker surfing 111
Supertubes (Ventura) 97
Surf 82
Surf at Monterey 34
surf carnival 51, 61
Surf Channel 141
"Surf City" (song) 8
Surf Classic (1981, Bells Beach) 103
Surf Classics 82
Surf Crazy 46, 58, 59, 217
Surf Diva (La Jolla) 31
Surf Down Under 43
Surf Fever 56, 82, 84
surf film festivals 121, 125, 210, 211
Surf Happy 45
Surf Industry Manufacturers Association 8, 223n6
Surf Mania 33, 5, 53, 54
surf mat 74, 75, 83, 127, 129
surf music 1, 15, 27, 32, 50, 160; *see also* Beach Boys; Dale,

Dick; Jan & Dean, Packards; Sandals; Sunrays; Surf Raiders; Trashmen; Ventures
The Surf Network 209
The Surf Raiders 48
Surf Safari 82, 84
surf travel, surf trip 28–31, 43, 53, 57–68, 77, 78, 83, 88, 104, 106–108, 114, 120, 132, 154, 178–180, 207, 209, 211, 212, 217
Surf Trek to Hawaii 52
surfboard design 14, 15, 38, 51, 61, 68, 70, 74, 77, 127–129, 132, 135, 176; *see also* longboard revival; shortboard revolution; "vee-bottom"; *individual shapers*
surfboard destruction gag 59, 87
surfboard shaper as mentor *see* mentor
Surfer (magazine) 15, 27, 29–33, 43, 49, 52, 53, 71, 80, 82–85, 100, 101, 107, 111, 121, 130, 134, 141, 169, 175, 176
Surfer, Dude 7, 186, 193, 200, 201
Surfer.TV 141
The Surfer's Journal 1, 29, 33
Surfers: The Movie 116, 121
Surfing for Life 117
Surfing Hollow Days 60–62, 66, 209
Surfing Illustrated 52, 53
Surfing Life 141
Le Surfing: Sport national des îles Hawaii 37
Surfing the 50's 47, 48, 49
Surfing World 47
Surfrider Beach 157
Surf's Up 174, 180, **181**, 182, 193
Surfside 6 160
Surfwise 33, 117
Sutherland, Jock 83, 94
Sutherland, Mark 125
Sutton, Cyrus 122, 132
Swarts, Lewis "Hoppy" 39
Swayze, Patrick **203**, 205
The Sweet Ride **87**, 163
Sydney 118, 187, 198

Tabeling, Mike 93
Tahiti 9, 10, 16, 41, 64, 65, **110**, 111, 114, 129, 139, 220; *see also* Teahupoo
Takayama, Donald 49
Tales of the Seven Seas 139
Talking Heads 122
Tall Timbers 147
Tallman, Jarrod 122
tandem surfing 44, 91, 149, 154, 159
Tashnick, Anthony **183**

Tavarua 99, 107
Taylor, Don 165
Teacher, Lee 161
Teahupoo 111, 114, 130, 139
Tears for Fears 135
Teen Beach Movie 164
Tennyson, Alfred Lord 20
Thailand 193, 194
Thatcher, Margaret 177
Thicker Than Water 129, 130, 177, 198, 212
This Time Tomorrow 43, 139, **140**, 196, 211
Thomas, G. Wayne 79
The Thomas Crowne Affair 128
Thompson, John 71
Thoms, Albie 1, 73, 121
Thoreau, Henry David 6, 132
Thurso East 118
Ticket to Ride 99, 100
Tijuana 171, 218
Tiki craze 14, 147
time travel 164, 177, 178
To Kill a Mockingbird 153
Todos Santos 99, 139, 196, 217
Tokyo Olympiad 168
Tom and Jerry 40
Tomson, Michael 116
Tomson, Shaun 82, 93, 97, 98, 100, 101, 103, 107, 108, 120, 195, 197, 210
Tonga 99
Topanga Canyon 94, 95
Torquay 198
tow-in surfing 16, 107, 108, 110, 111, 113, 194, 195–197, 199
Towne, Robert 170
Townend, Peter 95, 97, 99–101, 171
Tracks 76
Tracy, Terry "Tubesteak" 51, 144
TransWorld Surf 122
Trapton, George 95
The Trashmen 15
travel *see* surf trip
travelogue 25, 28, 36, 37, 74, 108, 224n15
Trek to Makaha 42, 43
Treloar, David "Baddy" 75
Trent, Buzzy 32, **41**, 42–46, 153, 178, 209
Trestles 43, 61, 123
Trew, James 142
Tristar Productions 194
Tubular Swells see *In Search of Tubular Swells*
Tudor, Joel 126, 127, 132
Turner, J.M.W. 19, 138
Twain, Mark 153, 170
20th Century Fox 74, **87**

Ultimate Sessions 99, 100
Uluwatu 77, **78**, 79, 103
Universal Studios 190, 194
Upton, Gabrielle 153, 156, 186

The Val Dusty Experiment 125
Van Artsdalen, Butch 46, 91, 165
Van Bastolaer, Raimana 129
Van Dyke, Fred 14, 53, 82
Van Hamersveld, John **29**, 64, 105
"vee-bottom" surfboard 72, 74
Velzy, Dale 7, 57, 58, 132, 212
Velzy & Jacobs Surfboards 7, 58, 132
Velzyland 61, 95, 97
Ventura 69, 95; *see also* Supertubes
The Ventures 58
Victoria 72
video 1, 24, 28, 31, 33, 47, 48, 53, 68, 82, 84, 85, 88, 94, 101, 103–105, 112, 113, 115–143, 164, 167, 170, 207, 210–212
Vidler, Steven 189
Vidor, King 147
Vietnam 138
Vietnam War 63, 80, 110, 111, 157, 160, 163, 169, 170, 171, 173
"View of Honmoku" 35
The Village Voice 164
Villégiature: Premiers bains 35
Vincent, Jan-Michael 101, 170, **172**
Viola, Bill 76
Virostko, Darryl "Flea" 124
visual effects 72, 73, 77, 83, 104, 124, 128, 134, 168, 194
Volcom 84, 123, 210

Waikiki Beach 7, 13, 22, 26, 36–39, 41, 42, 61, 88, **146**, 147, 159, 177
Waikiki Wedding 147
Waimea Bay 16, **41**, 42, 44, 46, 47, 49, 51, 52, 54, 59, 70, 82, 84, 97, 99, 106, 112, 113, 165–167, 200
Waimea Falls 58, 167
wake boarding 47
Wake of the Red Witch 148
Walker, Isaiah Helekunihi 113, 224n62
Walley, Debra 159
Walt Disney Studios 148, 163, 164, 193
Warbrick, Doug 198
Warhol, Andy 164
Warner Brothers 85, 169
Warren, Tyler 131, 132
Warshaw, Matt 1, 6, 7, 27, 66, 113, 114, 126, 214, 223n3

water camerawork 38, 39, 44, 48, 51, 61, 75, 76, 84, 86, **87**–89, 97, 100, 101, 107, 111, 114, 116, 122, 124, 129, 133–135, 166, 168, 170, 178, 181, 184, 199, 202, 218
water skiing 159
Water Sportites 37
Waterlogged 62
Watts Riots 163, 171
Wave Warriors 121
Waveriders 117, 133
"Waves and Thrills at Waikiki" 38
Waves of Change 44, 88, 92, 94, 96, 138
Wayne, John 148
We Got Surf 97
Weatherley, Benji 17, 137
Weaver, Robert "Wingnut" 106–108, 110
Weber, Dewey 45, 46, 49, 132
Webster, Dale 110, 115
The Wedge 44, 45, 47, 50, 60, 65, 86
Wegener, Tom 127
Weiser, John 45
Wendkos, Paul 155
Weston, Jonny **183**
Westwick, Peter, and Peter Neushul 6, 7, 223n3
Wet Side Story 164
wetsuits 15, 39, 198
Whaley, Ed "Blackout" 42
What Youth 141
Where the Boys Are 159
The White Album 79
The White Flower **146**, 147
Whitman, Walt 21, 144, 177
Whitmore, John 107
Wide World of Sports 168
Williams, Ross 130, 133
Williams, Tennessee 45
Wilson, Brian 12, 48, 89, 158; *see also* The Beach Boys
Wilson, Jane 138
Wilson, Sloan 56
The Wind and the Lion 169
Windansea 39, 161
Windansea Surf Club 74
Winnicott, Donald 173
Winton, Tim 115, 126, 174
wipeouts 7, 42, 48, 49, 59, 64, 106, 111, 114, 124, 133, 161, 184, 191, 196, 197, 210
wise elder in surf films *see* mentor
Witchita 63, 167
Witzig, John 71, 101
Witzig, Paul 52, 65, 68, 70, **71**–73, 78, 81, 93, 211

The Women and the Waves 31, 117, 190
women in surfing and surf films 6, 8, 16, 31, 46, 47, 54, 55, 81, 92, 93, 96, 97, 104, *110*, 111, 128, *146*, 147, 149, 151, *155*–158, 166, 177–180, 186–193, 214; *see also Blue Crush*; *Dear and Yonder*; *Into the Sea*; *Gidget*; *One Winter Story*; *Soul Surfer*; *The Women and the Waves*; *individual surfers*
Women Outside 190
Women's International Surfing Association Championship (1975, Malibu) 96, 97
Woodman, Nicholas 142
Woodshed Films 129
Woodstock 85
Woolcott, Richard 123
Woolf, Virginia 21
Wordsworth, William 19, 84, 88, 173
World Championships (1966, San Diego) 71, 73, 86
World Championships (1968, Puerto Rico) 72, 73
World Surf League (WSL) 16, 28, 32, 98, 101, 120, 122, 141, 142, 176, 177, 197, 210; *see also* International Professional Surfers
Worthington, Sam 198, 199
Wreyford, Tim *137*

Yallingup Beach 136
Yeats, W.B. 34, 208
Yokahama Bay 58, 82
Yoshinaga, Jun 219
Young, Beau 131
Young, Neil 93
Young, Robert (actor) 148
Young, Robert "Nat" 60, 65, 70, *71*–74, 76, 86, 88, 91, 97, 100, 107, 108, 125, 126, 136
The Young Wave Hunters 60
YouTube 30, 84, 114, 116, 141, 142, 211

Zerfas, JoAnn 93
Zeta-Jones, Catherine 179
Zuckerman, Kathy Kohner *see* Kohner, Kathy
Zuckerman, Marvin 144
Zulus *66*, 108

www.ingramcontent.com/pod-product-compliance
Ingram Content Group UK Ltd.
Pitfield, Milton Keynes, MK11 3LW, UK
UKHW050702160426
5217IPUK00038B/1951